MALCOLM LOWRY

Malcolm Lowry

A BIOGRAPHY BY DOUGLAS DAY

New York   Oxford
OXFORD UNIVERSITY PRESS

OXFORD UNIVERSITY PRESS
Oxford   London   Glasgow
New York   Toronto   Melbourne   Auckland
Delhi   Bombay   Calcutta   Madras   Karachi
Kuala Lumpur   Singapore   Hong Kong   Tokyo
Nairobi   Dar es Salaam   Cape Town

and associate companies in
Beirut   Berlin   Ibadan   Mexico City   Nicosia

Library of Congress Cataloging in Publication Data

Day, Douglas.
Malcolm Lowry.

Edition of 1973 reissued with corrections.
Bibliography: p.
Includes index.
1. Lowry, Malcolm, 1909–1957. 2. Novelists, English—
20th century—Biography. I. Title.
PR6023.096Z598   1984   813'.54   84-12213
ISBN: 978-0-19-503523-0

Printed in the United States of America

For
Elisabeth

SPECIAL ACKNOWLEDGMENT

Anyone who reads this work will come away from it convinced, as I am, of the courage of Margerie Bonner Lowry. But I am bound to say here that this biography is evidence of another sort of courage than that which Mrs. Lowry brought to her life with her husband: the courage to give me much of my material, and then to leave me alone with it, to make of it what I might. She agreed with me from the first that my aim was not to write fantasy or hagiography, but truth. This biography is not always flattering to either Malcolm or Margerie Lowry, but it is as close as I could get to the truth I was seeking—and I would have come nowhere near it if Margerie Lowry had not been so patient, honest, and brave.

D. D.

ACKNOWLEDGMENTS

The man who was originally to have been Malcolm Lowry's biographer, Conrad Knickerbocker, committed suicide in the spring of 1966. He had been making notes and conducting interviews for two years, but had not yet begun to write when he died. His notes were made available to me, and—as will become apparent in the early chapters of this work—I have made extensive use of them.

I wish to thank Margerie Bonner Lowry for permission to quote from the unpublished letters, notebooks, and diaries of her husband; and Jonathan Cape, Ltd., the J. B. Lippincott Company, New American Library—World, and Oxford University Press for permission to quote from the works cited in my biography.

My thanks also to the following for their thoughtfulness and courtesy in the course of my correspondence and conversation with them: in England, Martin and Ralph Case, William Empson, Charlotte Haldane, Eric Estorick, Edwina Mason, James and Tania Stern, Sir Paul Mallinson, George Northcroft, Dr. Michael Raymond, John Sommerfield, Arthur and Ara Calder-Marshall, Ronald Hill, Robert Pocock, Julian Trevelyan, Edgar D. Brooke, and Dr. James Troupe; in Canada, Harvey and Dorothy Burt, Einar and Muriel Neilson, William and Alice McConnell, Dr. Clarence McNeill, and Marjorie Kirk; in Zürich, Dr. Aniela Jaffé and Dr. C. A. Meier; and in the United States, Conrad Aiken, Clarissa Lorenz Aiken, David Markson, Albert Erskine, and Dr. Sylvan Keiser.

The various editors who have presided over the writing of this book have been uniformly wise and tactful, and I am happy to thank them: Arabel Porter, Tracy Tothill, Whitney Blake, James Raimes, Sally Dufek, and Catharine Carver.

More friends and colleagues than I could possibly name here have read pieces of the book and offered advice and encouragement. I should like most especially to mention Mary Hill Caperton, Dr. Ian Stevenson, Anthony Winner, Martin and Ruthe Battestin, Robert Langbaum, Robert Kellogg, James Boatwright, Robert Scholes, Fredson Bowers, Andrew MacAndrew, E. D. Hirsch, Alistair Duckworth, Francis Hart, Peter Taylor, Jacob Levenson, Michael and Linda Mewshaw, Jon Schueler, Alastair Reid, Ronald Williams, Dr. H. J. Strasser, Ruthven Todd, and Denise Baker, the ablest of research assistants.

My thanks also to the three typists who worked on the manuscript: Karen Czerlinsky, Donna Purvis, and Carolyn Robertson.

I am grateful to the University of Virginia for an appointment as Sesquicentennial Fellow of the Center for Advanced Research in 1969–1970, and for grants from the Faculty Research Committee; and to Basil Stuart-Stubbs of the Special Collections Section of the University of British Columbia Library.

Finally, I should like to acknowledge the forbearance of my family: my wife, Elisabeth, who has read, criticized, and finally approved of the whole "bolus" (as Malcolm Lowry used to call his manuscripts); my parents, Admiral and Mrs. Turner Day; my wife's parents, Dr. and Mrs. Herbert Hölscher; and, at the end of all, my four children, who have been less bloody-minded about the whole business than they had a right to be: Douglas, Ian, Patrick, and Emily Forsyth.

D. D.

CHRONOLOGY

1909   Clarence Malcolm Lowry born at "Warren Crest," North Drive, Liscard, Cheshire, to Arthur Osborne and Evelyn Boden Lowry.

1915–   At the Braeside School, Wirral, and the Caldicote School,
1923   Hitchin.

1923–   At the Leys School, Cambridge. May–October 1927: to the Far
1927   East aboard *S.S. Pyrrhus*.

1928   At Weber's School of Modern German, Bonn.

1929   April–September: to Cambridge, Mass., to study under Conrad Aiken. October: enters St. Catharine's College, Cambridge, England.

1930   July–September: to Norway to meet Nordahl Grieg.

1932   May: graduates from Cambridge with third-class honors in English tripos. May–December: London. December: Paris.

1933   January–March: Paris. March–May: Spain with the Aikens; meets Jan Gabrial. November: *Ultramarine* published by Jonathan Cape.

1934   January 6: marries Jan in Paris. Jan leaves several weeks later for United States. Autumn: Lowry returns briefly to England, then sails to New York; reconciled briefly with Jan.

1935   June: admitted to Psychiatric Wing of Bellevue Hospital for ten-day stay; after release, begins writing early version of *Lunar Caustic*.

1936   September: leaves with Jan for Los Angeles. October–December: sails with Jan from San Diego for Acapulco; settles in Cuernavaca and begins *Under the Volcano*.

1937 Working on *Under the Volcano*. May–July: Aiken and friends visit Cuernavaca. September: Arthur and Ara Calder-Marshall arrive for short stay. December: Mexico City, where Jan leaves Lowry for last time; Oaxaca, friendship with Juan Fernando Márquez; Christmas in jail.

1938 April–July: Acapulco and Mexico City, leaving Mexico via Nogales in July, en route to Los Angeles. Begins work on second draft of *Under the Volcano*.

1939 June 7: meets Margerie Bonner. July: leaves for Vancouver, British Columbia. Joined one month later by Margerie. Work on third draft of *Under the Volcano*.

1940 August: moves to squatter's shack in Dollarton, on Burrard Inlet. November 1: divorce from Jan final. December 2: marries Margerie. April: buys second shack.

1941– Working constantly on fourth draft of *Under the Volcano*. June
1944 7, 1944; shack burns. Two weeks later, leaves for Oakville and Niagara-on-the-Lake, where fourth draft of *Under the Volcano* is completed on Christmas Eve.

1945 February: back to Dollarton, to rebuild shack. November 28: begins flight to Mexico to gather material for *Dark as the Grave Wherein my Friend Is Laid;* from Mexico City to Cuernavaca, with excursion to Oaxaca.

1946 March 8: Acapulco. March 13: arrested for not having paid fine in 1938. April 6: both Jonathan Cape and Reynal and Hitchcock wire acceptances of *Under the Volcano*. May 4: deported from Mexico at Nuevo Laredo; returns to Vancouver. November: leaves Dollarton by bus for New Orleans. December 26: sails for Haiti from New Orleans; arrives New Year's Eve.

1947 February: flies from Haiti to Miami; goes by bus to New York. February 19: arrives in New York on day *Under the Volcano* is published there. March 4: Niagara-on-the-Lake. March 10: Lowry returns to Vancouver; Margerie follows several days later. November 7: sails with Margerie aboard French cargo ship *Brest* to Europe via Panama Canal. *Under the Volcano* published in England by Jonathan Cape. December 23: arrives in Le Havre, travels to Paris.

1948– In Paris and surrounding countryside; travels to Cassis, back to
1949 Paris for stay in American Hospital; to Florence, Venice, Rome,

Naples, Pompeii, Capri, Brittany. Early January 1949: to London on first leg of return flight to Canada. In Dollarton, work resumed on *Dark as the Grave Wherein my Friend Is Laid*, *La Mordida*, stories in *Hear Us O Lord from Heaven Thy Dwelling Place*, and film script for F. Scott Fitzgerald's *Tender Is the Night*. July 14, 1949: breaks back in fall from pier.

1950– In Dollarton, work on *October Ferry to Gabriola*, stories, poems.
1954 January 6, 1954: dropped by Random House. August 11, 1954: leaves Dollarton for last time, for New York via Los Angeles. September: from New York to Milan aboard Italian ship *S. S. Giacomo*. November: Taormina, Sicily.

1955 June: London. November 25: to Atkinson Morley's Hospital for psychiatric treatment.

1956 February 7: Ripe, Sussex. At work on *October Ferry*, stories, political essay.

1957 June: tour of Lake District. June 27: death by misadventure. July 5: burial in the churchyard of St. John the Baptist, Ripe.

CONTENTS

MALCOLM LOWRY

The village of Ripe is in East Sussex, about five miles due east of the town of Lewes, just north of the South Downs. Ripe is an antique sort of place. Two of its cottages are listed in the Domesday Book, its church is early thirteenth century, and it seems to be populated mostly by elderly ladies and middle-aged urban weekenders from London. There is the one church, one pub, one store. Ripe is quiet, "quaint," and lovely in a faintly seedy way. It is hard to believe that raffish, rackety Brighton is only a half-hour's drive to the southwest.

In spite of its air of having gone almost unnoticed by the last five centuries, Ripe has one rather considerable claim to contemporary fame. Just at the edge of the consecrated ground in the churchyard is a small gravestone, usually almost hidden by unmown grass, that commemorates the village's most famous resident:

MALCOLM LOWRY

1909–1957

For the first five or so years after this man's death, until there began appearing in Ripe a steady stream of earnest academic researchers, journalists, broadcasters in antennae-waggling BBC vans, and literary entrepreneurs in general, probably not more than a dozen inhabitants of the village remembered Malcolm Lowry more than vaguely as the nice writing chap who had died so suddenly a while back. Their memories might have been jogged if Lowry's widow had had engraved on his headstone the epitaph he himself had composed:

> Malcolm Lowry
> Late of the Bowery
> His prose was flowery
> And often glowery
> He lived, nightly, and drank, daily,
> And died playing the ukulele.

But probably not: Lowry's connections with the Bowery were fleeting, at best; he drank very little (publicly, at least) while in Ripe; and—sadly—he did not die playing the ukulele, or taropatch, as for some obscure reason he insisted on calling it, which he had carried about with him for so many years. The part about the flowery-glowery prose is apt enough, given Lowry's penchant for self-deprecation; but the inhabitants of Ripe would not have known that.

What they *would* have known was what was written up in the Brighton *Argus* a week after Lowry's death:

SHE BROKE
GIN BOTTLE
FOUND HUSBAND DEAD

One evening last week Mrs. Margerie Lowry, of White Cottage, Ripe, tried to stop her 47-year-old writer husband, Clarence, from starting on the gin.

She smashed the bottle on the floor. And he hit her.

Afraid, Mrs. Lowry fled next door, and did not go back to the cottage until nine o'clock the next morning.

When she did she found her husband dead.

This was the story told at the Eastbourne Inquest, when The Coroner, Dr. A. C. Sommerville, recorded a verdict of death by misadventure.

INCURABLE

Mrs. Lowry said her husband had been treated in a hospital for alcoholism, but was discharged last year as incurable.

"When he hit me," she said, "he was under the influence and in a bad temper."

P. C. William Ford said he found Mr. Lowry on the floor beside his bed.

Near him was a smashed gin bottle and a smashed orange-squash bottle.

A bottle of 20 sodium amytal sleeping tablets belonging to his wife was missing.

This was found later, empty.

"In the house," said P. C. Ford, "I found a number of bottles prescribed for Mrs. Lowry."

Medical evidence showed that Mr. Lowry died from acute barbituric poisoning associated with a state of chronic alcoholism.

As epitaph, the newspaper report is more nearly accurate than Lowry's poetic version; but it still misses the important points. Nowhere does it mention, for instance, why "Clarence" Lowry (Clarence Malcolm Lowry had been running all his life from his first name, and it does seem cruel that the *Argus*, at the last, did not let him escape it) should have been hiding out in a place like Ripe—this fugitive from Liverpool, Cambridge, London, Paris, New York, Hollywood, Cuernavaca, Vancouver, Haiti, the Western Pacific, the Mediterranean. Nor does the *Argus* mention anywhere that this sad suicide was one of the century's greatest novelists, a man of such awesome talent that the word *genius* must be used to describe him.

How did the author of *Under the Volcano* come to be in Ripe, and what, precisely, was the manner of his death? Like everything else about Lowry, the answers are complicated.

To begin with, one must go back almost three years, to September 1954. Lowry and Margerie were just about to sail on the Italian freighter *S. S. Giacomo* from New York to Genoa, with their lives, as they felt, in tatters. In August they had flown east from Vancouver, by way of Los Angeles, after having surrendered finally to the threats of eviction from their squatters' home on Burrard Inlet, near Dollarton—the only place where Lowry ever felt at ease, able to work, able to exercise some control over his drinking. (Lowry later told his London psychiatrist that they had left Canada not only because they were about to be evicted, but also because Margerie was bored there, and wanted to live where being the wife of a prominent writer might count for something. However much truth there might be in this, Lowry's letters from this time mention only the eviction threats, financial problems, and his depression at having been, he believed, deserted at a crucial time by his editor in New York, Albert Erskine—whose superiors at Random House had recently terminated Lowry's contract.)

As generally happened to Lowry, his suitcases—containing, among other manuscripts, the only draft of *October Ferry to Gabriola*, the novel which he was sure would eclipse *Under the Volcano*—were lost en route to New York. They turned up, as they always did one way or another, three days later, but not before Lowry had used his anxiety over their absence as an excuse to go on his biggest binge in years.

The task of caring for Lowry in Manhattan was shared between Margerie and David Markson, a young New York novelist who had in 1952 written his Columbia Master's thesis on *Volcano* and had afterwards become a close friend of Lowry's, and who now offered his small apartment on West 113th Street to his visitors during their two-week stay in the city. From the first, Lowry was difficult:

> The man could not shave himself. In lieu of a belt, he knotted a rope or a discarded necktie around his waist. Mornings, he needed two or three ounces of gin in his orange juice if he was to steady his hand to eat the breakfast that would very likely prove his only meal of the day. Thereafter a diminishing yellow tint in the glass might belie the fact that now he was drinking the gin neat, which he did for as many hours as it took him to. Ultimately he would collapse— sometimes sensible enough of his condition to lurch toward a bed, though more often he would crash down into a chair, and once it was across my phonograph. Then he would hack and sputter through the night like some great defective machine breaking apart.[1]

1. David Markson, "Malcolm Lowry: A Reminiscence," *Nation*, CCII (February 7, 1966), 164–67.

And when morning came, Markson would awake to find a cheery Lowry standing over him: "I say, you do have the decency to offer me a drink?"

One afternoon in New York both Margerie and Markson had to go out, leaving Lowry alone in the apartment. Markson had hidden his supply of gin behind a bookshelf, but he had underestimated Lowry's thirst and ingenuity. When he returned, about three hours after having left, he was met by a smirking, mischievous-faced Lowry: "I have a funny story to tell you, about something that happened when you were out." The funny story, it developed, was that Lowry had, during his time alone, found a newly purchased seven-ounce bottle of Markson's shaving lotion, and drunk it all. With little harm done, apparently, since by five that evening he was (at least outwardly) quite fit and happy, freshly shaven and dressed by Margerie, and off to an apartment in the East Thirties, where a party was to be given for him, and where it had been arranged for him to see again Conrad Aiken, his old friend, tutor, and father-surrogate. According to Markson other Lowry friends were also present: the writers James Agee and James Stern, his former editors Frank Taylor and Albert Erskine, and two or three wives. The evening was hot and sticky, a typical late-summer Manhattan evening, but Lowry scarcely seemed to notice the discomfort—or anything else. After a few minutes' embarrassed literary conversation with the 65-year-old Aiken, who had come all the way down from his Cape Cod home to see his protégé, Lowry

> drifted into a kind of rapt silence . . . sweating profusely, gazing at nothing; perhaps an hour passed in which he spoke to no one at all, nor did he move from his chair. Then, suddenly, cupping his hands to his mouth, he began to make sounds that can only be called "beeps"—though one who knew could infer jazz, and more specifically tunes associated with Bix Beiderbecke: "Singin' the Blues"; "I'm Comin', Virginia"; "In a Mist." For thirty minutes at least, even more absolutely lost to the rest of us now, the man rendered the Dixieland he had loved as a youth.
>
> (Markson, p. 167)

This "private recital," as Markson calls it, or "alcohol-induced regression," as a psychiatrist would describe it, was ended only when Aiken, who was both hurt and distressed by Lowry's obviously poor condition, and by his apparently capricious neglect of his old mentor, came up to Lowry and laughingly exclaimed, "Good night, disgrace!" Then, says Markson,

> Lowry insisted upon seeing [Aiken] home—this with no idea where Aiken was headed, and, chances were, with no money in his possession either, since Margerie normally handled all cash. In the street, in jest but in sadness, Aiken had to wrestle him off as a taxi drew up. Breaking Lowry's hold, the older man tumbled to the floor as the vehicle took him away.

As Aiken's cab drove off, Lowry suddenly turned sober and despondent. "He is an old man," he muttered to no one in particular, "and now I will never see him again." And he did not; but not because Aiken was an old man. Lowry ended the evening in tears.

The Lowrys spent the weekend before their voyage with their friends "Peter" Churchill (Victor Spencer, Viscount Churchill) and his wife, Joan Black, in the old frame house the Churchills had rented at Sneden's Landing on the Hudson River. In his autobiography, Churchill recalls a typical Lowryan adventure, this one occasioned by the approach from the south of a hurricane code-named Edna.

> The evening before the Lowrys left had been hilarious, and, one must admit, somewhat drunken. Next morning we were due to make an early departure. Joan and I were still in bed when Margerie burst in upon us and announced with a suitably dramatic gesture that Malcolm had vanished. She had searched the house. He was gone. Edna had not yet arrived, and in fact, as I remember, never did reach New York but a high wind was blowing. I put on some clothes and went to look for Malcolm. In passing I saw that a full bottle of gin had disappeared also. I noticed that one of the low-sweeping

branches of a huge Pawlownia tree seemed to be swaying rather more than was accounted for by the wind. Through the mass of enormous leaves I could see Malcolm in pyjamas clinging to it desperately. When he saw me he shouted, "Hang On! Here comes Edna. Don't let go!" I subdued Edna slightly by leaning heavily against the swaying branch and in a matter-of-fact tone asked Malcolm if he could lend me a razor blade as all mine seemed to be blunt. Edna forgotten, he followed me into the house and duly found me a razor blade.[2]

Delivered later in the day to the Hoboken pier from which the *Giacomo* was to sail, the Lowrys were initially enthusiastic. Lowry kept repeating, in bogus southern accent, a line he insisted came from Faulkner: "Ah can stand anything. Ain't nothing wrong with me that a good bour-bon won't cure," and buoyantly saying farewell to the long-suffering Markson: "I'm a pretty bad man, but you really should come to Sicily with us. We love you, you know, but not so that you have to shove a cork up your arse, old man."

The Churchills drove back up the Hudson, Markson returned to his ravaged apartment; and Lowry, as he so often did as soon as his friends were out of sight, began sliding into a deep depression. The sailing was delayed for eight hours, by the end of which time Lowry was lying almost comatose in his bunk.

Even the sea was not enough to improve his black mood. One evening shortly after their departure he behaved so badly at dinner that the Captain told him either to shut up or to be taken to the brig. Lowry shut up, though possibly only because he had found out how to cadge bottles of *Lacrima Christi* from the stewards. No one was ever really able to stop Lowry when he wanted to drink, not even the dogged Margerie.

After a couple of days in Genoa, they went on to Milan, where Lowry wanted to meet Eric Linder, his European agent, and Giorgio Monicelli, who was translating *Volcano* for the Italian publisher,

2. Victor Alexander Spencer, Viscount Churchill, *Be All My Sins Remembered*, (New York, 1965), p. 199.

Lowry and Margerie in Milan, Fall 1954.

Feltrinelli. With Monicelli he tried valiantly to sober up and be helpful; which he was, until—after a long morning's work one day—he keeled over in his chair and began vomiting "great gouts of black blood" (Lowry's glowery and possibly somewhat exaggerated description). He was rushed to a local hospital, and spent a week in bed listening wide-eyed and repentant to his doctor's ominous prophecies; and then "bounced out," as Margerie put it, "fit as a fiddle." The Milanese doctor was not the first physician to be confounded by Lowry's recuperative ability—nor the last, unhappily: for Lowry could look healthier than he was, and subsequent specialists were to assume that, because he was physically robust, his psyche was robust as well. From Milan he sent a card to Dave Markson. "Bang!" it said.

Lowry seems to have had it in the back of his mind to find some sort of Mediterranean replacement for his lost Canadian *Paradiso*, because he insisted that they fly next to Sicily, and look for a seaside town where he could begin writing again. This they did, landing at the airport in Catania, then going on to Syracuse. Which they liked—so much so that one night soon after their arrival there, Lowry crept out of their hotel room to look over the town. Some hours later Margerie got an angry call from the police. They had picked up a berserk Englishman; would she please come get him? Margerie trotted down to the jail, accepted responsibility for a very shamefaced Lowry, and popped a handful of Vitamin B pills in his mouth.

Next, on to Taormina, to the Villa Eden, a little *pensione* perched on a cliff high above the sea, with a splendid view of nearby Etna, spouting fire and smoke. At first, Lowry was enthusiastic: here was a new volcano to add to his collection (next to storms at sea, Lowry liked volcanoes best), the Mediterranean was below them, and their room was Number Seven in a particularly auspiciously named villa. All the right portents; so the typewriters were unpacked, and Lowry began writing; but not *October Ferry to Gabriola*, alas, only letters. To Markson, in early November, he sent a card:

Taormina
Day of the Dead
Villa Eden
Via San Pancrazio 52
Room no. 7

Dear old Dave:

(the numerology will not escape you) Am situated . . .
here at last, immediately above the cemetery to which a pro-
cession of people are taking chrysanthemums Christian an-
thems if not quite like that old Typhoeus, adjacent. Margie is
getting better by leaps and bounds. We bathe daily in the
ancient city of Naxos. I swim to and fro, contemplate a short
story called Tremor in Taormina, and we both miss you
much.

But this breeziness was assumed, not real. The pain of having lost
their Canadian Eden was too great for Lowry to encompass or dis-
guise. To Giorgio and Daniela Monicelli in Milan he wrote:

I have tried ten times to write this letter and have not yet
succeeded. I believe I am not going to succeed this time either too well but at least perhaps I can finish this sentence
before my consciousness fails me again: which will be a sort
of beginning, if not an end. . . . all has so far been anything
but heavenly with us, largely due to my own ghastly inca-
pacity to look my own grief in the face which, not liking
not to be looked at, becomes all the greater each time I fail;
fail because I am still half unconvinced that it is not a Me-
dusa that has to be grappled with from behind, else I turn to
stone.

A few days after this, Lowry was reporting his grief more specifically, again to the Monicellis:

My eyes are failing—can scarcely see under electric light
at all—hence this scrawl. By daylight I can see fairly well,
intermittently. Which is something. I try to write, but the
writing is mostly bad, so I tear it up.

Moreover, this new paradise was of itself not measuring up: "I
loathe Sicily," he wrote, "just as much as I love Italy. Dramatic and

formidable though it may be, it is the worst and most hypocritical place in the world . . . endless are the hypocrite lectures I receive about drinking their bloody wine even at the moment I am being overcharged for it and cheated everywhere." Lowry had, years before, made similar claims against Mexicans in general: that they encouraged him to drink, then piously condemned him for being drunk.

In December Lowry and Margerie moved to the Villa Margherita, nearby; and things looked better, momentarily. On December 20 Margerie wrote to Albert Erskine that the typewriter had again been set up, the manuscripts unpacked, and Malcolm swimming happily in the sea below. Lowry himself apologized in a letter to the Monicellis [3] for his earlier maudlin effusions; announced that he was gaining weight—"becoming my abnormal deranged fat self again," as he put it—and cheerfully complained about the terrain, the weather, and their servants: "a male Neanderthal orangutang [sic] in a flapping overcoat with a forehead like the infant Mozart and a female gorilla with a heart of gold and a mind that thinks of nothing else, unless it be food, most of which is inedible."

Partly to escape this pair, and partly to live closer to the sea, the Lowrys moved, early in 1955, down to Mazzaro, the beach below Taormina. That this was an improvement in their standard of living was almost immediately dubious: Lowry could indeed swim more conveniently now, but their *pensione*, the Villa Mazzullo, was only a few yards from both a railway and the highway that ran around the coast of Sicily; and their new maid had many small children, all of whom hung about every day, "shouting in Malc's ears" as Margerie described it. The noise alone made writing impossible. There was the swimming, and the wine was cheap; and Lowry availed himself of both, in good weather and bad. According to Margerie, Lowry was "just slightly sozzled all the time." *Gabriola* receded even farther into the background.

At the end of May a visitor arrived at the Villa Mazzullo, via the train from Palermo. This was Dorothy Templeton, who had been,

3. Harvey Breit and Margerie Bonner Lowry, eds., *Selected Letters of Malcolm Lowry* (New York, 1965), 374–75.

Lowry, outside the house in Mazzaro, Winter 1954.

with her husband-to-be, Harvey Burt, the Lowrys' next-door neighbor on the beach at Dollarton. She was with the Lowrys for two months of that summer, and her letters to Burt in Canada are both revealing and depressing. Though Lowry at first seemed relatively normal, she reported, this was a deceptive impression. Actually, Lowry was sodden, numbed, and often out of touch with reality. Once he announced to Dorothy and Margerie that he had just seen a peasant girl eating a bird alive. He was, in fact, scarcely swimming at all; and he left the villa only to go to the dentist (who was, Lowry confided to Dorothy, a close friend of the Prime Minister of Finland), or to buy wine. He had originally been drinking gin and water more or less constantly throughout the day, but by early June Margerie had succeeded in imposing a bizarre sort of regimen on him. According to Dorothy Templeton, Margerie gave Lowry a cognac and two nembutal capsules at bedtime, which usually kept him unconscious until about 12:30 the following afternoon; at which time he awakened, to be given a stiff drink and a "daytime sedative," and some sort of meal, which he rarely was able to eat. Under the best of conditions, knives and forks—like shoes and socks, or cigarette packs—were too difficult to handle; and Dorothy recalled one especially painful meal at which she sat opposite Lowry and, over the course of two hours, watched him try to fumble a few pieces of cheese and bread into his mouth. One begins to understand why writing was impossible for him in Sicily.

Margerie, Dorothy Templeton wrote Harvey Burt, was almost completely out of patience with Lowry at this time. She tried often —and vainly—to lure Lowry to a barber shop in Taormina; and once, when he balked after having got as far as the Corso in that city, she lost her temper and punched him in the nose. (Margerie denies this. In a recent letter to me she observes, convincingly, that she was too afraid of Lowry's rages ever to have dared strike him.) Lowry, in his turn, spent many hours confiding to Dorothy that Margerie despised him, that she stayed with him only because she wanted his money, that she had agreed to a separation if he would only promise to pay her $100 each month; that she had nagged him until he established a joint account for them at the bank, then nagged until the account was put entirely in her name, then nagged until he made out a will signing everything over to her. Small wonder that Dorothy should have written Burt: "I am witnessing such a tragedy: two souls disintegrating." One suspects that Lowry, if he did in fact make such accusations, was at least in part trying for sympathy from Dorothy.

Sicily was, in short, a disaster. Margerie somehow managed to convince Lowry that they had to leave for a place where they could find not only quiet, but a good psychiatrist as well. On April 15, 1955, Margerie had written to Albert Erskine:

> Malc had been trying to write you for two weeks, but the letter became more and more involved, longer, and in trying to say something, poor soul, he ended by saying nothing comprehensible, so I'm trying to figure out what he really meant to say, and say it for him. From all of which you may gather that he isn't well, and that's right he isn't, though rather better now and I have hopes. Neither Malc nor I have been able to do much work here—the *noise* has nearly driven us crazy. And Malc, of course, cannot be driven to work (in that case he just gets frantic and *can't* work) nor can he be led (he just gets balky and blank). . . . As I say, the noise. He says it sounds like a continual invasion from Mars. For another, when he tried despite noise to get down to *Gabriola*, he found it still too immediately and personally anguishing, so, of course, it was going to become more and more involved, longer, and in trying etc. . . . However, it is there, and one day you'll have it, and it will be terrific.

Erskine had, as a matter of fact, long since lost patience with Lowry, and was almost certainly hoping that *October Ferry to Gabriola*, in whatever form, would never reach him at Random House.[4] But by this time Lowry had become so entangled in the convolutions of his manifold "Works in Progress" that he was probably incapable of suspecting that his followers were growing weary of letters explaining why *Gabriola* should have been delayed, why *La Mordida* and *Dark as the Grave Wherein My Friend Is*

4. Cf. my essay, "Malcolm Lowry: Letters to an Editor," *Shenandoah*, xv (Spring 1964), 3–15.

Laid should have been put aside indefinitely, why there was trouble with *Lunar Caustic* and why he was ashamed of *Ultramarine*— and even why *Under the Volcano* should be recalled and revised. To Lowry, these were constant, palpable problems: he lived with them all, daily. And, with his habitual naïve egocentricity, he would have found it hard to believe that others were not nearly so wrapped up in his creative and organizational problems as he himself was.

Before they left Italy for good, Lowry and Margerie took a boat trip around the Aeolian Islands. As might be expected, Stromboli appealed most to Lowry, and they spent a week at a little villa on the shore of that island, where he was fascinated by the black sand, the half-destroyed villages, and above all by the volcano itself, erupting every twenty minutes. Then on to Palermo for a few days before their flight to London in late June.

The next two months appear to have been spent chiefly in drifting about from one London hotel to another. Margerie does not recall precisely where they stayed or whom they saw—only that she was herself unwell, and that Lowry was drunk almost constantly. Dorothy Templeton, who followed the Lowrys to England, recalls that they stayed for a time in a flat in Earl's Court, then moved on July 26, 1955, to a larger place in Richmond. Lowry continued in bad shape. He shook constantly, and was often unable to move his fingers at all, requiring Margerie to light and hold his cigarettes for him. He was momentarily buoyed up by a present sent him by Harvey Burt, who was still in Canada: a detailed little model of the Lowrys' shack in Dollarton, complete with tiny, rickety pier over the painted blue water on the bottom of the cardboard box in which the present had come. The real pier had collapsed by this time, in the spring storms; but Lowry did not know this, and Margerie insisted that no one tell him. It had meant so much to him, she felt, that learning of its destruction would drive him even farther into his depression. And she was right, as it turned out.

Of this period there is only one clear reminiscence, by Lowry's old friend from Cambridge and Paris days, the painter Julian Trevelyan. One night in late July, Trevelyan remembers, the Lowrys,

The island of Vulcano, Sicily, Spring 1954.

James Stern, the Irish writer, and John Davenport, the critic-reviewer, another old Cambridge pal, all came to dinner at his studio on Durham Wharf. As soon as they arrived, Davenport called Trevelyan aside and warned him to put away the spirits and serve only wine. They all went to a nearby pub, the Black Lion, for a couple of glasses of wine, then returned to the studio for dinner. Lowry would not eat, and was so tense that he made everyone else edgy. Then, as Mary Trevelyan was getting coffee, Lowry saw a bottle of cooking sherry in the cupboard. "Hello, there," he said, "do you mind if I take a swig?" He drank the whole bottle in an instant and was immediately reeling drunk.

Davenport was quite anxious to get Lowry away, and, with Margerie's help, had got him almost to the door when Lowry noticed the wooden beams across the studio's ceiling. "See those? I'm going to sleep on one of them," he announced. He was ill, and quite drunk, but even at his worst Lowry was stronger than most men, especially when he felt stubborn, as he did now, and it took the efforts of everyone there to get him away from Trevelyan's. The guests finally caught the last underground train back to London. As they waited for it at Hammersmith Station, Lowry lay down on the station platform, and let them roll him through the train's doors when it arrived.

By the third week in August, Margerie was convinced that she needed her gall bladder out, and wrote to David Markson that she would be at a London Hospital and Lowry would be staying at John Davenport's flat on Flood Street. According to Dorothy Templeton, the Lowrys were being evicted from the Richmond flat because of general fighting and drunkenness; and Davenport proved to be the only friend willing to take Lowry in during Margerie's stay in hospital.

Before all this could take place, however, Lowry called another old Cambridge friend, George Northcroft, now a neurosurgeon. Lowry dined one evening with Northcroft, who was immediately impressed by the gravity of his friend's condition. According to Dorothy Templeton, Northcroft asked her if Lowry might be persuaded to join Alcoholics Anonymous. But Dorothy felt, probably correctly, that Lowry had not enough willpower left. By September 12, Northcroft had arranged for Lowry to be admitted to Brook General Hospital in Woolwich where he was a consultant. Margerie went into the same hospital a week later to have her gall bladder out (or, at least, to rest), and Malcolm was to undergo a series of tests in the neurological wing.

According to Margerie, Northcroft suggested to her at this time that Lowry might require surgery; Margerie recalls describing his proposal as " a small brain operation to relieve the tensions and anxiety." The form of surgery known as lobotomy, or leucotomy, was frequently performed in America between roughly 1940 and 1955; and a modified form of the operation continued to be performed in England even beyond that time (indeed, one well-known psychiatrist in Great Britain still advocates it). But even in its heyday, the lobotomy was always regarded as a treatment of last resort, to be undertaken only after other medical and psychiatric methods had failed. Lobotomy, after all, makes irreversible cuts in the brain, producing in the patient a state that has been described as "surgical childhood." He becomes content and placid, to be sure; but inert and deprived of the full octaves of deeper emotion. A lobotomy would have been the end of Lowry's creative work just as surely as his death was.

Although Margerie appears to have reacted strongly against Northcroft's suggestion, she did mention to Lowry the possibility of surgery. His response was surprisingly meek. If such a procedure might make him less of a burden to her, then he would agree to it. Margerie was at this time certainly not very hopeful about Lowry's condition, as she revealed in a letter to Markson dated September 17:

> They say he's only a "secondary alcoholic" which I could have told them and the trouble is actually his mind— which of course I've known for years. . . . But he's written nothing for over a year, can't even write letters, as you see, and was losing all contact with reality.

This assessment was not, strictly speaking, entirely accurate. Lowry was certainly in poor mental and emotional condition, and physically debilitated by acute alcoholism. It was probably true enough that when drunk he lost "all contact with reality"; and there is no evidence that he had done so much as one day's work on his fiction since leaving Dollarton. But Lowry *was* writing letters, and those that have survived demonstrate rather forcefully that his mind was—or could be, when he chose—as good as ever. One of these, to Albert Erskine, is included in *Selected Letters*,[5] and in this he says that he is indeed having an operation at Brook—for piles. His recent eye trouble, he reports, is just "the usual weakening of the muscles that can occur at my age." Margerie, in fact, is far more ill than he is. The manuscript of *Gabriola* has been brought to his bedside, but he cannot bring himself to face it just yet. He regrets having been dropped by Random House, and expresses eagerness to return to his work. A totally coherent, even witty, letter—from a man who might at any moment expect to be subjected to radical brain surgery. What is one to make of this? The most plausible answer is that Lowry was indeed gravely ill, but that, as was the case up to the end of his life, he could almost invariably manage to seem, for however brief a time, much better than he really was. Most particularly when he wrote to David Markson and Albert Erskine, Lowry was able to pull himself together and be wise, mature, subtle, or clownishly witty.

In general, Lowry's condition at this time could best be described as depressed, resigned, acquiescent. He was full of guilt for what he had done, or believed he had done, to Margerie's health—so full of guilt, in fact, that one suspects he might have been looking on the prospect of surgery as a kind of deserved punishment for his sins against those he loved. His always amazing constitution brought him back to physical health quite rapidly as the weeks at Brook passed; so much so, in fact, that he could write to Erskine in October that he was spending most of his time "shirtless on the cricket

5. Pp. 380–83. The date supplied by the editors for this letter (July 1955) is clearly incorrect. Internal evidence indicates an October date.

pitch in the dew." But Robert Pocock and John Sommerfield, boozing companions from the early London days, both visited Lowry at Brook, and felt that he had changed greatly from the Lowry they had known: he seemed much older, rather confused, inclined to live in the past. Lowry was only forty-five, and it is true that in photographs taken of him during this time, he looked much older than that. He had been living on his psychic capital for many years, and he was finding it increasingly difficult to hold himself together.

Margerie was allowed to see her husband for only thirty minutes each day, but each visit to his ward made her a little more optimistic about Lowry's chances for recovery. Apparently, she was being encouraged in this by Northcroft, who told her in mid-October that if Lowry "were not yet out of the woods there was at least a light at the end of the tunnel." Margerie wrote to Markson, on October 16, that "his genius is intact, memory still phenomenal, and his wit and sense of humor are now in great form." Again, the problem is to discover who was deceiving whom here; and the solution, again, is to see a little deception, and self-deception, on the part of both the Lowrys.

The whole scene at Brook blew up ten days later, quite suddenly, when Margerie discovered one day that in all their time there Lowry had never seen a psychiatrist, and had received no treatment at all. Northcroft recalls that Lowry, having drunk nothing at all in his weeks in hospital, went out on October 26 with one of his visitors, to a pub, and in a few hours, undid the work of weeks. He was discharged from Brook two days later.

Again according to Margerie, Mr. Northcroft suggested that what Lowry needed now was a long rest in the country—away from Margerie. "You two need a rest from each other," he said to her. It was at this point that Margerie, infuriated, gathered Lowry up and took him away from Brook.[6] Northcroft's assessment was probably not a bad one: Malcolm and Margerie Lowry needed each

6. Dorothy Templeton in a letter to Harvey Burt dated October 26, 1955, provides us with an alternative—or at least supplementary—version of this debacle. She writes that "Northcroft told Margerie two days ago to go off to Cornwall, that he would be responsible for Malcolm. He will keep him in hospital for some time,

other badly, but their need was not always a completely healthy one. There is every reason to believe that they often brought out the worst in each other, and could be in fact mutually quite destructive—all unknowingly, one assumes. They might indeed have profited from extended separate vacations.

But back into London went the Lowrys, this time to the Frobisher Hotel on Cromwell Road. There seemed nowhere to go, nothing to do. Lowry of course began drinking again, as heavily as ever; and Margerie as usual was desperate. Fortunately for them both, Lowry did have several good friends in London, not all of whom were fellow alcoholics. Two of Lowry's old Cambridge cronies, the Case brothers, Ralph and Robert, were on hand (a third brother, Martin, was in Kenya), and the Lowrys saw them often during the month following the departure from Brook.

The Cases, both doctors, recognized the seriousness of Lowry's condition at once; and Ralph noticed, in the days that followed, that the drinking was steadily worsening. "The least I could do," says Ralph, "was to make some kind of gesture." This was to put them in touch with Sir Paul Mallinson, a psychiatrist of real prominence, with offices at 50 Wimpole Street, the old address of Elizabeth Barrett, as Lowry noted with delight. An initial appointment was made with Sir Paul, and one afternoon during the first week in November, Lowry appeared at the Wimpole Street address— frightened, sweating, grinning, and unsteady. It was immediately obvious to Sir Paul [7] that treatment of Lowry would necessitate

---

then arrange to take half of Malc's check, get him into a boarding house where he'd be fed, and give him two pounds a week to spend. If he spent it as he would, at first, all in one day, he'd get no more. George could put him up if necessary, and he could always put him in a sanitarium, so he felt he'd always have the whip hand. 'After all, Margerie, he has opened his heart to me as to no other. And Margerie, I feel that he has a better side, and all we need to do is appeal to it. He won't break his word to me.'" He could scarcely have hoped to win Margerie's friendship and trust by telling her that she was not her husband's chief *confidante*; and anyone with any knowledge at all of alcoholics must be aware that appeals to better sides and unbroken words are bootless notions. One is inclined to suspect the accuracy of the reporting.

7. Material dealing with Sir Paul Mallinson's observations of Lowry comes from interviews conducted by Conrad Knickerbocker in the summer of 1964, and by me in the summer of 1967.

hospitalization. Since he was a consultant at Atkinson Morley's, a neuropsychiatric hospital in Wimbledon, this was rather easy to arrange. But Atkinson Morley's had 150 beds, of which only 46 were for psychiatric patients, and as a matter of policy not more than a few of these could be alcoholics. So Lowry would have to wait almost three weeks for admission. "Good; I can enjoy myself before coming in," he told Sir Paul.

On the evening of November 28, 1955, Lowry, Margerie, and John Davenport arrived at Atkinson Morley's. The two men had spent most of the afternoon in a pub, and Lowry, at least, was quite drunk. An orderly came to check him in, and to lead him to his ward. Lowry followed the orderly obediently down the corridor, while Margerie and Davenport watched from the admissions room. Then, as he was about to turn a corner, Lowry stopped, turned around, danced a little jig, waved, and winked at his wife and his friend—then skipped around the corner after the orderly. It was difficult, Sir Paul Mallinson later recalled, to persuade the new patient to go to bed that evening.

Atkinson Morley's was Lowry's home until his release on February 7, 1956. Margerie took a bed-sitting room in Earl's Court, near the underground that could take her to Wimbledon; but she was not allowed to see Lowry for three weeks. Initially, his treatment consisted of direct interviews conducted by either Sir Paul or Dr. Michael Raymond, then Senior Registrar and First Assistant at Atkinson Morley's. Lowry was uncooperative at first, and so depressed that he could scarcely bring himself to say "Good morning" to the psychiatrists when they came to his bedside. When questioned, he remained silent, his face to the wall. Sir Paul sensed immediately that Lowry was "not at all keen on being cured."

Lowry was reluctant for several reasons. First, he was skeptical about the whole profession of psychiatry. Second, seeing a psychiatrist was what Margerie wanted him to do; and that this was *her* idea, and not his, made him balky. Third, there was the old bugaboo about analysis as the destroyer of genius: if his neuroses were exorcised, or at least brought under control, would not his creative ability go as well? (Practically speaking, Lowry's neuroses had pretty effectively done away with his ability to write for almost two years by now; but he did not think of it this way.) And finally, there was a very real sense in which Lowry wished to continue being an alcoholic. For him, intellectually at least, alcoholism was not necessarily only a weakness, or disease: it could also be a source of spiritual strength, even of mystical insights—a positive force, one of which any man might be proud. Or, put more simply, he *liked* to drink: standing drunk at a bar was a joyous experience for him, and he did not want to be deprived of this pleasure, especially since it was by now very nearly the only pleasure left to him. If he cooperated with the psychiatrists, he might very well lose all that. Hence his silence.

Under sodium pentothal, however, Lowry became quite talkative, even garrulous, though it took all of Sir Paul's store of the drug, and then some, to produce any appreciable effect. Some of the things he told the psychiatrists were manifestly untrue ("My father was an alcoholic"), but most of his admissions were neither true nor false, being for the most part that strange mixture of the grotesque and the pathetic that psychiatrists invariably dig up out of the foul rag-and-bone shops of our psyches. Sexual insecurity, as one might expect, was basic. He had been, he claimed, ridiculed in school because his penis was too small. He had started drinking in his teens chiefly because alcohol could serve as a sexual substitute, necessary because of a lack of confidence. He had tried his luck with prostitutes, and had been a miserable failure. This last was not a very surprising revelation when one considers that Lowry's upbringing had been strongly Low Church fundamentalist; and that he had been a true syphilophobe ever since his oldest brother Stuart, then about nineteen, had taken him, aged five, to an anatomical museum in Liverpool's Paradise Street which specialized in depicting, by a large number of pallid plaster casts, the ravages of venereal diseases.[8]

8. For much of the psychiatric material in this work, I am greatly indebted to information supplied me in correspondence and conversation by Dr. Ian Stevenson, Professor of Psychiatry in the University of Virginia Medical School. On the subject of Lowry as syphilophobe, Dr. Stevenson wrote me the following note on July 9, 1968:

> It would certainly seem to me an oversimplification to attribute Lowry's syphilophobia to the visit to the Anatomical Museum in Liverpool. I would suspect that this is a surface rationalization of the

There was resentment of Margerie, which must have been no sur-prise to Lowry's analysts,[9] and excessive respect for (and fear of) his father and Stuart. Of his mother, significantly, he never spoke —except once, to say that if he ever did anything nice for her, Stuart resented it.

As distasteful as this sort of revelation is, it is important to us, and must be discussed. It is distressing to imagine this brilliant, funda-mentally benign and innocent man demeaning himself so ("I'm given to self-aggrandizement and self-deprecation." "I'm always vulnerable, anxious to appear stronger than I am"); but such admis-sions, justified or not, help us understand the man better than any number of external details do; so we must use them, even at the cost of feeling like voyeurs. Whether or not the accusations he made against himself and others are true, Lowry *believed* them to be true, subconsciously, at any rate, and if he described himself as a pla-giarist who deserved because of this crime to remain obscure, then the essential consideration is not for us whether or not Malcolm Lowry was in truth a plagiarist (he was not), but why he should have thought that he was and what effect this had on his life. It helps us to understand, for instance, something more about why Lowry should have gone into such agonies over the wide and favorable reception that *Under the Volcano* had received: he was, among other things, literally terrified that some reviewer might check his first novel *Ultramarine* out of a library and discover that it con-

syphilophobia, [which] nearly always seems to derive from severe guilt over sexual experiences and impulses. It seems very likely that Lowry suffered from such severe guilt and this naturally fits in with his religious upbringing. I suspect that the memory of the visit to the Anatomical Museum is what the psychoanalysts call a "screen mem-ory," lying over memories of sexual impulses and experiences which are loaded with guilt and accompanied by fears of punishment.

As we shall see, Doctor Stevenson's point is well taken.

9. On December 15, 1955, Dorothy Templeton wrote Harvey Burt that Margerie was very upset over an interview she had just had with Sir Paul Mallinson, in which Sir Paul had said to her, "Is it not true, Mrs. Lowry, that you are jealous of your husband's success and have tried to keep him from his work?" Outraged, Margerie, reporting this query to Dorothy, assumed that Dr. Northcroft had been behind it all, somehow. But a better assumption is that Lowry himself, under sodium pento-thal, had made this accusation against his wife.

tained material stolen from Conrad Aiken and Nordahl Grieg (which it did not) and expose Lowry as a fraud. Most importantly, it helps us to understand the formidable intensity that one senses in such poems as "After Publication of *Under the Volcano*": [10]

Success is like some horrible disaster
Worse than your house burning, the sounds of ruination
As the roof tree falls following each other faster
While you stand, the helpless witness of your damnation.
Fame like a drunkard consumes the house of the soul
Exposing that you have worked for only this—
Ah, that I had never suffered this treacherous kiss
And had been left in darkness forever to founder and fail.

According to Margerie, in a letter to Markson dated December 17, she was allowed to see Lowry the day after a seven-hour session under sodium pentothal,[11] and he was so shaken by his experience that she was frightened. It was because of his extreme reaction to this procedure she said, that his physicians decided on "a series of electric shock treatments to try and bring him up before they probed his poor brain any further." According to Sir Paul, however, it was Lowry's pathological depression after withdrawal from alcohol that necessitated the shock treatments, of which a total of seven were given.

The results of the first two of these were, so far as Margerie was concerned, mixed: on the one hand, Lowry seemed alert, cheerful, and able to dress himself for the first time in months; and on the other, he seemed fuzzy, disoriented, and panicky about the amnesia he was experiencing (no one, apparently, having told him that this was a common and temporary effect of electro-shock therapy).

10. *Selected Poems of Malcolm Lowry* (San Francisco, 1962), p. 78.
11. Seven hours is a most improbable length for an interview with a patient under sodium pentothal sedation. Such sessions rarely last more than two hours at the longest, although the total effects of the drug may extend much longer and certainly could last over seven hours. It seems likely that Lowry, when he next saw Margerie after this interview, mentioned to her that he had felt under the influence of the drug for seven hours or so, and she misunderstood him to mean that the actual interview had been of such marathon length.

How Margerie could have seen Lowry as both alert and fuzzy at the same time is not immediately understandable; perhaps it was his faulty memory that prompted the latter adjective: one can, after all, be alert in the present and yet fuzzy about the past.

So long as alcoholism remained Lowry's most conspicuous aberration, his doctors would have been unable to do much in the way of defining any others. Psychiatrists see alcoholism as a mask: it distorts and hides the mental disorders that have caused it. It was therefore necessary to take heroic measures to free Lowry, at least temporarily, from his craving for alcohol. Accordingly, he was now subjected to a procedure that sounds barbaric in the extreme to laymen: apomorphine aversion treatment. Lowry was to be totally isolated, placed in a tiny cell illuminated only by a small red bulb ("It adds to the mounting horror," a cheerful orderly told Lowry) for ten days, during which time he would be given injections of apomorphine and allowed to drink as much alcohol as he wished. The apomorphine was to induce nausea and vomiting which, in theory, Lowry was then to associate with the experience of drinking alcohol, creating in him a conditioned aversion to drinking. Very little food was to be given him, and very little water; the emphasis was to be on alcohol, whenever he wanted it. "I got so thirsty I drank my own piss," Lowry afterwards said to Margerie.

Most victims of this savage rite collapsed after five days; few lasted out the whole ten. After ten days with very little food, water, or sleep, Lowry was going strong, and in better spirits than he had been in for months. He was pulled out, given forty-eight hours' rest, saline solution, glucose, tomato juice, and a little food. Then back into the cell for another treatment.

Lowry, nonpareil self-punisher, lasted twenty-one days. On Christmas Eve, only a couple of days after completing the treatment, he and another alcoholic burst out of Atkinson Morley's and, as Margerie said, "simply raised hell." The hospital, aware of his aggressive feelings toward Margerie, sent a policeman to her flat as protection; but Lowry never appeared there. Police all over London were alerted. Forty-eight hours after his escape, Lowry returned to Atkinson Morley's on his own, roaring and very pleased with himself. So much for apomorphine aversion treatment.

But, in spite of the rather splendid uncooperativeness of their patient, the staff at Atkinson Morley's were coming to some tentative diagnoses. A physical examination had revealed that Lowry had suffered some damage to his brain and his peripheral nervous system; some injury to his liver ("My God, why only *some* only God and Malcolm know!" exclaimed Margerie to Markson); and an extensive impairment of reflexes.

Mentally, the picture was not so clear. Insofar as it was possible to label Lowry's illness, one might have called him a cyclothymic, or small-scale, manic-depressive. By this is meant that his highs were not so high, nor his lows so low, as with classic, psychotic manic-depressives. The depressions that impelled this cycle were endogenous, that is, originating from within, rather than being a result of external causes. Precisely what there was in Lowry's psyche that prompted these depressions was never clear. Dr. Raymond, the Chief Assistant, told Margerie that Lowry possessed a "free-floating anxiety neurosis," which means, one supposes, that Lowry was able to be afraid of almost anything. Fear of life, fear of sex, fear of failure, fear of authority—fear of literally dozens of things; guilt, self-loathing; possible latent homosexuality; love of death, desire for oblivion: all of these things undoubtedly played a part in destroying Malcolm Lowry.

Sir Paul was, however, quite sure about one aspect of the case: the only reason Lowry knew for becoming sober was to be able to write. Julian Trevelyan had been prophetically correct many years before when he told Lowry that he did not need a psychiatrist, he needed to sit down and get to work on his book. Of course, there is another side to this coin, not necessarily incompatible with the first: Lowry was frightened of writing, or frightened of failing at writing; and drunkenness offered a very good excuse for not writing, and so not failing. More than once during his interviews with Sir Paul and Dr. Raymond, Lowry said that he could not imagine life without alcohol, and believed he would end as a suicide. Years later

Sir Paul noted, with regard to Lowry's drinking: "His life was so lopsided. If his writing was not going well, his life was not worth living." Lowry drank in order to avoid writing, sobered up in order to write, then drank in order to avoid writing—and so on.

To any psychiatrist, a severe alcoholic is always a potential suicide, alcoholism itself being rather obviously a kind of self-destruction. Apparently, no one ever told the psychiatrists at Atkinson Morley's that Lowry had in fact attempted to kill himself at least three times before they ever saw him, or, for that matter, that he had tried at least twice to do Margerie in. In other words, Lowry was probably a good deal closer to being a classic sort of manic-depressive than they imagined. Nor did they know that for years he had been swallowing barbiturates at a rate that would have been dangerous for even the hardiest of men. It seemed to them by February 1956, that Lowry might safely be released.

They turned him over to Margerie with many admonitions. He would in all likelihood require psychiatric care for the rest of his life. He would almost certainly have other deep depressions and aggressive periods, even violent ones. But if she could find a quiet, secluded place for him, no more than a day's journey from London, then he might just make it, and he might even be able to write again. No more traveling, no more cities, no more bad companions; no excitement, no change, ever again.

But Margerie was so buoyed up by Lowry's apparent improvement that all these restrictions bothered her not at all. To Markson, on January 14, she wrote: "I have not seen him in ten yrs. so collected, so *aware*, and though bewildered (Christ! who wouldn't be with what he's had) sometimes (but he is *always* bewildered by life, poor blessed damned old monster), so clear-headed and *definite*." And, in another letter, twelve days later: "Now he is the old Malc, the best, the good Malc, the Malc who wrote the *Volcano*. He is *mad* to get to work again, is trying to write even in the hospital. . . . Malc is not just all right, he is *Malc*." In other, less poignant and more realistic words, he was a manic-depressive who had just emerged from a low and was heading toward a high. And beyond that high lay another low.

During Lowry's remaining days at Atkinson Morley's, Margerie roamed over the south coast of England looking for a place, and by the end of January she wrote Markson:

> I have found a dream house. A beautiful 300-yr.-old cottage of whitewashed brick in a tiny town called Ripe, in Sussex. . . . It has living room, dining room (which shall be Malc's workroom), huge country kitchen, dairy, on first floor! 2 bedrooms, bath, on second floor, attic bedroom and storeroom on 3rd floor. Front rooms look across meadow, with sheep and thatch-roofed farm, brook, and up to the Great South Downs. We have a walled garden with flowers, and a kitchen garden, where I can grow lettuce, herbs, etc. I have a char to come in and do the cleaning for a few shillings. 2 of the houses in our town are in the Domesday Book but you won't find the town on any map, it's too small.

However reserved one might be over Margerie's ebullience, there is no denying that she had indeed found them a lovely spot. If there ever was to be enacted an idyll starring Malcolm and Margerie Lowry, which was more or less what the always Hollywood-oriented Margerie had in mind, this Ripe was the perfect place for it.

Their landlady, Mrs. Edwina Mason, was also their next-door neighbor. Margerie had told her that her husband could not be released from hospital unless there were some secluded and quiet place for him to go to, and the kind-hearted (and brave) Mrs. Mason took them in immediately. She was to see a great deal of the Lowrys for the next sixteen months, and her observations about them carry an air of truth and reliability—so long as we keep in mind that an elderly and pious gentlewoman, a schoolmaster's widow used only to the peaceful goings-on in Ripe, might perhaps not always be aware of just what these formidable strangers next door were up to.

Mrs. Mason concurs [12] with Margerie that, for most of their stay in Ripe, conditions for the Lowrys were indeed close to idyllic. Margerie gardened, cooked, and spent many of her mornings typing what Lowry had written the previous night (it was his custom to

12. In her interviews with Conrad Knickerbocker and me, during the summers of 1964 and 1967.

Mrs. Edwina Mason by the White Cottage in Ripe. The room in which Lowry died is on the second floor, directly above her.

begin writing at eight or nine in the evening, and work until two or three in the morning). They sunbathed often, in the garden behind the cottage, and went on frequent walks in the woods and fields around Ripe.

The "work in progress" progressed steadily. *October Ferry to Gabriola*, which had been like most of Lowry's other novels begun as a short story, was soon half again as long as *Under the Volcano*, and showed no signs of completing itself. There were three short stories, begun earlier, "Through the Panama," "Elephant and Colosseum," and "The Forest Path to the Spring," which were later included in the posthumous collection, *Hear Us O Lord from Heaven Thy Dwelling Place*. There were many—perhaps forty—poems. And, finally, there was "Halt! I Protest!" which began as Lowry's indignant comments on a newspaper report of some domestic scrape a young English writer had got into, and which expanded itself into a long and surprisingly astute treatise on the evils of McCarthyism and the responsibilities of freedom. In March 1956, Margerie reported to Dr. Raymond (whom they saw in London twice a month) that Lowry was working hard, which was surely no exaggeration. In April she told Raymond that Lowry was thinking of having a drink or two; but the danger apparently subsided, for in May she told Raymond that "his mind is clearer than I've ever known it. He is thinking of other people more."

Some of these other people were visitors. Ralph Case came down several times, and reported afterwards that Lowry had indeed seemed a new man. He was writing again at last; he was drinking only Cydrax, a sort of non-alcoholic cider; and he and Margerie were getting along quite well together. There was much less bickering than he had noticed earlier in London.

Viscount Churchill and his wife, Joan, came to the White Cottage at least twice, and he and Lowry spent hours happily advising one another about their respective books. To Churchill, Lowry looked better by far than he had during the time of Hurricane Edna in New York.

As usual, Lowry kept on writing letters at a great rate, and almost all from this period are characteristic of Lowry at his most mature and thoughtful. To old James Craige, his Manx boatbuilder friend in Dollarton, he sent birthday greetings and some copied-out poems by John Clare. He congratulated Clarisse Francillon, his French translator, on her edition of *Lunar Caustic;* and David Markson on a story of his that had been accepted by the *Saturday Evening Post.* He wrote to his agents in New York of his happiness that José Quintero was thinking of directing a film version of *Volcano.* (Nothing came of Quintero's notion, of course: he was merely the first of many directors—including Luis Buñuel—seriously to consider making a film of this most cinematic of novels.)

But all this was the calm before a very sudden storm. On May 22, Dorothy Templeton, in London, got a telephone call from a nearly hysterical Margerie. Would she please come down to Ripe, and help her do something about Malcolm? The Lowrys had been in London themselves earlier that day, so that Malcolm could see Dr. Raymond. After this appointment the Lowrys were having one of their rare good days in the city, visiting the Tower of London and Westminster Abbey, and walking along the Thames, admiring the houses that were set on the river's edge. These, inevitably, reminded Lowry of his beloved shack on Burrard Inlet, and he grew despondent. Then they passed a pub, and Lowry brightened. "Think I'll have a drink," he said. By the time Margerie had got him back to Ripe, he was in no mood to stop drinking, so he walked to The Lamb, Ripe's only pub, and bought a bottle of gin. While Margerie swore so at the owner of The Lamb, Mrs. Evans, that she vowed never to admit either of the Lowrys again, Lowry sat calmly and silently, draining the bottle, remorselessly erasing in one day all the progress he had made since February.

There was nothing of pleasure in this night's drinking, nor in the drinking which followed it over the next two days. Margerie (alone, since Dorothy Templeton had not been able to come to Ripe) called Dr. David Troupe, a general practitioner in the nearby town of Alfriston. Troupe arrived, took one look at the wild-eyed and incoherent Lowry, and called for the Health Department ambulance. Under heavy sedation Lowry went quietly enough to the hospital in Brighton, where he was put to bed in the receiving ward. But within a matter of days he was manic again, and Troupe realized that he would have to be taken back to Atkinson Morley's. Only one thing more remained to complete the shattering of Lowry's fragile stability. Harvey Burt now arrived in England, and came down with Dorothy to visit the patient. Margerie once again warned Burt to say nothing to Lowry about the collapse of his pier the preceding spring in Dollarton and reminded him of what tremendous symbolic and sentimental significance the pier had for Lowry. But Burt insisted on doing so. Lowry, he reasoned, was after all 47, and might have been presumed mature enough to bear up under the shock. So he told him, in spite of Margerie's pleas, and in spite of something Lowry himself, in his eerily clairvoyant fashion, had written to Burt in Canada that spring: "To me, too, childish though it may seem, there is the pier, which we built, which I cannot imagine myself living without, even if it isn't there or myself am dead" (*Selected Letters*, p. 378).

Lowry took the bad news calmly enough at first, and was even able to write about it to Burt a few days later, in one of his most touching letters:

> I am writing without my glasses so the contents of this note
> may be a little awry. Also I am very tired: I cannot believe
> our poor pier has been swept away: that pier, that gave so
> much happiness to many and us, *was us* in a sense; we risked
> our lives building it, especially on the further reaches you
> never saw, where there was a 35-foot perpendicular drop on
> to the granite and barnacles if you made a mistake: nobody
> could understand how it survived so long, not even engi-
> neers, and it was nicknamed "The Crazy Wonder" on the
> beach. Ramshackle from certain angles though it was, and
> the handrails puerile (but oh the washing hung out on the
> line there, like great white stationary birds beating their
> wings against the gale). Margie and I built it together with
> practically no tools and I am broken hearted it has gone. (*Se-
> lected Letters*, p. 388).

The old pier, was, in short, vitally symbolic to Lowry: it was his manhood, his sanity, his marriage, his work. It was clumsily built, precarious, flimsy, even ludicrous—but there was much of love in it, and no harm. That the pier should have collapsed must have seemed to Lowry, obsessed as he always was by omens and portents, a clear and ominous signal to him from the Beyond: his own spring storm was on its way. On June 30, 1956, after five months of freedom and work and steady improvement, Lowry was readmitted to Atkinson Morley's.

While they were waiting for Lowry to be well enough to resume his interviews with them, Sir Paul Mallinson and Dr. Raymond spoke several times to Margerie, who was anxious to tell them how afraid she was of her husband's violence. When she told them also that Lowry had for some time been wetting his bed when drunk, they took this very seriously, as evidence of his reversion to the infantile. Margerie, according to Sir Paul, also informed the psychiatrists that she and Lowry had had no sexual relations for two years, and that she had "a horror of Malcolm's touching her." Lowry, on his part, had told Margerie that he had lost all desire for her, though he "had never been so fond of her" according to Margerie. When drunk, Lowry had called her "a money-grubbing bitch, wanting to get all my money." (Margerie demurs: her recollection is that she told Sir Paul—and others—that after Lowry got out of the hospital and was sober, their sex life was better than it ever had been. In a letter to me of March 7, 1973, she writes: "It was only when he was drinking heavily and passing out every night in Sicily that he was, quite naturally, impotent or at least sound asleep. He certainly never lost all desire for me nor I for him.")

After all this, it must have come as no surprise to anyone that when Lowry did begin his talks with the psychiatrists, his chief theme was resentment of Margerie. He hated her for being afraid of him. For being over-protective. For causing him to be impotent. For causing his almost total lack of libido. For his own dependence on her: "She's always wanted a child, and I guess that's what I've become. She flies into hysterical fits and rages if thwarted but I can't do without her." And he hated her for *her* drinking: she had, he said, been drinking heavily, getting drunk every night. "This must be worse than Alcoholics Anonymous. It must be Alcoholics Synonymous." Finally, he accused Margerie of tearing up his manuscripts, then sticking them back together again to suit her own taste. This was clearly Lowry's overwrought way of expressing his intense dislike of the way in which he had always relied so heavily on Margerie as editor, even co-author. He had allowed her to take over large areas of authorial responsibility from him; and now he hated her for having done so. (Much as Geoffrey Firmin of *Under the Volcano* despised his wife for having cuckolded him, even though he had himself all but tossed her into other mens' beds.)

Again, the *truth* of these accusations is secondary. The important point is that the resentment was there, in such virulent proportions that it could literally madden Lowry. Margerie was the victim of a pattern of aberrant behavior that had been growing in Lowry for many years. The victim, and the cause. She and Lowry existed together in a curious sort of symbiotic relationship: he required a woman to take care of him, mother him, protect him; and she fell too readily in with this demand, having to pay the penalty when he came to hate her, unconsciously, for "unmanning" him. The worst that one can say for Margerie is that she appears to have relished her husband's dependence, that she was perhaps a little too willing to become a martyr; but then, with Malcolm Lowry she was out of her depth—as who would not have been?

(One recalls, suddenly, the passage in Chapter IV of *Under the Volcano* in which Hugh Firmin and Yvonne, Geoffrey Firmin's estranged wife, discuss an armadillo which Yvonne wants to buy. Hugh says, "You couldn't make a pet of it. . . . if you let the thing loose in your garden it'll merely tunnel down into the ground and never come back. . . . not only never come back, Yvonne, but if you try to stop it it will do its damnedest to pull you down the hole too.")

Once again, it was decided that the apomorphine aversion treatment was indicated. Lowry courageously agreed, and went back into the windowless cell. After only a couple of days, however, his blood pressure began decreasing so rapidly that the treatment had to be stopped. Lowry was furious: "This won't work with me, make it *worse* if you can," he cried. "I'll do it for a month if you can make it work! *Why*, find out *why*, so I can stop!"

But Atkinson Morley's had done all it could for Lowry. According to Margerie, after this last treatment the head of the hospital called her in and told her that so far as he was concerned Lowry was a hopeless case, that he was done for, and that they would not accept him at Atkinson Morley's again: aside from his intractability, he was disturbing the other patients. Sir Paul disagreed with this bleak prognosis, and said he would continue to see Lowry in his London offices. Dr. Raymond concurred. On August 11 Lowry was discharged once again, and returned to Ripe with Margerie.

This time there were not even the outward appearances of an idyll. A month later it was Margerie's turn: the strain had finally caused her to break down completely (". . . it will do its damnedest to pull you down the hole, too"). She could neither eat nor sleep, and sat all day in their living room, shaking and crying. Somehow she was able to pull herself together enough to make several train trips up to London to undergo physical examinations, while Lowry waited anxiously for her in Ripe; and when it was established that there were no organic causes for her illness, she was admitted to St. Luke's Woodside Hospital in London and put under extremely heavy sedation—the idea being to keep her asleep for several days so as to give her nervous system a chance to recuperate. When she woke up, after what Lowry called her "Rip van Winkle snooze," she went into a severe withdrawal reaction, with convulsions. At the end of this treatment she weighed seventy pounds. Lowry, full of remorse for, as he felt, having caused her breakdown, brought her back to Ripe on November 16 and, on his very best behavior, nursed her back to health.

While Margerie had been in hospital, Lowry had moved into a room in the nearby rectory, where he would be looked after, and be out of harm's way. He seems to have managed very well by himself, writing Margerie every day, and sending encouraging letters to various aspiring writers, coping with the problem of whether or not to tell Margerie that her mother, in Los Angeles, had died during her daughter's "snooze," chatting with the neighbors, many of whom he had never met before (Margerie had told Mrs. Mason when they arrived in Ripe that they would rather know no one than meet "the wrong people"), and going for long walks by himself.

Once she was back at the White Cottage Margerie's strength slowly returned, and her anxiety over Lowry's condition abated somewhat as she saw him happily writing again. On December 11 Lowry wrote to Markson that "We are having a grand life now and I am working like absolute sin on *Gabriola* with which I have completely fallen in love but I am managing to eat it a little more than it eats me so far. Back to work now, boys and girls" (*Selected Letters*, pp. 393–94).

Margerie was well enough to go up to London with Lowry over Christmas. They went to a service at Westminster Abbey, saw a film, ate in good restaurants. Lowry seemed in top form, and she allowed herself once again to become optimistic. There was a small amount of drinking now, but nothing consequential. Since they could not go to The Lamb in Ripe for beer any longer, they began walking frequently to the village of Chalvington, almost a mile away, to have their pint at The Yew Tree, Chalvington's local. Mrs. Mason, their landlady, says that Lowry was deeply happy during this time. When he was not working, or sunbathing when spring came, he spent many hours in the house next door, talking about spiritualism and mysticism with Mrs. Mason's invalid sister. With these ladies he was invariably charming, witty, courtly. But Mrs. Mason thought she detected something below the surface: "He was always searching for something unapprehensible. . . . He had second sight and knew he was going to die. His eyes looked *through* things." And if one looks closely at pages of *Gabriola* and "Halt! I Protest!" that were written at this time, one often sees, inscribed marginally in Lowry's minuscule script, "St. Jude help me"; or "God help me." Saint Jude, the patron saint of desperate and dangerous causes. Obviously, more trouble was brewing; and one is curious to know how Lowry was able to hide this from his wife, Mrs. Mason (her premonition notwithstanding), the psychiatrists, and such perceptive friends as Ralph Case and Viscount Churchill, both of whom had resumed their occasional visits to Ripe. To everyone who saw him, Lowry seemed in fine fettle; and one is sure that Margerie had by now long since forgotten what a doctor in the American Hospital in Paris had told her in 1948, after one of Lowry's most violent seizures: "Leave him. Get out

Lowry and Margerie at the door of the White Cottage, Ripe.

from under right now. He's going to kill either you or himself if you don't." To Margerie, at this time, what was most noticeable about her husband was a newly assumed air of maturity, even of solemnity: he seemed suddenly to have tired of frivolity and variety, to be almost without curiosity. Often she would find him sitting outside, bemused and silent, "his gaze turned inward." One evening he broke a long silence to announce to her that he was through with jazz: it belonged to his adolescence, not to his maturity.

In March of 1957 Lowry signed a contract with Knopf for the Vintage paperback edition of *Under the Volcano*, and he and Margerie began thinking of an extended holiday. Lowry had always wanted to visit the Lake District, and had never been able to do so. He suggested to Margerie that they go on a walking tour there, and she responded eagerly. According to Viscount Churchill, Lowry and Margerie had by this time begun to bicker a great deal, and "the walking tour was a kind of attempt at a sort of honeymoon re-union" (from a letter to Conrad Knickerbocker dated May 22, 1964). Margerie insists that Churchill is wrong about the bickering; that, in fact, she and Lowry were now closer than ever before. In any case, just before they left for the north Margerie reported to Dr. Raymond that everything was fine, and that Lowry was having no trouble controlling his drinking. This was the last news of their patient that his psychiatrists had. Lowry had one month to live.

Lowry and Margerie went first to the Farne Islands, on the border between England and Scotland, where there was a famous bird sanctuary. (The Lowrys were great bird-watchers and members of the Royal Society for the Protection of Birds.) They stayed in a monastery on the mainland, and went in boats to the islands, where there were eider ducks so tame one could smooth their feathers as they nested on the ground, and where they could watch roseate and arctic terns in their mating dances.

Then down to the Lake District, where they took a room in a hotel on the lake near Grasmere. During the two weeks they were there, Lowry often swam in the icy water of the lake—the first time he had been swimming since the bad days in Sicily, two years earlier. Several times they rowed out to a small island in the middle

In the Lake District, June 1957.

of the lake, and picnicked there, recalling sadly how many times
back in Dollarton they had set out in their dinghy to picnic on one
or another of the upriver islands. They visited Wordsworth's house.
Almost every morning they would pack sandwiches and a flask of
tea into a knapsack, then hike off into the hills for hours. Margerie
took several snapshots of Lowry during this time, and if one looks
closely at them one sees more than a middle-aged bearded man, pipe
clenched in teeth as he sits atop a hill, "all chest, though in that
aging athlete's way of going to fat so that chest and stomach had become one, stumplike," as David Markson once described his friend.
One sees a man who seems full of a sense of deep and ironic resigna-

tion, a man rendered gentle by fatigue. It is surely not only hindsight that makes one recognize that the awesomely wise face in these photographs was that of a man who felt himself to be burntout, used-up, ready to die. When one begins to wonder why so many people were willing to tolerate such an impossible man as Malcolm Lowry for so many years, he should look at these pictures. There had been Lowry the trickster, Lowry the buffoon, Lowry the charming disgrace, Lowry the ruined genius—and now there was Lowry the old wise man. One remembers how proud Lowry was on overhearing a man in a bar say about him, "The very sight of that old bastard makes me happy for five days. No bloody fooling"; and then one realizes that there was nothing in the look of Malcolm Lowry in the spring of 1957 that should have made anyone happy. One would have approached him quietly. Or left him alone with his thoughts.

The nights are practically white during the month of June in the Lake District, with the sun setting in late evening and rising before midnight. On one such night, toward the end of their stay there, Margerie and Lowry went into a pub for a Pimm's Cup, the specialty of the house. After this, they walked slowly back to their hotel, and paused for a moment on a bridge, while what seemed to be dozens of waterfalls cascaded around them. But for Lowry there was not much pleasure, even in this; for by now he had learned of the sudden death of Joan Black, Viscount Churchill's wife, and one of his closest friends. She had died on May 7 of hepatitis after having been ill only six days, and his grief over her death was more than enough to destroy once more Lowry's delicate balance. He and Margerie returned to Ripe on June 21, and he began dropping rapidly into another depression. He did manage several times to call Churchill (who wrote in his autobiography that, after his wife's death, Lowry's "was the one voice left that I wanted to hear") and to write him a final, comforting letter. And he tried to work on a poem for Margerie, about the bower bird of New Guinea, who builds his mate a home which serves also as an elegant temple in which he can worship her. It is a very bad poem, as if that mattered.

45

Obviously, whenever Lowry turned sorrowful his mind focused on his lost Canadian home.

Possibly to cheer him up, Margerie suggested to Lowry shortly after tea on the evening of June 26 that they walk to The Yew Tree in Chalvington. The weather was good, the sun still warm, and Lowry was willing. By this time he was on very good terms with the owners of the pub, Mr. and Mrs. Charles Baker, and had spent many quiet evenings with them. Charles Baker described these on a BBC interview in 1967: [13]

> Malcolm would come round into cellar and order his drink and we'd come out into the Public Bar and sit down on the seat. He never used to say a lot. I used to do a lot of talking and he used to just say "Yes, yes" and he would drink up his drink and say good-night and go out in the most orderly manner.

But this night, with Margerie, there was something wrong. The two sat huddled together at a table in the Public Bar, and Margerie was obviously upset about something. Lowry whispered to the Bakers that she was crying because of their lost home in Canada, and that he was trying to comfort her. But Margerie was inconsolable; and the longer she wept, the more shaken Lowry became. Finally, he bought a bottle of gin from the Bakers—to cheer Margerie up, he said. She began complaining about his buying it, and he hustled her out of The Yew Tree. The last the Bakers saw of them, Margerie was stalking off down the road back to Ripe, and Lowry was rolling along some yards behind her, the bottle tucked under his arm. What follows is, in essence, Margerie's version of the story. There are other versions; some, indeed, by Margerie herself.

There was to be a Stravinsky concert on the BBC that evening at 7:30, and they had planned to listen to it on the radio in their bedroom. As soon as they reached the White Cottage, Lowry went up-

13. "A Portrait of Malcolm Lowry," compiled and narrated by Arthur Calder-Marshall and produced by Robert Pocock, and broadcast on the Third Programme on September 16, 1967; hereafter cited in text as BBC "Portrait of Malcolm Lowry." An edited transcript of this production was published in *The Listener*, Vol. 78, no. 2011 (Thursday, October 12, 1967), 461–63.

The Yew Tree, near Ripe.

stairs to turn on the radio, while Margerie stayed downstairs in the kitchen preparing a cold supper. After perhaps twenty minutes she walked upstairs, carrying their supper on a tray—to find Lowry huddled wild-eyed in a corner of the bedroom, the half-empty gin bottle clutched to his chest.

Without saying anything, she turned on the radio, softly since she knew Mrs. Mason was next door listening to a Bach program. The evening was a warm one, and all the windows were open. Then Lowry, without loosening his grasp on the bottle, lurched across the room and turned the volume up full, drowning out Bach with Stravinsky. Margerie begged him to turn it down. He refused. For perhaps thirty minutes they sat there—eating the supper was impossible —while Lowry drank and the radio played *Le Sacre du Printemps:* one last outrageous Lowryan coincidence. Had he been sober enough to notice it, he would have been pleased.

Finally Margerie lost her temper and tried to snatch what was left of the gin from her husband. He struck at her, but she got the bottle away from him and smashed it against the wall next to the fire grate. Lowry, enraged, picked up the shattered neck of the bottle and came at her. He chased her down the narrow stairs, shrieking, "with a fiendish look on his face." It was ten o'clock.

She ran next door to Mrs. Mason's, where she could wait until Lowry calmed down. (It is curious to reflect that the distance from the Lowrys' front door to that of Mrs. Mason is perhaps fifteen feet; surely an incongruously short distance to flee when being pursued by a man bent on homicide. But people behave strangely at such moments, and Mrs. Mason's house must for one reason or another have seemed quite safe to Margerie—perhaps she knew Lowry was fond of Mrs. Mason, and would never harm her or behave badly in front of her, no matter how drunk.) She knew he could get nothing more to drink that evening—since they would not serve him in The Lamb, and since The Yew Tree would have been closed by the time he could have got back to Chalvington— and she hoped he would settle down and eat his supper, still untouched in the bedroom.

Margerie explained to Mrs. Mason that she and Lowry had had a row, and asked if she might stay there for a while. Mrs. Mason fixed tea, and they talked about gardening until midnight, when Margerie stepped outside to see if Lowry had gone to bed, she having heard nothing from the White Cottage since fleeing it. The light in the bedroom was still on, so Margerie went back into Mrs. Mason's. An hour later the light was still on, and Margerie decided to accept Mrs. Mason's invitation to sleep there. She took a sodium amytal tablet and slept soundly until nine in the morning.

Then she rose and said to Mrs. Mason: "Well, I suppose I must go out and get poor old Malcolm a cup of tea. But I know what I'm going to do: I'm going to go up to Liverpool to see if I can get part of the estate to hold over him when he has these attacks."

At the foot of the stairs in their cottage she called to Lowry, and got no answer. She climbed slowly up to the bedroom, and found him motionless on the floor, his almost untouched supper scattered about the room—as if he had suddenly collapsed while holding the plate in his hands. Beside him were the remains of the gin bottle and a fragmented orange-squash bottle. Margerie noticed almost at once that her bottle of sleeping pills—sodium amytal, of three-grain strength—was missing from the bedside table.

Without hesitating, Margerie ran back to Mrs. Mason's. "Oh, Winnie," she cried, "he's gone!" "Where, Liverpool?" asked Mrs. Mason. "No, he's dead." And so he was.

Margerie Lowry and Mrs. Mason called doctors and police, then —just in case—ran back to the White Cottage with blankets and hot water bottles. But Malcolm Lowry was, of course, far past needing them, or anything else. He had, in fact, already been dead for several hours by the time Margerie discovered him. There remained nothing to do except wait for the whole business to be taken out of their hands, so the two women returned to the Bosky Barn, Mrs. Mason's house next door, to drink tea and wait for the Authorities (the *Authorities:* Lowry would have been terrified).

They did not have long to wait. Within an hour the body had been removed and Margerie was having to guide Police Constable William Ford about the cottage. It was then that they found Margerie's sodium amytal bottle, empty, in the room across the hall, hidden under a pair of gloves in a dresser drawer. (The Coroner subsequently speculated that Lowry had swallowed as many as 50 sleeping pills—or at least 25 more than this bottle had contained. Margerie's answer to this was that there had been yet another bottle, in a medicine cabinet; and that Lowry had emptied this one, as well.)

Since there were no witnesses, it would of course forever be impossible to determine precisely the manner of Lowry's death. But there have always been plenty of theories, a few of which are even plausible. Mrs. Mason could not bring herself to believe that a gentleman like Malcolm Lowry would deliberately kill himself, and felt sure that he had suffered a heart attack, perhaps precipitated by all the gin and barbiturates he had ingested that night. But Dr. A. C. Sommerville, the Coroner of Eastbourne, reported at the inquest a week after Lowry's death that his heart was perfectly sound—as, rather miraculously, were his liver and other organs.

When Margerie was able to begin telling their friends about Lowry's death, her extreme disorientation manifested itself in the number of confused and widely varying versions she told. Clearly, her chief aim was to protect her husband's name from the stigma of suicide. She wrote to Downie Kirk, their schoolmaster friend in Vancouver, that Lowry had been completely sober, and working hard on *October Ferry to Gabriola;* that he had fixed himself a midnight snack, had choked on a piece of food, and strangled. This version of the death was, indeed, the prevailing one for several years. In 1961, *Time's* review of *Hear Us O Lord from Heaven Thy Dwelling Place* mentioned that Lowry had died of autostrangulation; and Conrad Knickerbocker, in a 1963 essay for *Prairie Schooner*,[1] modified the version only slightly: "On the night of June 27, 1957, he sat up late drinking, ate a midnight lunch, and took phenobarbital to sleep. He became sick and began to vomit. Alone, on his back on the cottage floor, he strangled to death. His wife, who had been asleep, found his body in the morning." (The Coroner's autopsy had indeed found some evidence that Lowry had eaten a bite or two of his "midnight lunch.") Presumably, this was the story Margerie chose to tell Knickerbocker at this time. (She also told him that Lowry had gone *alone* to Chalvington earlier in the afternoon, ostensibly to buy groceries; and had returned with a bottle of gin instead.)

Three years later, in a *Paris Review* essay,[2] Knickerbocker gave the screw another turn:

> That night he had gone to Chalvington for cheese and instead returned with a bottle of gin from The Yew Tree. He had been writing a poem to his wife, remembering the nest

1. "The Voyages of Malcolm Lowry," *Prairie Schooner* (Winter, 1963–64), pp. 301–14.
2. "Swinging the Paradise Street Blues: Malcolm Lowry in England," *Paris Review* (Summer 1966), pp. 13–38.

they had built for themselves in Canada, but then he threatened her with the bottle when she tried to take it away from him. The bottle broke. She ran next door, and he, full of the rage of a husband who jumps into his car and drives anywhere at all right into a tree, popped down twenty sodium amytal tablets. A miscalculation.

A miscalculation? Martin Case disbelieves in the suicide theories, and is convinced that Lowry was drunk, upset, and anxious to sleep; and that he "popped down" whatever pills were handy, without counting the number or considering the consequences. Now Lowry, classic oral-compulsive that he was, might indeed, in his rage and frustration, have clapped several pills of whatever kind in his mouth without thinking or counting, and without consciously intending to kill himself; but swallowing twenty-five pills all at once is hard work. (Ten such pills, incidentally, would have been ample to kill a man in Lowry's condition.) But 50 pills? (If there were 50.) And why would a man bent only on getting a good night's sleep hide the bottle that he had just emptied?

When I talked to her, Margerie Lowry came, I suspect, closer to the truth. Initially, she recalled that during the ugly scene in the northwest bedroom of the White Cottage, Lowry tripped and fell into the fireplace, breaking the gin bottle as he did so. But Mrs. Mason was able for years to point out a stain on the wall where, she claimed, the bottle, hurled by Lowry, had struck.

Still later Margerie presented the current version—that which is recounted in the previous chapter. In the main, one is disposed to accept it as reasonably accurate; but there are still two or three worrisome points. For one thing, a visitor to the White Cottage is struck immediately by how tiny it is: their bedroom was small, and only a midget would require more than three long steps to cross it in the direction of the hallway. The stairs themselves—which begin just at the doorway to the bedroom—are narrow and steep. From the bottom stair to the front door is perhaps one yard. It is difficult to see how Lowry, even drunk and angry as he surely was, could have failed to catch his wife before she escaped from the cottage. Either he was too drunk to chase her effectively, or too drunk to chase her at all. The best guess is that Lowry made a threatening lurch in her direction, and this—quite understandably—was enough to set her off down the stairs.

Dr. Sommerville proclaimed it "Death by Misadventure," which was certainly the wisest—indeed, the only—possibility open to him. Alcohol and barbiturates are famously synergistic: taken together in sufficient quantities, they can be absolutely lethal. (In one of his eerily prophetic literary asides, Lowry had once allowed his persona in "Through the Panama" to ask himself, "My faithful general Phenobarbus, treacherous to the last?") Lowry was drunk, and may indeed have failed to keep count of the number of tablets he was swallowing; but only a man determined to obliterate his consciousness—if not his whole self—would have so voraciously consumed so many of them. Sometime around midnight, full of shame, remorse, and anger (and, certainly, frightened at having been "deserted" by his wife), he went into the bedroom opposite, found her bottle of sleeping pills and proceeded to swallow them all, afterwards hiding the empty bottle in her dresser drawer; then, if the Coroner's hypothesis is accurate, he found the second bottle, and swallowed its contents as well. After this he returned to the bedroom, picked up his plate of food, took a bite or two—and fell backwards, dead.

Unfortunately, there are no useful answers to the mystery. Lowry's death may have been suicide; or it may simply have been the rather typical neurotic gambit of a man who *plays* at suicide: "Margerie has hurt me, I will give her a scare by injuring myself. She will find me in the nick of time and call the doctor, who will save me. And she will be sorry for having driven me to such extremes." But suicidal games all too often are clumsily played, and end in suicide. Let us, like Dr. Sommerville, leave it at "Death by Misadventure." No one will ever know precisely what happened that night. Grief and shock caused Margerie's recollections to be confused, one supposes permanently. She has not, certainly, meant to deceive anyone, and we must understand and forgive her confusion.

Fortunately, the Coroner's verdict meant that Lowry could be given a Church burial. Eight days after his death (the delay was caused by the difficulty in finding a suitable place for the inquest), Lowry was buried by the Reverend Frederick Talbot Baines in the churchyard of Saint John the Baptist.

The funeral must have been one of England's smallest literary burials. Shortly after Lowry's death, Mrs. Mason had said to the distraught Margerie, "You must tell someone. You must get someone to stay with you." Margerie obediently called Ralph Case and John Davenport, both of whom came immediately down to Ripe. She sent a telegram to the recently married Harvey and Dorothy Burt in Germany, and they arrived in time to see Margerie through the inquest, the funeral, and the bad days afterwards. James Stern arrived by train on the day of the funeral. Stuart Lowry flew in from Paris minutes before the ceremony began. He was the only member of Lowry's family to acknowledge the death of the wayward son.

To what doubtless would have been the approval of the dead man, a horrendous thunderstorm broke over Sussex minutes before the ceremony began. At the appointed time, Davenport and Stern entered the church on either side of the widow, who kept her eyes shut tight throughout. Stuart held her hand, across the pew, during the brief Anglican service. Afterwards, John Davenport placed a sprig of heather on the old-fashioned hummock of Lowry's grave; and the funeral was over. Margerie was packed off to Hellingly Hospital in Hailsham, the guests left Ripe, and Malcolm Lowry remained. Months later, Martin Case, newly returned from Kenya, went down to Ripe with Charlotte Haldane. They visited the grave, upon which Case, with consummate appropriateness, poured a bottle of Flower's Ale.

The subject of these obsequies was born Clarence Malcolm Lowry, on July 28, 1909, at "Warren Crest," North Drive, Liscard (now incorporated into the township of Wallasey), in the Birkenhead district of Cheshire, England. While he was still an infant, the Lowry family moved to what became their permanent home: Inglewood, in the town of Caldy, some six miles southwest of Wallasey. This area, known as the Wirral, is a large peninsula, bounded on

the north by the Irish Sea, on the east by the River Mersey and, a little further south, by the city of Liverpool, and on the west by the River Dee. Caldy lies on the banks of the Dee; and on a rare day when the sky is clear over Caldy Hill, one can see, silhouetted against the western horizon, the outlines of the distant mountains of Wales. Perhaps twice in a lifetime the summit of Snaefell in the Isle of Man appears just above the northwestern horizon.

"Those Wirral people are a hard lot," a woman once told Conrad Knickerbocker ("Malcolm Lowry in England," p. 17), with no little accuracy. The climate is harsh: the seas run high, and the north wind has frequently been known to come sweeping down at more than a hundred knots. Until fairly recent times, a substantial part of that hard Wirral lot made their living off the sea in unscrupulous

Lowry playing his "taropatch" at his parents' home in Caldy, Cheshire, 1932.

fashion. The main mass of the peninsula is Triassic sandstone, and the coastline is dotted with caves—ideally suited for smuggling, and so used for hundreds of years. The people of the Wirral were, however, even more famous as "wreckers" than as smugglers. The Report of the Royal Commission on the need of a Police Force, issued in 1839, observed: "Cheshire and Cornwall are the worst. On the Cheshire coast not far from Liverpool, they will rob those who have escaped the perils of the sea and come safe on shore, and mutilate dead bodies for the sake of rings and personal ornaments." [3] These wreckers would light fires on the Wirral shore to lure ships

3. For this and other information about the Wirral's history, I am indebted to Norman Ellison, *The Wirral Peninsula*, (London, 1955).

onto the treacherous Burko or Hoyle banks, there to break up in the heavy seas. Then they would gather on the beaches and wait for their plunder to wash ashore.

The Wirral's chief gift to history was, fittingly, a pirate: Captain Fortunatus Wright, who, like many of his profession in the early eighteenth century, became legitimized as a privateer and lionized by the press. He sank with his ship off Malta in a great storm in 1757, and was eulogized in the Liverpool *Chronicle and Marine Gazetteer* as "a gentleman of this town who in the last and present war, in a small privateer, gained immortal honour and the universal esteem of his country."

Culture has never been very obtrusive on the Wirral peninsula, manifesting itself for the most part in the flourishing seaside resort of New Brighton, which for a time rivaled Blackpool as the center of tawdriness in England. The list of artists and writers from the area is not long. There was one Olaf Stapleton, an early twentieth-century novelist of modest reputation; there was a painter named S. J. Lamorna Birch, R. A., who died in 1955, and who specialized in the painting of running water; and, best of all, there was Hetty King, the male impersonator, of whom it is said that her "electrifying personality dominated the music-halls for many years. She ranked second only to the great Vesta Tilley when she was at the height of her fame." Except for the occasion in 1794 when Anna Seward, the "Swan of Lichfield," visited the Royal Hotel at Hoylake and wrote one of her truly wretched poems to commemorate her stay, the Wirral has seen little else in the way of artistic endeavor.

The Wirral has at least some of the virtues of English rural life. If there are the down-at-heels communities of New Brighton and Birkenhead (that dreariest of places, a failed boom-town), there are also such pleasant villages as Caldy, which is very nearly an American's idea of what an English country town should be. The rough heathland which surrounds it is unspoiled, all golden gorse and purple heather. Caldy, too, is unspoiled, and for a very good reason: in 1832 a Manchester man, R. W. Barton, bought the whole township and either rebuilt or renovated every house in it. Caldy is all exposed-beam Tudor, ivy, and manicured lawns—just the sort of place in which a well-to-do, middle-class, Liverpool businessman like Arthur Osborne Lowry would want to buy a home. And the home he bought, Inglewood, was ideally suited to his needs: its grounds were large and well cared for; and the fifteen rooms in its spacious, oak-beamed house were ample for the large family he had accumulated by 1909. There was a tennis court on the grounds, and Caldy was not far to the south of the famous Royal Liverpool Links at Hoylake: important considerations for a father who demanded athletic prowess of his four sons. He himself was always fit: he won many swimming contests and on at least two occasions saved people from drowning in the Mersey—for which he was awarded the medal and certificate of the Liverpool Shipwreck and Humane Society.

Arthur O. Lowry, whose father had been a successful Liverpool contractor and architect, and whose family had come originally from the Lake District, was married to Evelyn Boden, the daughter of Captain Lyon Boden, a well-known Liverpool shipowner and mariner. When the young Malcolm Lowry began casting about for a way of adding a touch of glamour to his rather unexceptional ancestry, he settled quickly and predictably on old Captain Boden, and made him into a truly exotic figure. First, he became Norwegian instead of English. Then he became even more of a crusty old salt than he already was: in "Through the Panama," the Lowry-voice muses about his grandfather, captain of the windjammer *The Scottish Isles*, who

> went down with his ship in the Indian Ocean. He was bringing my mother a cockatoo. Remember the story about him by Old Hands in Liverpool. The owners loaded his ship badly: he complained: was forced to take it out. So he sailed it right bang down to the Cape, and right bang back again to Liverpool and made them load it correctly.

Lyon Boden was indeed captain of *The Scottish Isles*, but he was also part-owner of the ship; and it is rather unlikely that he as captain would load his own ship badly, or punish himself, as owner, for having done so. That he "went down with his ship in the Indian

Ocean" is probably young Lowry's debt to Joseph Conrad. As Lowry told the story to Margerie, Captain Boden, *The Scottish Isles* becalmed in the Indian Ocean, his crew dying of cholera, gave orders to a nearby British gunboat to blow up the ship, himself aboard. It is true that there once was an outbreak of cholera aboard *The Scottish Isles;* but it is also true that Captain Boden died peacefully in his bed, at the age of 90, in 1934. His romanticized self, though, lived on for another quarter-century, as his grandson continued to find ways to work one anecdote or another about the old sailor into his fiction.

Arthur O. Lowry was just as successful at making money as he was at rescuing drowning swimmers. His principal occupation was that of head partner in a cotton broking firm, with extensive interests and holdings in North and South America and the Near East; but he served also as a director in several sugar and oil corporations. By the time he bought Inglewood, the senior Lowry was very well off indeed—precisely to what degree, one can only guess from such clues as Malcolm and Margerie Lowry's share of the estate after his mother's death: £90,000.

Evelyn Boden Lowry appears to have been quiet, pious (in keeping with the earnest nonconformism that was the religious style of all the Lowrys except the wayward Malcolm, who liked to call himself a "conservative Christian anarchist"), and very much under the thumb of her autocratic husband. A. O. Lowry traveled a great deal, looking after the cotton, oil, and sugar; and Mrs. Lowry frequently accompanied him on these journeys. He usually required her to wait for him in their hotel lobby in whatever city they were visiting, it not being thought safe or proper for an English lady to go about alone in foreign communities. She was obedient to this restriction, except for one lapse in Jerusalem, when A. O. Lowry, emerging from a bank, spotted his wife serenely riding down the street on a donkey. It does not seem likely that he found this at all humorous.

Indeed, there is scant evidence that any of the Lowry clan ever found anything very humorous, always excepting, of course, the disreputable Malcolm, who generally was unable to take anything too seriously. The father may not quite have been, as Conrad Knickerbocker called him, "the incarnation of the worst of the imperial middle class" ("Malcolm Lowry in England," p. 14); but his wife and sons could never have felt very comfortable around him. For A. O. Lowry it was *mens sana in corpore sano* with a vengeance. No smoking. Perhaps a glass of port, at Christmas. (Malcolm took a kind of wry pleasure in reporting, years later, that his abstemious father had actually died of cirrhosis of the liver.) Cold baths, especially for the sons, even after modern showers had been installed at Inglewood. Plenty of rugger, tennis, swimming, shooting, golf, and walking—up to twenty or thirty miles in a day.

When Malcolm Lowry wrote, years later, to David Markson that he came from "a huntin' and shootin' family near Liverpool, who weren't interested in literary matters" (*Selected Letters*, p. 248), he was scarcely exaggerating. Nor was he in 1929, when he wrote to Conrad Aiken that "nobody reads at home: the only paper we take is *The British Weekly;* there are few books in the house more exciting than *Religions and Religion* by James Hope Moulton (although a careful searcher might find in a somewhat inaccessible region Donne, Chatterton, *The Smell of Lebanon,* Crabbe's *Inebriety* and *Blue Voyage)*" (*Selected Letters*, pp. 6–7). For the most part, he told Margerie, he got his early taste for literature from reading Blake's poetry and the various unobjectionable books that had come to Inglewood as school prizes.

This dearth of intellectual activity might have upset the youngest Lowry, but it does not appear to have distressed his parents or his three older brothers. Stuart Osborne, Wilfrid Malbon, and Arthur Russell Lowry were all sons after their father's heart. The eldest, Stuart, was fourteen when Malcolm was born; and he soon became, after his father, a vitally important authority-figure in Malcolm's life. Stuart was brave, Stuart was manly, and—apparently unlike the other two brothers—Stuart was fond of young Malcolm. And Malcolm reciprocated. With the other two, Wilfrid and Russell, nine and four years his senior, respectively, Malcolm would have almost nothing to do. So far as he was concerned, they were both bullies, fit only to go into their father's business; which is precisely what they did. (And so, for that matter, did Stuart.) For Wilfrid, Malcolm later admitted a grudging sort of respect: Wilfrid had been capped for England at rugby football, an achievement no rightminded English boy could fail to admire. Of Russell, he never spoke. Both of these brothers dropped Malcolm as soon as it became apparent that he had no intention of following them into the cotton business; and neither had anything further to do with him during his lifetime.

But Stuart was something else again. Clarise Francillon, in her essay, "Malcolm, mon ami," [4] records an anecdote that gives some measure of young Malcolm's hero-worship:

> The first world war called to the front the eldest of his brothers. A steel rooster surmounted a steeple that one could see from the Lowry garden. "If I return unhurt, I am going to climb up and take down that rooster," declared the soldier who, indeed, returned unhurt. With a wicked air, the father said to him, "Now, boy, what about that rooster?"
> Everyone laughed except the youngest son, Malcolm, who was silent, stunned. He adored this brother whose return he had awaited every day, every hour. He didn't understand the pleasantry; he believed that his father was really going to make the young man climb up the building and bring down the bird.

One does not have to be especially schooled in Freudian analytical theory to appreciate how crucial are the early years of a person's life. To understand completely everything that Malcolm Lowry did, in his life and in his writings, it would be necessary to collect and examine documents of his earliest years with the utmost thoroughness. Unfortunately, this cannot be done: too many of the principal actors are dead; and most of those who remain are either uncommunicative, misinformed or—sometimes for very understandable reasons—rather disingenuous.

Most important of all, obviously, is the person's relationship with his parents. We have already seen something (though by no means all) of what Lowry, in his last three years, told his psychiatrists

4. *Les Lettres Nouvelles* (July–Aug. 1960), 8–19. My translation.

about Arthur and Evelyn Lowry: that the two of them fought constantly; that his father was an alcoholic; that he had been a change-of-life baby, and unwanted by both his parents; that his mother had wanted a daughter, and had coddled him overmuch.

To Margerie, however, Lowry recalled that his mother had "neglected him terribly." She disappeared for long periods of time with her husband, leaving young Malcolm in the care of a series of nannies, all of whom were (in his telling) at best incompetent, and at worst maniacally sadistic. He had suffered from his ninth to his thirteenth year from a neglected eye infection which kept him more than half blind; and his mother, disgusted by the sight of the bandages which swathed his face, had refused to allow him to come home from the preparatory school to which she had sent him as soon as he was old enough. John Davenport confirms that Lowry spoke of his mother "only with hatred"; and there seems no reason to doubt him. Yet it is curious that in later years Evelyn Lowry and her youngest son conducted a long and affectionate correspondence. And when *Under the Volcano* was accepted in 1946, Lowry sent two excited telegrams to England—one to Stuart, and one to his mother. (*Selected Letters*, p. 89.) After her death in 1950, he was full of remorse that he had not seen more of her, and been closer to her.

We can learn something more from Lowry's friends. James Stern, commenting very perceptively on Lowry's fear of sex, speculates that it came from a basic fear of authority—specifically, of Arthur O. Lowry. To Davenport, and to Julian Trevelyan, Lowry always spoke of his father with admiration and respect; but Trevelyan notes that Lowry was nonetheless "terrified" of his father. To James Hepburn, another friend from the Cambridge and London days, he "talked lots about his father, with admiration." The general impression, then, is that Lowry loved but feared his father, and was—to some extent, at least—contemptuous of his mother. It is difficult to know how much weight to give to Stuart's complaint about this youngest brother's tales of neglect and mistreatment: "Malcolm was very much wanted and loved. His mother cherished him. You must realize that Malcolm over-dramatized this business of his parents." [5]

Most probably, Lowry did indeed want to construct for himself a dismal childhood; and, once again, what we should want to know is *why* he wanted to do so. To add a touch of pathos to his autobiography, as told to wives and friends? Probably; Lowry was never averse to a little pitying. To offer his parents (along with cruel and callous older brothers, bullying young friends, aberrant nannies, and others) up as scapegoats, so that Malcolm Lowry the grown man would not have to bear all the responsibility for having acquired so many shortcomings in such a brief time? Yes, certainly; one likes to think of oneself as a "self-made man" only if one regards oneself as an unqualified success—and Lowry seldom saw himself as anything but a failure. But Arthur O. Lowry was *not* a vicious or neglectful father, however much of a prig or Babbitt he might have been; and Evelyn Lowry was *not* a neglectful, unloving mother—not, at least, by the standards of the more ambitious elements of the English middle class.

Stuart, Wilfrid, and Russell seem to have thrived in this "robust, extrovert, and nonconformist household"; [6] why should only the fourth son have been blighted by it? Superficially, indeed, Malcolm's early life was not nearly as pathetic as he pretended it had been. As John Davenport wrote:

> According to conventional biographical pattern, the youngest boy should have been puny and sickly, a mother's darling, coddled and bookish. It is true that Mrs. Lowry had hoped for a daughter, it is true that she had the indiscretion to name her baby *Clarence* Malcolm—a guiltily guarded secret—but he was as healthy as his brothers. He became an excellent rifle-shot, the schoolboy champion golfer of

5. The material in this paragraph was drawn from interviews conducted either by Conrad Knickerbocker in 1964–65, or by myself in 1966–70.
6. John Davenport, unpublished preface to rev. ed. of *Ultramarine* (New York, 1962). This preface, one of the most useful and intelligent essays yet done on Lowry, was rejected by Margerie Lowry, who substituted for it her own introduction. Subsequent Davenport citations in this chapter are drawn from his preface.

Great Britain, was a magnificent swimmer, and later broke a record for lifting bar-bells.

In other words, there was little in his early life to suggest that Malcolm Lowry would become a voracious and self-destructive alcoholic—or, for that matter, that he would become a genius. Yet we have learned to be suspicious of the happy childhoods of our literary heroes: Dylan Thomas had a "normal" youth; and so did Ernest Hemingway. And both were, one way or another, self-punishers and suicides.

The way now becomes tenuous and dangerous. How can one generalize about the relationship between infantile trauma and subsequent literary achievement? Rilke was coddled by his mother, who had wanted a daughter. Thomas Mann's whole view of life and literature was controlled—distorted, some might say—by veneration of his sturdily bourgeois Lübeck father, and by his admitted embarrassment that his mother was not Aryan, but Latin. To Kafka *fils*, Kafka *père* seemed an ogre. Dostoevsky (if Freud is to be believed) rejoiced in the murder of his brutal father, and punished himself for this "unnatural" emotion by becoming an epileptic—and a genius. There are enough of such examples for there to have arisen in this century what now amounts almost to a truism: that in the background of every creative artist lies an aggravated Oedipal situation. If one is sufficiently conditioned, he need hear only a fragmentary description of the relationship between Arthur O. Lowry and his youngest son before the appropriate passage from Freud's "Dostoevsky and Parricide" comes to mind:

> The continuing pressure of a harsh, threatening superego may well account for a number of phenomena, including preoccupation with disease and death, self-punitive drinking and impairment of potency, both genital and creative.

One can well imagine that Arthur O. Lowry represented for young Malcolm a "harsh, threatening superego." Certainly, there is ample evidence to document the son's subsequent admiration-cum-fear of his father: a sure sign to analysts of an involvement of the superego. And Freud might almost have had Lowry in mind when he noted the characteristic psychic injuries of the superego-damaged man.

Margerie Lowry does not entirely agree that Lowry's father meant very much to him, and recalls that in 1945 in Dollarton, "when his mother wrote him that their old gardener and caretaker had died, Malcolm cried, terribly upset. When he learned his father had died, he was quiet for a few minutes, then said, 'Let's go for a swim.' " But then Lowry swam so far out into Burrard Inlet that Margerie lost sight of him, and began to grow anxious. Finally Lowry returned, climbed up the ladder onto their pier, and went inside, without speaking. Nor did he speak, except rarely and tersely, of his father again. To Margerie such conduct on her husband's part might have indicated a lack of feeling, or at least a lack of affection. But to others, Lowry's behavior in this instance might suggest just the opposite—especially when one learns that in Acapulco, sometime in 1938, Lowry attempted to commit suicide by swimming so far out into the Pacific that he would be unable to return to shore (at least, this is the story as Lowry told it to Margerie). One ought also to remember that Arthur O. Lowry was a famously strong swimmer. We shall have occasion later to speculate about the symbolic significance to Lowry of the sea, and of swimming; and of his association of his father, and hence Authority, with the sea. Let us for the time being simply postulate that Lowry was not only not indifferent to his father, as Margerie indicates; but also that he never escaped from his father's domination, and that his feelings for his father were a curious amalgam of love and terror. Why his father should have wished so to dominate his son, well into that son's maturity; and why the son should have tolerated, even welcomed that domination, are more complex questions, perhaps impossible to answer.

And yet Stuart, Wilfrid, and Russell were not, as far as we know, so traumatized by their austere, rigid father. There must, one supposes, have been more in Malcolm's early life to trouble him than the autocratic, unbending father, or the vague, ineffectual mother who overfondled him (and who, for what it is worth, is said to have looked extraordinarily like him). For one thing, being just that—the youngest son—in such an athletic, masculine-oriented household, with three very much older brothers, must certainly have contributed to young Malcolm's feeling alienated. For another, he *was* left for long periods during his early years in the care of nannies while his mother accompanied her husband on business trips abroad; and for the rest of his life he was to confide to one friend after another the cruelties of these women.

John Sommerfield recalls how Lowry, in the fall of 1932, just down from Cambridge, would reel drunkenly about the streets of London, muttering about terrible sexual insults at the hands of nannies—insults which had "ruined" him for good. Soon after she met him, Lowry told Margerie that on one occasion a governess had taken him and young Russell, who would have been about seven, out onto a lonely heath near Inglewood, pulled down Lowry's short trousers, and whipped him on his genitals while Russell watched. This same woman, he said, later tried to drown him by upending him into a rainbarrel; and he was saved only by the appearance of the gardner, who yanked him out, gasping and spitting.

In an essay in 1960,[7] Lowry's Vancouver friend William McConnell remembered a similar story:

> Unlike most of us, Malcolm had not lost the wide-eyed innocence of childhood. In fact, many of the incidents of his childhood remained in his mind vivid as current events. He told us on several occasions, for example, of a nurse his wealthy father employed when he was very young. She had loved his older brother and to his horror hated him. Once she had wheeled his cart along the cliff-edge, high above the rolling sea. He described with quiet exactitude her features as she leaned over with a blanket to smother him, how he screamed (the exact key), and then the saving running footsteps of his favoured older brother which interrupted the scene.

And, two months before his death, Lowry told Ralph Case, who was visiting him in Ripe, that "he had had a nurse in Wirral who

7. "Recollections of Malcolm Lowry." *Canadian Literature*, No. 6 (Autumn 1960), 24–31.

used to take him into a remote part of the garden and twist his arm, and beat him." [8]

How much truth there is to these unhappy stories is open to speculation. Lowry would certainly not have been the first rich man's son to feel neglected by his mother, or to have claimed to have been treated brutally by his nannies. But his near-obsession with these events for the rest of his life, and the dramatic intensity of his telling them (the "exact key" of his screaming), and his insistence that he had been permanently damaged by them—all suggest that the whole business of the sadistic nanny, or nannies, was (like the visit to the Syphilis Museum in Paradise Street that he, aged five, had made with Stuart) [9] a sort of "screen memory," as suggested in the preceding chapter. The assaults might have taken place, though they were probably neither as numerous nor as severe as Lowry claimed, but they were not of themselves primary determinants of Lowry's subsequent mental infirmities. If they did in fact occur, then to be sure they must indeed have contributed to his difficulties; and in all probability they would have been sufficiently impressive to have initiated severe psychic disturbances in sturdier types even than the young Lowry. But the suspicion remains that the guilt which tormented him throughout his life had its origins in something earlier and more harmful even than flagellation at the hands of his nanny—something which caused him to batten on the cruel nannies (and, later, on the visit to the Syphilis Museum) as substitute causes, more socially acceptable and more susceptible to cause-and-effect analysis than the truer, obscurer origins of his mental and emotional disorders.

What those origins are, we shall in all likelihood never know. Early religious upbringing must have had some bearing: one can easily imagine that the senior Lowry's brand of Methodism left little room for such accessories as forgiveness or mercy. A vengeful God was always after Lowry; and, more than once, figured in his work.

8. From an interview with Conrad Knickerbocker in 1964.
9. For a reconstruction of what this museum, for 6 shillings, had offered the young Lowry, see *Ultramarine*, pp. 110–11, when Dana Hilliot and his friends visit a similar place in Yokohama.

His vengeance was tied up in some murky fashion with sexual experience. In Chapter III of *Under the Volcano*, for instance, Geoffrey Firmin nervously awaits the frightening moment when he must attempt to have intercourse with his wife Yvonne, just returned after a year's separation. As the time draws near, Geoffrey thinks of Goethe's early poem, "Die Wandelne Glocke," in which a church bell drops from its steeple to pursue a little girl who is trying to avoid going to church:

> Yvonne, it was clear to him, dreaded the approaching scene as much as he, and now felt under some compulsion to go on talking about anything until the perfect inappropriate moment arrived, that moment too when, unseen by her, the awful bell would actually touch the doomed child with giant protruding tongue and hellish Wesleyan breath.[10]

Indeed, very nearly the only sort of theological system that never appealed to Malcolm Lowry in his adult years was Protestant Christianity. His religious sense was strong, yet diffuse: he could happily pray for remission of sins to Christ, Buddha, Yahweh, Mohammed, or the Spider God of Voodoo; and at one time or another he must have lit candles and offered up prayers to most of the Virgins in most of the cathedrals in central Mexico. But the church of his father attracted him not at all.

Yet the seeds of Lowry's later mental and emotional discord clearly lie still deeper and earlier than the forced instillation of the Nonconformist spirit in him in his childhood. Awareness of religion, after all, comes relatively late in the formation of a child's personality—even though one can well imagine that that rather formidable consciousness of guilt which characterizes Calvinism must have been all-pervasive in the Lowry household, and absorbed at a very early age by young Malcolm.

More than one of his friends have mentioned the strong element of infantilism that they saw in Lowry's personality. He was at all stages in his life given to tantrums when thwarted, and to sulking

10. *Under the Volcano* (New York: Lippincott, 1965), p. 74. Subsequent references will be to this edition of the novel.

when ignored. According to Viscount Churchill, Lowry was "puppy-like. He was all right as long as you didn't oppose him, while he was drunk. He was impossible in daily life; one had to use child psychology on him." [11] Tania Stern recalls that "he had tantrums like a child, or like an ape in captivity; and chiefly drink released this in him." [12]

Lowry was also, it seems, given to the more obvious manifestations of narcissism: the Sterns remember that they often came upon him staring long and broodingly at himself in a mirror. We should be very much mistaken if we were simply to label this "vanity," because it is a great deal more than that. Among other things, such self-absorption indicates strongly that Lowry carried with him into adulthood a state of mind which the American psychiatrist Harry Stack Sullivan called protaxis: he could scarcely distinguish himself from the universe. Lowry was not simply admiring himself when he stared at his image in mirrors; nor was he seeking to "understand" himself, except incidentally. Most adults, when trying to come to terms with what is going on in the world, will look around about them. But Lowry, seeking to understand the outside world, knew only to look at himself. Conventionally, this attitude is called solipsism; philosophically, idealism. Whatever name one chooses to give to Lowry's extreme self-absorption, it is symptomatic of a markedly regressive, infantile state.

Lowry was often able to startle his friends by revealing a striking amount of self-awareness: even when he was at his worst, he had a very good idea of what he was doing, and why he was doing it. His fictional selves were similarly gifted (as why should they not be, since they were never more than Malcolm Lowry with only the name and one or two trivial pieces of biographical data changed), and we can often gain real insights into Lowry by reading what these various personae have to say about themselves.

In *Lunar Caustic*,[13] for instance, the protagonist, who may or

11. Interview with Conrad Knickerbocker, 1964.
12. Interview with the author, 1967.
13. *Lunar Caustic* (London: Jonathan Cape, 1968), p. 18. Original English publication in *Paris Review* VIII, 29 (Winter–Spring 1063), 12–72.

may not be named William Plantagenet, awakens one morning to find himself in a psychiatric ward of Bellevue Hospital in New York. "What's wrong with me?" he asks the doctor who is standing over him. The doctor replies:

> "Alcohol. . . . And perhaps other things. Judging from your remarks in the last few days I'd say it's about as bad as you suspect."
> "What did I say?"
> The doctor smiled slightly. "You said, 'Hullo, father, return to the presexual revives the necessity for nutrition.' . . . You made some fine giveaways."

Presexual, indeed. Years of clinical psychiatric study have demonstrated quite convincingly that a condition like protaxis (to continue with Sullivan's terminology) has its origins in the very earliest stages of character formation: those which are subsumed under the general rubric of *orality*. In this developmental phase, the key transaction is "self-object differentiation," which Freud describes in this fashion:

> An infant at the breast does not as yet distinguish his ego from the external world as the source of the sensations flowing in upon him. He gradually learns to do so, in response to various promptings. He must be very strongly impressed by the fact that some sources of excitation, which he will later recognize as his own bodily organs, can provide him with sensations at any moment, whereas other sources evade him from time to time—among them what he most desires of all, his mother's breast—and only reappear as a result of his screaming for help. In this way there is for the first time set over against the ego an "object," in the form of something which exists "outside" and which is only forced to appear by a special action. . . . In this way, then, the ego detaches itself from the external world. Or, to put it more correctly, originally the ego includes everything, later it separates off an external world from itself. Our present ego-feeling is, therefore, only a shrunken residue of a much more inclusive—indeed, an all-embracing—feeling which corresponded to a more intimate bond between the ego and the world about it.[14]

14. Sigmund Freud, *Civilization and its Discontents* (New York, 1930 [1929]), Std. Edn., XXI, 65–68.

Or, as Norman Holland rewords Freud, "the very young child does not distinguish 'out there' from 'in here.' Only by being able to wait for, expect, trust in, the reappearance of a nurturing other, does he begin to sense that there is a world which is not a part of himself. Only by recognizing that other as a being separate from himself does he recognize himself as a bounded entity." [15]

When something—some event, or series of events—occurs to disrupt this early process of differentiation, the marks of that disruption will almost invariably remain with the subject for the rest of his life, and will exert a great influence over the direction of the subject's subsequent personality development. If the disruption is severe enough, the subject may well become fixated in this "oral" phase, so that he never is able to develop a fully integrated personality, and remains forever bound to this earliest of infantile stages. Whatever one later becomes, the signs of oral fixation will be there. It has become possible to speak with some confidence about "oral types," and to describe them in what will strike the layman as an ominously deterministic fashion. To cite Holland again:

> Because the oral phase occupies the earliest period when self and object are still not clearly differentiated, this first phase is important for establishing our ability to trust external realities, especially other people. It is important too, for establishing what we might call our abilities to do nothing, to be passive, to wait. These traits can become too overdone in the adult personality; typically, the malingerer, the addict, the alcoholic, have been disturbed in this first phase of orality. . . .

If the orally-fixated person becomes a writer, one can predict with some confidence not only the subjects he will choose to write about, but even the way in which he will write about them. Alcoholics, addicts—losers of one kind or another—will be his protagonists. What they do not swallow, will attempt to swallow them: the sea will drown them; the earth will smother them. Sea voyages

15. Norman N. Holland, *The Dynamics of Literary Response* (New York, 1968), p. 35.

will abound, as will journeys into labyrinths. The element of fantasy will be strong. According to Holland:

> The kinds of images in a literary work that would make you expect you are dealing with an oral situation are, naturally enough, almost anything to do with the mouth or with "taking in": biting, sucking, smoking, inhaling, talking, and the like; or their correlatives, food, liquor, tobacco, and especially words, particularly curses, threats, and vows, words which "bite," constituting a kind of action in themselves.
> . . . Characteristic of oral fantasies is either-or thinking; thus, absolute words often go with oral fantasies: every, all, never, no, and the like. . . .

Ultimately, language—the emission of words—may come to be a defense against the dissolution of the personality. The death-wish, present in us all, is perhaps strongest in the oral type; who, having never really separated himself from the all-encompassing maternal element, is in gravest danger of subsiding back into it. If he is as acute as Malcolm Lowry was, he may recognize the lethal attraction of silence, and may write copiously, compulsively, in order not to die.[16] Thus, however passive his exterior self may be (and *accidia* is the besetting sin of such authors), the writing of the oral type is likely to be marked by a high degree of energy and apparent lack of discipline. He will probably find his reviewers—with more cogency than they realize—calling him "word-drunk."

The dangers in this sort of psychoanalytic game-playing are all too obvious. One is easily led into compiling lists: Lowry, Dylan Thomas, O'Neill, and Poe are clear oral types; Swift, Henry James, Mann, and Rilke are anal types—and so on, until all Western literature is classified as oral, anal, urethral, phallic, or oedipal. Or oral-anal, anal-urethral, urethro-phallic, whatever other improbable combinations occur to the psychologically ingenious. This sort of

16. For an elaboration of this theory, see Edmund Bergler, *The Writer and Psychoanalysis* (New York, 1950). Relevant also are Otto Fenichel, *The Psychoanalytic Theory of Neurosis* (New York, 1945); Erik Erikson, "The Theory of Infantile Sexuality," *Childhood and Society* (New York, 1963), and Edward Glover, "Some Notes on Oral Character Formation," *International Journal of Psychoanalysis*, VI (1925), 131–54.

thing may be interesting, but it still does not satisfy: what good, after all, does it do to suggest that the basis of Lowry's illness— and achievement—was a severe oral disturbance, if we can only speculate about what such a disturbance might have been (if, indeed, there *was* such a disturbance)? And even if we accept the designation of Lowry as an oral type (which he surely was, with a vengeance), and see in his works the signs of his orality, how does this help us make qualitative evaluations about those works? What makes a great oral writer better than a poor oral writer?

There are answers to such questions, although they will fail to lessen the skepticism of those who still cringe at the introduction of psychoanalytic theory into literary biography. We shall probably never know what occurred during his earliest months to trouble Lowry so severely; but from the way in which his personality developed, one can deduce some sort of trauma in the oral phase, without its being necessary to know precisely the nature of that trauma. And, the diagnosis of oral fixation once made, it would be possible to speculate more systematically about why Lowry became the man he was: why he behaved as he did in social groups; why he treated women as he did; why he drank; why he swallowed every sort of pill with almost hysterical eagerness; why he needed always to feel dominated, dependent on others; and why he killed himself. One would not be able simply by proclaiming Lowry's orality to say why he was a great writer (or why he was a bad one, as he often was); but one could say something about why he chose the characters, plots, and settings that he did; or why he used the language he did; or the images. To learn such things from psychoanalytic techniques is a far from worthless occupation.

Let us suppose then that Malcolm Lowry suffered some sort of emotional injury during the oral phase of his psychic development. Let us suppose also (to return to what many will consider firmer ground) that this injury was continued, or perhaps even intensified, by the Calvinistic austerity of his home; that the young Lowry resented the frequent departures of his mother, and regarded them as her desertions of him in favor of his father. Let us speculate that he later chose to modify the direction of his resentment, and did so by inventing the stories of his mistreatment by the nannies who were his mother-substitutes (or, if he did not invent them, by exaggerating them). Let us imagine that Lowry was a particularly sensitive child, and that he was in fact overfondled by his mother. We should not then find it difficult to believe that Malcolm Lowry felt, throughout his childhood and beyond, increasingly alienated from his home, his parents, and his "huntin' and shootin' " brothers. He very soon learned to find escape in fantasy—Stuart, in fact, once reminisced about what a dreamy and vague little boy Malcolm had been—and, more and more often, as he grew older, his fantasies were markedly "oral" in character. There was, in other words, more than enough in his early life to engender neurosis; and when these neuroses emerged, they took the shape that one would expect in one who had been orally fixated. We are still not satisfied; but, lacking more data, we cannot speculate more accurately than this about what took place in the early years of Malcolm Lowry's life.

Lowry may have become an accomplished athlete, as John Davenport claims; but he certainly showed few signs of becoming one during his childhood. As a little boy (and, indeed, until he was well into his public school years) he was fat, clumsy, and inept at any sort of physical activity. During his sixth year Lowry attended the Braeside School, in the Wirral; and it was at this time—as Stuart recalls—that he suffered a very bad fall from his bicycle, injuring his knee badly enough to require minor surgery. The accident left a jagged, lightning-shaped scar; and Davenport remembers that years afterwards, at Cambridge, Lowry liked to describe the "many months of crippling torture" that the accident had caused. To Margerie, in 1939, Lowry accounted for the scar by saying that, during his 1927 sea voyage to the Orient, his ship somehow had got itself into the middle of a Tong war along the Chinese coast, and he had been shot in the knee.

In the autumn of 1916 Lowry, aged seven, was sent to the Caldicote School, where he remained until his fourteenth year. Caldicote, now defunct, was near Hitchin, a small town twenty-five miles southwest of Cambridge. It had at that time a close link with The Leys, the public school where Lowry was eventually to be sent (as all three older brothers had been). There were perhaps 100 boys at Caldicote, and young Lowry managed to become friendly with almost none of them. One of his schoolmates, K. N. Hargreaves, recalls:

> We were at Caldicote together, but we were never friends in the ordinary sense of the word. I don't remember how he got his nickname ("Lobs"), but as a boy of ten or eleven he was somewhat fat and clumsy, with a very uncertain temper. He . . . was not particularly interested in or good at athletic pursuits. Nor was he a very enthusiastic scout, where we served in the same patrol.
>
> By nature he was a nonconformist with no close friends . . . . I don't recall that he went out of his way to be a rebel against authority, but it would I think be fair to describe him as something of a rebel against society.[17]

Lowry was often to hint darkly to Margerie about how savagely he had been bullied as a Cub scout (which, if true, might explain why he should have been a "not very enthusiastic scout"); but his unhappiest recollections about Caldicote had to do with another injury, worse even than the wounded knee. His account, as given to Margerie, went like this: at nine, playing ball at Caldicote, he was struck in the eye. An infection resulted, which the school physician neglected so badly that for the next four years Lowry was more than half-blind. More often than not, he was forced to cover one or the other of his eyes with heavy bandages, which, of course, made it almost impossible for him either to study or to engage in sports. Mostly, he told Margerie, he had only one daily duty during these years of semi-blindness: to walk the headmaster's dog into Hitchin, and fetch back a bottle of port for the man. For the rest of the time, he was left alone—not only during term, but on vacations as well, since his mother, unable to bear the sight of her youngest boy so disfigured, refused to let him come home. Since none of his schoolmates invited him home with them, he was forced to remain alone at school, looked after by the bibulous headmaster.

Finally, as he told Margerie, Lowry was taken by a new school

17. In 1964, Mr. M. F. Howard, Careers Master at The Leys, very kindly collected a number of notes and reminiscences about the young Lowry, of which this is one.

doctor to a specialist in London, who diagnosed the ailment as ulcerated cornea, then scraped his young patient's eyeballs with a scalpel, "removing the thick crust that had accumulated there," and put some drops in the eyes. The cure was instantaneous, and Lowry never again had a moment's trouble with his vision until 1955, when middle-aged myopia set in.

Again, Stuart—backed up by John Davenport, who understood Lowry better than most—advises extreme skepticism about the severity of his youngest brother's eye trouble. One can guess that there was indeed some sort of troublesome infection, perhaps neglected, perhaps even requiring treatment by a specialist. But four years of crippling near-blindness? Not likely—especially since no one who knew him at Caldicote remembers "Lobs" Lowry as having been anything like an invalid.

But even if his schoolmates do not recall Lowry's eye trouble, and if Stuart remembers it only faintly, as a minor difficulty, for Lowry himself it was severe and humiliating and unforgettable. There is scarcely a Lowry protagonist from Dana Hilliot of *Ultramarine* to Ethan Llewelyn of *October Ferry to Gabriola*, who is not made to have suffered a debilitating eye infection during his youth. In *October Ferry*, for instance, Llewelyn thinks back to a poster he had seen in a London tube station "because it had been just after his eyes got better." [18] Suffering through insomniac nights, Llewelyn is deluged by fears, and

> out of the fears wild hatreds, great unreasoning esemplastic hatreds; hatred of people who looked at him so strangely in the street; long-forgotten hatreds of schoolmates who'd persecuted him about his eyes at school; hatred of the day that ever gave him birth to be the suffering creature he was . . . hatred of himself, and out of all this hatred did not grow sleep.

And a poem like "Autopsy," however much or little it comes from actual occurrences, tells us a great deal about Lowry's unhappiness during these years:

18. *October Ferry to Gabriola* (New York, 1970), p. 134. The second quotation is from page 124.

An autopsy on this childhood then reveals:
That he was flayed at seven, crucified at eleven.
And he was blind as well, and jeered at
For his blindness. Small wonder that the man
Is embittered and full of hate, but wait.
All this time, and always lost, he struggled.
In pain he prayed that none other
In the world should suffer so. Christ's
Life, compared with his, was full of tumult,
Praise, excitement, final triumph.
For him were no hosannas. He writes them now.
Matriculated into life by this, remembering how
This laggard self was last in the school Marathon,
Or that he was last, last in everything,
Devoid of all save wandering attention—
Wandering is the word defines our man—
But turned, to discover Clare in the poor snail,
And weave a fearful vision of his own.[19]

The poem is maudlin and hyperbolic, to be sure, but still convincing as a testament of schoolboy misery. Small boys, as we knew
even before *Lord of the Flies,* are merciless savages; and young
Lowry, fat, inept, and possibly ill, must have come in for a lot of
abuse at the hands of his contemporaries at Caldicote.

There is only one suggestion, anywhere in his writings, that
Lowry had during these years any friends at all. In spite of what he
told Margerie about not being allowed home in his "blind" years, he
did visit Inglewood on his vacations, and Stuart (then on leave from
the Front) remembers that his brother at this time went often on
long hikes through the Wirral with a group of boys. To Margerie
he once asserted that these friends were the fantasized progenitors for
the Taskersons of *Under the Volcano*—those hearty, beery, young
men who could each "drink seven pints in fourteen minutes or walk
fifty miles without dropping." Many have assumed, however, that the
family from whom Lowry constructed the Taskersons were the Hepburn boys, James and John, and their mother, the poet Anna Wickham; but Lowry did not meet the Hepburns until years afterwards,

19. *Canadian Literature, 8* (Spring 1961), p. 23.

though they very probably were in his mind when he created the Taskersons. (A likely possibility is that the Taskersons represented for Lowry the sort of family he would have preferred his own to have been: instead of the abstemious and philistine A. O. Lowry, there would be the wordsworthian Abraham Taskerson; and instead of the three muscular Christian Lowry brothers, he would have the boisterous and boozy Taskerson boys.) In any case, there is this brief passage from the manuscript of *The Ordeal of Sigbjørn Wilderness* [20] to help us: Martin Trumbaugh (who becomes Sigbjørn Wilderness midway through the manuscript, but who is nevertheless Malcolm Lowry throughout) lies with a broken back in a Vancouver hospital and thinks of "that time when one of the Furnaces—the original of the Taskersons in his novel—had come to his rescue when, because of his burst chilblains, some boys were abusing him for being unable to tie his tie." No one has so far been able to turn up signs of a Furnace family in the Wirral—none, at least, which answers Lowry's description. It is always possible, of course, that Furnace was not their real name. There is only, then, this one faint clue to tell us that Lowry was not entirely friendless in the long, unhappy years of his stay at Caldicote—and even this comforting information appears in a context of bullying. There can be little doubt that these years only exacerbated Lowry's problems.

In September 1923, Lowry, aged fourteen, was sent to The Leys, Cambridge, a well-known public school where most of the boys came from the same sort of home as himself: comfortably well-off, middle-class, and nonconformist. As English public schools go, The Leys was, even in Lowry's day, rather benign: the discipline was firm, but there was relatively little fagging or caning. Founded by a Methodist minister in 1875, The Leys had rather a definite religious air about it. Students in Lowry's day assembled for prayers twice daily during the week, and attended both morning and evening church services on Sundays. The school was also mildly mon-

---

20. An unpublished novel of 160 typed pages, begun in March, 1949 and abandoned by 1952; now on deposit at the University of British Columbia. The passage cited is from p. 96 of the typescript.

astic: the headmaster and most of his faculty were bachelors, and all but the prefects among the 250 students slept in dormitories containing twelve to fifteen beds.

The boys of The Leys were expected not only to study, but also to take part in athletics and in all manner of extra-curricular activities; and Lowry, no rebel, participated—even in the unpopular (but *de rigueur*) Officers' Training Corps, in which he was a conspicuously inept cadet. By the time he reached The Leys, he was no longer the fat child he had been at Caldicote. According to all reports by those who knew him at The Leys, he was now stocky, rather muscular, and considerably more self-confident than he had been when younger. S. C. Gillard, Lowry's Modern Languages master, remembers him as

> a small boy, tousle-headed, splay-footed, ruddy-faced—all teeth and perpetually grinning—frightfully jaunty and argumentative, rather untidy, terribly fond of talking, and especially fond of listening to sea yarns which I was rather too prone to tell in class, and he would often trap me into telling them. I can still see him in an outsize pair of Oxford bags. He wasn't any good at games, but he was a *personality*.

He was also, one might add, somewhat less than brilliant at modern languages—though he did learn enough in Gillard's French class to deceive those who knew even less into believing that he was a natural and accomplished linguist.

To R. Morris, a Classics and English master, Lowry was "a redfaced, untidy, stocky figure who had a reputation for writing essays 'pour epater le bourgeois' . . . I don't think he was ever regarded as a rebel—possibly as a freak." F. W. Ives, another English master, recalls that Lowry was "a rather shaggy, laconic boy, a 'cat that walked by itself.' "

One of Lowry's contemporaries at The Leys, W. F. Proudfoot, has a particularly sharp recollection:

> I think of Lowry as thick-set in appearance, not very tall, tough physically and mentally, a little blasé and casual in manner, something of a lone wolf, and with a questing mind

mature beyond his years. He had a sense of humor and his armory against foolishness included a rather cynical little smile which would flicker momentarily on his lips. It was very eloquent. I should imagine that much of school life bored him. . . . His scholastic achievements were limited, though his flair for the English language was already blossoming.

Simultaneous with this blossoming of his flair for the English language was the beginning of Lowry's desire ("compulsion" might be the more accurate term) to write the language. He had apparently picked up at Caldicote the habit of reading anything and everything he could find, and he arrived at The Leys not only with an almost awesome knowledge of the early plays of O'Neill, and the sea novels of Melville and Conrad, but with a desire to emulate these masters as well. Fortunately for Lowry, his literary ambitions soon came to the attention of one William Henry Balgarnie, an English master who was later to achieve a kind of immortality when another of his students at The Leys, James Hilton, wrote a novel about him: *Goodbye, Mr. Chips.* Balgarnie was Housemaster of Lowry's house, and also the presiding genius of *The Leys Fortnightly*, the school magazine.[21] In the early months of his second year in school, Lowry approached Balgarnie and rather offhandedly announced that he had written some pieces which the *Fortnightly* might like to print. Although customarily only boys in their third and fourth years wrote for the magazine, Balgarnie accepted young Lowry's first efforts; and in the issue of March 13, 1925, appeared Malcolm Lowry's first fiction: a perfectly ordinary short story called "The Light That Failed Not." A boy reads a novel during evening "prep"; is caught by the Master in charge, and asked to bring the offending book to him; is on his way to the front of the room, feeling humiliated, when the lights of the building suddenly fail, allowing him to escape. This slender tale won a prize as the best story to appear in *The Leys Fortnightly* during the year, thereby

21. The interested reader may wish to consult Suzanne Kim, "Les Œuvres de jeunesse de Malcolm Lowry," *Études Anglaises*, XVIII, No. 4 (1965), for a more detailed analysis of Lowry's work for this magazine.

giving its author (who had, at Balgarnie's suggestion, taken the pseudonym of CAMEL—his initials with the two vowels added) some measure of renown in the school. Lowry followed up this success quickly, with a poem in the next issue, and another story later that spring. The former, called "Der Tag," is typical public-school light verse, complete with scraps of Latin, references to sadistic masters, and noon - moon - hor-iz-oon rhymes; and the latter, "Travelling Light," recounts the author's adventures on a train, and his fortunate escape from an Officers' Training Corps drill. It would be pleasant to be able to say otherwise, but the fact is that there is nothing at all in the first published works of Malcolm Lowry to hint that from the same hand would, in twenty-two years, come *Under the Volcano*. There is nothing except perhaps a capacity for wry self-deprecation to connect Lowry's first flights with his subsequent soaring.

In his third year, CAMEL first attempted a parody of sophisticated crime fiction (a victim, shot, gasps "Police!" into the mouthpiece of his telephone, and then dies, "just before the close of the inverted commas"), and next moved on to an experiment with pathos: perhaps his best effort at The Leys, a story called "A Rainy Night." The narrator, this time not a schoolboy but a married man, is on a train from Yeovil to Liverpool. In his note-case are some sandwiches which he does not care to eat, preferring to wait for supper until he reaches home. At Manchester a filthy old derelict enters the man's compartment; and, when the narrator questions him, the old man introduces himself as a Swedish sailor whose wife and child have just died, and who is on his way to rejoin his ship in Liverpool. The narrator puts the Swede's obviously poor condition down to drinking; but the old man (who turns out to be a weathered thirty-two!) dies in the compartment after the narrator leaves, and we are told in a *coda* that he has died of starvation. It is then that the narrator remembers the sandwiches which he had left in his note-case. The level of sophistication is only slightly higher here than in the preceding mystery satire, but now there are at least some signs that Lowry might be beginning to try to move himself out of the world of the schoolboy; and here, for the first time, one encounters the true Lowryan hallmarks: fascination with drunkenness, and with the sea.

Next came more light verse ("Homeopathic Blues in J") and a curious sort of parable called "Satan in a Barrel," in which Lowry investigates the struggle of Judge Jeffreys (the infamous Jeffreys of the Bloody Assizes) imprisoned in the Tower of London and sentenced to die, with a voice which promises him Forgiveness. The story would be as forgettable as the rest of his fictional contributions to *The Leys Fortnightly*, were it not for this voice of Grace. Lowry had obviously discovered *Dr. Faustus* by this time, for "Satan in a Barrel" is full of Marlovian resonances; and when Lowry's Voice here whispers to Jeffreys, "You are not past forgiveness," and begs him to pray, we are immediately cast back to Marlowe's Old Man:

> I see an angel hovers o'er thy head,
> And, with a vial full of precious grace,
> Offers to pour the same into thy soul:
> Then call for mercy, and avoid despair.

Faustus falls, of course; and so does young Lowry's protagonist here—as will most of his heroes, most especially Geoffrey Firmin of *Under the Volcano*, who has his Voice, too: just as Firmin is at the point of sliding into the mortal sin of despair, it says (or seems to say) to him, "Alas, my poor little child, you do not feel any of these things really, only lost, only homeless." Lowry and his fictional personae were visited by many mocking familiars, were tormented and harangued by many demons; but they always listened as well for a Voice offering forgiveness.

Rather surprisingly, Lowry next appeared in the *Fortnightly* as a sports reporter, devoting himself to covering the school's field hockey matches. "Hockey," as he admitted in one of his first write-ups, "even at its best is rarely a very diverting game to watch." Nor was it very diverting to write about, apparently; but one must say for young Lowry that he did his best to introduce a little grace and wit into the tedium. A goalkeeper, compelled to "fox" for the majority of one game, saves the day with a "Panta-gruelian" kick; when the team loses, CAMEL comforts them by reminding them that Shakespeare had his *Pericles.* When the players perform dully, he looks elsewhere for his story:

> Indeed the only brilliant, and by far the most interesting incident in the whole game, was when one of the referees brought off a catch from a hard hit by one of our backs, not only with the utmost nonchalance, but with hardly removing one hand from his pocket, and with absolute immobility of expression. This feat brought one of the few outbursts of applause heard during the match.

Almost immediately, angry letters from students and Old Boys began arriving at the office of the *Fortnightly:* in English public schools, one does not make sport of Sport, and CAMEL had to be put in his place. Loudly crying their "amazement" and "disgust," they took him to task for his ellipises, his conceits, his flippancies, and most of all his arcane vocabulary: "And what does the First reporter mean by 'fox,' 'Pericles,' 'torpid,' 'Pantagruelian,' and such absurd words?" wrote one angry young dunce. To all of these complaints, Lowry published a reply:

> Sirs,
> I have not had the time, nor had I the time, would I take it, to deal with you all in detail, but I am tendering a statement —not an apology, nor yet an explanation—of a state of affairs for which I have not the slightest intention of apologizing. I cannot say I read your somewhat childish slating with any interest. . . . I do not know how long you have been, or were, at the School. Two years, is it, or was it? or only one? Perhaps then you have not had time to form your style: perhaps (indeed you almost admit it) you are not old enough to write for our excellent magazine. . . . There seems to be a yet further objection concerning my reports, on which I have attempted to bestow a little sadly needed originality; you ask "What can I mean by Pantagruelian?" It is a confession that you yourselves do not know your Rabelais, and perhaps a further confession that you are not old enough to read it? and "Fox"—what can I mean by

"fox" ? A fox, I may state for your benefit, is an animal which, in its spare time, foxes. Hence the verb, to fox. . . . Another point. One of you remarks that I have undoubted talent: this is an error of etiquette—you should never tell people that they have undoubted talent: you will find me making no such mistake with you.

Indeed, all of the complaints only spurred Lowry on to further violations of high seriousness. In subsequent reports, inept backs are said to have spent the game "wandering round like mislaid ewes and hitting at this and that"; and the final five minutes of one especially bad match "would have disgraced a tenth-pitch game with twenty-one sanatorium excuses." In April 1926, the team traveled to France for matches with the Sporting Club de Colombes, the Academie de Paris, and the University of Paris. Lowry was taken along (the team appears not to have resented his sardonic reportage as much as did the other readers of the *Fortnightly*) to cover these events, and did so amiably enough, reserving most of his scorn for the loudness and incompetence of the French players, and the venality of the gate-keepers.

Aside from his sportswriting, which was to continue fitfully through his fourth year, Lowry wrote little else of interest for the *Fortnightly*. There was one more story, remarkable only for its title: "The Repulsive Tragedy of the Incredulous Englishman"; and two more poems, one nonsense-verse and one "serious" (which, in public-school taste, means Graveyard School) called "The Rain Fell Heavily," in which are gaunt woods, corpulent toads, blackened hay, skeletal pines, and the obligatory poignant epitaph:

> *When I am dead*
> *Bring me not roses white,*
> *Nor austere lilies grimly bright;*
> *But bring me from the garden roses red,*
> *Roses red, wind-blown, sun-kissed;*
> *The roses that my life hath missed—*
> *When I am dead.*

For the rest of it, there was a review of what must have been a rather indifferent performance of *Macbeth*, in which the schoolboy lead acted with "hideous gusto," and in which "the cauldron [was] so obviously not a cauldron, and the thunder so obviously but indifferent work on the bass drum, and the chair at the head of the table in the banquet scene so obviously out of No. 6, and the witches more like respectable spinsters of West Kensington than witches, that it was very difficult to keep one's mind on the action." And, in CAMEL's concluding remarks, there is a breath of the mature Lowry, astute and gently mocking:

> There is nothing particularly funny about a fly on an old man's bald head, but in church, and if that old man happens to be sitting in front of you, it is one of the illicit joys of the spirit. Similarly there is nothing funnier in *Macbeth* than in any other of Shakespeare's tragedies, but well—you know what I mean. One watched it breathlessly, but breathlessly as one watches a preacher who is about to drop his notes.

There was one more letter to the editor on December 16, 1926, in which CAMEL castigated the *Fortnightly* for blandly having noted as a "good point" a statement made in a school debate to the effect that "Public School men are better than self-made men." One of Lowry's signal virtues was that he was without a trace of snobbery, and that he was often ready to take public stands against snobbish attitudes. It was, of course, very nearly a moral imperative (and a social one, too, for that matter) for the well-off Oxbridge youth of Lowry's generation to be class-conscious, to seek solidarity with the working classes, or even to identify with them. Lowry was shortly to do his share of this well-intentioned sort of posturing, but he never did it to be *in;* quite the reverse, if anything. By the time of this last letter, Lowry had decided, probably with some accuracy, that the boys of The Leys were a "horrid lot of prigs," as he later described them to John Davenport; and he was ready to seek his way among real people, in the real world—which for members of Lowry's class and generation almost inevitably meant the martyred

The Leys School's 1926 production of *Tilly of Bloomsbury*, with Lowry as Percy, fourth from left.

proletariat in their lives of grinding poverty (poverty was always "grinding" though occasionally it was "abject").

But it would be simplistic to present Lowry during his public school years only as fledgling aesthete, unwilling sportswriter, or crusading egalitarian. Writing for the *Fortnightly* was only a small part of his activity at The Leys. Among other things, one might wish also to note that he had by 1926 already acquired something of a reputation as a surreptitious drinker. Or that, with his friend Michael Rennie (later the actor), he became a trend setter of sorts: the two introduced to The Leys the daring concepts of long, pointed sideburns and cuffless trousers.

Nor should one overlook Lowry's dramatic career. *The Leys Fortnightly* for March 1926, printed its review of the school's production of Ian Hay's *Tilly of Bloomsbury*, and noted that "Lowry acted the character of Percy with a delightful breezy abandon which made one regret the unsatisfactory way in which the part peters out in the second act; if he had a fault, it was that he was a little too emphatically resolute." Something of a ham, in fact. And in March 1927, he took part in a production of *Oliver Cromwell*, and the reviewer this time commented that "There was a pleasing vigor about the 'General Fairfax' of C. M. Lowry, and he was suitably diabolical in his other capacity as agent to the Earl of Bedford."

In athletics, as well, Lowry appears to have emerged from his ugly duckling phase by the time he left Caldicote. At The Leys, he swam and played tennis and rugger with much enthusiasm, if not much brilliance. But golf was really his game. He began competing at the Hoylake course in the Wirral during vacations, and by the time he was fifteen, he was a champion. In 1947 he described his golfing career to Albert Erskine (*Selected Letters*, pp. 149–50):

> Yes, I was pretty good at golf once, I broke the boys under-15 record, and also later under-18, held for fifty-odd years by Johnny Ball (later open champ) in 1924: I did the first 8 at the Royal Liverpool (Hoylake) in 28 once in the annual boys' show there when I was 14½, broke down at the 9th a short hole took in six (still two under actual par so far) but came back in the last 9 in the late forties but still broke the record. But later I took to socketing and even beer perhaps and dreadful nervous twitchings on the green. When I began to think I was really good I became lousy. But should you care to—er—look you will still find my record inscribed on the wall in the Royal Liverpool to this day: there is a very nice pub beyond the 17th green, on the other side of the road, called The Bull also. My record isn't quite fair altogether because Johnny had to use a gutta-percha ball in them days. But I beat H. H. Hilton's winning score, too, who didn't, and several others who later became amateur or open champs. My record wasn't beaten until sometime in the 30's, balls and clubs were getting better or perhaps even the players: to me, the holes were getting longer and more complicated.

After these triumphs, Lowry seems very nearly to have given up golf entirely, but Martin Case remembers playing him once in the early Thirties, and being "wildly outclassed."

By his final years at The Leys, Lowry was in a fair way to becoming muscle-bound. For some time he had been lifting weights regularly, and by 1927 had all the usual stigmata of this dubious form of exercise: he was quite barrel-chested, which had the effect of making his arms, always conspicuously short, seem all the more like vestigial appendages of some sort. His thighs were so thick that he could walk only by affecting a rolling, nautical gait. It was about this time that he began saying that he wished to become physically strong, "not in order to defeat people, but in order to be more practically compassionate." And strong he became, but clumsily so: for the rest of his life any activity requiring the slightest agility reduced him to sweating and trembling.

Early in his final year at The Leys, Lowry befriended a student named Ronald Hill, two years younger than himself; and the two began a musical association that got them some notoriety, at least. Hill gave his account to Conrad Knickerbocker in 1965 ("Malcolm Lowry in England," p. 21):

> One day when I was fifteen, I was playing the piano in the music room at The Leys and Malcolm came in. He stood listening and then brought his ukulele, although he insisted on calling it a taropatch. We started to play jazz, "hot music" it was called. He was seventeen, a sub-prefect; so he had made some sort of accommodation with authority. I revered him.
> . . . One of our favorite tunes was "Hindu Babe," full of rhythmic breaks, and Lobs always passed wind during the breaks. Remarkable. He was allowed to perform at the year-end concert, but without the gas. We started writing tunes together and paid a few pounds to have our songs printed. I believe one was actually performed once on the BBC.

This was "Three Little Dog-Gone Mice: Just the Latest Charleston Fox-Trot Ever," with lyrics (undistinguished) by Lowry and score by Hill; and the cover of the sheet music announced that it had been "Featured with Great Success by Alfredo and His Band." The

ROLAND'S PIANOFORTE TUTOR THE BEST IN THE WORLD.
English Fingering   Feldmans 6D Edition   Continental Fingering

I'VE SAID GOOD-BYE TO SHANGHAI

VOCAL FOX-TROT
(with UKULELE accompt)

Written and Composed by

RONALD HILL AND MALCOLM LOWRY.

Copyright   LONDON. ENGLAND.   Price 6d net
B. FELDMAN & Co 125. 127. 129. Shaftesbury Avenue W.C. 2

WORTON 6d EDITION   COPYRIGHT

THREE LITTLE DOG-GONE MICE

Just the Latest Charleston Fox-Trot Ever

Written and Composed by

MALCOLM LOWRY and RONALD HILL

Featured with Great Success

by

ALFREDO
AND HIS BAND

WORTON DAVID LTD. 6 New Compton Street Charing Cross Road W.C.2.

two followed this venture with another fox-trot, "I've Said Good-bye to Shanghai," which does not seem to have been featured with great success by anybody. Though this was Lowry's last real venture into the profession of music, his various fictional selves were to continue his career: the protagonist of *Lunar Caustic* has led a group called "Bill Plantagenet and his Seven Hot Cantabs"; Hugh Firmin of *Under the Volcano* had tried unsuccessfully to launch himself as a songwriter in London; and the nameless narrator of "The Forest Path to the Spring" climaxes his career by composing a jazz opera. Lowry himself was, by all accounts, a genuine connoisseur of jazz, and a real virtuoso on his tenor ukulele. But he had one physical shortcoming that never let him be more than a clever amateur: his hands were impossibly small, and his fingers so short and clumsy that he could never stretch over an octave on the piano, and had to "fake it" constantly on the ukulele. These artisan's hands we·e a source of shame and frustration to Lowry all his life, and hands ·n general acquire very nearly an obsessive thematic quality in his works.

Arthur O. Lowry had, of course, expected Malcolm to follow his brothers on to Cambridge, and had accordingly sent his name to Christ's College for the fall of 1927. But the youngest Lowry had other plans. He was now in the Fifth Form Remove, a special class for those who had not satisfactorily completed all their subjects, and his interest in academe was at a very low ebb. (He never did pass all of the entrance examinations for Cambridge, and appears to have been admitted chiefly because of the intercession of W. H. Balgarnie and S. C. Gillard, his chief masters at The Leys.) When his father pressed him about his plans, he at length agreed to go to Cambridge—but only on the condition that he be allowed to spend a year at sea first. Eugene O'Neill's early sea plays and Jack London's *The Sea Wolf* had caught him, and he could see no way to becoming a man but by shipping out. His father finally agreed, and even cooperated, to the extent of choosing the ship—the Blue Funnel liner *Pyrrhus*—and having the young sailor, purple with shame, driven to dockside on the day of departure in the family Rolls. Continuing the disaster, reporters were on hand, and under the leader "Rich Boy as Deck Hand" quoted young Lowry as declaring: "No silk-cushion youth for me, I want to see the world, and rub shoulders with its oddities, and get some experience of life before I go back to Cambridge University." Mrs. Lowry was on hand to make things even worse: "He is bent on a literary career, and his short-story writing is all to him. Of course, he has taken his ukulele with him, and he hopes to compose some more Charlestons during the voyage." [22]

The following day the *Pyrrhus* trudged out of Liverpool into what the disillusioned Lowry was later (*Under the Volcano*, p. 187) to call the "nauseous overrated expanse" of the sea. It was not to return until the following September, and was to work primarily in Asiatic waters. It took the young deck-boy perhaps two days to lose all his illusions about life before the mast, but the cruise lasted six months. Details about the activities of the *Pyrrhus* at this time are scarce, and Lowry was too dispirited to write anyone about his folly; but at the end of the voyage he summarized his life at sea to another reporter:

> I do not regret my action, but I do not intend to go to sea again. . . . My hardest job was chipping the paint off winches, and what you cannot chip off you get off with your nails or your teeth. Another job I did was to paint the inside of a coal bunker with black paint. As a rule I worked from 5:30 in the morning until 7 at night, scrubbing decks, polishing brasswork, and carrying the meals to the seamen. I took my ukulele with me and tried to compose some fox-trots. I hope to go on to a university and compose some more fox-trots and write fiction.[23]

Lowry never said much more than this to anyone about his voyage (if we except the far-fetched tale of battle with Chinese ganglords in which, he told Margerie, he had been shot in the knee), but we can infer, probably with some accuracy, much from the fictional voyages in *Ultramarine* and *Under the Volcano*. He was, of

22. *The London Evening News* (May 14, 1927), 5.
23. "Once Quite Enough/Cotton Broker's Son as Deckhand," *The London Daily Mail* (September 30, 1927), 20.

Lowry's sketch made aboard the *Donald S. Wright*, Christmas 1946.

course, an outcast, alternately despised and cozened by the crew of
the *Pyrrhus*, who resented his wealth and his—to them—rosy
prospects. As the ship moved along at a steady seven knots toward
Japan via Port Said, Perim, Penang, Port Swettenham, Singapore,
Kowloon, and Shanghai, he often heard his shipmates saying about
him, "I hate those bloody toffs who come to sea for experience." By
signing on, he had "done a good lad out of his job." He was clumsy;
he was a nuisance. One senses that Hugh Firmin's recollections
about his cruise on the *S. S. Philoctetes* are a close match for what
Lowry's must have been:

> Meantime it is scarcely an overstatement to say (Jesus, Cock,
> did you see the bloody paper? We've got a bastard duke on
> board or something of that) that he was on a false footing
> with his shipmates. Not that their attitude was at all what
> might have been expected! Many of them at first seemed
> kind to him, but it turned out their motives were not en-

tirely altruistic. They suspected, rightly, that he had influence at the office. Some had sexual motives, of obscure origin. Many on the other hand seemed unbelievably spiteful and malignant, though in a petty way never before associated with the sea, and never since with the proletariat. They read his diary behind his back. They stole his money. They even stole his dungarees and made him buy them back again, on credit, since they had already virtually deprived themselves of his purchasing power. They hid chipping hammers in his bunk and in his seabag. Then, all at once, when he was cleaning out, say the petty officer's bathroom, some very young seaman might grow mysteriously obsequious and say something like, "Do you realize, mate, you're working for us, when we should be working for you?"

(*Under the Volcano*, p. 189)

But, even though he had had no experience of hazing at The Leys, such mistreatment (rather mild, actually) bothered Lowry not so much as did some other things. These were violations of his romantic sensibility. He had counted on bunking in something called a fo'c'sle, but found instead that he was to sleep in something called the "men's quarters"—and this rankled. As Hugh Firmin complains, "To him a fo'c'sle—and where else should the crew of a ship live?—meant inescapably a single evil-smelling room forward with bunks around a table, under a swinging kerosene lamp, where men fought, whored, drank, and murdered." But on the *Pyrrhus* there was no fighting, whoring, or murdering going on in the "men's quarters," and precious little drinking. Worse, not only was the food not bad, it was positively delicious when compared with what The Leys had been offering him for the past four years.

Nor did their various ports of call offer much in the way of sin. On a salary of fifty shillings per month, one's capacity for vice is restricted; and Lowry gave himself up to only two iniquities: going ashore and getting drunk, or remaining aboard and getting drunk. He seems to have observed a good deal of fornication—the coolie longshoremen and their women used regularly to couple in the cargo holds of the *Pyrrhus* during working hours—but to have taken part in none. Perhaps he was, like Dana Hilliot of *Ultrama-*

rine, keeping himself pure for a girl back in England (Conrad Aiken has said that the original for *Ultramarine's* Janet was a girl in Liverpool named Tessa, but there are no more clues to help us, here.)

It is just possible that two more of Lowry's recollections about this voyage have some truth in them. He often claimed (and eventually—in "Elephant and Colosseum"—made a story out of it) that the *Pyrrhus* had brought back from Singapore, bound for the Dublin Zoo, a cargo of five black panthers, a wild boar, ten poisonous snakes, and an elephant named Rosemary. Since Lowry had turned out to be very nearly useless in any other sort of shipboard work, the Bos'un had made him the zoo-keeper for the return voyage; and Lowry had crossed the Pacific for the most part stumbling about in a hold of the *Pyrrhus*, trying to calm the frightened and seasick animals. It may have happened: this sort of thing did, to Lowry.

And, in the same story, Lowry lets his protagonist, the Manxman Kennish Drumgold Cosnahan, recall a rather heroic feat in which he had taken part during a typhoon as his ship lay at anchor in Yokohama harbor. A nearby Japanese fishing boat had begun to founder, and Cosnahan found himself in the crew of a whaleboat lowered to rescue the screaming fishermen. Lowry always insisted that this was a true account, and that the Japanese government had even given him an award for bravery.

In general, though, what Lowry seems to have learned from his grand adventure was that the sea is almost always boring, and that grandeur is seldom in men: valuable lessons for an eighteen-year-old, but not precisely the lessons he had sought. He did learn something about his own limitations and aspirations, and he lost some— though by no means all—of his illusions about the world. He had developed by this time one of the best eyes in modern literature for detecting the bogus and describing the squalid. He was to go to sea again, though not in search of epiphanies (for one thing, he was not much good as a seaman: too clumsy); and his later writings are very nearly always waterborne: the sea was from now on one of his prime symbols, more important even than alcohol. He knew its tedium, its nastiness; but he also had experienced, like everyone who goes to sea, one or two halcyon moments that almost—not quite, but almost—redeem the time:

> And the sun and wind danced through our clothes, strung on the line. All around us was the morning's blue crystal; the sun sparkled with a thousand flashes on the waves' gentle fall. The sun shone on deck as I washed and scrubbed my coal-black dungarees, stiff from dust and ashes, red lead and dust and grease; I stole a heaving line from the poop, and my washing dangled along the line, so that the forecastle was quite dark. But the sun spun around in its might towards the evening land of clouds, the atmosphere turned to evening with the burning of pale red stars. . . .
>
> (*Ultramarine*, p. 82)

One day in October 1927, a friend rushed up to Ronald Hill at The Leys and said, "Lowry is back, and he's in your bathroom." Hill hurried to his rooms, and, sure enough, there was Malcolm Lowry, roaring drunk, wearing a seaman's windbreaker, shouting songs at the top of his voice and playing his ukulele. "I was terrified," Hill said long afterward; "he'd moved into a man's world and I was still a schoolboy."

Indeed, the change in Lowry could hardly have been greater. He had left The Leys seven months before, a clever, boisterous, rather articulate schoolboy; and he appeared before the startled Hill now, loud, coarse, smelly, and drunk. The loudness would change often to sullen silence; but the Lowry that Hill watched was the new Lowry, the face that he would show the world for some years to come.

Why Lowry should have decided now to play the diamond-in-the-rough, the coarse speaker of truth, the loutish genius, is by no means certain. Eugene O'Neill and Jack London were undoubtedly unwitting instigators still, as they had been when their works sent the seventeen-year-old Lowry from public school to the decks of the *Pyrrhus*. Certainly, the months at sea must have had their effect on the boy; but they were not so very many months, as such things go, and they do not appear to have been unduly traumatic. (He had even come to feel accepted by the crew toward the end of the cruise, especially when at docking they packed his bag for him —until he found that they had packed it with stale bread.) He was under no very lasting impression that he had in six months become a real mariner, and therefore destined forever to feel ill at ease on land. For one thing, he was no fool, and knew that his nautical career had been after all rather fraudulent. As he let Hugh Firmin reflect (*Under the Volcano*, p. 197):

> To the sailor life at sea was no senseless publicity stunt. It was dead serious. Hugh was horribly ashamed of ever having so exploited it. Years of crashing dullness, of exposure to every kind of obscure peril and disgrace, your destiny at the mercy of a company interested in your health only because it might have to pay your insurance, your home life reduced to a hip-bath with your wife on the kitchen mat every eighteen months, that was the sea.

No, there was nothing especially romantic about the sea. But a very romantic pose indeed might be that of the simple sailor come ashore, compelled to live amongst all the sham and hypocrisy, an honest man fallen among dilettantes. Lowry kept himself as unwashed as possible, affected a nautical gait so pronounced that his friends often claimed it made them seasick to watch him walk, and wore clothes that—he hoped—made him look the worst sort of briny derelict. When he spoke, he bellowed; when silent, he contrived to glower.

And now, too, he drank, constantly and conspicuously. How much the role created the drinking, and how much the drinking made the role appropriate, is a difficult question. We have already noted Lowry's reputation as a "surreptitious drinker" while still at The Leys; and if *Ultramarine* may be taken at least in part as an autobiographical statement, then Lowry must have been drunk at every opportunity during the voyage of the *Pyrrhus*. Orally fixated types are prone to excessive drinking. Sons of austere and autocratic fathers are apt to express their rebellion against that parent by drinking. Guilt and fear, of sexual origin, are likely to express themselves in drinking. Reaction against a rigidly authoritarian religious upbringing may manifest itself in drinking. Lowry drank now partly because the sailor home from the sea was expected to be something of a boozer; but he drank not so much because he chose to, as because he *had* to: from one source or another, he had acquired, by the age of eighteen, enough guilt—sexual and otherwise—and resentment and insecurity to have made it almost impossible for him to be anything but an alcoholic. He must have been an utterly miserable young man.

And yet. For anyone writing about Malcolm Lowry there is (or ought to be) a small voice in the back of the mind that is always saying, *Do not take me quite so seriously.* Lowry could be sodden, sullen, wracked with shame and remorse: a figure of total anguish. And then, say his friends, you would catch him looking at you out of the corner of his eye, seeing what sort of effect his performance was having. If you caught him gauging you thus, he was perfectly capable of breaking out into his foxy grin, throwing his arm over your shoulders, and telling you a long, intricate, and hilarious joke —of which he was usually the butt. Lowry was often miserable, all right, and with ample justification; but he was also capable of watching Malcolm Lowry being miserable, and laughing at the sorry spectacle. Sometimes it is difficult to do so, but it is essential to keep in mind that Lowry was a comedian first and foremost, and a great ham actor. We need to keep Conrad Aiken's reminder before us, lest we be taken in by the tragic aspects of Lowry's life: "his whole life was a joke: never was there a gayer Shakespearean jester. A fact that I think we must remember, when everyone is saying What Gloom, What Despair, What Riddles! Nonsense. He was the merriest of men." [1] On the other hand, we need also to keep before us the undeniable evidence that he was an alcoholic of Gargantuan proportions, an occasionally dangerous manic-depressive, and a suicide.

The *Pyrrhus* deposited Lowry back in Liverpool too late for him to go up to Cambridge that fall, and Arthur O. Lowry had to find some way of keeping the prodigal son out of trouble for another year. He settled on Weber's School of Modern German in Bonn, and packed Lowry off to Germany in late December 1927,

1. Letter to *Times* [London] *Literary Supplement* (February 16, 1967), 127.

hoping that he could be kept out of difficulties for a few months. This "English College" (as it was generally called) was a rather expensive institution on the Koblenzerstrasse that had as its aim the teaching of German to well-to-do young Britons who were destined either for the diplomatic corps or for businesses connected in some fashion with Germany. Lowry, of course, fell into neither category (even his father had by now begun to admit to himself that his youngest son was a queer sort, with no interest at all in following his brothers into the family cotton brokerage); he was simply there to learn German. Captain Weber, a retired army officer, maintained a staff of six teachers, three of whom served also as housemasters of the three houses which constituted the school. Lowry's teacher and housemaster was Karlheinz Schmidthüs, who seems to have inspired great respect and fondness in his pupil. In 1951, when Lowry was writing Clemens ten Holder, the first German translator of *Under the Volcano*, he waxed enthusiastic about Schmidthüs and all things German (*Selected Letters*, pp. 237–40):

> There was indeed a teacher, when I was at Bonn-Koblenzerstrasse, in 1928, named Schmidhus [sic], and one of whom I entertain the kindliest and most affectionate memories, for he was not only the most brilliant of the teachers there and the most well-liked—as brilliant a teacher as I was a dummkopf of a pupil—but he was a person of such great goodness and wisdom that I not only have never forgotten him but can describe him in absolute detail, even though this is 23 years ago, and my sojourn in Bonn only 8 weeks. . . .
> He needed a lot of patience with me, as I had an almost abnormally slow mind, which caused me to suffer a great deal; however I can read German aloud today almost as well as a German—that was about the only class I took with Herr Schmidhus, who mostly dealt with advanced students, but then that was almost the only thing I learned at all in Bonn, outside the bar of the Hotel Rheinischer Hof.

He pleased Schmidthüs, he recalled, by showing a genuine appreciation of German theater, especially of Georg Kaiser and Ernst Toller, and by insisting that O'Neill could never have written *The Great God Brown* without Kaiser's influence. He hoped that Schmidthüs might take some pride in his old pupil because the influences that have formed the *Volcano* are in a profound degree and largely German, though it may be hard to see where they come from. (It was in Bonn I saw Murnau's *Sonnenaufgang;* seventy minutes of this wonderful movie . . . have influenced me almost as much as any book I ever read, even though I've never seen it since.)

There were also, Lowry remembered, occasional adventures during his stay at the school:

> Indeed I was arrested in the street once in Bonn for playing and singing [my] guitar, in company with some of your countrymen and one of mine, on the occasion when we were celebrating the defeat of Essen *Verein* at hockey, I having played inside left for Bonn *Verein*, a refrain that went, every now and then, *Zwei-null!* We having defeated Essen 2-0. Also there was another song to the refrain: *Drei Segelmann. . . .* But the policeman didn't like it. Finally he decided he did like it but would fine us all a little bit just the same. Whereupon your countrymen swore gallantly they would go to gaol rather than be fined. Whereupon we swore gallantly we would go to gaol rather than they be fined. Whereupon we all repaired to the Hotel Kaiserhof, and were fined just the same, though nobody, it seems to me mysteriously, paid.

There is a curious discrepancy between Lowry's experiences as described by himself, and as recalled by Herr Schmidthüs. Writing to Conrad Knickerbocker on July 17, 1964, he noted that "Lowry was not at all unpopular with his fellow students; they certainly thought him odd . . . but he had quite a number of friends." But as for Lowry's close attachment to his former teacher: Herr Schmidthüs was embarrassed to have to say that he did not remember having had very much at all to do with Lowry, who rather

> gave the impression of a mute, dumb, inarticulate fellow, who even at that time was already drinking very heavily. I remember several times when he came home at night nearly unconsciously drunk. The discipline in the school was rather strict, and the students worked rather hard to learn their

German. So you can imagine that Lowry was not exactly popular with the staff. I personally did not find Lowry very attractive, but he interested me as you could guess behind his dumb appearance some sort of intelligence. He surprised me one day by showing himself to be a rather good jazz player on the piano. . . . he was certainly not one of my favorite pupils, but certainly there did not exist a special antipathy between us. I remembered that I often wondered what would become of him.

In any case, Schmidthüs was kind to Lowry, and listened to the young man's effusions about German novels and films; and it is unlikely that Lowry's eight weeks in Bonn did him any great harm. Certainly it did little to interfere with what he once called "his flawless incompetence as a linguist" [2]; and it did at least leave him with another small role into which he was to drop from time to time until his death: that of the quiet Englishman with "formal, faintly German manners." Sigbjørn Wilderness in *Dark as the Grave Wherein My Friend Is Laid* has often to resist the temptation to click his heels together (especially when he is wearing only one of his shoes).

Lowry was back in England by late spring of 1928, and proving to be even more of a problem for his father than before. He refused to come home to Caldy, and showed no signs of living up to his old promise to go up to Cambridge. In desperation Arthur O. Lowry found him lodgings at 5 Woodville Road in London's Blackheath area, and arranged for him a weekly allowance of £7 per week—a very comfortable sum in those days. Lowry—who knew almost no one in London at this time—for the first time began to spend all his time writing. His goal was a "truly modern" novel of a youth's initiation into life, set at sea; and practically speaking, what he meant by this was the application of current fictional techniques to his own recent adventures aboard the *Pyrrhus*. He began filling notebooks with material for what was to become *Ultramarine*, but nothing that he wrote satisfied him: too callow, too trivial, too ob-

2. "Elephant and Colosseum," *Hear Us O Lord From Heaven Thy Dwelling Place*, p. 129.

viously the work of a public school boy who had read a little Joyce.

Then, quite by accident, he came upon Conrad Aiken's novel, *Blue Voyage* (published only the year before), and his future lay clear before him: he would absorb all of Aiken's works, then go to Aiken and sit at his feet until he had absorbed all of the American's genius as well. Lowry, for all his apparent experimentalism, was never really a "modernist." Gerald Noxon, who became one of Lowry's closest literary friends at Cambridge, recalled in 1963 the way they had worried about "how a serious novelist should write in 1930":

> Naturally we discussed the kinds of solutions put forward by such writers as Joyce, Faulkner, and Hemingway. . . .
>
> Basically Malcolm was unwilling to repudiate the legacy which he had found awaiting him in the works of the nineteenth-century novelists. While discarding the aridity of a purely realistic style, he was unwilling to adopt the kind of personal stenography which made the works of writers like Joyce and Faulkner superficially difficult for the reader but still insisting that his writing must be capable of carrying meaning at many different levels of intellectual and emotional communication which he discerned in Melville, for instance.[3]

We shall have more to say later about a theory which supposes that Lowry's psychological values were largely Elizabethan, and his fictional values primarily those of the late nineteenth century. Suffice it now to say only that Noxon's citation of Melville is most appropriate; for if Lowry learned much of his technique from Aiken, it was from Melville that his poetic vision came, more so than from any other single source. (And for that matter, if Lowry were now the Hairy Ape and Wolf Larsen, he was also Melville's Redburn, standing lonely at Easton Station, inept at sea, homeless on land.)

But Lowry could not write his young-man-at-sea novel after the fashion of Melville: Melville had already exhausted the possibilities in that direction. He needed his own voice, his own way of saying; and there was something about the way Conrad Aiken wrote that

3. "Malcolm Lowry: 1930," *Prairie Schooner*, XXXVII (Winter 1963–64), 317–18.

made Lowry believe that the American was destined to become his master. So, saturated with multiple readings of "The House of Dust" and *Blue Voyage*, in late December 1928, he wrote to Aiken, care of his home in Rye, Sussex. The letter began, "I have lived only nineteen years and all of them more or less badly," turned itself into a little tone-poem about thinking of "The House of Dust" while sitting in a grubby London tearoom, and then concluded:

> Sometime when you come to London, Conrad Aiken, wilst hog it over the way somewhere with me? You will forgive my presumption, I think, in asking you this.
>   I am in fact hardly conscious myself of my own presumption. It seems quite fated that I should write this letter just like this, on this warm bright day while outside a man shouts Rag-a-bone, Rag-a-bone. It may not even interest you, my letter. It may not be your intention *ever* to come to London even to chivy up your publishers. . . . You could also tell me whether you are coming to London any time, you would have any time to see me. Charing X is only a quarter of an hour away from here. But perhaps this letter has infuriated you so much that you have not read this far.
>
> te-thrum te-thrum
te-thrum te-thrum
Malcolm Lowry[4]

Aiken replied optimistically to Lowry's application for a position as adulator; but by the time his reply reached Lowry, Aiken had left England for Cambridge, Massachusetts, where he was to begin conducting a tutorial at Harvard. He apparently did not tell Lowry of his impending departure from England; or else the young man, beside himself with happiness that Aiken should have bothered to answer him, failed to register any such information: because Lowry now (March 13, 1929) wrote Aiken a second letter, and mailed it, like the first, to the Rye address (*Selected Letters*, pp. 4–7).

> I cannot remember what you said. You were pleased that I ended off my letter to you with *te-thrum, te-thrum, te-*

4. *Selected Letters*, pp. 3–4. The "te-thrum" is a refrain in *Blue Voyage*.

thrum, te-thrum; but I can't remember anything else except your handwriting. Of course it was, as I realized bitterly when I woke up, merely a rose-festooned illusion. You had no intention of writing me. You didn't like the way I asked if you would have time ever to see me in London when you might have time but hardly time enough to trouble about having a lunch on someone you'd never seen. I perhaps didn't make it clear enough that I'd go anywhere within my reach from Pimlico to the Isle of Dogs if only there was half a chance of seeing *you*.

Then Lowry got down to specific terms for Aiken, who was, it seemed, to be asked not only to teach but also to serve *in loco parentis* to Lowry:

> I suppose there are few things you would hate more than to be invested with any academic authority. Well, this I shall say. Next October I am going to Cambridge for three or four years to try and get an English Tripos and a degree. Until October I am more or less of a free lance and a perpetual source of anxiety to a bewildered parent. The bewildered parent in question would be willing to pay you 5 or 6 guineas a week (I should say six personally, but tactilly) if you would tolerate me for any period you would like to name between now and then as a member of your household. Let me hasten to say that I would efface myself and not get in the way of your inspiration when it comes toddling along, that my appetite is flexible and usually entirely satisfied by cheese, that although I can't play chess and know little of the intricacies of gladioli, I too have heard the sea sound in strange waters—sh-sh-sh like the hush in a conch shell— and I can wield a fair tennis racket.

He goes on to praise Aiken's writing, and to lament his family's lack of sympathy for his ambitions: "and although I have had a certain amount of youthful success as a writer of slow and slippery blues it is as much as my life is worth to play anything in the house—that doesn't worry me so much—but when they see me writing anything serious they don't exactly discourage me but tell me that it should be subordinate to my real work." But his real work, he knows, is writing; and he pleads once more with Aiken to see him in London, or at least to write him affirmatively about the guardian-*cum*-tutor arrangement.

Aiken wrote from America, agreeing to give it a try. Lowry, overjoyed, raced up to Caldy to say good-bye to his parents, and to arrange for his father to send Aiken's fee on to him; then ran by The Leys briefly, in order to leave one last poem ("Number 8 Fireman") with the *Fortnightly;* and finally, in late April, sailed from Liverpool as a steerage passenger aboard a cargo ship that was headed to Boston via Bermuda and the West Indies.

Unfortunately, one has to rely for information about this second voyage almost entirely on what Lowry chose to tell Margerie Lowry about it, and the romanticizer was all too obviously at work in the anecdotes that he recalled for her. The ship had, he said, put into most of the islands of the Antilles group; and he had spent many nights on shore, paying for his food and rum by playing his taropatch in one sporting-house after another. While on Montserrat, moreover, he had, taropatch in hand (and drunk to boot) climbed a mountain never before ascended, and helped a pair of creoles survey the peak. Far-fetched? Yes, of course; except for a titillating passage in "Through the Panama," [5] which suggests that there might be at least a grain of truth in the second anecdote:

> Montserrat not far to starboard where I altered geography
> books by climbing Chance's Mountain in 1929, in company
> with two Roman Catholics: Lindsey, a Negro, and Gomez, a
> Portuguese.

In any case, Lowry's ship reached Boston in early July; and he passed through Customs and into the United States carrying with him his taropatch and a little broken suitcase containing nothing but the notebooks for *Ultramarine.* He found Aiken in his apartment at 8 Plympton Street, above the Grolier bookstore, and the two hit it off at once. "We were natural father and son," Aiken has often remarked, and justly so; but their first evening together was rather

5. *Hear Us O Lord From Heaven Thy Dwelling Place,* p. 72.

less solemn than one might be led to expect from Aiken's words. The two, joined by Aiken's brother, Robert P. A. Taylor, celebrated by throwing a grand beano, and ended by wrestling for possession of a porcelain toilet seat. Lowry tossed Aiken into the stone fireplace with such force that the man's skull was fractured. "That," says Aiken, "was the beginning of a beautiful friendship."

It was also the beginning of a month in bed for Aiken, during which time he was entirely dependent on Lowry for care (Aiken being at the moment more or less between marriages, and living alone). Every day Lowry would work for a few hours on *Ultramarine*, after which Aiken would try to explain something to him about the architectonics of fiction. Lowry, Aiken felt, could not understand the importance of ebb and flow, of contraction and expansion: he was trying to write *Ultramarine* entirely in a tone of muted, injured brooding, and Aiken tried to convince him that he could not sustain this for the length of the book.

They worked on poetry as well. Here, Aiken felt (accurately), Lowry was destined never to be more than a "gifted amateur"; but he gave him complicated exercises, requiring him to change caesuras in verses, or to rewrite various poems using different meters. Lowry worked diligently at the tasks Aiken set him, and no doubt profited much from them; but he would never acquire much technical facility, either in prose or verse: with Lowry, it was always to be strong lines and bass chords, or nothing (saving verbal slapstick, a facility of his which has usually gone unremarked).

Lowry was happier than he had ever been. In Aiken he had found the father-figure for whom he had so obviously (as witness his rather poignant attitude toward Herr Schmidthüs in Bonn) been searching. Arthur O. Lowry was for his youngest son a creature from an alien world: a world in which men *did* things, made money, amounted to something. There could never have been any way for Lowry to have approached his stern, decent father; but with Aiken it was different. "The fact is," Aiken wrote, "that we were uncannily alike in almost everything, found instantly that we spoke the same language, were astonishingly *en rapport*." [6]

6. "Malcolm Lowry: A Note," *Canadian Literature*, No. 8 (Spring 1961), 30.

Toward the end of August, Lowry went with Aiken down to South Yarmouth, on Cape Cod, where Aiken had a house that was about to be thrown into the divorce pot. They stayed there off and on for perhaps a month, while Aiken was seeing to the removal of his furniture from the house; and here Lowry had (if we except the perhaps mythical Tessa of Liverpool, hypothetical original of Janet in *Ultramarine*) his first brush with love.

Doris ("Dolly") Lewis was the step-daughter of Charles D. Voorhis, an old friend of Aiken's. She was in her late teens in 1929, and quite competent as a painter and writer. Malcolm, says Aiken, "quite fell for her—his type, the boy-girl." [7] In the remaining weeks of the summer the two went often for long, barefoot walks along the beach; talked about poetry and painting; and sometimes went up to Boston to the theater. He was apparently quite proper and restrained with her; and she appears to have been impressed mainly with his eccentricity:

> Malcolm had no clothes or very few—he played the ukulele *all* the time. Carried it with him quite a bit and sang funny songs. . . . I can see Malcolm's face always shiny with the dampness—a pair of too large gray flannel slacks (Conrad's) draped and folded about his waist and a very *tight* white shirt that clung to him—open at the neck. He was writing too—he came and spent some time with us. . . . His only baggage was the ukulele and a very large sponge which he left behind when he went to Cambridge. . . . He had black patent leather shoes, rather pointed. We swam a lot in the Bass River. I can remember taking several long walks with him along sand roads where the cranberry bogs were—back of S. Yarmouth village. . . . Malcolm read a lot of very odd books then—the only ones we had in that house since it was often rented and I remember him searching all day for sea stories (we had so few!) and reading aloud passages from one or two things. I was a frightful priggish high-brow at the moment and was shocked to see what he read! [8]

When the time came for him to return to England, he spent one last weekend at Dolly Lewis's house in South Yarmouth, then returned

7. Letter to Conrad Knickerbocker, September 21, 1964.
8. Letter of August 31, 1964.

to Boston—leaving behind one of those rather pointed black patent leather shoes, perhaps as a dubious memento of his infatuation.

In September he left Boston at the end of what Aiken was to call "that wonderful summer of 1929," and sailed on the Cunard White Star Liner *S. S. Cedric* back to England.

Lowry was already a formidable correspondent, able to tear off a twenty-page letter to anyone at all with ease; and he spent considerable time during his voyage home writing copiously back to Dolly Lewis. Sitting in the smoking room of the *Cedric* (the very place in which Aiken had written a chapter of *Blue Voyage*, he noted with satisfaction), he wrote her that life aboard ship was lively:

> I ought to be having a good time. A party of Americans & four architectural students bound for Rome adopted me & unintellectual whoopee has been made every night. Amazons of liquor flow. Ukuleles are played, songs are sung. There are heaps of pretty girls on board and I have kissed three so far. It is all only too easy. One is even sure she loves me. That is ocean air and gin.

Once into the letter, he cannot resist the temptation to try out a few of the tricks he had been taught by Aiken during the summer. He composes a central, recurring motif for Dolly: "But you do not love me"; and develops, each time he uses the motif, a conceit having to do with his clumsy ardor and her carefree refusal to take him seriously. These segments he tries to space out by interposing, for counterpoint's sake, impressions and observations about other passengers, descriptions of the seascape ("At night one sits on the boat deck and watches . . . the moon sweeping in great circles round the horizon"), and snippets of dialogue from *Blue Voyage*. But he is too young, and too lovesick, to be so artful for very long; and by his twelfth page he is agonizing over what Dolly's mother must think of him:

> . . . that also maybe your mother (kind to me as she was and desperately grateful to her though I am) even now is telling you that she dislikes me, that I am not enough of a he-man for her, or that she thinks my hands, which God was not

quite sure to make those of an artist or a bricklayer, and decided on an unsuccessful compromise between the two, are effeminate. She will undoubtedly tell you that I am bound to have an unsuccessful life and having enumerated the times I have stumblingly contradicted myself will show you just when and where, and how corrupt a liar I am.

By page thirteen he was perhaps beginning to feel that he was not representing himself strongly enough: it was necessary for him to convince her of the depth of his love. His attempt at this is remarkable, and possibly unique in the history of erotic correspondence:

I cannot kiss anybody else without wiping my mouth afterwards. There is only you, forever and forever you: in bars and out of bars, in fields and out of fields, in boats and out of boats . . . there is only love and tenderness of everything about you, our comings in and our goings forth, I would rather use your tooth brush than my own: I would wish, when with you on a boat, that you would be sick merely so that I could comfort you. Nor is there one ounce of criticism in this. I do not conceal in my heart the physical repulsion which, not admitted to oneself hardly, exists usually in the filthy male. I would love you the same if you had one ear, or one eye: if you were bald or dumb: if you had syphilis, I would be the same; it is the love that one stronger algebraic symbol in a bracket has for its multiple—or complement . . . it cannot live without the other.

No nineteen-year-old girl could ask for more passionate intensity than this, certainly: here is Malcolm Lowry laying himself open utterly, even to the telltale inclusion of the syphilitic detail. But unless Dolly Lewis were an unusually sophisticated young lady, she was most probably rather appalled by such carryings-on, and not much pleased at being made wonder how she would look if seasick (with not even a toothbrush to call her own), one-eared-or-eyed, bald, dumb, and possibly syphilitic. Not, one would say, a manner of wooing very likely to succeed; but absolutely typical of Malcolm Lowry: earnest, vulnerable, bumbling, and—however obscurely —brilliant.

By October, Lowry's unrequited passion for Dolly Lewis had subsided enough for him to look forward to entering Cambridge. His old teachers at The Leys had written to A. G. Chater, then Master of St. Catharine's College, to propose that Lowry be admitted without passing the School Certificate exam; Chater agreed. Lowry stopped briefly in Caldy after his return to England, collected his books and the minimal wardrobe that always seemed sufficient to him, and set off to find digs in Cambridge.

He settled into a rather down-at-heels rooming house on Bateman Street, near the train station. He was by now at least a year older than his classmates, and had certainly seen more of "life" than most of them; and he was under no illusions that he was going to fit in easily at Cambridge. Ronald Hill, his old musical partner from The Leys, was there now, at Christ's. He was, he recalls, "living in digs in New Square. Malc came over to see me, to renew friendship; but after the bathroom experience at The Leys in 1927, I was frightened of him as an idea and rejected him at first meeting. Malc was hurt but didn't press the friendship. I had a feeling of suppressed violence in Malc, and I was afraid of being possessed. Maybe Malc was looking for an element of stability." [9]

But Lowry was determined in any case to make a name for himself with the literary set, and commenced almost immediately to establish connections. During his first week at the University he went by Trinity College to call on Gerald Noxon, one of the editors of *Experiment*, and to announce that he would shortly be offering Noxon several pieces from a large work-in-progress. Then, still in October, he paid a visit to John Davenport in his rooms in Corpus Christi. Davenport was an editor of *Cambridge Poetry*, and Lowry approached him (Davenport afterwards recalled) "with the solemnity of a Frenchman seeking election to the academy." [10] It was late

9. Interview with Conrad Knickerbocker, 1964.
10. This quotation, and those which follow, are from Davenport's unpublished preface to the 1962 edition of *Ultramarine*. Davenport gave Knickerbocker a somewhat different account of his meeting with Lowry, which Knickerbocker included in his 1966 *Paris Review* essay: "I first met him in Robin Fedden's rooms at Magdalene during the October term of 1929. 'Are you Mr. Fedden?' he said. 'No,' I replied, 'John Davenport.' 'Oh yes, the poet,' And we had drinks, many drinks."

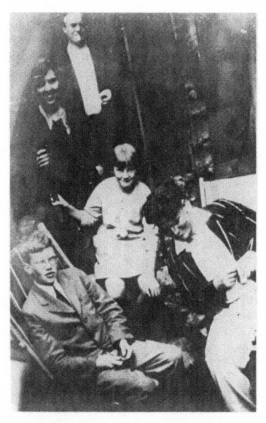

Conrad Aiken, Catherine Freeman, Aiken's daughter Jane and son John, and Lowry, Jeake's House, Rye, 1931.

afternoon, and dark as only Cambridge can be, and Davenport asked Lowry if he would like something to drink. Lowry (he later confessed to Davenport) was afraid he was going to be offered tea —but a decanter of whiskey soon put him at ease, and by suppertime he was insisting that he and Davenport become blood brothers, with all appropriate ceremonies.

Davenport returned Lowry's call the following day, and found him in his drab lodgings, seated amidst a confusion of books, papers, bottles, and phonograph records. There were a pair of barbells and a ukulele. Pinned on the walls were restaurant bills from many countries, reproductions of paintings by Chagall and Henri Rousseau, and other objects, all of which obviously had some totemic significance for their owner. Davenport sensed that a mysterious order somehow underlay the chaos:

> The books revealed the eclecticism of the literary workman. Like other undergraduates of that time he had the Elizabethans, Joyce, and Eliot, but few undergraduates then knew Knut Hamsun and Herman Bang, B. Traven and Nordahl Grieg. Nor had they read the whole of Ibsen and Strindberg. E. E. Cummings, Hart Crane, Wallace Stevens, and Conrad Aiken himself had merely been names to most of us. Henry James had not been rediscovered, but Malcolm had volume after heavily annotated volume of the Master's works. . . . Three novellas he had an especial affection for were Mann's "Tonio Kroger," Melville's "Bartleby," and Bunin's "The Gentleman from San Francisco." Many young men of twenty are well-read, but Malcolm's reading was integrated in an unusual way. Dante and Faulkner were made to seem part of a whole.[11]

Lowry's supervisor during his first year at St. Catharine's was L. J. Potts,[12] a mild and kindly scholar who—Lowry was pleased to discover—was something of a specialist in Scandinavian literature, and had translated a volume of Strindberg's short stories. Potts was friendly toward Lowry, but unable to interest him much either in

11. There is no particular reason to doubt Davenport's recollection of Lowry's prodigious reading, except perhaps for the reference to Faulkner. Even supposing Lowry to have been exposed to Faulkner's works by Aiken in Massachusetts during the preceding summer, there was in 1929 no way Lowry could have read more of Faulkner than *Soldiers' Pay* (1926) or *Mosquitoes* (1927)—and not even a Lowry could have made connections, however arcane, between these two novels and *The Divine Comedy*.

12. According to Davenport, at least, the supervisor was Potts. According to T. R. Henn, then director of Studies in English for St. Catharine's and Trinity Colleges, he himself was Lowry's tutor during the young man's first two years, and Potts in the third. Lowry himself is no help in this puzzle: in letters to his friends, he always referred to his supervisor only as "Old Lupus."

Some of Charlotte Haldane's "addled salon," on the lawn behind Roebuck House, Cambridge, 1932. From left to right: William Empson, J. L. Cowan, Lowry, Ronald Burghes (Charlotte's son), unknown, Charlotte, Robert Lazarus.

his first year's reading, which was supposed to be a general survey of English literature, or in attending very many University lectures. Lowry could spare Cambridge little time: his own private reading schedule, his work on *Ultramarine*, and his drinking occupied most of his waking hours. This last was done chiefly in the company of friends he had met through Davenport: Christopher Saltmarshe, who, with Basil Wright, was the rest of the editorial staff of *Cambridge Poetry;* Henry Boys, who generally attended Potts' supervisions with Lowry; and Julian Trevelyan, who was at Trinity College doing English, and occasionally writing for *Experiment.* With Trevelyan, who left shortly afterward for Paris to paint, Lowry spent much time at a pub called the Maypole, discussing his enthusiasm for Chagall—a taste which Trevelyan found rather curious, not to say romantic, in such a roughneck type as Lowry.

Later in the fall of 1929, Davenport took Lowry around to Roebuck House, the residence of J. B. S. Haldane, then a University official in biochemistry, to meet Haldane's young wife Charlotte, who conducted a sort of informal salon or open house for Cambridge's young aesthetes. Here, for the next two-and-a-half years, Lowry was almost a fixture, spending long hours being "literary" with such as Michael Redgrave, Wynyard Browne, William Empson, Hugh Sykes-Davies and the young lady he was shortly to marry, Kathleen Raine, and Douglas Cooper, the art historian and collector.

Lowry's introduction to what he was later, in *The Ordeal of Sigbjørn Wilderness,* to call "Chatty Haldane's addled salon" was not exactly auspicious. Davenport dragged Lowry up to Mrs. Haldane, told her that Lowry was unhappy in his Bateman Street lodgings because his landlord was a clubfoot, a condition which Lowry was sure had been caused by syphilis. Lowry, said Davenport, was slowly starving to death because he was afraid to eat or drink anything the landlord had touched. Throughout this account Lowry stood silently behind Davenport, looking wildly about for a way of escape. Nearby, playing jazz quietly on Mrs. Haldane's magnificent piano (nothing about her gatherings was ever very noisy, because all her young men were terrified lest they bring down the wrath of the formidable Professor J. B. S., who detested them all) was a young research student in biochemistry named Martin Case. Mrs. Haldane took the stricken Lowry by the hand, marched him over to Case, and whispered in Case's ear: "This young man has syphilis or thinks he has." Presumably Case, a biochemist, might have been able to prescribe something.

The initial result of Lowry's first exposure to Roebuck House was not his introduction into the literary-social life of Cambridge; that came later. What his first evening brought him was his friendship with Martin Case, who came within a short time to know Lowry very well indeed, and who remained a lifelong friend. Case was not at all "literary": he liked to drink beer, he played jazz superbly well, he could swim better than Lowry, and perform mightier feats with the barbells. In fact, he so impressed Lowry in this last respect that Lowry made him a present of his own set of weights, which Case later carted off to Kenya and never used. From then on, whenever Lowry was not locked up in his digs, huddled under a table (so to lie reminded him of being in his bunk at sea, he claimed) with a bottle of whiskey, a tin of sardines, and a book, he was likely to be out with Martin Case, moving from pub to pub until the two finished up the evening by getting into good-natured fistfights after dinner at the "Red Cow."

> Malcolm had decided that he ought to teach me something about boxing, of which I was completely ignorant, and practice bouts always seemed inexplicably to crop up at the time of day and in the place that I have indicated. Beginning academically, scientifically, correctly, they invariably degenerated into slogging matches (unmotivated by the faintest malice or ill-will, though) which frequently sent us home with bloody noses, split lips, and black eyes that we had difficulty in laughing off later. It was also difficult for the proprietor of the pub, who knew us well, to explain to the rest of his bewildered clientele that these were a couple of friends of his and of each other who often chose this alternative to a quiet game of billiards or a visit to the cinema after their evening meal.[13]

13. From a reminiscence written by Martin Case for use by the Canadian Broadcasting Corporation in 1962.

The work on *Ultramarine* was, what with all the diversions, going very slowly. According to Davenport, a first draft was complete by January 1930. He remembered it as being "a perfectly straightforward account" of Lowry's trip to China. But Lowry was dissatisfied with it, and kept trying for a montage effect—·something like Aiken's technique in *Blue Voyage*. He wanted time past to move in and out of time present; he wanted conversations superimposed on one another; he wanted his protagonist's fantasy life to blend with his real life aboard ship. He wanted hallucinations, literary allusions, copied-out notices and advertisements—he wanted, in short, to give to his rather ordinary story an effect of richness of texture and motion that belonged more characteristically to cinema than to fiction. Indeed, one can scarcely make too much of the lifelong influence of film on Lowry's work: recall, for instance, his remarks (see p. 100), about Murnau's *Sonnenaufgang;* and note also another letter, still unpublished, to Ten Holder dated October 31, 1951:

> I think I have seen nearly all the great German films, since
> the days of *Caligari*, some of them many times, risking my
> neck even when at school (where movies were forbidden) to
> see . . . Conrad Veidt in *The Student of Prague*, and Mur-
> nau's wonderful things, all the films of the great Ufa days,
> and other later masterpieces. . . . and it is an enthusiasm that
> has not deserted me, for only recently we [Lowry and Mar-
> gerie] have trekked through the snow . . . just to keep up
> with the times, to see Murnau's *Last Laugh*, Fritz Lang's
> *Destiny* (a pioneer piece if there ever was one) and other
> contemporary films and Klangfilms at the local Vancouver
> Film Society.

But, putting aside for now the very real connection between German Expressionist cinema and Lowry's fiction,[14] one must insist that the major influences on his work at this time were two writers: Conrad Aiken, still; and Nordahl Grieg, the Norwegian author

14. The surface of this most interesting aspect of Lowry's career has only just been scratched. For a beginning, see Paul G. Tiessen, "Malcolm Lowry and the Cinema," *Canadian Literature*, 44 (Spring 1970), 38–49.

whose novel John Davenport had noticed in his early calls on Lowry at Bateman Street.

Grieg, distantly related to the composer, had in 1924 written a novel, *Skibet Gaar Videre*, which was translated for Knopf in 1927 as *The Ship Sails On*. The translator was none other than A. G. Chater, Master of St. Catharine's; and there is little doubt that it was Chater who introduced Lowry to Grieg's novel. When, in later years, Lowry would insist that *Ultramarine* was worthless, being only a pastiche of techniques and plots stolen from Conrad Aiken and Nordahl Grieg, he was being too harsh on himself; but he did indeed in *Ultramarine* make conscious use of *The Ship Sails On*, as he did of *Blue Voyage*. According to Margerie Lowry, he told her that "these two books had in some ways influenced him more than anything else, and he wished to combine the poetry and style of Aiken with the power and purity of Grieg." [15]

Presumably, Lowry was preoccupied with Grieg's novel primarily during the fall, winter, and spring of 1929–30 at Cambridge, as he struggled to organize the plot of *Ultramarine* into the "perfectly straightforward account" that Davenport recalled. His first reading of *The Ship Sails On* must have given Lowry a real shock of recognition: for here was a young toff, Benjamin Hall, "a ship-broker's son who wanted to find out what the sea was like before he took to the business" (p. 17), who sets out as an ordinary seaman aboard the *Mignon*, a Norwegian freighter en route to Cape Town. For young Benjamin, as for young Lowry and his *Pyrrhus*, the *Mignon* is not for long an object of happy romantic illusions; she is, instead, "a warehouse that moves from port to port. . . . A Moloch that crushes the lives of men between its iron jaws, then calmly turns its face to the solitudes as though nothing had happened" (p. 2). The crew of the *Mignon* are coarse, sentimental, sly, superficial, boastful. In port, they keep their bunks filled with fat prostitutes, who seem uniformly to have coarse, ravaged faces, tattooed arms, and greasy hair. And the *Mignon* could boast of the sort of forecastle

15. Margerie Bonner Lowry, "Biographical Note on Malcolm Lowry," a pamphlet prepared by Lippincott as part of its publicity campaign for the 1961 publication of *Hear Us O Lord From Heaven Thy Dwelling Place*.

that Lowry had hoped to find in the *Pyrrhus*, but did not: it is at the end of a narrow, pitch-dark alleyway, and when Benjamin opens the door to it, a "stifling, putrid stench" meets him:

> The forecastle was half in darkness; the lamp could barely burn with a sickly little flame in the heavy atmosphere. But after a while he saw that four men were sitting at the long table which almost filled the space. Behind them on the starboard side ran a row of bunks, most of them hidden by dirty, ragged curtains. . . . The table was slimy with remains of fish which blended with soda in a sickening stench. A filthy tin plate was filled to the brim with a disgusting mixture of syrup and melted butter.
>
> (*The Ship Sails On*, pp. 3, 5)

Clearly, whatever else Lowry learned from Nordahl Grieg, how to use adjectives sparingly was not to be included among the lessons.

The voyage of the *Mignon* is alternately boring and dangerous for the crew, and Benjamin spends most of his watches either chipping paint or shoveling coal, too exhausted to wax lyrical about life at sea. He misses his Oslo sweetheart, Eva, and prays that there will be a letter from her waiting for him in Cape Town. When there is not, he angrily goes ashore with the crew, bent on expunging his memory of Eva by a night of drinking and whoring. He should have known better, because Grieg has prepared him—and the reader—very thoroughly for the inevitable: the *leitmotif* of venereal disease surfaces throughout the book, as one after another of the crew reveals himself to be a sufferer from either syphilis or gonorrhea (Grieg fastidiously mentions neither disease; but we know, we know). So, when the delayed letter from Eva does finally reach Benjamin, it is too late: he has heard the one, fatal word from his doctor, and "Now everything was finished. . . . the tears slowly trickled down his cheeks. He was so helplessly young and unhappy, so faint and shattered by life's cruel blow. He was only nineteen, a little clod of soft springtime mould after all." Benjamin thinks of suicide, and does indeed stand for a moment at the rail on the poopdeck, the mangy ship's dog clutched in his arms, ready to leap overboard; [16] but in a last spasm of contempt for the ship he decides to live and to continue as part of the crew, thereby contributing further to her squalor and corruption.

However melodramatic *The Ship Sails On* may appear to us, to Lowry it possessed "power and purity"; and he always kept Grieg near the top of his list of "masters"—perhaps slightly below Conrad Aiken; but generally above, say, Henry James or Dostoevsky. One might also note that *The Ship Sails On* was, like *Ultramarine*, the work of a very young man: Grieg was only five years older than Lowry, and so was only twenty when his novel was published. It is, therefore, not surprising that Grieg's youthful lugubriousness should not be obvious to Lowry, who was twenty when he first read *The Ship Sails On*. In 1938 Lowry wrote to Grieg that "My identity with *Benjamin* [Lowry's italics] eventually led me into mental trouble. Much of *Ultramarine* is paraphrase, plagiarism, or pastiche from you" (*Selected Letters*, pp. 15–16). Lowry was overstating things, certainly; but one can see that, coming upon Grieg's novel after having labored for more than a year, now, on his own sensitive-youth-at-sea novel, Lowry must have felt that whatever *he* could do now would be to a large extent what Grieg had already done.

His fascination with Grieg and his work shortly led to a pilgrimage to Norway. He wrote several admiring letters to Grieg in Oslo, but—characteristically—found himself unable to mail them; and then determined to sail to Norway during his summer vacation of 1930, to congratulate Grieg in person.

Before he could sail, however, two complications arose: Conrad Aiken returned from America to his home in Rye, Sussex, newly remarried and anxious to resume his friendship with his young

16. It is this moment that gave to Lowry almost the only lines that he was to lift directly from Grieg: as Benjamin prepares to jump, he says to Santos, the dog, "Santos, this day shalt thou be with me in paradise" (*The Ship Sails On*, p. 217). Near the end of Chapter VII of *Under the Volcano* (p. 229), Geoffrey Firmin declaims to his ubiquitous pariah dog: "Yet this day, pichicho, shalt thou be with me in ——." Geoffrey breaks off before he can say the final word for two reasons: the dog has limped from the room; and Geoffrey will never see paradise.

protégé; and Arthur O. Lowry, having become alarmed at what he presumed to be the spectacular excesses of his son at Cambridge, came from Liverpool to London to set him straight. Young Lowry spent several happy days with the Aikens in Rye, then went with Aiken up to London to meet the father. They all had lunch together, then went to see *The White Hell of Pitzpalu*, the famous German film. Mr. Lowry somehow found time during the afternoon to confide to Aiken that he was very concerned about his son: not only did Malcolm seem determined to pursue a literary career —which was bad enough—but he had recently found an obscene letter from a friend at St. Catharine's in Malcolm's dresser drawer, and feared that his son was on his way to a life of real depravity. Aiken suggested to the elder Lowry that there had been several quite respectable men in English literary history, and that obscene letters were perfectly normal in the life of a young male. Mr. Lowry was so impressed with Aiken's own apparent probity that he offered to pay Aiken a salary to serve *in loco parentis* to Malcolm, to portion out his son's allowance, and generally to watch over him. Aiken was happy to do this: he was genuinely fond of Malcolm; and he needed the money. It was the time of the Great Depression, his first divorce had been costly, and he had officially been certified as "destitute" in the United States, where he had most recently been employed by the Works Project Administration as a writer helping to compile *The Massachusetts Guide*. Mr. Lowry returned to Cheshire, presumably relieved at having the burden of responsibility at least partially lifted from him; while the two respectable authors returned to Rye, where they celebrated by staging a "javelin-throwing contest," tossing branches across the little river at the foot of Mermaid Street—until Aiken neglected to release his "javelin" on his last throw, and "launched himself into space," falling ten feet down into a bed of mud.[17]

In July Lowry left Rye for Liverpool, and in Preston, a small

17. Conrad Aiken, *Ushant: An Essay* (New York, 1971), p. 226. This very curious autobiography, in which Lowry appears as "Hambo," was originally published in 1952. When Lowry first read it, he wrote Aiken that *Ushant* was "A masterwork, but Ow how it hurts!" (Letter from Aiken to *The Times* [London] *Literary Supplement*, February 16, 1967, p. 127).

port nearby, found a Norwegian tramp steamer that was about to sail in ballast (that is, with no cargo, empty except for the necessary ballasting weight in the holds) for Archangel in the White Sea, and signed on as fireman. What then happened on his journey to meet Nordahl Grieg is not quite certain. According to the often inaccurate biographical sketch that Margerie Lowry wrote for Lippincott, "The ship never reached Archangel: they stopped at a small town in northern Norway, Aalesund, hoping to take on cargo; the captain failed in this and the crew was paid off. While in this town Malcolm learned that Nordahl Grieg was living under an assumed name in Oslo. So he went by train to Oslo, where he met Grieg by another coincidence, and they became fast friends." This was the story as Lowry had given it to her, and it coincides rather closely with his account of the journey as he narrated it in a typescript draft of *Dark as the Grave Wherein My Friend Is Laid*, where there is much amplification of detail.[18] The other "coincidence" to which Margerie Lowry refers has to do with the manner in which Lowry located Grieg in Oslo: he apparently took a cab to the street on which he knew Grieg was living, Bygdo Allee, stopped the first man he saw, asked him whether he knew Grieg—and the man led him straight to Grieg's door.

For his friend James Stern, Lowry had another version of this adventure. According to Stern,[19] Lowry told him during one of their

18. Malcolm Lowry, *Dark as the Grave Wherein My Friend Is Laid* (New York, 1967), ed. by Douglas Day and Margerie Bonner Lowry. The original typescript from which this edition came contained 705 pages; those dealing with the journey to meet Grieg (in this work called "Guldbransen") are chiefly pp. 345–52. Perhaps one ought to note here, however pedantically, that Aalesund is not in the north of Norway, where Mrs. Lowry places it, but in the southern third of the country, more than 300 miles south of the Arctic Circle.

19. "Malcolm Lowry: A First Impression," *Encounter*, XXIX (September 1967), 58–68. Stern and his wife Tania were among the most perceptive of Lowry's friends; but one must note that, in this otherwise excellent essay, Stern, himself a linguist of some distinction, (he and his wife have done, among other things, superb translations of Kafka and Hoffmannsthal), errs in supposing Lowry to have been talented in learning languages. Lowry was, all his life, a truly miserable linguist. But he told Stern that he had, like Joyce, taught himself Norwegian in order to read Ibsen in the original; and when Stern heard him exchange a few words with the barman in a Scandinavian restaurant in Paris, he was convinced. Lowry was, apparently, able to *read* French, but he resolutely refused to *speak* it; and all

drinking evenings in Paris, in the winter of 1933, the story of "how he had once jumped ship in the port of Oslo, with the express purpose of meeting the Norwegian poet, Nordahl Grieg":

> He . . . arrived in Oslo . . . without a clue as to the whereabouts of the man he intended to visit. Only after hours of wandering about the city did he discover that Grieg lived not in Oslo at all, but Heaven knows how many scores of miles away in the north of the country. Never one for short-cuts, for modern means of transport . . . Lowry acquired a map and there and then, armed presumably with a compass, set out into the foreign land on foot through the snow. That he eventually succeeded in finding Nordahl Grieg I know, but how long the journey took him, how far he walked, how he was greeted on arrival, I cannot remember. There remains in my mind, after thirty-four years only a vague memory of Malcolm, footsore and hungry, knocking diffidently on the door of a remote mountain cabin in the middle of the night. . . .

As Stern observes, it would never have occurred to Lowry that enquiries at the Norwegian consulate in London, for instance, might have helped him locate Grieg. All his life Lowry relied on the long shot, the amazing coincidence, for his most important contacts with the world that existed so improbably outside himself; and one can well imagine him appearing in Oslo with nothing but Grieg's name as his guide. In his 1938 letter to Grieg mentioned earlier, Lowry wrote, "I wish I could tell you all the extraordinary coincidences which led up to our meeting." Apparently, not even Grieg ever knew all the details of how the two men came together.

Whether in fact Lowry's ship ever did put into Aalesund, we do not know. But this much *is* verifiable: we learn from an undated letter to Conrad Aiken that Lowry was in Oslo at some point in his journey, staying at the Hotel Parkheimen, while his ship, the *S. S. Fagervik*, was laid up for repairs. While he waited "a few days for another ship," he found the language barrier insurmountable, and spent most of his time in his hotel room, reading the novels of Julien

---

agree that he never learned more than a drinker's vocabulary in Spanish, or in German—or, so far as one can tell, in Norwegian.

Green in Tauschnitz editions. Possibly what happened is that one day Lowry tired of this, went out and hailed his cab, and set off for Bygdo Allee and Grieg. In any case, the two *did* meet, and in the course of their short time together (one afternoon and evening, apparently) Grieg was so impressed with Lowry's knowledge and understanding of *The Ship Sails On* that he gave Lowry permission to turn the novel into a play. Like most of Lowry's projects, this remained "in progress" for many years, accumulating notes and partial drafts, and never reaching completion.

The summer voyage of 1930 provided Lowry with a second literary project, as well: a novel which he proposed to call *In Ballast to the White Sea*, and which was to become part of his fictional master-plan until it was almost completely destroyed in Dollarton, on June 7, 1944, when Lowry's shack went up in flames. Before he went down from Cambridge Lowry began making notes for this novel, though he did not really commence the actual writing until his stay in New York in 1934. By the late thirties, *In Ballast to the White Sea*, in some form, was in the hands of Lowry's then agent, Ann Watkins; in 1941, when he put it aside to complete *Under the Volcano*, it amounted to "1000 pages of eccentric word-spinning" (*Selected Letters*, p. 63); and, according to Margerie Lowry, when it burned in 1944, it—and the notes that went with it—came to more than 2000 pages.

In Ballast to the White Sea was an extremely important project for Lowry, and not simply because of its monolithic proportions. In 1946 he wrote Albert Erskine, who was just beginning the task of editing *Under the Volcano* for Reynal and Hitchcock, that

> *Under the Volcano* was originally planned as the inferno part of a Dantesque trilogy to be called *The Voyage that Never Ends. Lunar Caustic* was the purgatorial part, but was to be much expanded. . . . The Paradiso part was called *In Ballast to the White Sea*, was a good deal longer than the *Volcano* and was completely destroyed in the fire here which took our house and all our books.

Although *In Ballast* was, in fact, not *completely* destroyed—fourteen pages of manuscript draft and two typescript pages from

Chapter One have survived—our only real information about this novel is contained in a single, nineteen-page letter he wrote from Dollarton to David Markson on August 25, 1951 (*Selected Letters*, pp. 247–66). The plot summary he did for Markson was typical Lowry: full of qualifications, amplifications, mystifications—so convoluted, ultimately, that one almost finds it hard to regret the loss of such an impossibly complex novel.

The protagonist, who is called "A" in Lowry's letter to Markson, is identified in the surviving fragments as "Sigbjørn"—which would indicate either that Lowry had begun to formulate the Sigbjørn Wilderness persona very early indeed in his career, or—more probably—that the fragments are from a relatively late draft. Briefly, A. is an undergraduate at Cambridge who has been to sea, is writing a novel about his experiences, reads a novel in translation, by a Scandinavian author, X., and is quite overpowered by Y., the principal character in X.'s book; and not merely that, but "X.'s book uncannily resembles the one A.'s been trying to write himself, which it seems to have rendered futile."

For A., obviously, read Malcolm Lowry; for X., Grieg; and for Y., Benjamin Hall. Possession by the spirits of others was a lifelong Lowry obsession, and it is not surprising to see him fascinated by the idea of his personality's being absorbed, first by the character of Benjamin, and then by that of Benjamin's creator. The pathetic instability of Lowry's own ego is more than manifest in this description to Markson: he is drawn to Y. not because he is looking for a hero to emulate, for Y. is no hero: "his experiences are not enviable, he is not even wise—he isn't even physically described in X.'s book, for that matter, so that he has no features or stature and is quite impossible to picture." But what Y. *does* possess are simple virtues that Lowry feels himself to lack: "loyalty, simplicity, decency, and a capacity to be reverent, in the bloodiest of circumstances, before the mystery of life, and a hatred of falsehood." Whereas those who knew Lowry best would say those were *precisely* his own best qualities, and those which made him loveable even at his most trying, Lowry sees himself as "an almost pathological liar—unable to give any rational account of himself, he invents the most fantastic tales about himself at every point that are so vivid they have a kind of life of their own."

Though admitting to Markson that A. equals himself, Lowry does make some attempts at the creation of non-autobiographical fiction. A. is troubled at Cambridge by a number of things: a "stormy" love affair with an older woman (probably a fantasy of Lowry's, erected about the person of Charlotte Haldane); the fact that he is a man and yet is treated as a child at Cambridge; a "Dostoevskian" brother (called "Tor" in the fragments of *In Ballast*); the "ghoulishness" of his contemporaries; the ideology of the English faculty; his own doubts about whether he is a writer at all—and so on. He neglects his studies, starts to drink, is instrumental in causing his brother's death, sails for Norway to meet X., does so after a series of coincidences which may or may not coincide with reality—and finds X., as close to despair as he is himself. Somehow, both men "are realigned on the side of life"; and, as Lowry writes Markson, "Plot of *In Ballast* has a triumphant outcome." The Paradiso is attained:

> A.'s action has also resulted in his salvation by his girl; in effect both the life of the imagination and life itself has also been saved by A.'s having listened finally to the promptings of his own spirit, and acted upon those promptings, rather than the analytical reductions of reason, though it is reason too—by virtue of harmony with the great forces within the soul—that has been saved, and on this note the story and the trilogy closes.
>
> (*Selected Letters*, p. 263)

As Lowry concludes to Markson: "Well, what a hell of a plot, you say, a kind of Strindbergian Tonio Kruger [sic], by Maeterlinck, out of Melville. That may be, but the point is that with a few exceptions . . . I didn't make the story up." It is indeed a hell of a plot, and not necessarily a good one; but his description of it does at least tell us something about the way Lowry saw himself, and about the way he *wished* things would happen. Whatever the literary merit of *In Ballast to the White Sea*, the book meant a great deal to

Lowry: he risked his life to save it from the fire that destroyed it, and never ceased lamenting its loss. Perhaps it represented to him his closest approach to the "power and purity" that were Grieg's, and not—he felt—his.

Lowry returned from Norway in September 1930, and went, without stopping in Cheshire to see his parents, directly to Jeake's House, Aiken's home in Rye—where, in fact, he spent all his long vacations from then until his graduation in the spring of 1932. Almost immediately upon reaching Rye he ran into Gerald Noxon, who was passing through Sussex on his way back to Cambridge. The weather was warm, the sky was clear, and Lowry appeared in splendid shape; so Noxon stayed on in Rye for two or three days, during which time he and Lowry roamed about the town, going from pub to pub, comparing pipe tobaccos—and becoming fast friends. "In those few days," Noxon has written,[20] "I discovered a new Malcolm, a man full of laughter and joy, conscious, though never confident, of his talent and ability." According to Noxon,

> During those few days Malcolm proved himself a fascinating companion. The brilliance of his mind, his extraordinary memory, the amazing range and depth of his knowledge, his fund of really funny stories in which the jokes were most often at his own expense, all astonished and captivated me as did the warmth and friendliness of his nature, which was revealed to me in its true condition for the first time.

Obviously, Lowry's voyage to Norway had been good for him; and one is fortunate to have such records as Noxon's as evidence that Lowry seemed to almost everyone who knew him a much better person than he thought himself to be. There is little doubt, also, that Lowry was never in his life happier and brighter than he was during his vacations at Jeake's House with Conrad Aiken. One thinks here of Aiken's reflections about young "Hambo" in *Ushant* (p. 292) at about this time, as "that most engaging and volatile and unpredictable of geniuses":

> for surely of all the literary folk D. [Aiken] had ever encountered, there had been none among them who had been

20. "Malcolm Lowry: 1930," *Prairie Schooner*, XXXVII (Winter 1963/64), 315–20.

so visibly or happily alight with genius—not that Tsetse [T. S. Eliot] hadn't manifested something of the same thing, to be sure—controlling it, moreover, to better purpose; but in Hambo it had been the more moving, and convincing, and alive, for its very *un*controlledness, its spontaneity and gay recklessness, not to mention its infectiously gleeful delight in itself. And why—he had always seemed in the act of asking—shouldn't genius damned well enjoy itself—? What was wrong with that—? Enjoy itself his genius did; here, there was never any secret hoarding, all was communicable and communicated, life itself was a picnic of genius in which everyone could share alike.

This sort of accolade is difficult for a biographer to assess. How does a writer manifest his genius before he has written anything? Why were so many dissimilar people so utterly convinced of the brilliance of Malcolm Lowry, long before there was any visible evidence of that brilliance? Apparently, when Lowry was in a good mood, as he generally was in Rye, or when he was with Martin Case and his brothers, or with James Stern—or with any of a number of other very astute people—he could be so full of joyous energy that "genius" seemed the only appropriate word for him. Unhappily for the biographer, there is no way of recording this quality, or of transmitting it; one simply accepts it as a matter of faith.

One can say about Lowry's brilliance, however, that real though it clearly was, it was not a stable element in his character. It often —and increasingly—had to be induced and sustained by alcohol. And one can say the same for his phases of joyousness; in Rye, or much later, in Dollarton, perhaps, one can suppose him to have been genuinely happy; but there was always the remorse of conscience, the self-doubt, the conviction that he was only a poseur, never far beneath the surface of the radiant exterior. Even Aiken, that most psychoanalytically oriented of authors, was unaware, until the final years of Lowry's life, of these increasingly potent destructive forces in his protégé.

When he returned to Cambridge for the fall term of 1930, Lowry had rooms in college, on the ground floor of the big court at St. Catharine's. This situation was better than that on Bateman Street the preceding year, but only barely: according to John Davenport (in his unpublished preface to *Ultramarine*), Lowry "very much disliked being on the ground floor because of the lack of privacy. The door would often be locked for days, although an occasional jazz record could sometimes be heard: Joe Venuti and Eddie Lang, perhaps, playing 'Going Places' or 'Doing Things.' " [21] When he was visible, he was more than ever playing the part of rough seafaring man, though he was now more assertive than before about his promise as a writer. To T. R. Henn, who was now (if he had not been so earlier) Lowry's supervisor at St. Catharine's, his pupil's brilliance was not so obvious as it was to others. For Conrad Knickerbocker, in 1964, Henn recalled that "Lowry was withdrawn, slow-spoken, and rather idle." He frequently did not bother to appear for his supervisions, attended rather few lectures, and came in for a certain amount of disciplinary actions at the hands of the college authorities. He collected, it seems, a number of "gate bills." (Henn explained to Knickerbocker that students were supposed to be back in college each night by ten o'clock. If one came in at eleven, he was fined a penny. If an excessive number of fines was accumulated, one was reported to his tutor. We might recall here Lowry's complaints about having been treated as a child at Cambridge.) Henn, who had indeed around this time had a part in supervising the work of several very promising authors, such as T. H. White, Richard Eberhart, and William Empson, was "not impressed" by the quality of Lowry's writing. But Lowry's worst failings to Henn, seemed to be that he showed no interest at all in rowing, and that he refused to attend Henn's Monday evening "at homes," where undergraduates gathered over fruit, coffee, and snuff to hear Henn, I. A. Richards, or E. M. W. Tillyard read poetry. And, Henn concluded to Knickerbocker, Lowry proved to be a very poor sort of "Old Boy" at St. Catharine's: after graduation, "he never came back."

Clearly, Lowry was pursuing no sort of academic life at Cam-

---

21. The subject of Lowry and jazz is, like that of Lowry and film, one with which scholars will have to deal. A very shrewd initial essay is that of Perle Epstein, "Swinging the Maelstrom: Malcolm Lowry and Jazz," *Canadian Literature*, 44 (Spring 1970), 57–66.

bridge. What, then, other than working fitfully on *Ultramarine* and convincing everyone but the dons of his genius, *was* he doing? For one thing, according to Martin Case (in his 1962 CBC reminiscence), he was playing a passable forward on the St. Catharine's rugby team. For another, still according to Case,[22] he was spending long hours, in his rooms or in Case's, listening to records of American "white" jazz. Lowry's idol "above all other players was Bix Beiderbecke, but very close to him came Eddie Lang (guitar), Joe Venuti (violin), and Frankie Trumbauer (saxophone)." And he and Case often performed in various Cambridge pubs, Case playing the piano and Lowry his tenor ukulele,

> with four plucked strings tuned normally to A, D, F sharp and B, or their equivalents in any other scale. . . . The resources of such an instrument by itself are of course very limited, as it is not capable of much more than a strumming effect; but this he used with great skill in accompanying the human voice, more often than not his own. He had an untrained but pleasing and resonant tenor voice, and a very good instinctive ear for chords and harmonic progressions, so that besides being able to fit in readily with existing tunes, whether he knew them or not, he could improvise new ones with considerable facility.
>
> It was a favorite trick of his to seize upon some instrumental passage that he liked in a record and then to compose words of his own to fit the melody thus dissected out, as it were. Quite often, after he had sung it enough times, he would tend to forget that the tune had never been his, strictly speaking, in the first place; and as a result of this he enjoyed, among the uncritical and uninitiated, a higher reputation as an original jazz "composer" than perhaps he strictly deserved.

There were, besides the music, the continued boxing lessons, as described earlier by Martin Case; and a few curious but not particularly aberrant undergraduate disgraces, generally centering on alcohol, usually involving John Davenport, and occasionally Case. "One night late," Case recalled for Knickerbocker ("Malcolm Lowry in

22. Letter to Suzanne Kim, September 16, 1963.

England," *Paris Review,* p. 27), "we were on our way back to Malcolm's digs from the Cambridge station. A hideous old bag—which meant she must have been thirty—waylaid Malcolm, and the two disappeared behind a shed in a builder's yard. . . . Later, he said it had been a marvelous experience, being tossed off with a fur glove." [23]

Lowry went with Martin Case during the Christmas vacations of 1930, 1931, and 1932 to stay with the Cases in their large Victorian house in Edgbaston, a suburb of Birmingham. There for the first time, in 1930, he met Martin's younger brother Ralph, then a medical student at the University of Birmingham. Soon after their meeting, Ralph brought in one of his textbooks showing the effects of *adiposis dolorosa*, a particularly repellent form of obesity; and then gravely diagnosed Lowry's slight beer belly as manifesting that disease's first symptoms. Lowry took this seriously for all of five minutes, and needed considerable reassuring before regaining his composure.

Shortly after this, the Case brothers took Lowry to the University Club in Birmingham for an evening's drinking. The

23. This seems an appropriate place to deal with one particular legend which John Davenport, through Knickerbocker, insisted on perpetuating. Davenport told Knickerbocker: "You must remember that Malcolm was a masturbator," and Knickerbocker duly reported this information ("Malcolm Lowry in England," p. 23). If one consults Constantine Fitzgibbon's biography of Dylan Thomas (Boston, 1965, p. 108), he will notice that Davenport leveled the same charge against Thomas. Indeed, according to Martin Case, in a letter to me dated July 24, 1967, "it was a strange obsession with John to make this assertion indiscriminately about nearly all his acquaintances, so far as I could see. He certainly made it to me, or in my hearing, regarding at least six or seven people, eminent and obscure, whom we both knew." The whole business of masturbation, then, would seem to be the concern, not of Lowry's biographer, but of Davenport's. But it is also true that Lowry causes Dana Hilliot of *Ultramarine* to be accused of being a masturbator; and the notebook which Lowry kept during his 1947 hospitalization in Haiti contains this curious fragment: "fear of seeming to stay too long in lavatory is doubtless fear of being thought masturbating: but why should a pretty nurse think that he was masturbating, especially when that was precisely what he was doing?" When one observes also that Ethan Llewelyn of *October Ferry to Gabriola* remembers with shame his father's denunciation of him as a masturbator, it begins to seem plausible that with Lowry, at least, Davenport's favorite accusation is not entirely unwarranted. If Lowry must be considered as harboring guilt-feelings over masturbation, this would of course be an important causative factor in his continuing preoccupation with the *hands* of his various protagonists.

three went to the mens' room at one point, and Malcolm retired to a cubicle. Ralph began "to impersonate the janitor, yelling in a janitorial voice, 'I'm pretty well fed up with these buggers stinking with drink!' Malcolm cowered in the cubicle and would not come out until we told him the pubs closed in ten minutes" ("Malcolm Lowry in England," p. 29). The absolute fear of authority which Lowry always felt apparently extended as far down as the janitorial level.

Perhaps to atone for his terrorizing of Lowry, Ralph during this first vacation presented him with an old, brown Trilby hat. For some time afterwards, Lowry slept with it down over his ears, or wore it as he lay beneath various tables in various places, playing his ukulele and singing.

He got on famously with all the Cases, perhaps most especially the mother, who loved him at once, and continued to do so even though Lowry insisted on wearing the same blue shirt each day throughout the three-week vacation. To all of them, as Ralph Case told Knickerbocker, "he was the kind of man one meets once or twice in a lifetime if one's lucky. He had a defenseless air that was irresistible. He placed himself in one's hands. The result was that various people were always adopting him. In those days he was a perennial mascot" ("Malcolm Lowry in England," p. 29).

When they were not pub-crawling or playing jazz with him, the Case brothers gave Lowry an intensive introduction into "a rather esoteric Sports Club" that the Cases had founded, primarily for the purpose of playing a game that the family had invented, and that Martin Case describes, in his CBC remarks, as "one of the most murderous and diabolical recreations ever devised."

> Combining some of the features of squash rackets and fives, with the addition of some irregular natural hazards, a smaller space than is allotted to either of those games, and a very much heavier ball, which moreover was permanently attached to a length of powerful rubber cord, so that the speeds attained were inconceivable, this sport necessitated the wearing of protective clothing, especially on the head, and even so was notably destructive. . . . In spite of the fact that

Lowry at 8 Plympton Street, Cambridge, Mass., July, 1929.

Malcolm attained a laudable degree of proficiency, he is known to have complained in later life that the physical and mental trauma arising from this pastime had had an adverse effect upon his subsequent character and development. I can only hope that this was not really true.

Life was, to say the least, strenuous at the Cases'; and when Martin recalls having come upon Lowry one evening talking earnestly into the earpiece in the telephone booth of a pub, one almost begins to wonder whether this error was caused by alcohol—or by concussion.

At any rate, Lowry survived, and enjoyed, these harrowing vacations. Between them and his long summer vacations, which he spent at Jeake's House in Rye with the Aikens, he survived Cambridge as well, though without much enjoyment. After supervisions, however, there was time for beer at the Bath or the Eagle. There were other friends, like Tom Harrisson, later a prominent sociologist; Tom Forman, who owned his own airplane, and later gave Lowry an old MG Magna—the only car Lowry ever drove, let alone owned; James Hepburn, who became a close companion in the London days that followed Cambridge; and James Travers, whom John Davenport described, in a letter to Knickerbocker dated June 27, 1964, as "a vague, amiable drunk who later farmed in an amateurish way. We all got to know him in Cambridge. Malc liked him very much as he was an agreeable boozing-companion and totally uncritical of his friends. He was by no means a fool, but a bit too languid for me. A hanger-on without being precisely a parasite, if you know what I mean." Travers, for reasons which are only partially clear, became an especially important figure in Lowry's life, even though they knew one another only between 1931 and 1934.

With such as these, and Martin Case and John Davenport, Lowry passed what one might call his boisterous hours. He seems not really to have been concerned with what was going on around him in England, to say nothing of Europe or the rest of the world. Nowhere did he record, in his letters or other writings, any awareness of economic collapse in the Western World, of the rise of communism in the East—or of what his Oxbridge contemporaries were making of these events. And this is very curious, since his Cambridge years were precisely those in which socio-economic awareness became *de rigueur* for young intellectuals. The "Auden Group" was becoming prominent, chiefly through the annual volumes of *Oxford Poetry; New Signatures* was beginning to flourish; John Cornford, who died later in the Spanish Civil War, was about to go up to Trinity College, Cambridge; Julian Bell, who also died in the Spanish Civil War, had been at King's College, Cambridge, since 1927, and remained there until 1932, when Lowry was graduated. *Experiment*, in which Lowry published the first piece of *Ultramarine*, was not only Cambridge's closest approximation to an avant-garde magazine: it aimed at representing the University's Left element as well (as opposed to *The Venture*, which was generally held to be conservative and Neo-Georgian in character).[24] One *had*, suddenly, to be committed: no more Twenties aestheticism. If one were expected to have had his brush with homosexuality at the University, he must now also (or instead) have his brush with communism. Or at least explain why he was not having it. But none of this sudden political activism reached Malcolm Lowry, apparently. As a schoolboy at The Leys in 1926, he cannot have failed to be aware of the General Strike, even if only because so many students at nearby Cambridge were involved in it. And at Cambridge himself from 1930 through 1932, he must have been exposed to the enormous amount of political excitement that was replacing the languid introspection of the Twenties.[25] But not so: Lowry's only real recognition at Cambridge of the plight of the working classes was to affect to be one of them —which to him meant rough dress, rough speech, rough manners.

His chief audience for this show of solidarity with the proletariat

24. Although Lowry seems to have given his literary allegiance primarily to *Experiment*, he did in fact publish one story in *The Venture*: "Goya the Obscure," in No. 6, June, 1930. It is of awesome badness, "experimental" in the worst way, a stream-of-consciousness portrait of a syphilitic sailor who, worried about having got his girl friend pregnant, visits the Liverpool Anatomical Museum on Paradise Street.
25. In the years to come he felt some degree of guilt at not having joined those friends who fought for the Republic in Spain, and this guilt indeed becomes a major refrain in *Under the Volcano* ("They are losing the Battle of the Ebro"); but at the time—nothing.

was that group of aesthetes who continued to gather at Roebuck House around Charlotte Haldane. With most of the salon he was now much more aggressive and assertive than he had been during his first year; to several of the more effeminate members, especially, he was openly contemptuous. We do not know very much about how any of the salon responded to the roughneck persona he was displaying for them, but we do know something of how Charlotte Haldane herself reacted. Until one night in the winter of 1932 when Lowry and John Davenport showed up at Roebuck House "too drunk to admit," and so ended their welcome there, Mrs. Haldane was delighted to have the roughneck. With her, for one thing, he was not loud, or coarse, but extremely shy. "Though he needed a drink in order to speak at all, he wanted very badly to be a tough guy, to prove he was tough and could take it. I felt at once there was a strong streak of infantilism in him." [26] He would have liked to be taller (one thinks of Hugh Firmin in *Under the Volcano*, stretching himself to his full mental height of six feet two, while still remaining his actual height of five feet eleven), but Mrs. Haldane found him quite attractive as he was: to her, Lowry seemed "extremely beautiful; golden hair, small triangular blue eyes, white teeth. One noticed his sweetness, beautiful manners, intelligence, and charm." [27]

In her autobiography, Charlotte Haldane writes of her third novel, *I Bring Not Peace* (London, 1932), "The character of the hero of this novel was partly synthesised from my friendship with a remarkable young man, Malcolm Lowry, the most romantic undergraduate of that period in Cambridge, who several years later was to become famous as the author of a powerful novel, *Under the Volcano. . . .*" [28] This hero of *I Bring Not Peace*, one James Dowd, may be, as Martin Case has said (in his CBC essay), "A decidedly distorted travesty" of Lowry; and Lowry was certainly correct in describing Dowd as "a preposterous character." [29] Yet even though Dowd is an American, and employs a diction so "American" that

26. Interview with me, summer 1967.
27. Interview with Conrad Knickerbocker, summer 1964.
28. *Truth Will Out* (New York, 1950), pp. 29–30.
29. *The Ordeal of Sigbjørn Wilderness*, p. 67.

his countrymen, reading the novel, can only wince whenever he speaks; and even though the novel is set not in Cambridge but almost entirely in Paris—nonetheless, James Dowd *is* Malcolm Lowry. Or, more precisely, Malcolm Lowry as a character in an erotic fantasy in which he stands at center stage, entirely vulnerable to the ogling and mental fondling of the author.

The heroine is Michal, a vivid, daring, dark-eyed young woman of thirty. Her father is English; her mother, a French Jewess. She is a divorcée, leading a decidedly carefree life in *beau monde* Paris. One evening, as she is bathing, Michal hears a crash in the dark hallway outside her flat. She throws her robe about her, dashes out, and finds a drunk, slowly picking himself up after having fallen:

> He had his back to her. . . . He was testing with clumsy groping fingers the strings of a ukulele and muttering softly in accents of vindictive hate. . . . She put her hand inside the lavatory door and turned the switch. At first she saw, looking down blinkingly at her, the red puckered face of the small boy caught by mother in irresistible naughtiness. The next moment the pucker slowly changed, not to the relaxation of a bursting howl (which would not, somehow, to her have seemed unnatural) but to a smile hardly less absurd, an ashamed, sheepish smile that spread slowly from eyes to lips, displaying white teeth. He held his head down and to one side: the eyes looked up from under their lids and yellow brows, twinkling. He seemed not to know that his lower lip was bleeding. He leant against the wall and fumblingly tore the shabby black hat from his head, disclosing a pile of tousled yellow hair which seemed to be standing straight up, Gorgon-wise, all round it. (*I Bring Not Peace*, pp. 34–35)

This rumpled child-Adonis is James Dowd, Cambridge undergraduate, seaman, medical student, professional boxer, "cabaret singer in most of the brothels in the West Indies," and drunk. Michal, fascinated to say the least, invites him into her flat, where she gets a better look at him.

> He was a light-heavy-weight dressed in old grey flannel trousers and a navy-blue jersey with pale-blue letterings

across the chest. The jersey bulged, stretching tightly across the colossal pectoral muscles beneath it. . . . The peculiar slanting blue eyes, the yellow hair, the way he clutched the battered uke with one hand while the other impatiently dropped the rusty black hat on the floor, confirmed the impression: sailor—ashore and lost. S. O. S. S. O. S. A bright splash of blood dribbling slowly from his lip completed the spectacle of a powerful male animal at bay, temporarily dazed and out of its element.

(*I Bring Not Peace*, pp. 36–37)

The powerful male animal, we soon learn, has rich parents, lifts weights, admires Beiderbecke, Eddie Lang, and Trumbauer—and is obsessed with the ugliness and clumsiness of his hands. Of course, Dowd falls promptly in love with Michal; and she—obviously—is drawn to him. But, of course, it is impossible: he is wild and young; she is mature and sophisticated. So, sadly, she relinquishes him (the affair, incidentally, is never consummated—he is too shy and respectful, and the moment is lost).

The single curious twist in this otherwise embarrassing wish-fulfillment of a novel is that Michal relinquishes Dowd to a young man. This is Dennis Carling, a wan dandy recently sent down from Cambridge. He openly pursues Dowd, ogles him just as frankly as Michal had done, and is quite distraught when Dowd does not respond. At the novel's ending, Dennis is being blackmailed for having written some compromising letters to another man. Back in England, he threatens suicide to Dowd, whose response is, "I think it'd be a damned good riddance." Dowd refuses to offer compassion, Carling does in fact kill himself—and the novel ends with Michal's reflecting that Dennis had been brave, and Dowd cowardly. For Dennis had loved life, and been willing to lose what he loved; whereas James had been afraid of life, and able only to run from it.

Life for James was like the sea, silent, deep as the soul itself, fertile of beauty and horror. James was afraid of the sea, as he had been afraid of life, and run away from sea, as in the beginning, being no wiser, he had run away to sea. But there was no peace for him on earth, on dry land or water, and never would be peace until he learned surrender and acceptance.

(*I Bring Not Peace*, p. 310)

Charlotte Haldane dedicated this novel to Malcolm Lowry, and wrote most of it during Lowry's final year at Cambridge, even including in her text three lyrics by Lowry. Chatto and Windus published the book in June 1932, just after Lowry had gone down to London from Cambridge. There are certain rather obvious conclusions to be made about the *I Bring Not Peace* incident; but let us be content with saying that, at some stage of his life at Cambridge, Lowry was probably shyly and chastely infatuated with Charlotte Haldane; that she was clearly—and not so chastely—infatuated with him (according to one former member of the salon who has asked to remain anonymous, Mrs. Haldane literally terrified Lowry with her amatory aggressiveness, and "practically chased him around the dinner table at Roebuck House"); and that something happened to destroy this sort of cat-stalking-bird-paralyzed-with-fear flirtation. Perhaps it was indeed only that Lowry, with Davenport, turned up one night "too drunk to admit." Or perhaps it had to do with the suicide of an undergraduate, for which Charlotte Haldane held Lowry at least partly to blame.

If this last conjecture sounds melodramatic enough to have come from *I Bring Not Peace*, so be it. And it is just that: conjecture. To me, Mrs. Haldane professed no recollection of any such incident during her time at Cambridge. But Lowry spoke often of just such an event, to his friends and in his writings. He often told Margerie, for instance, about a very rich undergraduate, handsome and flaxen-haired, who had pursued him relentlessly during his Cambridge years, until at last he swore to kill himself if Lowry would not respond to his advances. Lowry, disgusted, went out to a nearby pub, met some friends, and told them there was someone back in his digs who wanted to kill himself. "Let the bastard die!" exclaimed one of the friends, and Lowry stayed at the pub. The young man did kill himself that evening, there was a more-or-less hushed-up inquest at which Lowry testified, and Lowry felt remorse for his callousness from that time on.

Now, Lowry told Margerie many things that were not true, or that he only wished were true, about his early years. Sometimes he created these fantasies to protect her feelings, sometimes simply to tease her or amuse himself. But there is something about this particular tale that prods the intuition more than most of Lowry's other self-dramatizations. This youth, who Lowry claimed was so strikingly handsome that he had been the model for the illustration of the young sailor on the packets of Players Cigarettes, appears as an offstage character in three Lowry works: in the unpublished typescript of *The Ordeal of Sigbjørn Wilderness*, and in the typescript drafts of *Dark as the Grave Wherein My Friend Is Laid*, in *October Ferry to Gabriola;* and surfaces briefly as the protagonist's younger brother in the few pages that remain of *In Ballast to the White Sea.*

In early July 1949, while Margerie was in Los Angeles visiting her mother, Lowry, left alone in Dollarton, fell from the pier outside their shack onto the rocks several feet below. He was taken to a Catholic hospital in Vancouver, where—after he had sobered up enough to be examined—his injury was diagnosed as "a very slight wedge of the fourth dorsal body indicative of compression fracture here, with slight depression of its antero-superior margin." [30] Though the damage was minor enough so that Lowry could be released in a couple of weeks with only a temporary brace to strap around himself, he appears to have thought of his "broken back" episode as lastingly traumatic, perhaps psychically more than physically. In the hospital, after several injections of a sedative, he began to experience mild forms of hallucination. But, being Lowry, he saw all of this rather ordinary drama as material for a novel; and, while still in the hospital, began compiling data for what was to become the work called *The Ordeal of Sigbjørn Wilderness.*

The typescript of this judiciously abandoned novel is like every other Lowry work-in-progress: a great hash concocted of everything he could get his hands on at the time, whether out of his own

30. Letter from V. Drache, M. D., a Vancouver surgeon, to E. B. Woolfan, M. D., Margerie's brother-in-law, dated July 10, 1949.

imagination, *The Vancouver Sun*, letters from Margerie, long passages from whatever theosophical or popular psychological books he had about him, or physicians' reports—anything at all would do. What makes this otherwise bootless exercise important for us, now, is that on page seven of the typescript, dutifully typed by Margerie into the draft, is a letter from Lowry to none other than T. R. Henn, in which Lowry begins to explain to his old supervisor the circumstances of his accident. The letter is discarded, as the "fiction" begins. For some reason Lowry's mind was strongly focused now on his Cambridge days, because he reports that during his first evening in the hospital he gradually, under sedation, became aware that he was being visited by the ghost of James Travers, the "vague, amiable drunk" Davenport remembered as having been a hanger-on at Cambridge. In the interim, Travers had died in a blazing tank in a battle in the Western Desert in 1942. (Travers is generally called "James Winton" in this typescript, but not invariably; and Lowry begins by calling himself "Martin Striven," then "Martin Sigbjørn Wilderness," and finally simply "Sigbjørn Wilderness.") Travers makes his presence known to the ailing narrator through his voice, and a whiff of his old pipe tobacco, and then suddenly he is *there*, in the hospital room with Lowry:

> James had hair so fair it was almost white, a wisp of a mustache . . . an unusually gentle almost beautiful face, and one might have mistaken his mouth for being weak, it was also in a way a curiously old face. And he had an unusually deep beautiful and old and extremely *slow* voice.
>
> (*The Ordeal of Sigbjørn Wilderness*, p. 11)

There are several pages of fond description of Travers, "historian and silver fox farmer, writer and iconoclast, beer drinker and wit, seven years dead, but as live as a barrel full of monkeys" (p. 134). Though he and Travers were never particularly close friends (p. 13), Lowry—who freely admitted throughout his life that he was "unusually weak at physical descriptions" (p. 12)—can surprisingly picture now not only Travers's features, but his clothes as well: he recalls his old golf shoes with crepe soles, his grey flannel trousers, and his tweed sportscoat. He remembers (indeed, now *smells*) Travers's tobacco: a John Sinclair mixture called Old Castle. Travers and Martin-Sigbjørn-Lowry talk for a few pages rather cheerfully about nothing much, and then he fades away—to be replaced shortly by the shade of Charlotte Haldane herself (here variously called "Charlotte," "Rocksie Ann," "Roxy McEwin," and finally "Roxy Anne Sully"). She has, in this second hallucination of Lowry's, come to Vancouver to see him, and he is very much embarrassed that she should find him in such a helpless, undignified condition: he is lying on a small hospital bed with only a blanket over him; his belly is bloated, and he is attached to a stomach pump. Charlotte—or Roxy Anne—and an impatient, drunken Englishman who appears to be her close companion, look down at the stricken Lowry, who feigns sleep, and comment on his virility (or lack of it), his skill as a writer (or lack of it), and his disgraceful conduct while at Cambridge. Lowry, inwardly seething, thinks of "that godawful book of hers" (p. 67), remembers with contempt "the preponderance of homosexuals in her addled *salon*" (p. 122), and laughs as she tries to pretend to her companion that she had slept with Lowry; for at Cambridge, "in spite of his amorous record he was careful to create, he was a virgin" (pp. 87–88). Later, while her friend is outside trying to move his automobile, Charlotte speaks to Lowry about "a dear friend they had in common"— Martin Case. Solemnly, Lowry intones, "He was a good man."

Charlotte and her friend fade out, but not before Lowry recognizes the man as an old prep school acquaintance, a bully and successful journalist (his name here is "Izzard"), and "the very man who was mysteriously yet equally responsible for Wensleydale's death" (p. 130). There is one other, totally enigmatic reference to Wensleydale (p. 141); and then *The Ordeal of Sigbjørn Wilderness* fades out in a welter of notes on the nature of the afterlife, taken from a book by Annie Besant, and something called "Notes from the Catholic Church in Action."

When Margerie reached Vancouver, she found her husband in a general hospital, in a strait-jacket and raving. He had been evicted from the Catholic hospital, he insisted (and was always to insist), because of the apparitions that had appeared to him there. Furthermore, after his departure his ward had had to be totally vacated, so that it could be ritually cleansed and an exorcism performed. Another mystery—except that the Catholic hospital has no records of any such bizarre carryings-on. But it is curious that physical trauma, combined with alcohol and drugs, took Lowry so precisely back to his Cambridge years, to his happy recollections of James Travers, and to his darker memories of Charlotte Haldane, "Izzard," and the elusive Wensleydale.

In 1947, after *Under the Volcano* had been accepted and the Lowrys had returned from a trip to Mexico, Lowry began work on the novel called *Dark as the Grave Wherein My Friend Is Laid*. In the 705 pages of typescript from which the novel was ultimately to emerge, Wensleydale figures often—always as a character for whose death, long before the work begins, the protagonist (again, Sigbjørn Wilderness) feels some obscure guilt. These references begin on typescript page 90, when Lowry, thinking of various murders in his work, writes a reminder to himself: "bring in Wensleydale." On page 116, we read, of Sigbjørn-Malcolm: "Nov. 10, or 7, or 13, his unlucky day—why? (Wensleydale)." On page 157 he thinks again of Wensleydale, this time in connection with friends who have committed suicide. On page 226 he lists his major griefs and fears: the loss of the shack of Dollarton; the death of Nordahl Grieg in a bombing raid over Berlin in December 1943; his fear of failing Margerie; the probable failure of *Under the Volcano*—and the death of Wensleydale. Not, surely, a catalogue of minor catastrophies for Lowry. That Wensleydale should be included here offers ample evidence that his death was extremely important, if not crucial, as a component in Lowry's psychic makeup for most of his adult life.

Then, on page 356, the protagonist of *Dark as the Grave* is describing the plot of *In Ballast to the White Sea* to some friends, and mentions that the novel contains a certain crime. When asked about this, he responds:

> In this book I used, I should say I began it—I disguised it, of course, out of consideration for the parents—an unfortunate experience that happened to me at college. A friend of mine named Wensleydale . . . Wensleydale committed sui-

cide, I knew he was going to do it—in fact I told him to
—instead of sympathising with him beyond a point. I won't
go into it. There's no point in bothering his ghost by telling
you what actually was bothering Wensleydale. . . . I was
not blamed at the inquest, and even if I had told the more
exact truth I don't see how I could have been legally
implicated—it would have shattered even more lives than
those that were shattered by it. Moreover, it would have
been hard, if not impossible, to tell the truth about Wensleydale, without making matters a thousand times worse if possible.

And that, very nearly, is all we are to know about this murky and
inconclusive, but undoubtedly traumatic, event in Lowry's last
Cambridge year. Later in the typescript of *Dark as the Grave* we
are told that the quarrel which arose between Lowry and his friend
began when Wensleydale expressed his hatred for both *Blue Voyage* and *The Ship Sails On;* and Lowry, taking this to be a spiritual
affront upon himself, was led to be "hardhearted" when he should
have been "compassionate." The Lowry figure ultimately tells his
friends that the brother of the protagonist of *In Ballast to the White
Sea,* for whose death the protagonist is partially responsible, is
modelled on Wensleydale. If we glance again at the fourteen pages
of *In Ballast* manuscript that were not burned, we see that the protagonist's flaxen-haired younger brother, Tor, worships the elder,
Sigbjørn, who has been to sea, finds Cambridge an absurd and
childish place, and is for the most part rude and condescending to
the vulnerable, affectionate Tor. And finally, Ethan Llewelyn, the
protagonist of Lowry's last work, *October Ferry to Gabriola,* broods
incessantly over his guilt in having provoked his undergraduate
friend, Peter Cordwainer, to suicide.

Is it too far-fetched to suppose that, among other things, Lowry
was using his fiction, as we use our dreams, for the purpose of what
in classical Freudian terminology is called displacement—that is,
the attachment of affect to an object other than that to which it
normally belongs, or originally belonged? I think not: Lowry's fiction abounds in situations involving sibling, or near-sibling,
conflicts—all of which are clear variations on the common pat-

tern of displacing onto a sibling—either real or imaginary—the affection that one really feels for a person not acceptable to the psyche or to society as a proper recipient for that affection. Wensleydale, whoever he was, did apparently love Lowry; and Lowry rejected that love—and worried and punished himself thereafter for having thus been partly responsible for his friend's suicide. His fictional attempts to come to terms with this guilt began with *In Ballast to the White Sea*, and quite possibly found their resolution in *Under the Volcano*, in which Lowry killed off the older-brother figure, after having condemned him for having been unable to love. As I admitted earlier, this all remains conjecture; but we do know what Charlotte Haldane wrote about James Dowd and Dennis Carling in *her* displaced "fiction"; we know what Lowry told Margerie about the incident; and we know how Lowry returned, almost obsessively, to the incident in his own writing. Some of the Wensleydale situation is clearly invention, on the part of both Lowry and Charlotte Haldane; some, just as clearly, is not.[31]

By the spring of his third year at Cambridge, Lowry had had enough. He had somehow managed to persuade T. R. Henn to accept the completed *Ultramarine* in lieu of the usual thesis, and during the Easter vacation he and John Davenport holed up in a little hotel at Hartland Point, in North Devon. Davenport had taken Lowry there because Lowry's father, realizing that his son had done no work at all in two-and-a-half years, had hired him to act as his son's "tutor," to help him prepare for his final examinations. But there was far too much to be done, and so Lowry instead spent his vacation in polishing *Ultramarine*, having resolved not to touch it during his last term. Nor did he, but concentrated on doing, in the few weeks that remained to him, all the work that he had been neglecting for so long. His final examinations consisted of six three-hour papers, and he emerged from them with a third-class honors degree—which in those days meant that he was in the bottom third of his class. "He could have done much better if he had worked," Henn remarked to Knickerbocker.

---

31. M. C. Bradbrook, in her *Malcolm Lowry: His Art and Early Life* (Cambridge, 1974, p. 15), identifies Wensleydale as Paul Fitte, who committed suicide during his

So there we have him as he was at Cambridge: for his supervisor, a rather ordinary sort of under-achiever; for his drinking and rambling and jazz-playing cronies, a great companion, a rowdy, happy, hard-drinking friend; for the intellectual element who knew him at Cambridge, a somewhat mysterious and moody figure of undoubted genius; for Charlotte Haldane (and perhaps for the enigmatic Wensleydale, as well), a sex-object of sorts: "the most romantic undergraduate of that period in Cambridge."[32] The only completely negative portrait of Lowry in these years comes, predictably, from Lowry himself. In *The Ordeal of Sigbjørn Wilderness* (p. 58), he (as Sigbjørn) describes himself as having been

> fat, out of training, dishonest, disgusting, carrying around a ukulele from pub to pub, a poseur whose pose, having been to sea, was to be the only honest person in Cambridge when in fact he had not grown up yet.

first term at Cambridge.
32. Gerald Noxon, in his *Prairie Schooner* essay, remembers Lowry's degree as having been a first; and several who have written on Lowry have mentioned his "first-class honors degree in classics"; but the *Cambridge University Calendar* of 1933–1934 lists Lowry's degree under "English Tripos" as "Third Class."

By the time of his graduation from Cambridge, Lowry was becoming too difficult for even the fond and patient Conrad Aiken to handle. At Jeake's House, when Lowry came down to Rye, there were still long, late-night literary conversations. They still played ping-pong, went for extended walks. But their pub-crawls had begun stirring gossip in Rye, and their casual timetable annoyed Clarissa Lorenz, Aiken's second wife, who grew tired of sitting "by the front windows chafing, while the dinner dried up in the oven." [1] She wrote in her diary: "How much longer will Conrad put up with this madman?" Lowry was not deliberately disrupting the Aiken household, for—as we have seen—he loved it. But even at his most benign, he was difficult. According to Clarissa Lorenz,

> Malcolm tried hard not to be a nuisance. A creature of extremes, he either starved himself or gorged—on everything but fish (choking on the bones happened to be one of his many phobias). I kept fearing he would absentmindedly set fire to his mattress or break a leg falling downstairs. He moved like a somnambulist, his blue blazer spotted and rumpled, a necktie holding up his trousers. Keeping him laundered and presentable called for finesse. His socks created minor crises.

Finally, even though the Aikens would miss the check for twenty

1. Clarissa Lorenz, "Call it Misadventure," *The Atlantic*, Vol. 225, no. 6 (June 1970), 106–12. Subsequent quotations by Ms. Lorenz are from this essay.

guineas that Arthur O. Lowry was sending them each month for looking after his son, they were relieved when Lowry left them, in the early summer of 1932, for London. He was anxious to have *Ultramarine* published, and apparently had been able to convince his father that he would have much better luck if he were right on the scene. The elder Lowry consented to let Malcolm go to London, but only if he agreed to live in a temperance hotel. So, with a weekly allowance of £7, the manuscript of the much-revised *Ultramarine*, the ubiquitous ukulele, and the noisome wardrobe, off he went to make his way in literary London.

Staying in a temperance hotel (near the British Museum, and probably the Kenilworth, according to Ralph Case) was no problem for Lowry, because there was a pub next door to the hotel. Ralph Case stayed with him one night shortly after his arrival, and remembers that "the next morning we were getting up about half past seven and Malcolm, even before dressing, helped himself to a good snorter of whiskey. This was really the first occasion in which I'd observed anything really abnormal about his drinking" (BBC "Portrait of Malcolm Lowry").

And, initially at least, there was no problem with *Ultramarine*, either. After he and Lowry had returned from what was supposed to have been their cramming session at Hartland Point the preceding spring, John Davenport had suggested that Lowry send the novel, now thoroughly revised and as polished as it was ever likely to be, to Ian Parsons at Chatto and Windus. This he did, in September. Parsons, who had only just come down from Cambridge himself a short while before Lowry, read the manuscript and recommended publication. The reader at Chatto and Windus, Oliver Warner, agreed with Parsons' recommendations, though with some misgivings. In his reader's report, Warner wrote, "This is an unsatisfactory work because it is potentially so good and so original. . . . The man has a real flair for reporting, in which he is brilliant, and he has an ear for conversation which is remarkable. My conclusions are these: (1) I agree with I.M.P. [Parsons] that we should do him, for his potentiality rather than his achievement. (2) I don't think we shall make a penny, and I think he'll get very mixed reviews. . . .

He will never, I think, do four-square circulating-library books, but his talent is one to be encouraged." [2]

But this acceptance did not come until September. Until that time Lowry was on his own in London; and the summer of 1932 became his initiation into such *vie bohème* as London could offer. By July he was out of the temperance hotel and living a life that John Davenport remembered as "extraordinarily squalid" (the unpublished preface to *Ultramarine*). According to Davenport, Lowry "moved from one room to another in the Bloomsbury area—rooms that had no heat; rooms that had no light; one room that could only be entered by squeezing through a broken panel in the permanently bolted door. He became a familiar figure in the pubs and bars of the neighborhood—the doomed sailor of genius. It was then that the Lowry legend really began."

He seems to have stayed longest in the rooms with the permanently bolted door; and it was in this singularly seedy flat on Devonshire Street, in Marylebone, that he came to be "at home" to both old friends and new. Martin Case recalls sleeping on the floor there one night, and awakening to see a hand slipping through the broken panel on the door. The hand belonged to James Travers, over from his silver fox farm in Devonshire to see his old hero.

The flat on Devonshire Street had not been luxurious before Lowry moved into it, but he certainly did nothing to improve its condition during his time there. Visitors to the flat remember a few pieces of continually collapsing furniture, orange crates full of books, great furry balls of dust everywhere, pipes, spilled tobacco —and bottles, dozens of bottles, displayed in their emptiness with obvious pride on the part of the consumer, or simply piled up anyhow. There was no way to bathe, nor any indication that the young tenant cared to do so.

Lowry blamed this squalor on poverty, but he was—or ought to have been—by no means in financial straits during his months in London. His father, according again to John Davenport (preface to *Ultramarine*), was allowing him £7 per week,

2. From a letter by Ian Parsons to the London *Times Literary Supplement* (Thursday, April 13, 1967), 317.

on condition that he appeared personally and collected it at the London office of his firm. These terms were really neither harsh nor humiliating, as the poor man simply wanted to be assured that his son was alive week by week. He was disappointed. Malcolm refused to go—he was too dirty, had no shoes, didn't want to shave. He was forcibly cleaned up one day and I accompanied him to the City . . . to a rather dreary sort of office in Leadenhall Street. He walked into the office quite briskly, exchanged a few words with the chief accountant, and was handed an envelope which must have contained £70. Of course he enjoyed pretending to be destitute. It was another of his masks. He also enjoyed spending the money in forty-eight hours on the sad detritus of humanity that haunted London's Quartier Latin.

This "Quartier Latin" in 1932 was not, strictly speaking, confined to Soho. For Lowry, it began near the British Museum, at a pub called the Plough, which was then still a favorite haunt of literary and scholarly types. By the time Martin Case had located him at his flat on Devonshire Street, Lowry was chiefly using the Duke of York, a pub in Upper Rathbone Place just off Charlotte Street. It was a sort of headquarters for painters and writers, and it probably seemed too bourgeois for Lowry; for he soon shifted his allegiance to two other places: the Marquis of Granby, nearby; and the Fitzroy Tavern, on Charlotte Street, north of Oxford Street, and therefore north of what was then thought of as "Soho proper"; and west of Tottenham Court Road, and therefore west of Bloomsbury. In 1932, this rather indeterminate area was just beginning to be called "Fitzrovia," in honor not of Fitzroy Square, but of the tavern to which most of bohemian London now found itself drawn. Though Lowry and Martin Case (who was now often in London, trying to find work after having completed his Ph.D. at Cambridge) occasionally performed for the generally annoyed patrons at the Marquis of Granby—Case on an old mahogany upright piano, and Lowry on his ukulele—they were more comfortable at the Fitzroy and spent no one knows how many evenings there during the fall of 1932.

It would be a mistake to suppose that the pubs in either Soho or

Fitzrovia served primarily as gathering places for artists and intellectuals. The depression still prevailed in England, and those who drank in pubs were with few exceptions those who had no other choice. Most of the faces one saw belonged to working-class people; and the "bohemians" in these pubs were distinctly in a minority, consisting for the most part of those artists who were either genuinely poor, and so could not afford to entertain in their homes or in restaurants—or those who were slumming, or very self-consciously ignoring class barriers. Of these, not a few were poseurs even as artists. In his autobiography, Arthur Calder-Marshall recalls his impressions of this scene:

> The Fitzroy Tavern in those days was the headquarters of most undergraduates with bohemian tastes. . . . I enormously enjoyed evenings at the Fitzroy, the Marquis of Granby, and the Plough, and the companionship of painters, writers, and models older than myself. The illusion that I was at the center of the intellectual and artistic life of the great city was at first complete; then gradually it began to dawn on me that the painters and writers whom I met there were only part-time artists and their main occupation was drinking.[3]

The presence in these pubs of the bohemians, who were almost without exception bourgeois in origin, was often not appreciated by the workers who spent their evenings at them. This attitude was not easily understood by the bohemians. As Constantine Fitzgibbon has written, "The poor young who wanted to write or paint were . . . almost all of left-wing views. They believed that their and the world's future lay with the workers, and though they came almost entirely . . . from the middle class, 'bourgeois' was the dirtiest French word in their English dictionary. To go to the pubs, to mix with the workers, was therefore not only economically attractive but also politically virtuous" (*The Life of Dylan Thomas*, p. 148). But, of course, there was very little mixing: the workers cared little for writing; and the writers cared little for work.

3. *The Magic of My Youth* (London, 1951), p. 175.

Even with his weekly £7, a man with the thirst of Malcolm Lowry could not have afforded the more elegant bohemianism of Hampstead or Bloomsbury; and besides, he would have had to be "literary" in either of those areas (even supposing him to have had access to the inner circles of London intellectual life, which is dubious), and this would have been impossible for him. His digs on Bateman Street in Cambridge might, in Davenport's recollection, have been full of the works of every sort of author, ancient and modern; but he seems not to have read a great deal of the books he owned, or not to have absorbed what he did read—and he had just escaped from his formal education at Cambridge with about as little learning as he could manage. He simply was not, in 1932, equipped with enough intellectual experience to handle himself in the more rarefied atmosphere of Hampstead or Bloomsbury. Nor, for that matter, could his almost pathological shyness have allowed him to function in any ambience save that of rowdy, crowded Fitzrovia.

There, he was thought of as a "comer"; there, he could stand and drink not only with his old friends, but with men like Liam O'Flaherty, or—slightly later—with young Dylan Thomas, who arrived in London from Swansea in 1933. There were, according to Martin and Ralph Case, a few—Louis MacNeice was one —who thought Lowry only an unkempt waster; but most of the crowd (the bourgeois element of the crowd, anyway) at the Fitzroy took him for the real thing: a true, seagoing, brawly genius, who was sure to produce great work any day now.

He was known principally at the Fitzroy for two special attributes: his ability to sit at the bar, for hours, at something like a forty-five degree angle to one side or the other; and for what the Cases named "Malcolm-staggering": a particularly happy little lurch, or shuffle, which Lowry went into when approaching the bar. This was much imitated by Lowry's followers, especially James Travers.

And, of course, there were the hangovers, often of monolithic proportions for Lowry. Martin Case remembers one instance of Lowry's post-drinking depressions:

One day we were walking along some street off Charing Cross Road. Malcolm was feeling particularly persecuted and wronged that afternoon. While we were passing a horse standing in the shafts of a cart, the horse made one of those snorting, raspberry, rubber-lip sounds that horses do, unutterably contemptuous, derision of the Fates. Beasts and inanimate objects were always conspiring against Malcolm. He swung. His fist connected just below the cart-horse's ear, and the animal quivered and sank to its knees. Although no real harm was done to the horse, Malcolm was overwhelmed with a remorse that lasted for weeks.[4]

Lowry was strong, even though he was running rather to fat by now, subsisting as he was principally on beer or gin at the Fitzroy, and on the pasta at Bertorelli's Italian restaurant just across the street. But even if he could still fell horses in their tracks, there were now definite signs that his fondness for alcohol was running away with him. To Martin Case, one hungover morning at the Fitzroy gave clear evidence of the pathological nature of Lowry's drinking. There had been a late party the night before, and all of Lowry's group asked the publican, an enormous Russian named Kleinfeld, for halfpints of bitter—except for Lowry, who demanded a treble gin in a loud, clear voice, with emphasis on *treble*.

One of Lowry's closest friends during his London days was John Sommerfield, a young man who had been to sea and written a novel based on his experiences, *They Die Young*. Lowry read the book, and decided he must meet Sommerfield.

Instead of writing to my publisher, he very typically started looking for me around London. I was working as a carpenter in a little workshop off the Old Kent Road that made scenery. I was carpentering away lateish one afternoon, and somebody said, "Oh, there's a chap to see you." And there was Malcolm, dressed in jeans and a dungaree jacket—at this time what working chaps wore. He was carrying a small ukulele and he had half a bottle of whiskey in his pocket and he was slightly swaying about, not because he was tight— he used to stand that way—and I thought, who is this

4. In Conrad Knickerbocker's *Paris Review* essay, "Malcolm Lowry in England."

rather splendid looking chap? He explained that he'd been looking for me and I was terribly flattered. And he sat on a bench and I sat on a bench and he said, "Is the boatswain about?" So I said, "That's all right," and we drank some of this whiskey and we went off to the local pub and oh, for the next two years, I saw a great deal of his company. (BBC "Portrait of Malcolm Lowry")

It would not at all be an exaggeration to say that John Sommerfield came to know Lowry at this time far better than anyone else. Certainly it is the case that his descriptions of Lowry strike one immediately as being absolutely precise, even profound. Sometimes Sommerfield's reminiscences are cheery, as when he remembers their coming upon a pair of elephants one evening:

We were walking after closing time along Fitzroy Street, and Malcolm suddenly said, "My God, look!" I looked round and just going round the corner of Charlotte Street were two large elephants. And I looked at him, and he looked at me. I thought, "Well, if we're both seeing them, it's all right," but he was worried and we ran like blazes around the corner. No sign of an elephant at all, but we did discover a heap of steaming elephant dung. (BBC, "Portrait of Malcolm Lowry")

"Lowry believed that it was his destiny," Sommerfield explained to me years afterward, "that his deepest sorrows and greatest joys should be turned to grotesque ridiculousness by some mocking pantomime incident." When Lowry lamented to Sommerfield that a malign fate should so deliberately outrage his sense of dignity by placing elephants, and then—infinitely worse—elephant dung before his eyes, late at night in London, Sommerfield could only reply, "Malcolm, you have a touch of persecution mania, but in your case it's perfectly justified."

A short time after Lowry left London, John Sommerfield wrote a novel, *The Last Weekend*, which was never published, but which Lowry later read, and admired. One of the central characters of Sommerfield's book is named David Nordall (Lowry must have spoken often to Sommerfield about Grieg), a young, drunken writer in London. David is troubled, and troubled in exactly the way that Sir Paul Mallinson was to describe Lowry's difficulties 24 years later. In Sommerfield's prescient words, "David's conflicts can only resolve themselves through his work, and to effect this, he must cease from destroying himself with drink; yet he only drinks because of the nature of his conflicts" (*The Last Weekend*, p. 88).

And, in Sommerfield's manuscript, David is seldom sober. Or silent. Most of the time he is coherent enough to talk; not to converse, strictly speaking, but to deliver monologues. He might choose to tell the narrator, while stumbling from one lamp post to another during a late-night walk through London's streets, about his unhappy early years, "talking about nurses and little boy's sexual organs . . . maundering psychoanalytically about his childhood." (Lowry had by this time apparently already formulated, or at least conceived, the anecdotes about his sadistic nannies which he was to tell even to casual acquaintances in subsequent years.)

In his flat, which is obviously Lowry's Devonshire Street lodging, David speaks at length to his friends:

> David, whose hair is standing on end, is swaying about in his chair. When he talks he splutters, runs out of words, and everyone waits tensely for the end of his remarks; his pipe keeps on going out and he continually loses his matches. This, I imagine, is the way he conducts all the practical affairs of his life; now he burns his fingers trying to light a dead match at the gas fire; now Pat hands him a lighter, which he cannot get to function.
>
> (*The Last Weekend*, p. 95)

Later, David is telling his friends some "long, very complicated story that, everyone felt sure, was leading to a tremendously funny climax, that continually receded behind a mist of parentheses" (p. 127). This is, of course, exactly Lowry's manner of discourse—except, presumably, that Lowry *was* occasionally able to reach the hilarious conclusion of his monologue. How else explain that there were so many intelligent people who were willing to go about with him, sitting silently through these monologues?

And sometimes, again exactly like Lowry (and Geoffrey Firmin, and Sigbjørn Wilderness, as well as most of the rest of the Lowry personae), David will break into a silly conversation suddenly, to say, in a lecturing sort of voice: "Regent's Park, like Dante's Inferno, is divided into circles" (p. 125).

Like Lowry, David also becomes drunk beyond the range of his hard-drinking friends; terrifyingly drunk, in fact.

> David kept laughing, a wild laugh in which he bared his teeth and seemed to grin ferociously. There was something alarming, almost dangerous, about him when he was drunk like this. He exceeded the stages of comic or foolish drunkenness, but he didn't go through the sagging, slobbering, repulsive last stages of ordinary boozing. After days of hard drinking he became like this, only a little way from delirium, and his behavior quite incalculable.
>
> (p. 134)

Sommerfield's novel leaves its Lowry-figure sitting drunk in his flat, with eyes staring stupidly ahead and mouth fixed in a wolfish grin; and so must the real Lowry have been, at the end of a long binge. What the Cases had by this time observed in his behavior, and what Sommerfield analyzed so perceptively about him, were the unmistakable stigmata of the most savage and self-destructive sort of alcoholic.

And yet. Not everyone saw with such clarity what was happening to Lowry: people noticed that he drank more than most, but not many thought much about it. For one thing, he often seemed proud of his consumption; and when he would beamingly announce in a morning session at the Fitzroy that he had the preceding evening drunk sixteen pints of beer and one-half bottle of whiskey, most ignored this boasting (if, indeed, it was boasting: Lowry's capacity was astonishing, both then and later). And, of course, there was his loveable vulnerability, as described by Ralph Case in the preceding chapter. Lowry might have needed caring for, being so obviously nearly helpless most of the time; but there were many who were happy to care for him. This was a phenomenon that Lowry discovered early in his life: that the world is full of people eager to become nursemaids to the incompetent, the vulnerable, even the impossible—if only one is *engagingly* incompetent, vulnerable, impossible. Lowry had charm; he could dazzle not only mamas, maids, and the middle-aged, but tough, shrewd men like John Sommerfield as well. And, if a drunk can ever be attractive, Lowry can be said to have been so—most of the time.

It was this charm (or, as I called it in the preceding chapter, "genius") that kept him afloat in London in 1932. In the early fall of that year, James Hepburn, one of his Cambridge friends, saw that Lowry needed caring for, and carted him out of Devonshire Street up to Hampstead, where his mother, the Australian poet Anna Wickham, lived on Parliament Hill in a comfortable but eccentric house she called "Bourgeois Towers." Although Lowry never actually lived here, he stayed often at Bourgeois Towers in the succeeding months; and it became for him something of a replacement for Jeake's House, where he no longer felt quite welcome.

Anna Wickham, a very tall, imposing, deep-voiced woman, was the widow of Patrick Hepburn, who had been a solicitor and distinguished amateur astronomer, and who had died in a climbing accident. She lived in her Hampstead house with her three sons, James, John, and George, and kept a free-wheeling sort of salon-cum-boarding house for young writers. Davenport remembered Bourgeois Towers as "a large house through which a gale swept perpetually, tossing leaves and manuscripts in and out of the windows" (unpublished preface to *Ultramarine*). Conrad Knickerbocker, in his *Paris Review* article, erred greatly in equating the Hepburns with *Under the Volcano's* Taskersons; for Anna Wickham's sons were no "rough lot," as he calls them, but instead cultured, refined, sensitive—and talented. The two older brothers, James and John, made a living (and not a bad one) in their youth as music-hall dancers and singers, and, with their impressive mother, were among Fitzrovia's more glamorous attractions.

Lowry was impressed by the unselfconscious and talented exuberance of this singular family; and James, especially, was glad to have his old friend staying there, even though he often tired of Lowry's posing as the doomed young sailor-poet, and "thought he ran the entire destiny thing rather hard at times" (Knickerbocker, *Paris Review*, p. 32). On the whole, for the eldest Hepburn son, Lowry was "utterly marvelous. . . . He had a way of looking up at you from under his eyes, foxy and twinkling. Mischief, the real thing. Remembering him makes all those years seem—real" (Knickerbocker, *Paris Review*, p. 33). Anna Wickham and her sons took great care of Lowry, and if the fondness of James Hepburn's recollection is mixed with a tinge of exasperation, it was nonetheless real fondness. Bourgeois Towers must often have been as noisy as the Fitzroy Tavern, and very nearly as crowded; but it was a home, and Lowry (whose whole life might be said to have been a series of quests for a home) was at his best when he was there.

Another good friend in the London days was the young novelist, Arthur Calder-Marshall. Not long down from Oxford, Calder-Marshall was at a party one afternoon, given by Lawrence and Wishart at Gatti's, and at 5:30, going up the stairs, met John Davenport and Lowry, both very drunk, coming down. Davenport, who had thus far published nothing, was enraged at seeing Calder-Marshall, who had already produced two novels. For some minutes he swore at Calder-Marshall, while Lowry stood, smiling and swaying, on the stairs. Then, in spite of Calder-Marshall's pleading with him not to drive in his condition, Davenport tumbled out the door, pulling the smiling, mute Lowry after him, and leapt into his very old car that was parked just outside in Coventry Street. With Lowry beaming away beside him, Davenport tore down the street for perhaps twenty yards, when he was stopped and arrested for being drunk in charge. What became of Lowry that evening, Calder-Marshall does not remember.

Before Calder-Marshall met Lowry again, September came and *Ultramarine* was accepted by Chatto and Windus. Lowry was jubilant, but at the same time more than a little apprehensive; what if the reviewers caught him out at his plagiarisms of *Blue Voyage* and *The Ships Sail On?* (In fact, though *Ultramarine* was indeed held by its reviewers to be derivative, it was not Aiken or Grieg whom they named as the source, but Joyce—whom Lowry probably had not yet read very extensively.) But this anxiety was replaced by another, more serious one a month later, when Lowry was notified by Ian Parsons of Chatto's that he had lost the manuscript of *Ultramarine*.

On the afteroon of October 2, Parsons was heading out of town in his open three-litre Bentley, with his suitcase, containing the typescript of *Ultramarine*, in the back seat. He stopped at the office of Chatto and Windus for a moment to make a telephone call. When he came out, the suitcase was gone. Parsons was not too worried: it was, after all, only a typescript that had been stolen, and the author would surely have a copy. In any case, he advised his superiors and the police, and "arranged for a suitable reward to be advertised in a number of appropriate places" (Parsons, in a letter to the *Times Literary Supplement*, April 13, 1967). When no news of the whereabouts of *Ultramarine* was forthcoming, Parsons had to tell Lowry what had happened. Lowry, of course, had no carbon; but to Parsons he was brave about the loss, and said that he thought he might be able to rewrite the book if he were given enough time. Chatto's agreed to give Lowry a weekly salary until he should have completed the rewriting.

On June 22, 1946, from Dollarton, Lowry was to write Albert Erskine about *Ultramarine* that the book, "which set out to be good, is an inexcusable mess of which I've been ashamed for 13 years. The first and only real version was lost by Chatto and Windus and I rewrote it in two months from notes salvaged from a waste paper basket and a few published bits" (*Selected Letters*, p. 113). As Parsons says in his letter, this is not quite accurate. He remembers that toward the end of December he "suddenly received an urgent message from Malcolm" to meet him in a local pub. After many beers, Lowry suddenly came out with this story:

> He had gone home to try to reconstruct *Ultramarine*, but had found it quite impossible to work there. He had then visited, in turn, half-a-dozen places in which he had written parts of the book, in the hope that local inspiration would stimulate memory. All to no purpose. Finally he had gone to stay with the friend in whose house—somewhere near Birmingham, I think—he had finished the book.

Upon explaining the reason for his visit, the friend went straight to a drawer and pulled out a bundle of heavily corrected half-sheets of typescript. It was the torn-up draft of *Ultramarine*, rescued from the waste paper basket into which Malcolm had thrown it after typing out a fair copy.

The version of the story that Lowry told Parsons in the pub is close to the truth, and it was apparently the version that Lowry preferred, since, as Parsons observes, it was substantially the same version that he told to his friend and publisher, Frank Taylor, fifteen years later in America.

But, as usual, at this stage of Lowry's history, the closest approximation to truth about the whole sad—but far from tragic—business is the account by Martin Case, who was of course the friend in Birmingham of whom Lowry told Parsons. During the Christmas vacation of 1931 Case had spent many days helping Lowry by typing out what they assumed would be the final fair copy of *Ultramarine*. Case believed that it was this copy which Lowry gave to Chatto and Windus—though in fact it was not, since Lowry had made further revisions on the novel at Hartland Point with John Davenport the following Easter, so that what Lowry submitted to the publisher was undoubtedly in some form an emended copy of the Christmas 1931 version. Then, according to Case in his reminiscence prepared for CBC in 1962,

Some weeks or months later, when I . . . happened to be in Birmingham, I received a frantic and incoherent telephone call that turned out to be from Malcolm, who in fact was speaking from the railway station in that city. His typescript had been stolen from or lost by his publishers; he had kept no copy; the work of years had gone for nothing; he had fled from London and blindly taken a train to Birmingham to seek comfort, advice, oblivion, anything. I collected him from the station and brought him home. I don't know whether his joy was greater than mine at my being able to tell him that I had long ago retrieved discarded sheets, carbon copies and so on, from waste paper baskets and firegrates, had bound them together in a file for my own delectation, and was able to present him then and there with a complete and final version of *Ultramarine*.

It was not quite final, as we have seen; but it would do. We shall never know in what ways this retrieved copy differed from the revised version that Lowry had given to Chatto and Windus in September.[5] In his *Times* letter, Parsons says that he is "tolerably certain that the published version didn't differ materially from the original manuscript, despite Malcolm's reference to 'the only real version' and his subsequent plan to rewrite the book."

As soon as he was able to deliver another fair copy to Chatto and Windus, Lowry, curiously, begged Parsons not to accept it unless Chatto's really believed in its promise; he did not want it published just because of Chatto's embarrassment over Parsons' having lost the earlier typescript. Parsons was not the last editor to be surprised by such scrupulosity on Lowry's part, but in any event he showed great aplomb now, by taking Lowry at his word, and returning *Ultramarine* to him. We have already noted the tepid response of Oliver Warner, Chatto's reader, to *Ultramarine*. On December 21, before Lowry had announced the recovery of Case's draft of the novel, Chatto's had got in touch with Lowry's agent, John Farquharson, to say that they were not especially eager to publish the novel even if Lowry were able to rewrite it; but that they would of course honor their commitment to publish it if Lowry chose to have them do so. Parsons passed this information to Lowry, who took back his typescript with good grace.

Happily for Lowry, he—or Farquharson—was able to place the book almost immediately after this with Jonathan Cape, who expressed great pleasure in having it, put it on their list for Autumn 1933, and gave Lowry an advance royalty of £40. So it was that *Ultramarine*, after a voyage nearly as complicated as some of those its author had made aboard ship, found a publisher.

5. Conrad Aiken has since claimed that he himself at this time possessed at Jeake's House in Rye a complete draft of *Ultramarine*, but that Lowry never asked him for it. This would seem to support Case's recollection that Lowry went straight to Birmingham without ever visiting those "half a dozen places in which he had written parts of the book."

When *Ultramarine* was finally published, more than one reviewer characterized it as "experimental." Perhaps in 193; it might have seemed so to its more conservative readers; but it certainly was not "experimental" because Lowry had been deliberate y trying to make it so. When he and Gerald Noxon had spoken it Cambridge of writing, Lowry had been far more concerned with problems of language and style than he was with content. The question, Noxon recalled in his *Prairie Schooner* essay, always was "How should a serious novelist write in 1930?" The two undergraduates discussed what had been done in the way of innovation by such modern novelists as Joyce, Faulkner, and Hemingway, but Lowry was not especially responsive to their achievements.

> Basically Malcolm was unwilling to repudiate the legacy which he had found awaiting him in the works of nineteenth-century novelists. While discarding the aridity of a purely realistic style, he was unwilling to adopt the kind of personal stenography which made the works of writers like Joyce and Faulkner superficially difficult for the reader. Nor was Malcolm to be seduced by the apparent simplicity of Hemingway, whose writing he found much too flat for his own purposes. For Malcolm it was necessary that his writing should have a perfectly wrought surface meaning, in the sense of the term established by Flaubert. A competent and thoroughly understandable narrative technique, however complex it might be in form, was a necessity. . . . But while fulfilling all the conditions mentioned above, Malcolm insisted that his writing must be capable of carrying meaning at many different depths, on the many different levels of intellectual and emotional communication which he discerned so clearly in Melville, for instance.
>
> (Noxon, *Prairie Schooner*, pp. 317–18)

Melville, it is true, was at this time, and remained, one of Lowry's "masters"—ultimately, perhaps, after Aiken the greatest influence on his literary career. But, as we have already noted, it was to Aiken and Nordahl Grieg that he felt he owed most of *Ultramarine*. Grieg cannot be said to have given him his content in the novel; for it was, after all, based not primarily upon *The Ship Sails*

On, but his own experiences at sea in the spring, summer, and fall of
1927. But Grieg's novel certainly confirmed Lowry in his sense that
the best means of giving strength to a conflict was to depict it as
taking place on an elemental level: thus, if one wanted to write a
Künstlerroman (and Lowry, Albert Erskine once complained to
him, never wanted to write anything *else*), then it should be set, not
in *ateliers* and dancing parlors, as Mann had done in *Tonio Kröger*,
but at sea, where the young artist's struggle to realize himself could
gain impact from confrontation with existential extremes. Benjamin
Hall of *The Ship Sails On* has no artistic ambitions, but Dana Hilliot of *Ultramarine* most definitely does. He has gone to sea not to
learn the family's business, nor even to prove himself as a man
(though this is certainly *one* of his hopes), but to learn what he
needs to know in order to write. He comes aboard the *Oedipus
Tyrannus*[6] in Liverpool filled with all manner of Wordsworthian
foolishness ("I propose to myself to imitate and as far as possible to
adopt the very language of these men"); and he gradually learns, as
the voyage progresses, not only that one does not learn much by ac-
quiring the language of seamen, but also that the sea has a greater
lesson to teach than the art of fiction. In fact, *Ultramarine* is a real
rarity: a *Künstlerroman* in reverse. Nineteen-year-old Dana Hilliot
sails as a dedicated author (who has not yet, it is true, written anything), and proceeds through his stages of development until he
learns, midway through the novel, that his callowness or self-absorption will not let him be a writer:

> . . . the desire to write is a disease like any other disease; and
> what one writes, if one is to be any good, must be rooted in
> some sort of autocthony. And there I abdicate. I can no
> more create than fly. What I could achieve would be that
> usual self-conscious first novel, to be reviewed in the mor-
> tuary of *The Times Literary Supplement*, a 'crude and un-
> pleasant work,' something of that nature, of which the prin-

6. In the 1933 edition of *Ultramarine*, the ship's name was *Nawab*; but Lowry at
some time in the 1950's altered this, so as to make *Ultramarine* conform to his master-plan, in which it was to serve as the first novel in *The Voyage that Never
Ends*. The edition cited here is that of 1962 (New York: Lippincott), in which
there are other minor revisions from the original edition, now a collector's item.

cipal character would be no more and no less, whether in liquor or in love, than the abominable author himself. I fear also that the disease is a childlish one, diarrhoea scribendi simply.

(Ultramarine, p. 96)

If Lowry's first novel is about the coming to manhood of Dana Hilliot (whose given name probably came from Lowry's having read Richard Henry Dana's *Two Years Before the Mast*), it is also about the growing up out of the childish disease of the desire to write. By the end of *Ultramarine*, Dana opts for the *vita activa* over the *vita contemplativa*. He writes a not-to-be-posted letter to his sweetheart, Janet, which proclaims this:

> But in future I shall be more interested in biceps than forceps; I shall lift weights rather than pints. As for my books, I shall throw them overboard and buy new ones. . . . Let their writers sign on troismâts and learn how to swarm up a rope with passion? My writing? You or any woman can do that for me. I don't know a damn thing yet. But one day I shall find a land corrupted and depressed beyond all knowledge, where the children are starving for lack of milk, a land unhappy, although unenlightened, and cry, "I shall stay here until I have made this place good."

Young Hilliot may be embarrassing in the naïveté with which he speaks, here; but he is no more so than, say, the young Tonio Kröger—or perhaps even the young Stephen Dedalus. The important point is that *Ultramarine* (as no one seems to have noticed) shows us a Lowry writing, at the very beginning of his career, about the antithetical natures of the real hero and the hero *manqué*, the artist—or, at least, the inactive, introspective sort of artist he must have felt himself in danger of becoming. With the young Lowry, as for Thomas Mann, disease and genius went hand and hand, as did health and an ordered, normal life. And Lowry had his protagonist opt for normality.

Not so surprisingly, Lowry extends this equation between disease and genius to include considerations of his two great enemies, al-

coholism and venereal disease; the former real, the latter only a paranoid obsession—for Dana Hilliot as for Malcolm Lowry. For
three years Dana has remained faithful to his Janet (whose last
name, oddly, changes between Chapters Three and Four from Roh-
traut to Travena), who waits for him in Liverpool. Whenever the
Oedipus Tyrannus enters a new port, Dana either stays aboard the
ship, or goes ashore only to get drunk. "You've been oiled in every
port all the way up the bloody coast," a shipmate complains to him
(p. 34). "You're one of the most regular booze artists I ever struck,"
says another. "You drink enough to put out the bloody fires of the
ship. It's not natural at your age—that's what we all says"
(pp. 64–65).

The crew would think much better of him, Dana is convinced, if
he were to forget his vow of chastity. But he is terrified of disease,
and with some reason. As in *The Ship Sails On*, syphilis or gonorrhea are subjects that come up in almost every conversation; but in
Ultramarine Lowry allows his seamen to speak more graphically
than Grieg's had done. One of the novel's many fragmented conversations has to do with someone's recollection of a shipmate's illness:

> —And the next day he comes to me with tears in his eyes
> and shows me them. Caw— they were as big as your fist.
> And 'e'd let it rip—got it in Muji; he had, and never said
> damn all to anybody—Kept it to himself for thirteen
> months. Well, the doc sends him to the skipper, and the
> skipper says, "Get off my bridge, you *stinking beast*."
>
> (*Ultramarine*, p. 64)

And, of course, there is the anatomical museum in Tsjang-Tsjang,
imaginatively transported there by Lowry from Paradise Street in
Liverpool, with its missionary-lurid descriptions of its displays:

> THIRTY-SEVEN models in EIGHT glass cases portraying sec-
> ondary symptoms all taken from LIFE. Some of these diseases
> have been greatly exaggerated by the use of MERCURY and
> also wrong treatment. . . . The HEAD and NECK showing the
> awful and DEGRADED state in which MEN come when they
> DISOBEY the laws of GOD; the wages of sin is DEATH.
>
> (*Ultramarine*, p. 111)

In spite of such convincing arguments against sexual activity as these, Dana determines to prove his manhood. But he is too drunk, and Olga Sologub, the White Russian refugee-turned-prostitute with whom he had intended "going upstairs" at a dance-hall, moves on to another man: Andy, Dana's greatest enemy on the *Oedipus Tyrannus*.

One ought to note here another curious aspect of the disease-genius obsession: not only are drunkenness and syphilis given as instances of disease; they are almost invariably themselves equated. Seldom does mention of one appear, without mention of the other following hard after. Arthur O. Lowry's athletic Methodism had done its work. Drunkenness for Lowry was never to be simply an amiable weakness, or—as the Irish say—a strong man's failing: it was a moral abomination, just as loathsome as the worst sort of venereal disease.

The crew of the *Oedipus Tyrannus* despise Dana, as a pampered toff. He is "doin' a good lad out of his job." And he is inept: Andy's constant refrain is "I don't know what sort of bloody man you are at all." Dana detests himself just as much as the crew does: he is ashamed of his drunkenness, he spends anguished hours imagining his return, diseased, to Liverpool: "Pay attention to your trouser button and see him if you will for yourself, Dana Hilliot, the syphilitic, as he strolls aimlessly down great Homer Street. Look! How everyone he touches is smitten with the dire disease" (p. 73). Full of self-pity, he fantasizes about his death: "When the door of Dana Hilliot, old age pensioner, was forced, the police found him lying on the mattress in an emaciated and verminous condition. Death from exhaustion and self-neglect—" (p. 74). Most especially, he hates his clumsy, spatular *hands*, which are always filthy, always burned from the caustic soda with which he must polish brightwork. In one drunken fantasy, he imagines himself to be liable to stigmata, with "his bleeding hands enveloped in cloths" (p. 99). With Olga, the prostitute, he wonders about his "all-abiding sense of guilt" about his hands (p. 117). Why this particular piece of morbidity? For one thing, Dana's hands mark him as a toff, as someone who has never done real work. For another, there is the possibility of guilt over masturbation. When the boatswain tells Dana he is free to put on clean clothes and go ashore in Tsjang-Tsjang, he stops, winks evilly, and then adds to Dana, "Well, there's no need to do that. I forgot for the moment you were one of those who preferred your right hand—" (p. 84).

As long as the crew hate him, and as long as he hates himself, Dana must construct ugly fantasies not only about himself, but about his relatives and parents as well. All his father's brothers and sisters had died, obscurely but venereally, in early infancy; and his father "is now in a home eating the buttons off the chair at clairaudient intervals, and composing a sonnet sequence, *Songs of Second Childhood*" (p. 72), while his mother is going blind. Here we have another complex form of displacement: Lowry punishing his mother for her lack of compassion during his own years of near-blindness.

But once he is finally accepted, Dana can give up such punitive fantasies, as he gives up his desire to write:

> There is no further need to invent a venereal lineage for myself; it is no longer amusing; my innocent little aunts, and their equally innocent parents may rest in peace in Oslo cemetery. . . . as for my father we shall exhume him from his imaginary madhouse, reinstate him to his normal position of tutor, to his liver trouble, his pipe, his dog and his games of chess. . . .
>
> (*Ultramarine*, p. 185)

And his mother's approaching blindness becomes merely conjunctivitis.

What occasions this radical change in attitude? Ironically, given Dana's private detestation of himself ("this strong creature with a head of filthy, infected hair, and a maggoty brain and a rotting consciousness, who dreams of archetypal images"), the reversal comes when he learns a kind of humility. The crew are correct: he *is* a toff, and they cannot forgive him for treating as a romantic lark, or aesthetic experience, what is for them a harsh, glamourless life. They hate him because of his illusions; and it is only by abandoning those illusions that Dana can really join the men of the *Oedipus Tyrannus*.

He begins the voyage as an ordinary seaman, assigned the most demeaning tasks aboard ship. Like Benjamin Hall in Grieg's novel, he longs to think of the beauty of the sea and the sky; but, like Benjamin, he is too tired, or too harassed, to do so. The *Oedipus Tyrannus* is not only a tyrant: it is a filthy, floating shell concealing in its bowels a real inferno. The most consistent attitude of Dana throughout the voyage is that of looking downward. He will sit by the open skylight over the seamen's quarters, looking down at the crew, and listening to what they have to say about him. Or he will peer down into the deep rectangular well of one of the ship's hatches, watching stevedores, "their backs as glossy as moles," rolling boxes into place. Most importantly, however, Dana will stand, staring down into the hell of the engine and boiler rooms, into the very heart of the ship, where

> four stokers, foreshortened by the height, were dancing in front of four blazing chasms, driving in their slice bars. Shouts and cries floated up to him. . . . Cloom—cloom —cloom—cloom. Looking down he could see through the bulkhead doors where the red and gold of the furnaces mottled the reeking deck, and the tremulous roar of the cages' fires dominated a sibilant, continual splutter of steam. The *Oedipus Tyrannus'* firemen . . . half naked, gritty and black with coal, and pasty with ashes, came and went in the blazing light, and in the gloom; flaming nightmares, fire-lit demons. The furnace doors opened, and scorpions leapt out; spirals of gas spun and reeled over the bubbling mass of fuel, and sheets of violet flame sucked half-burned carbon over the quivering firewall into the flues.
>
> (*Ultramarine*, pp. 169, 171)

When, at the beginning of the voyage, Dana looks down into this frightening scene, he notices that "despite their work the firemen seemed to get more fun out of life than the seamen, and seemed somehow to be better, in some queer way to be nearer God" (p. 23); and at the end of the novel, Dana, having proven himself worthy, is invited to become a fireman—to descend himself into the inferno that provides the *Oedipus Tyrannus* with all its energy.

He proves himself by failing to be a hero—which is to say that he proves himself to be human, in no way superior to any of the crew of the ship. Shortly after the novel begins Dana is humiliated when he blusteringly proposes to rescue a carrier pigeon, a "mickey," that has been perched at the top of the mainmast for three days, where it will surely starve if not brought down. But the crew sense the vanity behind his gesture and tell him to mind his own business. Much later, in Chapter Five, the mickey, its wings clipped, slips from its leash and falls overboard, into what is assumed to be the shark-infested harbor water. Dana offers to dive in to the bird's rescue (like his author, he is an expert swimmer); and, though he is just as afraid of doing this as he had been of climbing the mainmast earlier, he is really willing to dive. The crewmen again restrain him, but this time they do so with respect: they know that he is not bluffing, and that he would try to save the bird not to demonstrate his bravery, but to rescue the beloved pet of one of his fellow sailors. Quietly but clearly, they make him one of them. Andy, the cook, who has bullied Dana throughout the voyage, invites him into the galley for a drink, and this clumsy ritual confirms Dana's acceptance by the crew.

If, as Gerald Noxon recalled, Lowry insisted that his writing must be capable of carrying meaning at many different depths, and on many different levels of intellectual and emotional communication, then the symbolic pattern he set up in *Ultramarine* was remarkably well-suited for this sort of multi-layered effect. Here was the ship *qua* ship; and here it was as a microcosmic little universe, with mainmast pointing to heaven, and searing inferno below. Dana cannot climb the mast: he is not worthy. But later he demonstrates his humanity by being willing, in effect, to sacrifice himself for a fellow man; and so he is rewarded by being taken into the hell of the engine-room, where the men are "in some queer way nearer to God." There is no salvation, or exaltation, by solitary ascent to heaven. There is only humanity, and the fellowship of the inferno as one's reward for manifesting his humanity. Somewhere, below, God exists. An inverted apocalyptic vision, to be sure; and one which not only establishes Lowry firmly in the company of *poètes maudits* from Baudelaire and Rimbaud to Céline and Genet, but which also was to become his greatest fictional concept—the very basis of all his work, the source of whatever greatness he ever possessed as a writer.

This is not to say that, simply because the majestic archetypal vision is there, *Ultramarine* is a great novel: it is not. For one thing, it is, as John Sommerfield described his fictional Lowry's conversation, constantly receding "behind a mist of parentheses." Lowry was determined to master Conrad Aiken's variety of stream-of-consciousness technique, and for Aiken's reasons: principally, what interested them both as writers was not what the artist-protagonist did, but what he thought and felt. (In their last meeting, in David Markson's New York apartment in 1954, Lowry laughingly reassured Aiken that "nothing at all was being allowed to *happen*" in his newest projected novel, *October Ferry to Gabriola*.)

In his "Author's Preface" to a 1965 one-volume edition of three of his novels,[7] Aiken explains his theory of what his novels had to be. Writing short stories was easy for him, he explains, because the method was basically similar to writing poetry; but the greater expanse of a novel caused special problems: how could one fill that expanse, and keep it *alive*, while still going about the "really fundamental business of saying one's say"? For *Blue Voyage* this problem was especially acute. At the time of writing it he was "steeped in the psychoanalytical movement and its concepts, notably those of Freud, Ferenczi and Adler."

> I was deeply concerned with the revolutions and revelations going on every day with regard to the understanding of the human psyche or ego which were then so rapidly developing, and the presentation of this in fiction, it seemed to me, could be a separate department of one's *poiesis*. . . .

For Aiken, his long fiction was to be an adjunct to his poetry, something used to fill in the outlines of his entire *œuvre*—in which he hopes to represent "a sort of totality of response to the universe with which we are faced, outer and inner."

7. Conrad Aiken, *Three Novels: Blue Voyage, Great Circle, King Coffin* (New York, 1965).

And the inner especially. For what I wanted above all to make of *Blue Voyage* . . . was a statement of the nature of the poet or novelist or critic at that particular moment in time, and then, to make it palatable, in terms of a novel. Here was the artist-hero-servant in a new predicament: he could understand his neurosis, and then proceed to create with it, on the one hand, while he analyzed both the neurosis and himself away with the other. . . . Anyway, this was the plan for *Blue Voyage:* it must appear to be a novel, in that it would have enough action, plot, and character, or design, to carry it forward; but more important, along with these elements, above and below them and embodied in them, there must be as complete a psychological statement of my own moral and social and aesthetic situation as I could possibly make.

Now, such a theory as Aiken's might work for *him:* he was at the time of *Blue Voyage* an established and mature author of thirty-six, and this novel was his twelfth published work. Such a man might be expected to have a rather fully developed "moral and social and aesthetic situation," so that a philosophical and psychoanalytically oriented autobiography masquerading as a "novel" might actually succeed, becoming a real portrait of a complex and highly sophisticated man, as seen at a crucial juncture of his life. (Northrop Frye has shown us all what a potent form of fiction the "confession" can be.) [8] In fact, *Blue Voyage* today seems dated, even tedious. Demarest, who stands for Aiken in the novel, may be intelligent, neurotic (as all good Freudians believe the artist must be), and able to analyze himself with great skill; yet even in *Blue Voyage* one feels the lack of things *happening:* there is Demarest, sailing second-class from America to England; there are fellow-passengers, none of whom amount to much, either in themselves or to Demarest—and there are Demarest's thoughts and emotions, delivered to us mostly through long interior monologues, fantasies, and dream sequences. This is not enough; self-absorption, even in so interesting a man as

8. Northrop Frye, *Anatomy of Criticism: Four Essays* (Princeton, 1957). See especially Frye's fourth essay, "Rhetorical Criticism: Theory of Genres," in which he defines his four "specific continuous forms" of prose fiction.

Aiken, is ultimately not sufficient to sustain a long piece of fiction.

And it was this approach to the novel that Lowry learned from Aiken, and tried to make his own. If concentrating on the inner life of Dana Hilliot (who is Malcolm Lowry just as surely as Demarest in *Blue Voyage* is Conrad Aiken) enabled him to transcend the rather shopworn conventions of the youthful sea voyage seen as *rite de passage*, it also placed him in the position of having to understand more about himself at twenty than he could do. From Aiken he was able to learn something of his tutor's modified stream-of-consciousness technique, and of the trick of superimposing several conversations upon one another, in order to achieve a sort of collage of fragmented statements. *Ultramarine*, like *Blue Voyage*, is full of imagined conversations; long, semi-coherent soliloquies; and drunken reveries, chiefly celebrations or excoriations of the self.[9] The lesson Aiken taught Lowry was heady stuff for so young a pupil, especially one so liable to an almost infantile concern with self. When Lowry has Dana, in a passage cited above, reflect that "what one writes, if one is to be any good, must be rooted in some sort of autocthony," and then admit that he is incapable of creating anything intended to have its own life outside himself, he was performing a very shrewd self-diagnosis—both as man and as novelist. At a time when Lowry should have been beginning to find himself in the world around him, and to root his fiction in what he found, Aiken was teaching him, principally by his own example in *Blue Voyage*, that the basis of fiction was introspection; that the external world mattered only in so far as it contributed to or illuminated the inner life of the author and of his fictional representative. Ultimately, Aiken's tutelage helped to cause Lowry, as man and as writer, to become fixated at an almost adolescent solipsistic level of development. Lowry had a powerful mind—more powerful, perhaps, even than Aiken's—and one of the delights of his fiction

9. In a letter to the *Times* [*London*] *Literary Supplement* (Thursday, February 16, 1967), p. 127, Aiken recalls that Lowry knew *Blue Voyage* by heart, and used its "styles, devices, etc." in *Ultramarine* and in his later work as well. "Even the title *Ultramarine*," says Aiken, "was intended as a reference to *Blue Voyage*, and I suggested why not go a step further and call it *Purple Passage?*"

could be the spectacle of that mind examining itself; but he was never on very sure ground when he tried to move outside that mind. In *Ultramarine*, we can admire the brilliance with which Lowry takes Dana Hilliot from a condition of near-despair to one of exhilaration; and we can understand that for him, as for Aiken, this psychic journey was meant to be one from neurosis to psychic stability, and hence from a condition in which the creation of art might be possible, to one in which it were quite impossible. But— except for the rather splendid evocations of the demonic apparent chaos in the engine-rooms of the *Oedipus Tyrannus*—much of the rest of *Ultramarine* is a muddle. How much of this was the fault of the loss of the final version, we can only guess. Not much, probably.[10]

One afternoon in early 1933, shortly after Jonathan Cape had taken *Ultramarine*, Arthur Calder-Marshall was having lunch at the Astoria Hotel, on Greek Street in Soho, with Hamish Miles, his editor at Cape, when Lowry walked disconsolately into the dining room, and sat down with them. He was carrying a small suitcase. Miles, who was also now Lowry's editor, smiled at Lowry and said, "Tell me, what are you doing now?" To which Lowry morosely replied, "I have a dead white rabbit in my suitcase and I'm trying to dispose of it." He then opened his suitcase to reveal what appeared to be a fully grown but thoroughly dead rabbit. Lowry, it turned out, had been sitting two nights before in front of the fireplace at Bourgeois Towers, talking and drinking with Anna Wickham and James Hepburn. Absent-mindedly Lowry had been fondling young George Hepburn's pet rabbit, holding it casually in his lap as he talked. The rabbit had suddenly gone limp: Lowry had broken its neck.[11] For two days, full of remorse and paranoia ("Destiny has struck again," he told James Hepburn; "look what happens when I

10. For other discussions of this subject, see Richard H. Costa, "The Lowry/Aiken Symbiosis," *Nation*, CCIV:26 (June 26, 1967), 823–26; and Costa's revised doctoral thesis, *Malcolm Lowry* (New York, 1972).
11. "He had large, coarse artisan's hands," Hepburn told Conrad Knickerbocker. "He occasionally reminded me of a wild boar." Perhaps, but the fact is that Lowry's hands only *seemed* large, possibly because they were so clumsy. Actually they were surprisingly small, as were his feet.

try to touch something beautiful"), he had wandered about Soho and Fitzrovia, afraid to go back to Bourgeois Towers, and unable to decide on a way of disposing of the rabbit's corpse. Calder-Marshall called a waiter, asked him to take away the rabbit, and offered Lowry a drink. They had several drinks, and he and Lowry became good friends.

For some reason, perhaps because he felt he had outstayed his welcome at Bourgeois Towers as he had at Jeake's House earlier, Lowry now insisted on leaving London for Paris. His father refused to give his permission unless Lowry could promise that he would study, preferably at the Sorbonne, and unless he could find a suitable guardian for himself in Paris. Promising to study was easy, though he had no intention of going near the Sorbonne: three years of Cambridge had been more than enough formal education, so far as he was concerned. But the business about the guardian was more difficult—until he remembered that Julian Trevelyan, his friend from Cambridge days, was living in Paris as a painter. Lowry went by boat-train to Paris, contacted Trevelyan, who was living in the Villa Brune, at the end of the Rue des Plantes, and persuaded Trevelyan (who was a year younger than he) to serve as his guardian. Trevelyan found him a two-room flat nearby, and Lowry settled in for what seems to have been a reasonably happy three-month stay in Paris. He would drop in every week or so to see Trevelyan, who would send Arthur O. Lowry a note saying that his son's studies were going well. (Trevelyan recalls that Lowry at this time could neither speak nor understand French, so that one wonders what Lowry could have studied even if he *had* gone to the Sorbonne.) How Lowry occupied himself between his weekly visits, Trevelyan did not know, though he recalls that Lowry did see something of S. William Hayter, the young English painter and print-maker to whom Trevelyan had introduced him. Perhaps it was also at this time that he saw something of another Cambridge contemporary, George Reavey, who was already translating Pasternak. Other than that, we know of Lowry during this period only that he sold to Whit Burnett, then editor of *Story*, a piece called "On Board the *West Hardaway*," which was to appear in the October 1933 issue of that magazine. But this can hardly have taken much of his time, since the story was only a slight re-working of the one he had originally called "Port Swettenham," and published in the February 1930 issue of *Experiment* (and which, re-worked again, was to become Chapter Five of *Ultramarine*).[12] "On Board the *West Hardaway*" is essentially the story of the rescue, and subsequent drowning, of the carrier pigeon; and its only noteworthy difference, from *Ultramarine*, aside from its being smoother and blander in tone than its version in the novel, is that here the protagonist is not Dana Hilliot, but Dana *Hall:* and this was far too clear an indicator of the debt to Nordahl Grieg for Lowry to allow it to remain unchanged in *Ultramarine*.

In any case, Lowry kept out of trouble in Paris, and returned to London in late March 1933, when the Aikens invited him to accompany them on a trip to Spain. The role of guardian reverted from Julian Trevelyan to Aiken, and on April 1, Lowry, Aiken, and Clarissa, sailed from Tilbury for Gibraltar. Clarissa noticed that Lowry had become quite fat since his last visit to Jeake's House, and that his drinking was even more of a problem than it had been before. In a bar in Ronda, on their way from Algeciras to Granada, Lowry and Aiken both ordered triple brandies, startling not only Clarissa but also the Spanish drinkers seated around them. For the remainder of the trip to Spain, Lowry received a considerable amount of not-so-friendly comment from the natives of Andalucía, for his potbelly, his drinking, and for his insistence on wearing everywhere one of those ten-gallon sombreros which no Spaniards wore, but which they sold (and, for that matter, still do sell) to tourists from northern Europe who imagine that they are buying authentic Iberian headgear.[13]

12. O'Brien had already published a re-titled version of "Punctum Indifferens Skibet Gaar Videre" (which had appeared originally in the Spring 1931 issue of *Experiment*) in his *Best British Short Stories of 1931*. He (or Lowry) changed its title to "Seductio ad Absurdum." This story was subsequently incorporated into Chapter Four of *Ultramarine*, and has to do with Dana's challenging Andy to a fight.

13. My information on the Spanish journey comes from two sources: Clarissa Lorenz' essay mentioned earlier, "Call it Misadventure," *The Atlantic* (June 1970); and Conrad Aiken, *Ushant*, to which I have also referred in the preceding chapter.

Lowry and Clarissa Aiken, Spain, 1932.

Lowry, sweating and hungover, tried to read *Ulysses* on the train that eventually took the three to Granada, where they were to meet the English surrealist painter, Ed Burra. They booked rooms at the Pensión Carmona, near the Alhambra. No one, apparently, had told any of them about the Spanish attitude toward drinking: here, a man drank, and drank often; but he must drink well. He might sit in a café for hours, swallowing one *copita* of *aguardiente* after another; but at the end he must pay his bill, rise decorously, and walk with dignity to his home. Courage is important to Spaniards, but *dignidad* is the crucial quality of manhood. And Lowry, drunk, was anything but dignified. Before many days in Granada had passed, he had become known all over the city as *"el borracho inglés,"* and people were openly mocking him. The *Guardia Civil* had their eye on him. Clarissa Lorenz recalls one especially unpleasant scene:

The day I caught sight of him he was lurching through the streets jeered and laughed at, children and adults turning around to poke fun at him. Scattering them would only have doubled his humiliation. He stopped at a music shop, listening to a flamenco record, a fixed smile on his face, then continued on his zigzag course.

Most of the time Lowry did not respond to this abuse. Once, when Ed Burra drew a rather cruel caricature of him as a blimp wearing a sombrero, and then allowed the son-in-law of the owners of the Pensión Carmona to scamper about the patio showing it to giggling customers, Lowry snatched the drawing away, drew a pipe in the mouth of the blimp, then tore the thing into pieces, flung them in the face of the son-in-law, and said—with amazing restraint—to Burra: "That was an unkind thing to do."

Another time, when the sadistic son-in-law was leading a group of friends behind Lowry as he climbed the Alhambra hill, aping his wobbly gait and sending catcalls after him, Lowry turned suddenly, grabbed the son-in-law "by the scruff of the neck, rammed him uphill a hundred yards or so, flung him down, picked him up again for a repeat performance, then left him in the dust" ("Call it Misadventure," p. 109).

Even though the Aikens had real need of the twenty guineas that Lowry's father was sending them each month, Aiken was thinking seriously of resigning as guardian, for his ward's behavior was almost past bearing. Then, suddenly, everything changed. In June two new lodgers came to the Pensión Carmona: an exotic young American girl, wearing high heels and a wide-brimmed hat, and her French gentleman friend. No one remembers the name of the Frenchman, but the girl was Jan Gabrial. Lowry fell instantly in love with this glamorous young woman, and soon was seen everywhere with her, "doing the town and roaming the foothills, falling into a brook one morning, he looking like a mesmerized owl, to quote Conrad" ("Call it Misadventure," p. 110). Clarissa was glad to see Lowry finally relating to someone other than her husband, but Aiken—not so surprisingly, perhaps—was quite put out. Lowry was transformed overnight: now he was sober; now he

Ed Burra, Clarissa Aiken, Lowry, and Conrad Aiken at breakfast in the Pension Carmona, Granada.

bathed daily, shined his shoes, cleaned his fingernails, and "absent-mindedly wore his shirts wrong side out" ("Call it Misadventure," p. 110). To his wife, Aiken complained, "All this primping and preening is positively revolting!"

Although she ultimately left Granada in the company of her Frenchman, Jan Gabrial had responded very definitely to Lowry's puppylike advances. On their first evening walk together (she later confided to John Davenport) they had stumbled while in the gardens of the Generalife, and Lowry had landed on top of her. She had expected to be seduced, and was rather surprised when, instead, Lowry took this opportunity to recount for her the plot of *Ultramarine*. Chiefly, it seemed, he was struck by the similarity between her name and that of Dana Hilliot's sweetheart, Janet. Nevertheless, she did leave Lowry in Granada—thus beginning a pattern which was to characterize their life together. She left him four more times before they parted finally in 1938.

After Jan had gone, Clarissa was alarmed late one night to come upon Lowry and Aiken in a loud and angry argument in the patio of the *pensión*. She heard Lowry threaten to kill Aiken. They said nothing to her subsequently about the reason for the fight, and it was not until 20 years later, reading her former husband's autobiography, *Ushant*, that she discovered what it had all been about.

According to Aiken (*Ushant*, p. 297), it was he who introduced Lowry to Jan (called "Nita" in the autobiography), in hopes that this "beautiful and swift little creature might be just the prescription he needed." It occurred to Aiken that perhaps Lowry's only hope for salvation might be a strong woman, to distract him from his increasingly morbid concern for himself and for alcohol. But it was more complicated than this, because Aiken wanted Jan for himself as well. In *Ushant* (pp. 352–53) Aiken remembers the quarrel in the *pensión* as having begun with Lowry's assertion that it was now his turn to "kill" Aiken, as Aiken had "killed" Lowry by so completely absorbing his personality:

> "You as much as admitted that now it was my turn—my turn to kill you. First, by taking Nita. Yes. For of course we both knew that both of us were powerfully drawn to that open wound—you first, but with your own obligations to Lorelei Two [Clarissa Lorenz], and therefore guiltily offering her up to me, but in effect proposing to share her. Not so? Yes—in the shadow of the Hundred Fountains, at the Alhambra, you proposed to share her, as foul a sort of voyeur's incest as any second-rate god could imagine."

Aiken admits that Lowry is right: that it has been his "visceral and feculent scheme" to hand her to Lowry, so that—vicariously, at least—he could possess her, too: "But to hand her on to you, I could thus keep her—at least, at one remove, and with your imagination to magnify it for me. Very simple. And twofold in function, too—for this might stop your drinking. Pull you together. Take you out of the endless chain of aguardientes, the daily round of cantinas, and the ultimate slobber of drunkenness in which you daily threatened to kill me."

Aiken and Lowry in the Generalife Gardens at the Alhambra.

But, for the moment at least, neither of them was to have her, whether actually or vicariously: she was gone. The bitterness between Lowry and Aiken made any further stay in Granada impossible, so the group packed up and entrained for Algeciras. Leaving Lowry brooding in Gibraltar for a few days, Aiken, Clarissa, and Ed Burra toured Spanish Morocco; and found, on their return, that the police were very rude to them. Lowry had evidently behaved quite badly in their absence, and they were anxious that he leave as soon as possible.

They sailed the next morning on the *Strathaird*. According to Clarissa Lorenz, it was an unhappy voyage: "Frayed nerves and edgy tempers prevailed. Conrad, almost knocked down by playful moppets, was tempted to pitch the noisy brats overboard. Malcolm shared a cabin on that hectic voyage with 'three Somerset Maugham colonels who were dying of the hiccups.'" They stopped briefly in Lisbon, where Lowry received a letter from Jan that was evidently quite discouraging.

By the time they reached England, he was also quite ill, suffering from some sort of Spanish intestinal bacillus as well as from the after-effects of several weeks of being able to buy *aguardiente* at a peseta the glass. He begged Aiken's forgiveness (Aiken has no recollection of *his* having begged *Lowry's* forgiveness), humbly asked for permission to come again to Jeake's House, and left for London. Clarissa Lorenz remembers that before two weeks had passed, they received a "suicidal" letter from Lowry. He was, he said, "being taken to a nursing home for dysentery complicated by alcoholism, thence to the 'pump room' to be dried out."

With typical resiliency, however, Lowry was out of the nursing home within a week, and searching around London for his old friends. He went to the flat of James Travers in early September, and there met Travers' roommate, Robert Pocock, then a policeman, and later a BBC executive. Within ten minutes after their meeting, Lowry had assumed his favorite attitude: he was lying under a table with his ukulele, singing a Negro spiritual. This seemed great fun to Pocock, and so did an adventure that took place a few days later. Tom Forman, one of Lowry's few Cambridge friends with money, had just given Lowry an old MG Magna, and—after perhaps three days' practice in driving— Lowry proposed to take Pocock and Travers out to the latter's silver fox farm in Chagford, South Devon. They reached Chagford safely enough, but one night soon afterward Lowry lost control of the car, and somehow disembowelled it on a great tombstone of a rock, jutting far out over the water. Lowry sadly abandoned the MG, walked to Chagford, and never drove again.

The first time that Robert Pocock noticed that Lowry's eccentricity had something to do with more than just youthful high spirits occurred when they were swimming in nearby Torbay. As Pocock recounted it in the 1967 BBC "Portrait of Malcolm Lowry":

> He had a terrible obsession that he was being shadowed by a male nurse whom his family had put on him, and he said one day, "I swam out three miles in Torbay this morning and I turned over to float, and, do you know, he was following me." And we said, "But where is he?" He said, "I don't know. He just appears and disappears."

Lowry was, as many of his friends have acknowledged, perfectly capable of giving an occasional nudge to his legend, whether it had to do with consumption of alcohol or with the strange way in which the most extraordinary coincidences were always occurring around him. But he seems to have been perfectly serious about being followed. Indeed, this classical symptom of paranoia became more and more conspicuous in him as the years went on, until in Mexico he was convinced that he was being trailed by secret police and informers; and during the Canada years it was obvious to him that the Authorities were tracking him down, or waiting for him at the Border. Most typically, these attacks of paranoia were set in motion by conflicts, real or imagined, between Lowry and his father, or between Lowry and one of his several father-surrogates. Some obscure guilt, of course, lay behind it all, amorphous and probably without basis in fact. A truly punitive superego like Lowry's did not need the commission of real, palpable sins; imaginary sins would do quite as well.

Back in London, in October, he went one evening to the Alhambra Palace, the music hall. There he ran into Jan Gabrial, who, having discarded her Frenchman, was in London for no one remembers what reason. The coincidence was too much for Lowry to withstand: she had left him at the Alhambra in Granada, and now here she was, at the Alhambra in London. Destiny was clearly at work again. Apparently he was able to convince Jan of this, too; because a real romance now began between them. For the next four months, until they left for Paris to be married, they were inseparable.

Robert Pocock and John Sommerfield often saw them in pubs in London, and noticed that they seemed totally absorbed in each other. They were an attractive pair. Jan was, by all accounts, small, neat, quick, strikingly beautiful in a dark, feral sort of way —a smart, tough New Yorker of no little ambition, walking directly, her high heels clicking on the pavement, toward whatever she wanted, and taking it. And rolling along beside her in his seaman's gait would be the ursine Lowry, his tie inevitably askew, his trousers threatening imminent collapse, a silly, absolutely happy grin on his face.

Like any lovesick bourgeois swain, he had to take Jan everywhere, to meet everyone who mattered to him—except that he never took her to Cheshire. Instead, he went with her to Birmingham, where they found Martin Case in a pub, playing the piano. Then they went down to Rye, to patch things up with the Aikens. But Conrad was in America (even though he was still technically *in loco parentis*, and still presumably being paid by Arthur O. Lowry), and the reunion did not take place. They went down to Chagford, so that Jan could meet Travers and Pocock. Back in London, they made plans to go to Paris. Jan wanted to live there, and not in England; and besides, she had her own work to do: she had (or affected to have) what Lowry did not—a social consciousness—and she proposed to do a study of the plight of Hungarian coal miners, and to write it all up for some left-wing American journal. This all seemed reasonable to Lowry; so in November 1933, he and Jan left for Paris.

Ultramarine was about to appear in England as Lowry and Jan departed. Two weeks before, in Torquay, they had gone with Robert Pocock into a bookshop where they had found a stack of brochures announcing Jonathan Cape's Fall list. Lowry grabbed one, read through the "rather glossy write-up" of *Ultramarine*, was delighted, and exclaimed, "Oh, that's marvellous!" As Pocock remarked, "Anyone would have thought he'd got a full-length notice in one of the Sundays or the *Times Literary Supplement*" (BBC "Portrait of Malcolm Lowry").

In Paris, Lowry and Jan paid little attention to *Ultramarine*, which began almost immediately to receive rather lukewarm reviews. In addition to being "experimental," it was derivative: the *Times Literary Supplement* reviewer had already said, in his prepublication essay of July 13, 1933, that, "if the art of writing is imitation, the author has mastered it." He went on to add with some justice that *Ultramarine* read less as a novel than as the first expansion of shorthand notes "taken with a view to making a novel out of a new experience." Most of the rest of the reviews followed the lead set by the *Times:* Lowry was praised moderately for his good ear for dialogue, noted—equivocally and ambiguously—for his "unorthodox manner"; but condemned for his having copied down so faithfully the crudities of his sailors' diction, and for the obvious weaknesses in his conception of Dana Hilliot's character.

Meanwhile, Lowry and Jan had gone immediately to Julian Trevelyan's villa in Paris to find out what one had to do in France in order to become married. Then, on January 6, 1934, in the office of the *Mairie, Quatorzième Arrondissement*, Lowry and Jan were married. Trevelyan served as best man. After the ceremony, he took the wedding party (himself, his girl friend Louise Scherpenberg, a New York model and painter, and the Lowrys) back to his studio, where he fixed a lunch of rice and prawns. There was a great deal of *vin ordinaire*, the groom became quite drunk, and he and the bride left in late afternoon. Before he departed, Lowry inscribed a copy of *Ultramarine* for Trevelyan: "To my guardian and witness angel and Louise from Malcolm."

Trevelyan remembers Jan as well able to hold her own with

Lowry: "She was rather an attractive little thing and she had a good way of handling Malcolm when he was difficult or wouldn't move. Somehow she gave him a certain amount of freedom and rope, and he adored her, I think, at that time" (BBC "Portrait of Malcolm Lowry"). She was quite pleased at the notion of being married to a genius, and in the first weeks of their marriage gave every evidence of being a devoted bride. But by February she was taking off on trips with companions, male and female, and it was obvious the idyll was over. To several of their friends she complained of Lowry's continual drunkenness. And there was the problem of impotence: she explained to more than one friend that she would not have been promiscuous if Lowry had been at all sexually competent. Moreover, there were times, she said, when he fairly flung her at other men (as Geoffrey Firmin did with Yvonne in *Under the Volcano*). It bothered her, too, that he was making so little money: if he were a genius, and if everyone knew he was a genius, then why were they so poor? When Jan returned to him in Paris, Lowry tried to placate her by taking her on journeys to places like Chartres; but Jan wanted action, and in the early summer of 1934 she left on the *Ile de France* from Le Havre for the United States.

So for all practical purposes Lowry was on his own in Paris from February 1934, until he himself left for England late the following summer. There can be no doubt that he did love Jan Gabrial, and that he blamed himself as much as he did her for the brevity of their relationship; but from what we know of him in Paris during the winter and summer of 1934, he managed very well.

For one thing, he formed new friendships. During the winter months his principal occupation seems to have been that of wandering about the streets of the city with James Stern, a young Anglo-Irish writer who had been living there for more than a year, in a flat in what was then the Rue René Pauline. Stern, who had lately returned from some years in Rhodesia, had recently published a collection of stories about Africa, called *The Heartless Land*. One night in early February, on his way to a party, Stern stepped into a bistro to buy a couple of bottles of wine. The place was almost empty: aside from the *patron* and one customer sitting at a table, there was only one other person.

. . . on the sawdust-covered floor there lay stretched, flat on his back, evidently asleep, a robust-looking fellow with a week of stiff red stubble on his face, and across his stomach a guitar. Round his neck the recumbent figure wore a scarlet bandanna, over his Herculean chest a jacket of royal blue tweed, and on his legs a pair of dirty grey flannel trousers.[14]

When Stern ordered his bottles of wine, the sleeping figure awakened, rose, surprised Stern by being considerably shorter than he had expected, and plodded over to stand next to Stern at the bar. Within minutes Stern was captivated by this amiable man, who had read *The Heartless Land,* and whose novel, *Ultramarine,* Stern had read. Their conversation began tentatively, as they sized one another up, and established their mutual British-ness; but then Lowry suddenly relaxed:

> He let out a chuckle. He smiled. His teeth were white, and even. Instantly his whole scrubby face lit up, expressing an indefinable charm. . . . And he put out his hand—a surprisingly small hand, I noticed later, with short stubby fingers. But I winced in their vise.

By midnight, "each had convinced the other that he was a budding genius." Lowry modestly asserted that he would soon be "out-Mobying Melville."

That night they went to the party to which Stern had been invited, where Stern managed promptly to smash his two bottles of wine, and then to burn his hand badly on a hot pipe leading from the stove. Lowry nursed him back to something like health, and around dawn the two young men began the. first of what they called their "little walks" about Paris. This one lasted 28 hours.

On this walk, as on all later ones, Stern was the navigator. Lowry seemed never to have the slightest idea where he was. One reason for this total lack of a sense of direction was that, as Stern notes, Lowry was not at all a visual person, at least not in the usual way.

14. James Stern, in his already cited *Encounter* essay, "Malcolm Lowry: A First Impression."

Whereas Stern was constantly "observing the faces of other pedestrians, searching for the name of an alley, looking at buildings," Lowry looked only for bars and stars. In fact, it was always to be the case that Lowry, drunk or sober, was almost completely unable to get about in any city unaided. He would walk along, as he did this night with Stern, delivering lectures on astronomy (probably bogus, since he knew nothing, really, of astronomy until years later, when Margerie, in Dollarton, gave him almost nightly lectures on the subject), stopping suddenly to point out constellations, ducking into very nearly every bar for a drink, walking blindly into rush-hour. traffic, absolutely unaware of where he was or where he was going.

At the end of his first remarkable *Fusswanderung*, which took them a night and a day, covered most of central Paris, and during which they paused often for drinks and occasionally for food, they wound up at Stern's sixth-floor flat. Lowry took a long time getting up all the flights of stairs, and drank most of a bottle of calvados on the way, pausing at each landing to "stoke up his boiler." Once safely inside Stern's doorway, he finally collapsed:

> Suddenly his head drooped, one leg buckled, and like a bull at the end of battle, he began to crumble. Down the wall he slowly slithered. Flat, prone he lay, his head in the crook of one arm, face to the floor. I bent over, laid my hand on his head. "Where's my guitar?" he gargled. And began to snore.

Aside from his frequent odysseys with Stern, Lowry seems also to have dipped, however slightly, into Parisian culture during his days without Jan. There is one especially intriguing passage in a letter which Lowry wrote, in March 1950, to Clarisse Francillon, French translator of *Under the Volcano*, which gives us the merest hint that Lowry may indeed have got to know, however slightly, literary Paris: "I wondered if you could somehow smuggle a copy, with my compliments, of your translation [of *Under the Volcano*] to Jean Cocteau, and tell him that I have never forgotten his kindness in giving me a seat for *La Machine Infernale* at the Champs Élysées in May, 1934: I went to see it on 2 successive days and I shall never forget the marvellous performance as long as I live—Whatever he personally may have thought of it" (*Selected Letters*, p. 192). We shall see this machine again, when it becomes a crucial symbol in *Under the Volcano*.

Since Lowry had gone through his three years at Cambridge without appearing to notice the social and literary upheaval going on around him, one would be unwise to suppose that he knew about, or was affected by, the rightist putsch in Paris during the early days of February, which almost toppled the Third Republic, or that he had made anything of Hitler's having become *Reichskanzler* in Germany the preceding year; or that he was aware, in June 1934, of Hitler's first major purge, in which the Brownshirt leader Roehm was murdered. But the passing reference to the Cocteau play does suggest that perhaps he did know something, after all, about, say, what the Surrealists were up to; or about how well Céline's *Voyage au bout de la nuit*, published in 1932, was doing in Paris, where in 1933 it had missed the Prix Goncourt by one vote; or about Artaud's advocacy, in one café after another, of his Theatre of Cruelty; or even about Giraudoux' new hit, *Intermezzo*. But if he was aware of anything beyond *La Machine Infernale*, we do not know of it.

We *do* know, however, that in the midst of all this activity, between walks with Stern and attempted reconciliations with Jan whenever she returned to Paris, Lowry was writing. He apparently began a novel at some time during the winter, and then quickly abandoned it. One fragment of it came, much later, into John Davenport's hands; and in the fall of 1949, without Lowry's permission, he published it as a story, "Economic Conference, 1934" in his magazine, *Arena*. One can only suppose that Davenport chose to publish it because it had been written by the suddenly famous author of *Under the Volcano*. It has little else to recommend it. An American writer on economics, Bill, meets a London cabbie, also named Bill; and ends up in the cabbie's flat in the small hours of the morning, arguing with his equally drunken host about the world's economic condition. Since both Bills are barely coherent, it is impossible to say whether or not the author of the story himself knew anything of the world's economic condition.

It seems that when Lowry went back to England in the summer of 1934, he left behind him somewhere in Paris two stories, "Bulls of the Resurrection" [15] and "China." The first of these was published in 1965, and concerns two Cambridge undergraduates who sit in a bar in Granada and brood while the girl they both love is driving around the city with yet another—but more dashing —Cambridge undergraduate. When the two forsaken lads in the bar compare their rather baldly portentous recent nightmares, they realize that some fatal disaster will shortly kill the girl they love and her debonair beau. "China," mercifully, is unavailable for scrutiny.

A fourth story, "June 30th, 1934," was written around this time. Its chief interest today is that it has as its protagonist a man named Firmin, who is a veteran of the Great War, and moderately disabled. This Firmin, obviously a prototype of the protagonist of *Under the Volcano*, is riding on a train through France, holding yet another long and Lowryan conversation with an unhappy ex-missionary in China, Bill Goodyear.[16]

The only works from this period that Lowry himself wanted published were two more short stories, "In Le Havre" and "Hotel Room in Chartres." [17] They established very definitely, when considered along with the other stories just mentioned, that at this time in his career Lowry saw just two subjects as appropriate to his short fiction: conversation on a train; or conversation in a bar. ("Economic Conference, 1934," may be considered as a minor variant of the latter subject.) The two published stories do at least have value for the biographer, if not for the literary critic, since they obviously are Lowry's attempts to deal fictionally with his unhappy marital situation.

"In Le Havre" takes place, of course, in a bar. Two men, one English, the other American, are talking. The Englishman is lamenting the recent departure of his wife, Lee, a New Yorker, for her homeland. He had just seen her off on the *Ile de France*. They had only

15. *Prism International*, Vol. V, no. 1 (Summer 1965), 5–11.
16. This story is on deposit in the Special Collections Division of the University of British Columbia Library.
17. The former was printed in *Life and Letters*, Vol. X, no. 55 (July 1934), 462–66; and the latter in *Story*, Vol. V, no. 26 (September 1934), 53–58.

been married five months, but she has had an operation, and there are complications. (There is some indication that she is pregnant, and hemorrhaging—which would seem to make a sea voyage unwise, to say the least.) Besides, she wants to see her mother. So the Englishman has let her go, and loving her deeply, has none the less picked a nasty fight with her that very morning, after he had got her aboard the ship:

> . . . she said something which angered me so that, in that extraordinary complete stillness which precedes a ship's sailing, I replied savagely, Oh, I don't love you; I never have loved you; it was just a caprice on my part. I married you to satisfy my own vanity, I was just getting one back on the old man. To hell with it all, I don't love you and never have done, and you can have the custody of the child.

Then, as drunken conversations do, this story about a drunken conversation breaks down, falls into maundering, and ends with the American's angrily getting up from the bar and leaving, hurling his conclusion at the Englishman: "Listen, the hell with you and your Lee. You only love your own misery." Which seems a reasonably accurate assessment of the situation—except that the story does somehow manage to convey that the Englishman loves his wife very much, and that he truly regrets having spoken so savagely to her.

In "Hotel Room in Chartres," similarly, there is the estrangement of a young couple. He, a former seaman, now possibly a musician, wishes to return with his wife to Chartres; where once, before their marriage went wrong, they had wandered in the cathedral, lit a candle to their love, and felt somehow that the town belonged to them, as young lovers. But now the marriage is imperilled, and the moment is wrong. It is too late to take the train from Paris to Chartres, and it is raining. The husband, hurt and angry, leaves anyway, determined to go alone. At the last moment, she catches up to him in Montparnasse, anxious for a reconciliation. He cannot unbend enough to offer her this, and they tensely board the train: "In the compartment he sat resolutely, his lips firmly shut, his eyes focused above his wife's head, on nothing, occasionally directing at her a look intended to punish; while she sat equally resolute, determined not to give way."

Four French merchant seamen enter their compartment happily drunk and singing; and the husband recalls with longing his own days at sea. He cruelly insults his wife (there is a suggestion that he is attacking her for her infidelity), who leaves the compartment. When she returns, he is drinking and singing with the sailors. Soon, he learns that he is mistaken in envying their imminent departure to sea: they have been at sea, but they are happy now because they are on their way home. Somehow (none too clearly) learning this breaks the tension between the husband and wife; and at the story's end the two are in their hotel room, sharing a precarious joy at being reunited. "And up in the only room in the world they were folded together in each other's arms crying with joy that they had found each other once again."

The story does have a certain poignancy, and it was obviously important to Lowry that he write about threatened lovers and the very small things that either tore them apart or brought them back together. Time and again in his career—in *Under the Volcano*, in several of the stories of *Hear Us O Lord From Heaven Thy Dwelling Place*, in *Dark as the Grave Wherein My Friend Is Laid*, and finally in *October Ferry to Gabriola*—he was to return to the anguished situation of the man and woman who love one another, and who know that even (indeed, *only*) the slightest gesture will bring them together, and who, knowing this, often cannot bring themselves to make that single restorative gesture.

Clearly, Lowry and Jan Gabrial were able to make no such gesture in 1934; for she left him in Chartres, for Le Havre and the United States. Lowry stayed for a bit in Chartres, working on his stories, and then went back to England later in the summer. He still loved his wife, and hoped, unrealistically, for a reconciliation; but he wanted to go back to London before he did anything else.

Once there, he took up for a while with his old friends. One bright moment came when he lunched again with Arthur Calder-Marshall and Hamish Miles, and Miles showed him a clipping from the *Times* saying that *Ultramarine* had been banned from the Hull

Public Library because of its obscenity. Miles said, "See, Malc, you're famous"; and Lowry was jubilant. He spent the rest of the evening wandering about Fitzrovia, showing the clipping to everyone he knew.

By mid-autumn Lowry had determined to follow Jan to New York, and to do whatever he could to patch things up between them. First, however, he wanted to make his peace with Conrad Aiken, who was rather huffy about not having been invited to Lowry's wedding the preceding January, and who had pointedly not asked Lowry down to Jeake's House upon his return from France.[18] Typically, Lowry could proceed only by indirection. So, one evening when Aiken was standing on the platform at Charing Cross station, waiting for the 5:12 to Rye, he was surprised to see Lowry sidling up to him almost furtively, his foxy grin about to break out. Looking at Aiken out of the corner of his eye, he whispered, "Remember, Conrad, how you were always at me to clean my fingernails? Well, I've cleaned them for you." He showed Aiken his freshly pared and scrubbed nails, then stood there beaming, waiting for the forgiveness he knew would come. Aiken shook his hand, then boarded the train; and Lowry went out to book passage on a ship bound for America.

18. Material in this paragraph comes from Conrad Knickerbocker's interview with Aiken, Summer, 1964.

Many years later, Lowry told Margerie that when the *Queen Mary* reached New York in the fall of 1934, and the Customs official asked him whether he had anything to declare, he had answered, "I don't know. Let's see." The official then had opened Lowry's single, large trunk and found that it contained one old football boot and a battered copy of *Moby-Dick*. The falsity of this anecdote cannot be proven, but one doubts it, somehow. For one thing, it echoes too closely the story of Lowry's *first* arrival in New York, in 1929, when he came to stay with Conrad Aiken, and turned out to have landed carrying only his ukulele and a small, broken suitcase containing his notebooks for *Ultramarine*. For another, we know that he brought with him this time the steadily lengthening manuscript of *In Ballast to the White Sea*. He did travel light, true enough; but the football-boot-and-*Moby-Dick* tale sounds ultimately like another instance of Lowry's nudging the legend along.

In any case, luggage or not, he reached New York, found Jan living with her mother, and somehow persuaded her to come back to him—temporarily, at least. They moved into a rather dismal two-room apartment on Central Park West, and stayed there more or less together for almost a year. Lowry detested New York, though it fascinated him. In 1954 he wrote David Markson about the city:

> In my own experience—odi et amo—that particular
> city—it favors brief and furious outbursts, but not the long
> haul. Moreover for all its drama and existential fury, or per-

haps because of it, it's a city where it can be remarkably hard—or so it seems to me—to get on the right side of one's despair.[1]

Though the pace of the city life was too fast for him, he did work on *In Ballast* during his first year in New York, apparently at some length: Conrad Aiken has said, in his February 16, 1967, letter to the *Times Literary Supplement*, that he read a complete draft of this novel while visiting Lowry in Mexico in 1937; and, since we know that Lowry did not work on it after the spring of 1936, and that he had already written a complete first draft of *Under the Volcano* by the time of Aiken's visit, it seems safe to assume that he spent most of 1935 and early 1936 producing a draft of *In Ballast*. Jan was, for a while, herself writing a novel, about the Hungarian coalminers whose plight she had looked into a year earlier. Other than this, it has been impossible to discover with any certainty what he was doing during these months, besides taking Jan for a short cruise on a Fall River sidewheeler, the *Providence*, to New Bedford: a voyage of homage to Melville and *Moby-Dick*, of course.

There was a certain amount of social life, as well, but one is not sure when it began and ended. Somehow, in 1934, Lowry and Jan came to know Waldo Frank, the prominent American critic and polemicist, and Michael Sayers, a young Dubliner then living and writing in New York. They were also at some point introduced to Donald Friede, who came to see quite a lot of both of them, especially Jan, during the following year. But Lowry's closest friend during the purgatorial New York phase was Eric Estorick, whom he met through Waldo Frank in early 1935.

Estorick, now director of the Grosvenor Gallery in London, was then a young man living in Brooklyn. He was intelligent, tolerant, and not obtrusively "literary," so Lowry took to him immediately. By midsummer 1934, Jan was taking extended vacations away from their apartment, and Lowry began to spend most of his leisure time in Estorick's company. The two of them passed many evenings in

1. *Canadian Literature*, 8 (Spring 1961), 42–46.

the kitchen of Estorick's Brooklyn home, where Estorick's mother (who, like all mothers who knew him, except perhaps his own, doted on Lowry) fed him great quantities of chopped chicken liver while he delivered lectures on Melville to them.

Lowry's love of jazz took them of course to Harlem, where Estorick was unable to convince Lowry that there were bars they should not visit, places they should not go. As a result of Lowry's naïveté, the two of them got into at least a couple of fairly dangerous situations involving muggers and pimps; and eventually Lowry learned, says Estorick, that his new fondness for pork chops and his old passion for jazz would have to be catered to elsewhere than in Harlem.

Estorick also remembers a brief phase during which Lowry was being pursued by a pair of aggressive English homosexuals, who were hoping to get him drunk enough to submit to them. Whether they ever succeeded, Estorick does not recall; but he *is* quite sure that there was a time when Lowry came to him, full of anxiety: he had been with these men a couple of evenings before, and had drunk himself into unconsciousness. He wasn't certain, but for all he knew he *might* have been had; if so, what, he wanted to know, were his chances of having contracted some sort of venereal disease? Again, there is scarcely enough evidence one way or the other for us to speculate on whether or not Lowry ever had any overt homosexual experiences. What one *can* say with some confidence, however, is that there were very few people who ever saw Malcolm Lowry in a state of complete unconsciousness from alcohol. In fact, almost without exception his friends have remarked on his almost preternatural ability to drink a great deal, and to *seem* to be unconscious—and then to demonstrate the next day (or the next year, or ten years later: his memory was truly phenomenal) that, not only had he *not* been unconscious, but that he had been alert enough to have heard every word that had been spoken around him. If, therefore, Lowry was seduced by these two men, the chances would seem to be very good that he knew he was being seduced. Whether he was too drunk to withstand their attacks is another question. He was, of course, stronger than most men.

Certainly his life with Jan, when she chose to come home to him, was hardly satisfying. She was far from discreet about her various liaisons; in Estorick's words, she was "rubbing her emotional life in Lowry's nose," taunting him for his drunkenness and lack of sexual prowess. Although Estorick never had the feeling that Lowry actively wanted to end his relationship with Jan, one suspects that when Jan finally left their apartment for the last time, in the fall of 1935, Lowry was at least partially relieved. They still continued to meet for drinks, or for an occasional restaurant meal; but by the end of the year Jan was living in a cheap hotel on the West Side, and Lowry had moved to a very squalid basement apartment in an old brownstone house, which he variously located in the West Seventies and in Columbus Circle.[2] As I noted in the preceding chapter, Lowry's sense of urban geography was very poor indeed; so we must regard the placing of Columbus Circle in the West Seventies, when it is actually several blocks downtown, as a very minor locational error for him.

Lowry rented his basement room from the janitor of the building, who had vacated it himself because "of the incidence therein . . . of certain rare insects" (*Selected Letters*, p. 277). His fellow boarders were in the habit of playing pinochle all night long in the basement kitchen, so that Lowry, unable to sleep, took to writing at night and sleeping during the day after the players had returned upstairs to their rooms. One morning, after having worked "perhaps for three nights and days on end," typing in the kitchen because the unnameable insects had driven him from the janitor's room, Lowry was sitting, unshaven and surrounded by a great deal of washing and "some seventy empty beer bottles" left by the pinochle players, when his landlady announced a caller.

"Mr. Kraken is upstairs, sir."

"What!"

"A kind gentleman—very well dressed—his suit is made of

2. Letter to Seymour Lawrence, editor of *Wake*, *Selected Letters*, pp. 277, 278. Originally published in *Wake*, no. 11 (1952), 80–89: a special Conrad Aiken issue.

real good material . . . Mr. Kraken would like to see you, sir, and is coming downstairs now."

It was, of course, Conrad Aiken, in New York for the day, and hoping to discover how his pupil was getting along. Lowry, who had been hoping to "produce an illusion of steady work and regular hours" for Aiken, could not have been more distressed if the mysterious caller *had* been the Scandinavian sea-monster, descending into the dark well of the brownstone.

Aiken remembers having gone to a restaurant near 42nd Street shortly after this with Lowry and Jan. They were in the middle of the meal when "a tall stranger came through the aisle, looked at Malc and Jan, then went out through the kitchen." Jan stood up quickly, excused herself, saying she had a newspaper job to do, and walked out. Lowry and Aiken finished lunch, then walked out onto Times Square, where the tall man was standing. Lowry, having recognized him as a lover of Jan's, went up to him, shook his hand, and said briskly, "We have something in common, don't we?" [3]

Lowry managed to pull himself together and seem quite fit during Aiken's occasional visits; but New York, Jan, a record heat-wave, and the stresses of alcholism were conspiring to break him down. By late spring it seemed to Estorick that Lowry was becoming more and more confused, and that his drinking was growing rapidly worse. He knew a girl who was engaged to a psychiatric resident at Bellevue, and through her initiated steps to get Lowry admitted to the hospital for observation if not for treatment. Estorick recalls that they had to find Jan so that she could give her permission to have Lowry committed to the Psychiatric Wing of Bellevue. She did so, and Lowry, incoherent, shaking, and hallucinating, went into the hospital in June 1935. He was afterwards to insist that his stay at Bellevue was not a "compulsory confinement," but "a deliberate pilgrimage" to that hospital to gain material for a story he wanted to write. [4] But compulsory confinement it was, and

3. Interview of Conrad Knickerbocker with Conrad Aiken, 1965.
4. In the early Fifties, Lowry gave Robert Giroux, of Harcourt, Brace, a 21-page statement of his "Work in Progress," in which he gives plot summaries of all the works that were to make up *The Voyage that Never Ends*. Lowry's words quoted above are from this source.

it lasted two to three weeks. He was released so soon not because he had recovered, but because he was a foreigner. Bellevue routinely informs consulates of their nationals who are admitted there; and apparently difficulties arose over Lowry's being treated as a charity patient at the hospital: American taxpayers supporting a foreigner, and so on. There seems even to have been some possibility that Lowry, as someone clearly liable to become a public charge, would be deported. Furious with Estorick for, as he thought, having got him into this mess, he marched out of the hospital, went on a two-day binge, then showed up, hungover but docile, at Estorick's house on the third day. He had found at Bellevue the material for a grand story, and he wanted to write it up immediately; so he sat down at the Estorick kitchen table and wrote the story—he said afterwards to Robert Giroux—in four days. This was "The Last Address," which after many transmogrifications ultimately became the novella called *Lunar Caustic*.

It would be helpful if there were some reliable way of determining precisely what happened to Lowry at Bellevue; but the psychiatric resident who was in charge of him, Dr. Sylvan Keiser, does not remember a Malcolm Lowry, nor do his personal records contain any reference to such a man. In a letter to me of August 30, 1971, Dr. Keiser, now in private practice in New York, says, "If I saw him during my work at Bellevue he was one of hundreds who would pass through my ward during a month." Lowry was, probably, just another drunk, and there was no way in overcrowded and understaffed Bellevue to spend very much time with men like Lowry. One would in fact have been very surprised if Dr. Keiser *had* remembered this man. Lowry certainly remembered *him*, and made him an important character in "The Last Address" and all its subsequent revised forms. Indeed, if we are to gain any information about Lowry at Bellevue, it is to this *Lunar Caustic* complex that we must go.

What we find is a happy hunting-ground for a textual analyst, but frustrating work for a literary critic or biographer. After Lowry had completed "The Last Address" as a short story, he sent it immediately to Whit Burnett, who had become editor of *Story*.

Burnett accepted it. Soon after that, Lowry realized that he was dissatisfied with what he had written, and asked Burnett to return the story. Burnett did so, and Lowry, now ready to leave New York for California, began a revision—which of course for him could mean only an expansion. Then, in California, Lowry completed this revision, which emerged as a novella, *The Last Address*. (The original short story disappeared soon afterwards, and has never turned up.) In 1940 he sent this novella to Harold Matson, who had by that time become Lowry's agent. Matson held out little hope for its publication—wrong length, too depressing, unclear—and so Lowry took it back, and began another revision. This became *Swinging the Maelstrom*, still a novella. It did not seem, when completed, to look any more saleable than *The Last Address* had done; so Lowry set it aside for a few years, "to gather a little dust," as he said. Then, when the Lowrys were in Paris in 1948, he gave a copy of it to Clarisse Francillon, his French translator of *Under the Volcano*. In 1956 she translated it into French and published it serially in the February, March, and April issues of *L'Esprit*. (Lowry was glad to have her do this, in part because it gave him insurance that he really did need: once published, the work could never be lost, and Lowry was probably the champion manuscript-loser of all time.) Then, in the last months of his life, he made a thorough revision of the novella one of his several literary projects, along with *October Ferry to Gabriola*, his political and philosophical tract, "Halt! I Protest," and some of the stories in *Hear Us O Lord from Heaven Thy Dwelling Place*. What he planned, according to Margerie Lowry, was a sort of conflation, or annealing, of *The Last Address* and *Swinging the Maelstrom*, with much new material incorporated as well. He had decided in the early Fifties that such an eclectic revision would have to be done, and he had determined (as early as 1946) that it should be called *Lunar Caustic*. He died without completing this project. Finally, in 1962, Lowry's old Vancouver friend, Earle Birney, a professor of English at the University of British Columbia, persuaded Margerie that the two of them should complete what Lowry had undertaken—that they should, in an approximation of Lowry's method and intent, "splice together" *The*

Last Address and *Swinging the Maelstrom,* making additions and deletions where Lowry had indicated that they should be made. *The Paris Review* published it, with a brief foreword by Conrad Knickerbocker, in its issue Number 29, winter and spring 1963. In 1968 Jonathan Cape republished this version, and there the matter rests.

With which versions are we to deal in discussing this *Lunar Caustic* complex? There are five typescript drafts of *The Last Address* on file in the Special Collections Division of the University of British Columbia Library, of which the fourth is the latest complete text. There are, filed with these, eight drafts of *Swinging the Maelstrom,* of which the last seems most nearly authoritative (certainly, it is the draft used by Clarisse Francillon in her translation). And there is the Margerie Lowry-Earle Birney "splicing," which is not, to be sure, entirely Malcolm Lowry's work. But Margerie wrote to Conrad Knickerbocker that "we have not added a line" to what Lowry had written. "Malcolm, of course, would then have rewritten, but who could do it as he would have?" Still, their *Lunar Caustic* does very probably represent a closer approximation to what Lowry himself wanted the book to become (Margerie says he hoped ultimately to stretch it out to novel length), and it does in many ways represent an advance over the earlier versions. Whatever its authenticity, the published *Lunar Caustic* is as close as we shall ever get to what Lowry had in mind for it. Accordingly, one ought to base a discussion of *Lunar Caustic* on the *Paris Review*-Cape text, and accompany this discussion with as many references to the texts of *The Last Address* and *Swinging the Maelstrom* as seem relevant.

One must begin by observing that his stay at Bellevue was Lowry's first actual experience of just how dreadful life can really be. He had been ashamed of this; guilty of that; an embarrassment, perhaps, to his parents; a disappointment to his tutors. There were his personal failures, in alcohol and—if Jan is to be believed—in sex. He was undoubtedly neurotic. But his tribulations and failures and flaws were, it might be said, middle-class, circumscribed: he was, after all, a young man from a rich, bourgeois family. He had been given very nearly the best that he could be given in the way of schooling. He had been allowed, more or less in the traditional pattern, his *Wanderjahre* abroad. His father was still supporting him, if modestly. He was unhappy, but unhappy in a limited sort of way. One thinks of Auden's "In Praise of Limestone," with its delineations of a region of short distances and definite places; a land based on malleable, permeable limestone, just suited to the moderate youth who lounges there, never doubting "That for all his faults he is loved; whose works are but/Extensions of his power to charm." Such youths are unable

> To conceive a god whose temper-tantrums are moral
> And not to be pacified by a clever line
> Or a good lay: for, accustomed to a stone that responds,
> They have never had to veil their faces in awe
> Of a crater whose blazing fury could not be fixed. . . .[5]

Lowry had, in effect, played about with the concepts of drunkenness, madness, oblivion; but now, suddenly, the doors of Bellevue closed behind him with a "dithering crack" [6] and he found himself in a world that was infinitely worse than anything he had imagined before. Here were *truly* broken lives; here were men whose brains had been *really* rotted by alcohol, or who were *really* dying of syphilis; or who were experiencing nightmare visions so shattering that they shrieked for hours on end. There is no better place in the world to learn how hideous life can be than in the psychiatric section of a large public hospital; and Lowry, who was no fool, must have seen this and realized what a poseur he was, and how protected he had been.

The point is that we can hardly begin to calculate how traumatic his stay at Bellevue must have been for Lowry. When he emerged, immediately to begin his story, or as he revised it, off and on over the next twenty-one years, he might have been able to use his famil-

5. W. H. Auden, "In Praise of Limestone," *Collected Shorter Poems* (New York, 1966), pp. 238–41.
6. *Lunar Caustic*, p. 11. This was a favorite expression of Lowry's: he had already used it, in "Economic Conference, 1934." He got it, like "horripilation," another of his favorites, from Conrad Aiken.

iar, Aiken-inspired, layering effect for the sake of distancing: but it would be a mistake to assume that *Lunar Caustic* is Lowry's symbolic tribute to Melville, or to jazz; or to take too seriously his oft-repeated assertion that the novella was the *Purgatorio* of his "drunken Divine Comedy." Melville, jazz, and Dante are there, from *The Last Address* through *Lunar Caustic;* but they are not used with such scholarly precision that one can spot consistent patterns of allusion or analogy throughout. *Lunar Caustic* is only after the fact a literary, allusive work: basically, essentially, it is an anguished and very nearly inchoate account of a young man's first real encounter with horror. If one misses the febrile quality of the work, then he misses what makes Lowry a good writer—as well as a bad one.

It is, indeed, as a poseur that the protagonist, Bill Plantagenet,[7] enters the hospital. He has been wandering about the East Side all day, during a heat wave so severe that 186 New Yorkers were dying from it at that very moment, making a circumferential pub-crawl about the tower of the Hospital, keeping it always in view. He enters the Hospital, finally, as he knew he must; and as he does so he is seeing himself as the young Rimbaud of *Une Saison en Enfer:*

> "I want to hear the song of the Negroes," he roars. "*Veut-on que je disparaisse, que je plonge, à la recherche de l'anneau* . . . I am sent to save my father, to find my son, to hear the eternal horror of three, to resolve the irremediable horror of opposites!"[8]

If we choose, we can see the tower of Bellevue as Dante's Mount of Purgatory, which Plantagenet knows he must ascend if he is to be saved; and, if we like, we can turn to the *Purgatorio* to remind ourselves that its inhabitants were guilty of various failures of love, and can speculate about whether Plantagenet is guilty of excessive love

7. That is, his name *may* be Plantagenet. In *The Last Address* he is Sigbjørn Lawhill; and in *Lunar Caustic* he gives his name originally as "the *S. S. Lawhill*." On p. 50 we learn that "the *Lawhill* was a windjammer that survived more disasters than any ship afloat."

8. *Lunar Caustic*, 11. References throughout will be to the Jonathan Cape edition.

(that is, guilty of pursuing worldly appetites without observing due limitations), defective love (being slothful, loving inadequately), or perverted love (taking a delight in evils that befall others). We can conclude that, though he may be innocent of the last, he is certainly guilty of both excessive love (of alcohol, at least) and defective love (of his wife, Ruth, and of himself). And we can note the purgatorial air of the psychiatric ward in which Plantagenet soon finds himself, with its patients who are neither alive nor dead, neither saved nor damned—quite. But the Dantean analogues very quickly become diffuse in Lowry's novella, which is, unlike the *Purgatorio*, a symbolist work, and not a precisely regulated allegory. Nothing *equals* anything else in *Lunar Caustic;* one thing only *suggests* or *evokes* another thing, or several things. Bellevue may be like Purgatory, but in many ways it is rather more like the Inferno. There may or may not be an earthly paradise atop the tower; but if there is, Plantagenet never ascends to it. Like Dana Hilliot, his younger self in *Ultramarine*, his gaze is always downward. And so, ultimately, is his path.

The early allusion to Rimbaud is not fortuitous, for Plantagenet obviously thinks of himself as *un bateau ivre*, thrown capriciously about by the malign forces of life, and as the spiritual kinsman of the young bourgeois who wrote in 1871 that

> Now, I am degrading myself as much as possible. Why? I want to be a poet, and am working hard to make myself a *seer*. . . . It is a question of reaching the unknown by the derangement of *all the senses*. The sufferings are enormous, but one has to be strong, one has to be born a poet, and I know I am a poet. . . . The poet makes himself a *seer* by a long, gigantic and rational *derangement* of *all the senses*. All forms of love, suffering, and madness. He searches himself. He exhausts all poisons in himself and keeps only their quintessences. Unspeakable torture where he needs all his faith, all his superhuman strength, where he becomes among all men the great patient, the great criminal, the one accursed —and the supreme Scholar!—Because he reaches the *unknown!* Since he cultivated his soul, rich already, more than any man! He reaches the unknown, and when, bewildered,

he ends by losing the intelligence of his visions, he has seen them. Let him die as he leaps through unheard of and unnamable things: other horrible workers will come; they will begin from the horizons where the other one collapsed! [9]

So Plantagenet, late of Cambridge where he led a jazz group known as "Bill Plantagenet and his Seven Hot Cantabs," which fell apart once in America, and a recent failure as a husband, reels like the speaker of *Une Saison en Enfer* about the searing and stinking alleys of the city. Compare Rimbaud: "Je me traînais dans les ruelles puantes et, les yeux fermés, je m'offrais au soleil, dieu de feu" ("I dragged myself through stinking alleys and, eyes closed, I offered myself to the sun, god of fire"). He imagines that, in entering the hospital, he will enter on a voyage into the abyss of himself, from which he will emerge perhaps shattered, but purged and cleansed, and ready, like Rimbaud, to be "responsible for humanity, even for the *animals*" (Fowlie ed., p. 309). Lowry's "drunken Divine Comedy" was, he said, to be constructed on a dynamic of "withdrawal and return"; like Rimbaud's seer, his various personae were to plunge into themselves, to extinguish their outer identities, usually with the aid of alcohol; and then to emerge from their own inner hells regenerated, now with their perilously gained vision able to join mankind, and to serve it.

Lowry seems really to have thought of his life in these Rimbaudian terms; and it is striking to observe how consistently throughout his works he was to point toward the symbolists' demented inner voyage as being necessary for the artist—even the artist who resigns from the role, like Dana Hilliot; or the failed artist, like Bill Plantagenet (or, later, like Geoffrey Firmin).

The place in which Plantagenet is to make his struggle toward rebirth is amply purgatorial, even hellish. Far below his ward, between the Hospital tower and the East River, is a stretch of coarse grass. Just beyond, aground against the edge of the grass plot, is a ruined coal barge, "sunken, abandoned, open, hull cracked, bollards

9. Arthur Rimbaud, *Rimbaud: Complete Works, Selected Letters*, ed. by Wallace Fowlie (Chicago, 1966), 303, 307. The material quoted is from Rimbaud's letters to George Izambard and Paul Demeny.

adrift, tiller smashed, its hold still choked with coal dust, silt, and earth through which emerald shoots had sprouted." Beyond the coal barge are two wharves. The one on the left seems vaguely friendly; at it are moored white and blue motor boats, "which seemed as they nudged and nibbled ceaselessly at the suicidal blackness of the streams to tell tender tales of girls in summer." At the right-hand pier is a ferry that goes to the Ice Palace at Rockaway. Across the river is the Jack Frost Sugar Works. Lowry could wring more portentousness out of a few signs than one would believe possible. How delighted he was later when, on Burrard Inlet across from his shack in Dollarton, the first letter of the giant neon sign over the oil refinery burned out, to leave its last four letters blinking and blazing across the night sky: HELL! So now, Ice Palace; Jack Frost: we know that they are taunting beacons to the inmates of Bellevue who are sweltering in the infernal summer heat. And if Bellevue is Purgatory, it stands in the midst of another, larger Purgatory: New York itself, with its imprisoned spirit, "that spirit haunting the abyss between Europe and America and brooding like futurity over the Western Ocean." The inmates on Plantagenet's ward rush to the windows whenever a ship passes below. If it is headed into port, the madmen burst out with a cry that is "partly a cheer and partly a wailing shriek"; if headed to sea, "there is a dead silence in the ward and a strange foreboding as though all hope were sailing with the tide." Apparently, if Lowry had survived long enough to give *Lunar Caustic* the full symbolic treatment, a journey from Europe to New York, and then to the rest of America—with Mexico and Canada—would have been something like a voyage from Inferno to Purgatory to Paradise. But Lowry, one is sure, would never have made it that simple: journeys for him are never only geographical; and hell never in only one place. The abyss is always with us— even in the midst of Paradise; and especially in Purgatory.

Plantagenet suffers a period of delirium tremens and hallucinations drawn mostly from images Baudelaire had concocted for *Fleurs du Mal* ("Music mounted to a screech, subsided. On a tumbled bloodstained bed in a house whose face was blasted away a large scorpion was gravely raping a one-armed Negress.") After some days of this, he slowly awakens to find "two people looking at him kindly, a small old man and a little boy." These are Kalowsky, an ancient Jewish Lithuanian, and Garry, a fair-haired little boy who seems about ten, and who makes Plantagenet think vaguely of "a portrait of Rimbaud at twelve or thereabouts." If Garry is the young Rimbaud, then Kalowsky (called Horowitz in *The Last Address*) is the Wandering Jew. Indeed, he wryly gives himself this title (*Lunar Caustic*, p. 28)—thereby allowing us to recall not only that the legend of Ahasuerus was one which always interested Lowry, but also that the Wandering Jew was a tangential if not central figure in the *poèmes-de-voyage* of the French symbolist tradition.[10]

Once fully conscious, the shaking and fragile Plantagenet begins to see that, however unhappy his plight, he is, finally, far saner than most of his fellow inmates. They are filthy, decaying, abandoned —so much so that one sees the symbolic appropriateness of the ruined coal barge which is rotting at the water's edge far below. These inmates, like the barge, were once fit for voyaging; now they are hulks. All but the feeblest spend most of their days in a hideous promenade around the ward, looking at nothing, thinking of nothing: no hope of heaven, not even hope of hell. And some of them, the oldest, show Plantagenet that Purgatory, or death-in-life, can be worse even than the Inferno:

> Later, when the nine high candles in their circular base were lighted above the old men who were considered too jittery or too obscene to eat with the others in the regular room, and they were bent over their stew in a grey, trembling despair, some seeming not to know they were eating at all, the food perhaps tasteless to them as they cuffed it slowly and

10. He is there, for instance, as "le Juif Errant" in Baudelaire's "Le Voyage," the ending of which must often have struck Lowry:

> Verse-nous ton poison pour qu'il nous réconforte!
> Nous voulons, tant ce feu nous brûle le cerveau,
> Plonger au fond du gouffre, Enfer ou Ciel, qu'importe?
> Au fond de l'Inconnu pour trouver du *nouveau!*
> [Pour out your poison so it can comfort us!
> This fire is burning our brain so much that we want
> To plunge into the abyss, whether hell or heaven who cares?
> To the bottom of the unknown to find the *new!*]

sleepily with their harmless spoons, others not even attempting to eat but wearing a fixed smile, as though the thought
even of misery afforded them some perverse comfort, Plantagenet, watching them, gradually thought he understood the
meaning of death, not as a sudden dispatch of violence, but
as a function of life.

(*Lunar Caustic*, pp. 26–27)

Plantagenet speaks to the ward's resident physician, Dr. Claggart
(whose literary ancestor is, of course, the villain of *Billy Budd*), who
sees quickly that Plantagenet is a different sort from the rest of his
patients. For one thing, he seems to know something about the
technical aspects of his neurosis. Shortly after Plantagenet's admission, Claggart had heard him mutter, "Hullo, father, return to the
presexual revives the necessity for nutrition." To Plantagenet he
says, "Sounds as though you once read a little book." Presumably,
then, Plantagenet is as aware as Claggart that his illness is closer to
infantilism than to demonism.

Plantagenet is a failed musician not only because he has been unable to hold his group together, but also because of the smallness of
his hands. "They're not big enough for a real pianist," he tells Claggart. "I can't stretch them over an octave on a piano. On a guitar I
fake all the time." But Claggart knows that Plantagenet's musical
shortcomings are not his worst trouble, and replies, "You didn't
leave Ruth because your hands couldn't stretch an octave." Plantagenet, unwilling to face discussion of this greater failure, tries to
dodge the accusation, both by an angry return to the musical complaint, and by denunciations of his wife: "Hell with her! She only
brought me back as a sort of souvenir from Europe." But Claggart,
tired yet persistent, has the last word: "Perhaps it was your heart
you couldn't make stretch an octave." Here we are, inevitably in a
Lowry work, at the theme of the inability to love (or, in Dantean,
purgatorial terms, of defective, slothful love). Whether Plantagenet's drinking (and with it, his impotence) [11] have caused him to fail

11. This is only hinted at in *Lunar Caustic:* "Four years ago I held the Cambridge
record for the two-arm press; matter of fact, the only weight I can't lift—" (p.
20).

Ruth, or whether his failure with her has caused him to drink, we are not told; but one suspects the former, this being a novella by Lowry.

After only a few days in the observation ward, Plantagenet comes to feel that Kalowsky and Garry, at least, do not belong in Bellevue. Kalowsky is 82, confused, and perhaps senile; but he should be moved to a sanatorium instead of kept where he is, without proper medical care. And Garry, the young Rimbaud, is a sane prophet in an insane world: he is a fabulist, an artist of sorts, and he prides himself on being able to tell stories anywhere, under any conditions:

> Do you know it's a funny thing, it's like a miracle, but wherever I am if I'm up in the air, or under the sea, or in the mountains, anywhere—I can tell a story. No matter where you put me, even in prison. I can be sitting, not sitting. Eating, not eating. I can put the whole thing into that story, that's what makes it a story.

Plantagenet acknowledges that all of Garry's stories are about disasters or collapses of one kind or another—he speaks constantly of that ruined coal barge, and has visions of the end of Pompeii, the cataclysmic destruction of the city, and of the hospital, that is to come—but he argues to Claggart that, if he were to read some of Garry's stories, the first thing he would notice

> would be the curious symbolism and if you had ever read any French poetry . . . you would see some similarity in the process of selectivity to, say, that of Rimbaud, taking an obvious example . . . Forests, soleils, rivers, savanes. Don't you see it's the same kind of thing? *Mêlant aux fleurs des yeux de panthères*—etc. And all his stories are about things collapsing, falling apart. Don't you see buried in all that wreckage his craving for freedom?

And Claggart answers, "His? Or yours?" He suggests to Plantagenet that in talking about Kalowsky (the rootless one, the homeless, the eternal wanderer) and Garry (the apocalyptic fabulist, the obsessive symbolist) he is really talking about himself. When

Plantagenet, anticipating R.D. Laing and *The Divided Self* by 24 years, says that "many who are supposed to be mad here, as opposed to the ones who are drunks, are simply people who perhaps once saw, however confusedly, the necessity for change in themselves, for *rebirth*, that's the word." Claggart again replies, "If you're talking about yourself, this is all very helpful. If not, I don't think you have a grasp of the facts." Plantagenet may, poetically or symbolically speaking, be right about the patients; but Claggart, in his pragmatic way, is right, too: the mad are, after all, mad: Kalowsky may be old and ill, a lifetime wanderer; but he has also been brought here by his brother because he was "always threatening people's lives and turning on the gas"; and little Garry, whose emotional age is ten, is actually a fifteen-year old who had been committed because he had, with a broken bottle, slit the throat of a young girl. Claggart is, finally, no villain: he simply will not allow poetic truth to exist outside pragmatic truth; and Plantagenet crumbles. He had hoped to perform a virtuous act here, and so to begin his own regeneration; but he cannot help his friends: he cannot even look them in the eye when he returns to the ward. He had thought of himself, hubristically, as an Icarian figure—though, unlike the arch and objective Stephen Dedalus, who sees himself as sailing above humanity, aloof and aesthetically distant, Plantagenet had, faithful to the *symboliste* example, imagined himself as "the tactile conscience, the lonely soul falling featherless into the abyss." It is all for nothing: he is a failure, and a fraud. Madness may take one into the abyss, but drunkenness won't. And, he admits, he *is* only a drunk, "though he had pretended for a while that he was not, that he was mad with the full dignity of madness."

The true initiates into the world of madness know that Plantagenet is a poseur. They mock him as he plays jazz on the ward piano, and drive him away from it—and cheer the slack-jawed degenerate who takes over from him: "You don't know nothing, you souse. . . . Lemme at that piano."

All his attempts at evoking a sense of kinship with the mad, or the threatened, or the great, are futile: he is no musician, no Rimbaud, no Melville—no matter how hard he reaches for allusions to *Billy*

Budd or *Moby-Dick*. Most certainly, he is no Dante: for he is compelled to leave this Purgatory of a hospital, to descend again, having failed to love (in spite of his fumbling efforts to do so), into the streets of the dreadful city. Like Lowry, Plantagenet, as an Englishman, cannot stay as a charity patient in a public hospital; well or not, he must leave.

The bottle with which he had entered the hospital is returned to him, and "once more, with a dithering crack," the hospital door shuts behind him. The best he can say for himself is that he has at least had a taste of what Purgatory really is: in the hospital, during a lull in a ghastly puppet-show, "He had the curious feeling that he had made a sort of descent into the maelstrom, a maelstrom terrifying for the last reason one would have expected: that there was about it sometimes just this loathsome, patient calm."

The calm may be awful, but the chaos of the summer streets is worse. Before he succumbs again to it, he manages to send back to Kalowsky a dollar's worth of oranges, and to Garry a packet of foreign stamps. Except for one last gesture, this is the best he can do in the way of helping others. He then goes into a sailor's tavern, where he sits down at a table and begins drinking. For a few moments he is exhilarated (very much like Dana Hilliot at the end of *Ultramarine*, in fact), thinking of himself as making heroic sacrifices, as striking blows for the right; then, in the washroom of the bar, he makes his gesture. He throws his whiskey bottle at an obscene drawing of a girl that is chalked on the washroom wall, and feels truly noble: "it seemed to him that he had flung that bottle against all the indecency, the cruelty, the hideousness, the filth and injustice in the world." Then, his empty altruism dissipated, he returns to the bar, and sits at a secluded place. But it is not secluded enough; and, "feeling he was being watched even then, he moved later, drink in hand, to the very obscurest corner of the bar, where, curled up like an embryo, he could not be seen at all."

There the novella ends, in total failure. Plantagenet has postured, done his best to be "significant," read all the necessary symbols into whatever came before his eyes, sympathized with his fellow patients, argued passionately with his antagonist, tried his hardest to be a madman suffering in Purgatory—but he is still only another drunk, another derelict in a city full of derelicts. Rimbaud ends his *Saison en Enfer* in glorious affirmation, after *his* descent into the abyss: "*Recevons tous les influx de vigueur et de tendresse réele. Et à l'aurore, armés d'une ardente patience, nous entrerons aux splendides villes*" ("Let us welcome all the influx of vigor and real tenderness. And, at dawn, armed with ardent patience, we shall enter magnificent cities"). But for Plantagenet there are no magnificent cities; there is only New York, a real enough Inferno, with "the whole mechanic calamity of the rocking city, with the screaming of suicides, of girls tortured in hotels for transients, of people burning to death in vice dens, through all of which a thousand ambulances were screeching like trumpets." Plantagenet hides, in his dark womb of a bar. Return to the presexual revives the necessity for nutrition: the embryo is feeding itself.

Tonally, *The Last Address* is rather like *Lunar Caustic*. The allusions to Melville are a little more frequent in the 1936 version (the title refers to the fact that, from Bellevue, the protagonist can almost see "the last address" of Melville as he was completing *Moby-Dick;* and Garry is thought of as being like *Moby-Dick's* Pip, the simple boy who became mad, and therefore visionary), but the outcome is the same: bitterness and futility prevail. With *The Last Address*, however, one is even less sure than with *Lunar Caustic* about what, precisely, is wrong with the protagonist (we do not know, for instance, that Sigbjørn Lawhill is a failed musician—but then, even when this flaw is given us in *Lunar Caustic*, we do not accept it as sufficient, any more than does Dr. Claggart.)

But *Swinging the Maelstrom*, written mostly in 1940, is far more optimistic than its earlier and later versions. This time, the protagonist is the cousin of the psychiatrist (here called Philip), and finds that Philip is at least as intuitive and sympathetic as he is. Thus though Plantagenet can do no more for Garry and Kalowsky than the protagonist of *Lunar Caustic* was to be able to do, he does not collapse so completely at the novella's conclusion. Instead, he resolves to join the world. He calls a relative of one of the patients, and then—quite like Hugh at the conclusion of *Under the*

Volcano—he decides to join the crew of a Spanish ship which is about to sail in hopes of bringing aid to the Republican forces in the Civil War. To do this is a gesture, and obviously intended by Lowry as a quixotic gesture at that (the Fascists had won in Spain a year before Lowry wrote this draft). But at least it is an active gesture, one requiring a man's functioning in a world of men—better by far than the impulsive hurling of a bottle at a dirty sketch on a bathroom wall.

Obviously, then, *The Last Address* and *Lunar Caustic* are closer to one another, thematically as well as tonally, than either is to *Swinging the Maelstrom*. There may be all sorts of reasons for this, among which might be that Margerie Lowry and Earle Birney thought the first draft better than the second, and therefore made it dominant in their edition. But there is the fact that Lowry did, after all, have a hand in the third version, and the return to the more pessimistic outlook of *The Last Address* was undoubtedly his notion. Even his title now, *Lunar Caustic*, suggests this; for lunar caustic is silver nitrate, so potent a cleanser that in full strength it can burn the skin from a man: a real purgatory, in fact, and a cruel one. To the biographer, a final possibility suggests itself: in 1936, Lowry was in near despair over what he had just gone through at Bellevue. It would have been unlike him to write an optimistic fable about so negative a reality. But in 1940 he saw his fortunes as finally on the upswing: he was out of the banal savagery of Mexico, he was writing well, and he had met the woman who later became his second wife. People he knew were doing amazing things in the new war; there was even the possibility that he himself might do something real in the way of virtuous action. Hence, the relatively greater optimism of *Swinging the Maelstrom*. And the man who revised the novella once again, in 1956, had been through more real hellishness than almost anyone he knew, including several approaches to real madness. If he had forgotten about despair in 1940, he had remembered it by 1956—well enough, after all, to kill himself less than a year later. Alterations in psychic well-being are not absolute determinants of literary endeavor; but they do, after all, have their part to play. In Lowry more than in most.

For Malcolm Lowry in August 1936, having just gone through the traumatic and ego-damaging experience at Bellevue, there was the necessity to write, and to let his writing be both his caustic and his balm. In *The Last Address* he could, with his unflinching honesty as an author, perform a ruthlessly thorough dissection of the person who had romanticized about madness until he discovered what madness was. Bellevue was, to him, yet another emblem of his failure, and he set about facing it in his novella. But, with the distancing that literary allusiveness can lend, he hoped also to soften for himself the impact of what he had to face. As in most of his works, the unadorned factual level of *Lunar Caustic* was too harsh for him to endure; it had to be festooned, and ultimately obscured, with evocations of jazz, Melville, Rimbaud, and Dante. While this allusive cushioning could give an effect of richness or density to Lowry's work, it could also annoy by its obfuscation. Somehow, in *Lunar Caustic*, we feel not only that Lowry is hiding behind Plantagenet, but also that Plantagenet is hiding behind Ahab or Ishmael, as types of lonely, doomed wanderers; and that it does little good to face one's trouble if one has to see that trouble as a white whale, or as the large pale hand of a puppeteer, or as a white seaplane buzzing about overhead. What would Lowry have been able to make of himself if, seated at Eric Estorick's kitchen table that hot August, he had instead been able to write, in unadorned, matter-of-fact prose, of his own horror at what he had seen, in himself as well as at Bellevue? And yet—there is what we might call the aesthetic of profusion, whereby beauty is created through proliferation of symbols. In this aesthetic, Lowry is a paradigm. If one prefers, however, the aesthetic of exclusion, whereby beauty is created through spareness of effect, then Lowry is not one's man.[12]

Somehow, Lowry contrived in early September 1936, to get together again with Jan. For reasons which we do not know— perhaps to look for work in films, perhaps simply to escape New

12. For useful discussions of *Lunar Caustic*, see David Benham, "Lowry's Purgatory: Versions of *Lunar Caustic*," *Canadian Literature*, 44 (Spring 1970), 28–37; and Dale Edmonds, "The Short Fiction of Malcolm Lowry," *Tulane Studies in English*, XV (1967), 59–80.

York—they decided to strike out for Los Angeles. Just after they had left, John Davenport and his wife arrived in New York from England, and tried to reach them. They called Jan's mother on Long Island, and were happy to hear that the Lowrys were on a bus headed for Los Angeles; for the Davenports were themselves on their way to Hollywood, where Davenport's friend, the actor Robert Donat, was having studio difficulties, and was in need of someone to write a script for him. Donat's studio had asked Davenport to do the job, and he had been glad to accept. Now, he went up to Cambridge for a few days to stay with Conrad Aiken, who had just met Mary Hoover, who later became his third wife. Aiken had no news of the Lowrys. Then Davenport, who had learned from Jan's mother the name of the bus company the Lowrys had taken, looked up its route to Los Angeles, and scattered telegrams all along their way, as he and his wife traveled by train to Los Angeles. It took a week or so to find a suitable house in Hollywood, but by the time they were settled in, they had somehow managed to locate the Lowrys, who came to stay with them.

In her biographical essay for Lippincott, Margerie Lowry wrote that John Davenport wanted Lowry to help him with his script-writing, and managed to persuade the studio to put Lowry under contract, "so Malcolm came to Hollywood and worked on several movie scripts, with John and others. He was always interested in the cinema and the theatre but he was unhappy in Hollywood; he didn't like their methods of working, or much of the results, and he found it difficult to work in tandem with several other writers on the same script." Davenport contradicted this story. According to him (in his unpublished preface to *Ultramarine*), Lowry indeed had hopes of working as a script writer, "but Hollywood was preparing for one of its periodic slumps," and Lowry was never hired by anyone in Hollywood for any sort of writing. No one has been able to locate a single piece of evidence to support Margerie Lowry, so it seems likely that Davenport's recollection is accurate. Without help from the film industry, then, Lowry presumably found that his small allowance sent him by his father was not enough to sustain him and Jan in Hollywood. Where better to go than Mexico, then, where they could live quite comfortably on his father's allowance?

Whether Davenport's memory is correct as to the date of the Lowrys' departure from Hollywood is, however, not so certain. Lowry always maintained that he and Jan sailed from San Diego aboard the cargo ship *S.S. Pennsylvania* for Acapulco, and arrived there on November 1, the "Day of the Dead." For Lowry, this date had talismanic proportions: several of the significant arrivals in *Under the Volcano* take place on the Day of the Dead; and again, in "Through the Panama." [13]

Davenport began by agreeing with Lowry on the November date: in his unpublished preface to *Ultramarine* he says that after about seven hectic weeks in Hollywood, the Lowrys "set off in November by cargo boat from San Diego for Acapulco." Later, however, Davenport decided that he had erred, and wrote to Conrad Knickerbocker on November 30, 1965, that Lowry had been with him in California "until December." Davenport's letter is quite emphatic about this date, but one suspects that here he is wrong, and Lowry right. On June 15, 1946, Lowry wrote to A. Ronald Button, a California attorney, to explain the calamitous nature of his second trip to Mexico, in 1945–46. In this letter, he says that "In November of 1936 I had originally entered Mexico through Acapulco, arriving by boat"; and there is no reason why Lowry, in a letter in which he was striving to be as precise and accurate as possible, should have insisted on the November date if he were not reasonably certain of it. (One ought to note here, perhaps, that though he probably had the correct month, he was wrong about November 1 being the Day of the Dead. The first day of that month is All Saints Day, in Mexico "el Día de Todos los Santos"; and the *second* day is All Souls Day, in Mexico "el Día de los Difuntos"—literally, the Day of the Dead.)

Let us suppose, then, that on either the first or second day of November Lowry and Jan went ashore like Martin Trumbaugh, "in a boat, the madman [presumably a fellow passenger] foaming at the mouth, correcting his watch; the mile-high bodiless vultures in the

13. "Through the Panama," *Here Us O Lord From Heaven Thy Dwelling Place* (New York, 1961).

thunder" ("Through the Panama," p. 42). They stayed in Acapulco only long enough for Lowry to discover mescal, tequila, pulque, and Mexico's splendid dark beer; and then took a bus inland, across the mountains to Mexico City. When they left Mexico City is not known, but it cannot have been longer than two weeks after their arrival there; because by Christmas of 1936 they had gone southward by bus along the Ajusco mountain range to Cuernavaca, and were living in a one-storey, three-room house: No. 15, Calle de Humboldt, complete with tiny swimming pool, a soon-to-be-ruined garden, and a spectacular view of the volcanoes Popocatepetl and Ixtaccihuatl, far to the east. In front of their cottage was the intersection of Calle de Humboldt and the Calle de Salazar, which ran westward toward the *zócalo*, or plaza, at the center of Cuernavaca. Just west of the *zócalo* lay the overgrown but still magnificent Borda gardens, with their apartments built for the unhappy Maximilian and Carlotta. Through the Lowrys' back yard ran one of the town's many *barrancas*, or ravines, so overgrown that one could not see it from the cottage; and, parallel to the *barranca*, but closer to the house, ran a smaller ravine: one of Cuernavaca's sewage ditches. If one looked from the rear windows of Number 15, Calle de Humboldt, southeast across the *barranca*, one could see in the middle-distance the small suburb of Acapantzingo, at the southern end of which was Maximilian's old shooting lodge. In the northeast one could see, across the railroad tracks, the hill on which was situated the rambling Hotel Casino de la Selva, where one could swim or play tennis. Beyond the hotel, to the north, lay the large *selva*, or forest, which had, in Aztec times, given Cuernavaca its name. (The Nahuatl name for the town had been Quauhnahuac: Among the Trees. The conquering Spaniards had chosen a word from their own language which came close to the Nahuatl, in sound if not in beauty of meaning. Cuernavaca means "Cow-horn.") The surroundings were spectacular, if the cottage was not; and the terrain was ideally suited to the eternally symbolizing Lowry: here was the ruined palace on the surface of the earth; the magic mountains in the distance, rising like the Mount of Purgatory to heaven; and at one's feet, apparently bottomless and certainly feculent, was the abyss.

He and Jan were probably drawn to Cuernavaca by nothing more romantic than the fact that there was a large foreign colony there, with many literary types in it; but if Lowry had been looking for Baudelaire's forest of symbols, with its myriads of correspondences, he could never have found a more appropriate spot than Cuernavaca. He began writing almost immediately.

Within a matter of weeks he had completed a short story, which he chose to call "Under the Volcano." It was divided into three equal parts, and came to around 7000 words. In the first section, an alcoholic English consul (called simply "the Consul"), his fair-haired daughter, Yvonne, and her sweetheart, Hugh, set off by bus from what is obviously Cuernavaca to attend a fiesta in Mexico City's Chapultepec Park. Always looming above them, as they meander northward, is Popocatepetl, which for the hungover Consul soon takes on a sinister quality: "like a sort of Moby Dick, it had the air of beckoning them on, as it swung from one side of the horizon to the other, to some disaster, unique and immedicable." [14] Hugh, a young man just arrived that day from Acapulco, is concentrating on Yvonne; but Yvonne is concerned mostly with her father, who for her sake is making the effort of going without liquor for the day. He free-associates after the manner of all of Lowry's tormented heroes, allowing signs along the way, vistas that open before them, sounds, and random words all to intersect and correspond, pointing toward some unspecified guilt that he feels. Across from him sits a drunken *pelado*, a "peeled one"—a petty thief, a hanger-on, an exploiter of those yet poorer than himself. The *pelado*, serene and poised despite the trembling of his large hands (the Consul has thrust his own hands guiltily into his pockets), has managed to achieve a sort of inebriated equilibrium, both physical and emotional, that the Consul quite envies: he is drunk, he is even ludicrous; but he is aware of everything that is going on around him —is even, in some obscure way, in control of events.

In the second section the crowded bus stops to allow the Consul

14. "Under the Volcano," *Prairie Schooner*, XXXVII, no. 4 (Winter 1963/64), 284–300. This short story, the original version of Chapter VIII of *Under the Volcano*, was unpublished until this issue, devoted to Lowry.

and Hugh to investigate what seems at first to be an accident: lying at the side of the road is a peon who is gravely injured; nearby, his horse grazes unconcernedly. They lift the sombrero which has covered the man's head, to see a terrible and bloody wound, as well as a few pesos in coins which lie beneath his head. Hugh is about to offer first aid of some kind when the others, the Consul among them, stop him: it is against the law to touch the victim of a crime or accident. The sense of futility grows in Hugh and the Consul (Yvonne, afraid of blood, has remained on the bus) as it becomes obvious that the man will die without immediate help. As they are about to board the bus (traffic is piling up, horns are honking), a group of vigilantes—members, perhaps, of the *Policia de Seguridad*—ride up, and ominously take charge of the scene. Hugh, threatened by one of them, reluctantly joins the Consul and Yvonne on the bus, which starts up again.

The short final section takes the bus to Chapultepec Park, where, as they are alighting, they notice that the smiling *pelado* now holds in his hands the blood-stained coins that had belonged to the dying peon. The story ends as the trio watch a grotesque apparition issuing from a bar: an old and lame Indian is carrying out of the bar another Indian, "yet older and more decrepit, on his back, by means of a strap clamped to his forehead."

Lowry cannot have long intended this short story to remain as it was. There was, true enough, the single sharp image—the dying man—on which one could focus attention; and there was a certain kind of geographical unity, at any rate: the plot began in one place, continued en route, and ended in another place. But who were these three gringo tourists? Why was it necessary to establish so emphatically the Consul's alcoholism, since it had nothing really to do with the plot? Why such detailed description of the *pelado?* And to what sort of vague symbolic pattern could one relate such details as the number seven branded on the horse's rump, or the volcano hovering about them, or the ubiquitous sign reading *Los* [sic] *Manos de Orlac: con Peter Lorre,* with its picture of "a murderer's hands laced with blood"? Ten years later, when the novel, *Under the Volcano,* appeared, one would be able to comprehend that sym-

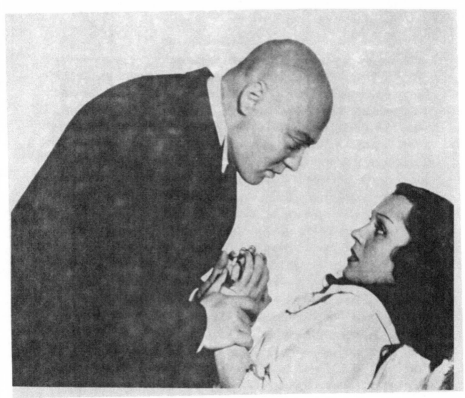

"*Las Manos de Orlac*, con Peter Lorre"

bolic pattern; but now everything pointed importantly toward nothing more than almost total opacity. This was nothing like slice-of-life realism: it was obviously homiletic as well as hermetic. As always in Lowry's work, every detail was "significant," having value only in so far as it thrust the reader outward or inward, beyond or beneath the surface level, but here, there was nowhere to go: signs indicated directions, but to non-existent places.

Lowry's mind functioned centrifugally: expansion and elaboration were his normal impulses. Before he had really begun it, obviously, he had started thinking of "Under the Volcano" not as a story but as a novel; and there was probably very little delay between the completion of the story (if, indeed, he ever regarded it as completed) and the commencement of its revision into something much longer. He had suddenly come upon a configuration of characters that was important to him, and workable; and he had found, in the terrain around him, an ideal setting for the working-out of the situation in which his characters were taking their positions. He did not know that terrain very well, yet, nor the language of the Mexicans who inhabited it (though he was quick at grasping the way those Mexicans spoke *English*); and there was something not quite right about casting Yvonne as the Consul's daughter—and who was Hugh, anyway?—but these were details that could be handled in revision. He had what was important: his self-tormented, symbol-seeking man of surrendered authority, his drunken, witty Consul; and he had his volcano, his exotic and dangerous land, and his *barranca*. Everything else would follow.

For the next three months Lowry wrote, until by mid-May he had a complete first draft of a novel of more than 40,000 words. At least, Conrad Aiken, who visited the Lowrys at that time, and stayed in Cuernavaca until July, claims to have seen such a manuscript; and Arthur Calder-Marshall, who arrived in Cuernavaca the following September, corroborates Aiken's claim.[15] This first full draft of *Under the Volcano* disappeared after Lowry left Mexico in July 1938: but it must indeed have existed, and existed much as Aiken and Calder-Marshall remember it: for the draft which Lowry completed in 1940, after reaching Canada, was labelled by him "2d Draft"—and it is very unlikely that he should have considered his little short story as a first draft.

But he was not only working in Cuernavaca: he was drinking as well, in sufficient quantity to make one wonder how he managed to come up with anything like those 40,000 words. When Aiken, in search of a Mexican divorce from Clarissa Lorenz, arrived by bus in Cuernavaca, bringing with him his next wife and—once again —Ed Burra, he was overjoyed to see "Hambo" marching toward

15. So, for that matter, does Frank Jellinek, in a letter of February 17, 1967 to Margerie Lowry. Jellinek, a journalist who was living on the Calle de Humboldt in 1937, recalls spending evenings together with Lowry and Calder-Marshall, during which Lowry would try out on them his 1937 version of *Under the Volcano*. Jellinek remembers thinking "how extremely funny parts of the book were," especially those having to do with Hugh.

them, carrying a long forked stick, and then walking slowly along-side the bus, grinning, his red face glaring up at them affection-ately, his "fat fist" lifting his stick toward them "in signal." [16] The stick, Aiken learned, had been borrowed from one of the rose-trees in the garden on Calle de Humboldt: Lowry had, he insisted to Aiken, contracted lumbago from his swimming pool, and could not walk unaided. He was an absurd figure, Aiken thought affection-ately, as Lowry approached them self-consciously and shyly, with his "fringe of blond beard making the round face look a little odd" (*A Heart for the Gods of Mexico*, p. 138), and with his trousers knotted around the waist with a necktie, looking as usual as if they were about to fall. He seemed at first to be his old delightful, foxy self, this "carelessly powerful and ingratiating figure, to which the curiously short arms, which he habitually thrust a little before him, lent an appealing appearance of helplessness" (*Ushant*, p. 348). But even though he *seemed* rather well, and able even to write, Lowry was really in almost desperate condition. He was, Aiken soon dis-covered, sinking daily ever deeper into marital and alcoholic misery, while he "grappled stubbornly and unremittingly with his unap-peasable vision, in that nest of old rags and blankets in which for the most part he lived, on the veranda of the villa" (*Ushant*, p. 348). Aiken's recollection is not a pleasant one: here was Lowry, lying —and, apparently, writing—on his squalid couch on the veranda, looking up with "longing and shamefaced devotion" as Jan paced irritatedly back and forth, her "pitiless and faithless heels" clicking on the tiles of this veranda as they had in the patio of the Pensión Carmona in Granada in 1933. For Aiken, Jan was still a "beautiful little creature," but now he was appalled to see her cold indifference to Lowry. It was painful to have to watch "the daily death of Hambo, the daily triumph of the faithless and pitiless heels, while the thunderheads punctually amassed themselves over the vol-cano for the tremendous assault of lightning and downpour at eve-ning" (*Ushant*, p. 349).

16. Conrad Aiken, *A Heart for the Gods of Mexico* (London, 1939), 130–31. This *roman à clef* about Aiken's Mexican journey tallies rather closely at points with material in *Ushant*; but in the novel Aiken has "Hambo" meet their train in Mex-ico City and then drive them to Cuernavaca—which he could not have done even if he had tried.

Jan was also, according to Aiken, again embarked on numerous and flagrant infidelities. On at least one occasion, she left Cuernavaca altogether, with no pretense of an excuse. This was "the pathetic episode of the earrings":

> For the faithless heels were all too faithlessly and obviously going away: they had announced it as if it were a challenge, which it was: they were going to the north, to the silvermines, and, quite frankly, to stay with those two friends of hers, the engineers: alone, too, and for a week, and no question of any chaperonage, either: it was, and publicly, too, a flat declaration that the heels were dammed well going to be unfaithful. From the parting at the bus station, where they had all gone to see her off, they had done their best to avoid their eyes. The stonily beautiful little profile avoided the anguished and hangdog gaze of poor Hambo, she was already looking ahead, over those propitious mountains, to the wealth of those silver-mines, and the promise of gay nights, and, as always on such occasions, the lavish and expensive gifts which awaited her there. And with this enthralling prospect before her, how could she possibly pay the slightest heed to the little gift of silver earrings? They were for her birthday—he murmured—handing them awkwardly and shyly through the *camión* window: they were for her birthday, day after tomorrow—did she remember? But, if she did, she expressed no surprise. She accepted them with a glance of suppressed annoyance, thrust them almost angrily into her handbag—as if they were a sort of rebuke, and perhaps they were—and then the bus shot away, the usual cloud of dust whirling up from it, over the square and its baroque bandstand, and she was gone.
>
> (*Ushant*, pp. 349–50)

It takes a callous commentator indeed to question such a sad scene, and something like this undoubtedly did take place. But let us, in passing, ask ourselves how difficult Malcolm Lowry must have been as a husband, and what Jan must have had to endure at his hands, in the way of drunkenness, sloth, promises unfulfilled, hope consistently defeated. And we might wonder how Aiken could know so precisely what was going through Jan's mind as she sat silently on the bus out of Cuernavaca. Perhaps she was merely being brave in her own behalf, resisting the rather blatant appeal to pity that Lowry was making—before an audience of his friends, not hers. Domestic issues are not to be judged too easily. She may, as Aiken suggests in *Ushant*, have betrayed her husband with the engineers at the silver mine, or with a *pelota* player, or a taxi-driver; but in what more private ways had Lowry betrayed her?

At any rate, Jan's departure accelerated Lowry's decline. He was almost unable to work, and his lumbago grew steadily worse; and he now

> began a series of alcoholic fugues from which they were often afraid he might never return. He would vanish for a night: he would vanish for two. His appearance became more and more disheveled, and if he kept his sense of humor, and his wonderful visionary gift of the gab, nevertheless it was with an increasing irritability, on the one hand, and an increasing indulgence in that fantastic mysticism of his, on the other.

This mysticism of Lowry's, which had always been a part of him in a rather muted, light-hearted way (as when he reported, during his undergraduate days with the Aikens, that he had come across the resident ghost of Jeake's House trying to learn the hunt-and-peck system on his Remington portable one midnight) or in his somewhat more tedious assertions that he was caught up in some giant network of cosmic correspondences, which embroiled him in all manner of predetermined coincidences and catastrophes, now took the form, with Aiken, of a series of discussions about psychic cannibalism. Aiken had absorbed him; now it was his turn to absorb Aiken. He intended, he said, wholly to consume Aiken, his spiritual father, as every son must consume his father. "You are a nation invaded," he told Aiken. "And as I'm younger, and as I'm stronger, in appetite, in will, in recklessness, in sense of direction, it will be no use your trying to compete with me, you will only appear to be echoing *me*, imitating *me*, parodying *me*—you will no longer have a personality of your own" (*Ushant*, p. 356). And, in fact, there *was* a certain amount of appropriating going on at all times. "Lowry was a giant sieve," Aiken told me in conversation. Sieve-like, now, he was sifting very carefully through Aiken's conversations, and retaining—subsequently to claim as his own—what he chose to retain. If Aiken made a joke about a cat's thinking he, whistling, was a bird in a tree, Lowry mentally filed it away, to use as part of the Consul's dialogue with his neighbor, Quincey, in Chapter Five of *Under the Volcano*. If he and Aiken discussed politics, then their conversation would be saved, to reappear, in Chapter Ten, with Aiken's conservative views given to the Consul, and Lowry's leftist opinions given to Hugh.

And he announced his intention to appropriate a story that Aiken held to be crucially important to himself: the history of William Blackstone. Aiken had had this on his mind, one way or another, since 1920; and during his Depression days on *The Massachusetts Guide*, he had come to feel that the saga of William Blackstone might be the core of his most important work, some day. Briefly, Blackstone was an Englishman who had arrived at what was to become Charlestown, together with a group of Puritans. Blackstone was a solitary by nature, however, and soon moved across the Charles River to live by himself in what was eventually to become Boston. There he made friends with the Indians, and was doing quite well until his former companions in Charlestown came to him to complain that their only drinking water was poisonous. Blackstone, in a magnanimous gesture, rode on the back of a bull down to the edge of the Charles, to let the settlers know that they might take their water from his pure spring. This they did—and moved in on him, to boot. So he left Massachusetts, and found privacy once again in Rhode Island. To Aiken, Blackstone became a perfect examplar of sturdy independence, and he resolved to use his story as the basis for a long portrayal of American individualism. But Lowry informed Aiken that Blackstone was now *his* property, and that he proposed to make full use of the story of "the man who went to live among the Indians" in *Under the Volcano*. Aiken was quite defeated—and deflated—by Lowry's aggressiveness in the Blackstone affair, until, much later, he came to see that the greatness of the notion—that of the pioneer who does what he does simply to be *alone*—could not be exhausted by one man, even if that man were the omnivorous Lowry. And, after all, Blackstone came to have a relatively minor, if distinct, function in the symbolic scaffolding of Lowry's novel.

The sorry climax to Aiken's visit came one night in early July when Lowry, staggering home drunk in the midst of a thunderstorm, fell headlong into the sewage ditch (which they had christened the Bilbo Canal) behind his cottage. Aiken and his friends "had heard his cry from the far end of the garden, in pitch darkness . . . and before they could find the flashlight, and go to his assistance, he had somehow missed the path to the little footbridge, and plunged in . . . and had had to be hauled out, and cleansed of the filth, and dried, and put to bed" (*Ushant*, pp. 351–52).

Lowry recovered from his real-life introduction to this small-scale but nonetheless equally cloacal sort of *barranca;* Jan returned from her vacation in the mountains; and so the Lowrys were able to appear with the Aiken group in Cuernavaca for the civil marriage ceremonies between Aiken and Mary Hoover. After the wedding, photographs were made; and a couple of them show Lowry and Jan seated, as Aiken says in *Ushant* (p. 357), like Sacred and Profane Love, on either side of the civic fountain. Lowry, in fact, looks absolutely proper, complete with pipe, cup and saucer, tweeds, and walking stick; and Jan does not look nearly so formidable as Lowry's friends have described her. The marriage day ended with one last round of cantinas, and the Aikens departed, taking Ed Burra with them. Lowry and Jan were left, presumably to see if there were something they could shore against the ruins of their own marriage.

One thing they did try was going on the wagon. Somehow, for one month, Lowry drank nothing, swam often, and exercised daily, with calisthenics and long walks. He was, after all, only twenty-eight, and not necessarily beyond reclaim as a useful citizen. Jan, if only to keep him company, also behaved very well for all of August.

This fragile tranquillity was broken after one month by the arrival in Cuernavaca of more visitors: Arthur Calder-Marshall and

Lowry and Jan, Cuernavaca, June 1937.

his wife, Ara. Calder-Marshall had been in Hollywood, writing scripts for MGM. When he was laid off after working for ten weeks, he and Ara decided to visit the Lowrys. They got the Calle de Humboldt address from John Davenport, and drove down without having let the Lowrys know they were coming. Once in Cuernavaca, they took rooms at the Casa Pepe, then drove over to the Lowrys'. They walked through the small grove of coffee and banana plants that screened the cottage from the dirt-and-gravel street, and were met by a rather startled Jan, who was wearing an old work shirt and dungarees. Lowry appeared shortly after, looking like a Somerset Maugham character, in appropriately scruffy white trousers and shirt. He was radiating good health and heartiness. Nothing to drink for six months, he boasted; and he was feeling wonderful. Lowry delivered several apostrophes to the sober

Lowry, Cuernavaca, June 1937.

life, the clean, simple life—he had heard this sort of talk from his father and brothers during most of his childhood and adolescence, and it must have done him good to be able to say it all now, himself. Then Ara Calder-Marshall asked, in her marvelously throaty voice, "Can we have a drink?" Rather condescendingly, Jan and Lowry agreed to meet them later, at a cantina in the *zócalo*, for "just *one*, perhaps." They all ended by driving, instead, to a dingy night club on a side street off the Pan American highway. They were the club's only visitors. At 11:30 in the evening Jan wanted to go home. Calder-Marshall drove her there, then returned to finish the evening with Lowry and Ara.

For the next few days and nights, Lowry was off again on his rounds of Cuernavaca's bars. One must not forget the almost *sportif* aspect of such odysseys for him, for it was not always sordid. Ara Calder-Marshall has recorded, in the BBC "Portrait of Malcolm Lowry" in 1967, this side of the drinking:

> Whatever state Malc was in, he was splendidly good-natured about it. Somehow, I always thought of a fox. Right, they've run me to earth. Then, in a flash, he'd be *away* through the gents, miraculously disappearing again anywhere—anywhere to go on with his fabulous mind—away from the ordinaries trying to sober him up. Sometimes it got rather boring having to be an ordinary.

One morning Jan called them at the Casa Pepe to say that Lowry was, as usual, missing; but that this time it was serious: she had hidden his allowance from him, and he had gone off with her alarm clock. "He's drinking the alarm clock," she cried to Ara Calder-Marshall. "I just don't care about him, but I can't buy another alarm clock." Then, since Lowry's favorite drink these days was pulque,[17] they searched for him in all the *pulquerías* Cuernavaca possessed.

17. Pulque is a rather thick, fermented derivative of the maguey plant. Lowry generally disdained it, claiming that it "continued to ferment in the guts"; and preferred instead either tequila or the more potent mescal, both distilled from a cousin of the maguey, the agave. Mescal is often erroneously supposed to possess some of the hallucinatory qualities of mescaline, the drug derived from peyote; and Lowry seems to have subscribed to this error.

No luck. Finally, late in the day, they ran him to earth in a cantina on the *zócalo*, just as he was coming out of the bathroom. He was wearing an indescribably filthy old trench coat, and seemed quite pleased to see them. Jan immediately asked him what he had done with her alarm clock. Lowry replied, "Don't worry, I've got it." From the pockets of the trench coat he first extracted three bottles of tequila, and then, with a magician's flourish, produced the largest alarm clock that Ara had ever seen. "Malc, why did you *take* it?" Jan asked him. "But my lovely," he answered gently, "how else should I know when to quit work?" Even Jan laughed at this, and Lowry was temporarily forgiven.

But only temporarily. Jan believed her husband to be a great writer, and was quite angry that he refused, as she thought, to allow any of his work to be published. The presence of the lovely and well-turned-out Ara Calder-Marshall upset her, too: why shouldn't *she* be able to dress as well as Ara? Finally, after a month of pursuing her husband from one cantina to another, her patience broke. Not too inconspicuously, she left for another vacation, this time in the southern seaport town of Veracruz, and this time accompanied by their next-door neighbor on Calle de Humboldt. Conrad Aiken remembers him as the British consul in Cuernavaca, but the Calder-Marshalls recall him as being the French consul. For the sake of subsequent references to Jacques Laruelle in *Under the Volcano*, one would like to think of the Calder-Marshalls as more accurate in this matter than Aiken; but there seems no way, now, to determine who was right.

In any case, Jan left, wearing her white sharkskin suit and her red high-heeled shoes; and Lowry was once again desolate. As Ara Calder-Marshall remarked (in the BBC program), now "he really began living Under the Volcano." It was obvious to them that he could not stay on in his cottage as he was, so the Calder-Marshalls took him to the Casa Pepe to live with them for four or five days. There they were virtually his jailers. In attempt to get him in some kind of shape, they took him to a Mexican doctor, who prescribed several doses daily of brandy and strychnine, with an occasional Moctezuma beer in between times. Three days of this were all Lowry could stand; then he went back to tequila. By the third week in October, the Calder-Marshalls had had enough, and announced to Lowry that they were leaving.

Lowry decided to go back to Calle de Humboldt to find a clean shirt in which to say good-bye. Soon afterwards Calder-Marshall, back at the hotel, got a telephone call from a very excited Lowry: "Arthur, the house has been robbed. Will you please call the police?" Calder-Marshall arrived there minutes later, with three police in his car, and two on the running boards. (The police in Cuernavaca, recalls Calder-Marshall, did not have very much to do.) Once inside the cottage, they ran around gathering clues—things like old cigarette-butts of Calder-Marshall's. During all the commotion, Lowry was otherwise occupied: he was trying to change into a clean pair of trousers, and was distressed to find that he had gained so much weight on his latest bender that he could not manage to get himself buttoned up. Nothing, it turned out, had been stolen. Lowry had sounded the alarm because he had looked on a coffee-table in the living room for an old copy of *Story* magazine, and found not one but *two* copies. This was clear evidence that someone had slipped into his house and, while presumably stealing something, had for whatever reason left an extra copy of *Story* as a sort of signature. The Calder-Marshalls apologized to the police, waved to Lowry, and left Cuernavaca as soon as possible.

Alone again, Lowry fell apart rapidly. He made an anguished telephone call to John Davenport in Hollywood. He tried to write a thank-you letter to Innes Rose, at that time his English agent, for sending some small royalties from *Ultramarine;* but succeeded only in scrawling "Please don't say I'm a shit . . . for not writing more when you have dealt so kindly with me. It's just that my mind won't work. . . . I am having a lot to contend with right now." He sat all one day in a place called Charlie's Bar, writing four poor poems to Conrad Aiken. He called these "strictly impersonal exercises on excess," and named them "Prelude to Mammon," and "Prelude to another Drink," numbers one through three. Two are in iambic pentameter, "just to show old Conrad I've did my lessons," in spite of "God and mescal." He ends the exercise by sending his blessing to the Aikens, and then writing, "Come to Charlie's, where I am, soon: old Aggie's got the orrors somethink orful." It seemed to Lowry, as he says in the last line of his fourth poem to Aiken, that he is "the last drunkard"; and, he adds, "I drink alone." Alone he was, to be sure. An American woman who was staying in Cuernavaca at the time remembers seeing Lowry "sitting on a cantina doorstep in the early morning holding his head, waiting to get another drink." [18]

In the first week of December Jan returned from Veracruz, but only to gather her belongings. She had finally had enough: Lowry was a hopeless case, and she felt that she had better get out while she still could. They took the bus together as far as Mexico City. There they put up at the Hotel Canada, and—Jan's firm intentions notwithstanding—Lowry made one more attempt to pull himself together and talk her into another reconciliation.

Dark as the Grave Wherein My Friend Is Laid contains Lowry's partially fictionalized account of his last days in Mexico City with Jan, who is called "Ruth" in this novel (as she had been in *Lunar Caustic*). Up until the last minute, according to Sigbjørn-Lowry, Ruth had kept her decision open, contingent on one thing only: that Lowry stop drinking. "Right off, today?" he had responded. "Yes, now." "Well, my answer to that is No. What do you expect? I'll carry your bag down." This he then did, to the open two-seater with rumble seat belonging to the two Americans who were waiting to take her to California. After one final acrimonious outburst, they parted for the last time, as Jan and her friends drove off, leaving Lowry standing in the doorway of the hotel.

Fortunately, Lowry's is not the only account of the last days and nights in Mexico City. In 1946, *Story* published a short piece by Jan Gabrial called "Not With a Bang." [19] Two months after its publica-

---

18. From a letter on file in the Special Collections Section of the University of British Columbia Library. The letter, dated December 23, 1964, is from a Miss Frederika Martin of Cuernavaca. It is she who quotes the woman who saw Lowry.

19. *Story*, XXIX, No. 121 (September–October 1946), 55–61. In the Notes on Contributors column of the magazine, Jan wrote, "I was born in New York, raised on Long Island, and spent three wonderful years wandering about Europe and North Africa. Have been at various times an actress, millinery model, salesgirl,

tion, when Lowry and Margerie were in New Orleans on their way to Haiti, Lowry ran across the story while browsing in a bookstall. It was an enormous shock to him, he later reported to Conrad Aiken, because it was a cruelly accurate record of his final breakup with Jan. In addition to being this, "Not With a Bang" is a rather good story: Jan was not only no fool; she was talented, too.

It opens with the husband, Michael, being helped by two bellboys into his hotel room, where his very tired wife, Catherine, has given up waiting for him to appear. Why, she wants to know, has he bothered to turn up at all? "I haven't any money, if that's what you want. We're out of money. We don't get a check until tomorrow. Tuesday, remember? You get your father's check on Tuesdays." As they snap back and forth at one another, Catherine discovers that Michael has brought with him, wrapped in his bunched-up coat, a very small and sick puppy. He has bought it from a man in the street, to bring to her. She resents this, because she sees it as a rather meager gesture on his part; she wants the nearness and tenderness of Michael, and he will not give her that. "He would give her a dog, a symbol, saying, in effect, 'This innocent, helpless, gentle creature is my husband Michael; look after it and mop up after it and cherish it and give it your protection.' "

The gesture rejected, Michael angrily gathers up the puppy and lumbers out of the room and down the hall. Sighing with weariness and pity, Catherine dresses and goes out to find him. She takes a cab to a cantina that had once been a favorite of theirs, and he is there, sitting disconsolately on the pavement beside the entrance, looking "forlorn and somehow inevitable, as though all the days of his life had prepared him for this moment of sitting on a curb on this street of violence and tragedies, as though there were no further place for him to go, as though the pages stopped here and there weren't any more." She pleads with him to go back to her, to try one more time, but he refuses: "It isn't any good. . . . The trimmers, not

---

dancer, ghost writer, editorial assistant, secretary (simultaneously to three of Hollywood's nicest people who refute the theory that all movie actors are dopes.) My enthusiasms include Stendhal, Gorki, Somerset Maugham, and a large Persian cat called Jezebel."

good enough for heaven, not bad enough for hell." (Michael, like Lowry, thinks often, apparently, of Dante.) Sobbing over his little puppy, which is still wrapped in his jacket, he goes into the bar. Catherine follows, still pleading, until he turns on her: " 'Let it alone,' he shouted. 'Let it alone, you hear? You think you can control me, don't you? You think you can manage me, don't you? You think I don't see it? Well, let me tell you, I know everything. Because I am a great person, all my life I am a great person, even though the stupid, mealy-mouthed, crumbling little bellboy people will want to destroy me for it.' "

Inside the bar, Michael props himself up at the counter and orders tequila, while Catherine sits at a table. A man at a neighboring table smiles at her, and she is tempted

> I could show Michael, she thought. It would help me to put up with Michael and I might get a night's sleep for a change. I could show Michael, she thought again, bitter because he had resisted her when she was open to him. Then she thought, I'm really too tired to drink. So I'd get back at Michael. I'd wake up tomorrow in a strange room with a guy I couldn't talk to. It isn't much good if you can't talk to him afterward. I ought to know.

So she frowns at the man, and looks back at Michael—to discover that he is leaning on the bar, with his left arm pressed down on his crumpled-up jacket, while he gesticulates with his right. He is crushing the puppy. Catherine jumps up to protest, and Michael, "sensing another rebuke," strikes out at her: "the back of his hand caught her across the neck so that she staggered backward and grabbed a chair to save herself from falling." The dog, they discover, is dead. Michael whimpers. " 'But I loved it,' he insisted, as though that could make all the difference. 'It's my little dog. I was going to look after it.' " As she stares white-faced at him, Catherine sees in him "all the things in him she had cherished, which had grown stretched and loose in his flight headlong from the meaning of his life, his backward flight to a lost world on which the walls of history were closing." She watches for a few more minutes, as Michael rants and postures at the bar; then turns and walks out, leaving him there. She catches herself worrying that someone might steal Michael's coat, then realizes that she doesn't have to worry about that sort of thing any more, that she doesn't have to worry about Michael any more at all:

> And harshly, violently, she began to cry, because she knew that the boat that was Michael had slipped its moorings in her life, and was even now putting out to the darker sea to which she could not follow him.

Even though Lowry was stunned by the harsh accuracy of Jan's story, we cannot be sure whether it was a general or a specific accuracy of which he spoke to Aiken. It sounds like Lowry, and—in so far as we know anything about her—it sounds like Jan. But whether, for instance, there was ever a sick puppy, we shall probably never know. It is possible that Jan was simply recalling the old anecdote of Lowry and the Hepburns' white rabbit. There is no doubt that Lowry did love Jan, and one feels it strongly probable that for one reason or another he ran from her, out of fear, mostly; or drove her away; or hid from her behind alcohol or behind his Work, his Genius. The Michael of Jan's story is absolutely credible as a portrait of Lowry in at least two major respects: his necessity to be loved, but as a child, or a near-helpless pet, and not as a man; and his refusal, or inability, to love anyone except for his various father- and mother-surrogates, and the few old friends who could tolerate his ultimately infantile behavior out of fondness for him, or out of respect for that brilliance that could, at the most surprising moments and in the most unexpected ways, leap out at one.

And Jan? Aiken, one remembers, insisted on thinking of her as "pitiless and faithless." Faithless she may have been; but pitiless she was not. Ara Calder-Marshall described her to me as I think she must have been: "I liked Jan," she said. "She simply didn't know what she was in for. He gave the impression of being a tough guy, just a two-fisted drinker." And he had turned out to be more than she could handle—more indeed, than anyone ought to have to handle. So she had rescued herself, got out in time, instead of being pulled into Lowry's self-constructed maelstrom with him. One would like to wish her well, but she has disappeared.

Now began a real *noche oscura* for Lowry, worse, perhaps even than his Bellevue experience had been. He had announced to the Calder-Marshalls that he intended, as soon as the trouble with Jan was cleared up, to go almost 300 miles south to Oaxaca, where one could find the best mescal in Mexico. Now, shortly before Christmas, he took the bus from Mexico City to what he was to call his own City of Dreadful Night, put up at the Hotel Francia (where D. H. Lawrence once wrote a famous letter to Middleton Murry), and set out to investigate the mescal. Oaxaca, to the average tourist, is one of Mexico's bright spots: a bustling city with a perfect climate, within easy reach of the majestic and mysterious old Zapotecan tomb-cities of Monte Albán and Mitla. But to Lowry it was a nightmare: he listened to a pair of fawns being slaughtered for his hotel's dining room; two enormous turtles, upended, bled to death on the pavement outside the hotel; a vulture perched on his washbasin. With these hallucinations (if they *were* hallucinations) came the old paranoia. He was being lured into drinking, then derided for being drunk. He was being spied upon by men in dark sun-glasses. Within a few days of reaching Oaxaca, he wrote John Davenport from the Hotel Francia:

S.O.S. Sinking Fast by both bow and stern
S.O.S. Worse than both the Morro Castle
S.O.S. and the *Titanic—*
S.O.S. No ship can think of anything else to do when it is in danger
S.O.S. But to ask its closest friend for help.
C.Q.D. Even if he cannot come.

PS
To
Arthur   JOHN:
love and
to Ara   My first letter to you was impounded by the po-
too and   lice here. It contained both congratulation for you
alas   and Clem [20] and commiseration for myself. . . .
to   No words exist to describe the terrible condition
Jan.   I am in.

20. The Davenports had recently become the parents of a daughter, Natalie.

Jan is not responsible for this—but from what I have heard, and from what she has written, I deduce only too perfectly where she is.

This I cannot stand.

In short, I am politely invited to write my wife, care of/Friede.[21] Schadenfreude!

I have, since being here, been in prison three times. . . .

Everywhere I go I am pursued and even now, as I write, no less than five policemen are watching me.

This is the perfect Kafka situation but you will pardon me if I do not consider it any longer funny. In fact its horror is almost perfect & will be completely so if this letter does not reach you, as I expect it will not.

At any rate an absolutely fantastic tragedy is involved—so tragic and so fantastic that I could almost wish you to have a look at it. One of the most amusing features of the thing is that even an attempt to play Sidney Carton has ended in a farce. I thought he was a good man but now my last illusion is destroyed. . . . For obvious and oblivious reasons I cannot write to my family; for reasons so obvious they are almost naked I may not write to my wife. I cannot believe this is true; it is a nightmare almost beyond belief. I looked around in the black recesses of what used to be a mind & saw two friends—yourself and Arthur Calder-Marshall. I also saw something else not so friendly: imminent insanity. I have no conceivable idea how you could help me; or anyone else, unless it is by sending money that will be inevitably ill-spent. I can only send greetings from death to birth and go to pray to what in Mexico they call "the virgin for those who have nobody with. . . ."

Incidentally, I smell. . . .

I am not at all sure about this but in a Mexican prison you have to drink out of a pisspot sometimes. (Especially, when you have no passport.)

21. Donald Friede, their friend from New York days, who was now seeing a great deal of Jan in Hollywood.

But, even without this, I am in horrible danger: & even with it.

Part of this, of course, is imaginary, as usual; but for once it is not as imaginary as usual. In fact danger both to mind and body threatens from all sides.

I am not sure that the danger is not ten times as bad as I make out.

This is not the cry of the boy who cried wolf. It is the wolf itself who cries for help. It is possible to say that this is less a cry than a howl.

What is impossible is to eat, sleep, work: & I fear it may rapidly be becoming impossible also to live.

I cannot even remotely imagine that I am writing these terrible words, but here I am, & outside is the sun, & inside—God only knows & he has already refused.

I cannot see Jan now. But for God's sake see she is all right. I foresaw my fate too deeply to involve her in it.

. . . . I fear the worst, & alas, my only friend is the Virgin for those who have nobody with, & she is not much help, while I am on this last tooloose-Lowrytrek.[22]

Love: & to Clem: & to Natalie: & to Malc.

This letter makes Lowry's condition in Oaxaca appear to be very bad, indeed—and so it was, as far as his drinking was concerned. The remorse over Jan's departure was real, certainly. But the "Sidney Carton" business is pure romance on Lowry's part, as it were by B. Traven out of paranoia. The role fascinated Lowry, and he spent some time in developing it. In a letter to James Stern in 1940, he elaborated on the details of his incarceration:

I was thrown, for a time, in Mexico, as a spy, into durance vile, by some fascistas in Oaxaca (by mistake; they were after another man. How it arose was: he was a friend of mine, very sober and a communist, and they could not believe, be-

22. The verbal play here belongs to Aiken: Lowry "eating" his father, still. The only full publication of this letter is in the Lowry issue of *Prairie Schooner*. A slightly abridged version is in *Selected Letters*, pp. 11–13.

cause he was sober, that he was an agitator and therefore thought he must be me, who was not sober, but, nevertheless, not an agitator, not a communist). I subsequently found it difficult to explain why I had absolutely had to be drawing a map of the Sierra Madre in tequila on the bar counter (sole reason was, I liked the shape of them). Jan had left me some months before, so I had no alibi. On Christmas Day they let out all the prisoners except me. Myself, I had the Oaxaquenian third degree for turkey. Hissed they (as *Time* would say), "You say you a wrider but we read all your wridings and dey don't make sense. You no wrider, you an espider and we shoota de espiders in Mexico." But it was an improving experience. . . . They tried to castrate me too, one fine night, unsuccessfully, I regret (sometimes) to report. It ended up with a sort of Toulouse-Lautrec scene, myself, gaolers and all, simple walking, roaring with mescal, out into the night. They are looking for me yet.

(*Selected Letters*, p. 29)

The idea of suffering wrongly for another's political activities turns up at least twice in Lowry's work: Geoffrey Firmin dies in *Under the Volcano* at least in part because the authorities have found in his pocket his half-brother Hugh's membership card in the *Federación Anarquista Ibérica;* and Sigbjørn Wilderness, in *Dark as the Grave Wherein My Friend Is Laid*, recalls the time when, in Oaxaca, he went to jail in order to protect a communist named Mensch, whom he later helped to escape by way of Veracruz. But, however important this political-scapegoat action was to Lowry, it appears to have no basis in the facts of his life.

Jail does, however, seem to have been real. To his father Lowry sent a letter at about this time in which he tried to appear as cheery and respectable as possible, pluckily overcoming a number of obstacles: "We've had a good deal of bother lately, what with our house being robbed & leaving Mexico. . . . so we decided each to get jobs, Jan going to Los Angeles for a bit, I on assignment here of an innocent nature." Then, having performed this bit of camouflaging, he recounts to Arthur O. Lowry a less fevered version of his imprisonment:

After expressing mildly a liberal opinion I was promptly clapped in the local chokey where, having no papers to prove who I was, I had to remain indefinitely, sleeping with no cover on a cold floor, with a bunch of criminals, who were a great deal more courteous, I am thankful to say, than the municipality.

After a time there it struck even them that it was mildly absurd for me to be there, and I was let out into the outer world only to be shadowed everywhere by detectives wearing dark glasses.

I then assumed dark glasses myself but was promptly arrested again, this time as a spy.[23]

The probability is that Lowry came to the attention of the police through his conspicuous and continuous drunkenness, and that, after some difficulties over his passport (or lack of it) he was put in jail, where he spent Christmas 1937. Whatever did happen, the experience gave him the material for a poem which he seems to have written after 1940, and which he called "In the Oaxaca Jail" :

I have known a city of dreadful night,
Dreadfuller far than Kipling knew, or Thomson. . . .
This is the night when hope's last seed is flown
From the evanescent mind of a winter's grandson.
In the dungeon shivers the alcoholic child,
Comforted by the murderer, since compassion is here too;
The noises of the night are cries for help
From the town and from the garden which evicts those who destroy!
The policeman's shadow swings against the wall,
The lantern's shadow is darkness against the wall;
And on the cathedral's coast slowly sways the cross
—Wires and the tall pole moving in the wind—
And I crucified myself between two continents.

23. This undated letter is on file in the University of British Columbia Library. Near it is another letter, to someone in Mexico City named "Alfred," which goes a little further into the political dimension of Lowry's imbroglio in Oaxaca. Lowry asserts that the Chief of Police there is a Fascist, and that the picture of President Cárdenas displayed in the police station is only a front to hide the sinister goings-on of the police. He complains to Alfred that they have confiscated two letters which he had written to Jan, "the lack of which must leave her devilishly worried."

But no message whines through for me here, of multitudinous,
To me here—(where they cure syphilis with Sloans liniment,
And clap, with another dose.) [24]

One could have written such a poem without ever have gone near
the jail in Oaxaca, to be sure; but Lowry's complaints about harassment and detention are frequent and emphatic enough to make us
believe that he did indeed see the inside of the jail, and probably
over the Christmas holidays—which in Oaxaca last for nine days.
To Aiken, with whom he generally kept his exaggerations to a minimum, he wrote a letter which, though undated, must have been
posted some time shortly after January 4, 1938, his wedding anniversary:

> Dear old bird:
> Have now reached condition of amnesia, breakdown,
> heartbreak, consumption, cholera, alcoholic poisoning, and
> God will not like to know what else, if he has to, which is
> damned doubtful.
> All change here, all change here, for Oakshot, Cockshot,
> Poxshot and fuck the whole bloody lot!
> My only friend here is a tertiary who pins a medal of the
> Virgin of Quadalupe on my coat; follows me in the street
> (when I am not in prison, and he followed me there too sev-
> eral times); and who thinks I am Jesus Christ, which, as you
> know, I am not yet, though I may be progressing towards
> thinking I am myself.
> I have been imprisoned as a spy in a dungeon compared
> with which the Château d'If—in the film—is a little cot-
> tage in the country overlooking the sea.
> I spent Christmas—New Year's—Wedding Day there.
> All my mail is late. When it does arrive it is all contradiction
> and yours is cut up into little holes.
> Don't think I can go on. Where I am it is dark.
> Lost.
>
> Happy New Year,
> Malcolm
> (*Selected Letters*, p. 15)

24. *Selected Poems of Malcolm Lowry*, ed. by Earle Birney with the assistance of
Margerie Lowry (San Francisco, 1962), 28.

239

Whatever else in this letter is true, there is one really curious deviation from veracity: Lowry's assertion that his only friend in Oaxaca is the syphilitic who believes him to be Jesus. The fact is that Lowry did during his stay in Oaxaca establish one of the major friendships of his life, with a mysterious Zapotecan man named Juan Fernando Márquez. This obscure figure, who was to appear in *Under the Volcano* as Juan Cerillo (and as Dr. Vigil as well), and in *Dark as the Grave Wherein My Friend Is Laid* as Juan Fernando Martínez, and who may *really* have been named Fernando Atonalzin, came to represent for Lowry his ideal of manhood: a true (as opposed to literary) hero. In a short essay called "Garden of Etla" which he wrote for the June 1950 issue of *United Nations World* (pp. 45–47), Lowry described his friend, whom he calls Fernando Atonalzin:

> About twenty-four when I knew him, Fernando stood six foot three—thus contradicting ethnology, for the Zapotecans are supposed to be shorter than the Mixtecans—and in features he rather resembled an Italian. I have said that he was, and he always thought of himself as, Zapotecan, but he owned some Spanish blood.
>
> For sleeping under the stars and eating tortillas and beans he had a literal preference; doubtless he would have been equally at home at the Hotel Crillon in Paris. He had attended Mexico University where he had been trained as a chemist; apart from this, and a visit to New Orleans, where a relative was in the diplomatic service, he had spent most of his life in Oaxaca. With somewhat of the careless, noble bearing of a king, Fernando would have met with scant opposition had he claimed descent from his regal namesake.

In *Dark as the Grave*, Lowry elaborates a little more on Juan Fernando's ancestry, and then provides us with vague (and possibly invented) information about his friend's recent past:

> But what is important is that his father had been a man of intellectual persuasion, his mother had been a pure-blooded Zapotecan, and that somewhere among his collateral relations was an English renegade, who had drunk himself to

death in Oaxaca, where he was allowed to remain because he was under the protection of the British Consul, likewise a relative. Fernando had been trained as a chemist: but the horrible incident of his operation on his sister, for whom his father would not call a doctor, his father who even stopped the operation before Fernando was finished, had resulted in his leaving home forever.

(*Dark as the Grave*, p. 59)

If this account is accurate, it would explain why such a sophisticate as Juan Fernando would have been working at a job to which he was frankly dedicated, but which was hardly the profession of an educated man: as a rider for the *Banco Nacional de Crédito y Ejidal*. The *ejidos* were tracts of land belonging in common to all the natives of a village, and were a Mexican tradition going back to pre-Hispanic times. Until the presidency of Lázaro Cárdenas, the *ejidos* were for the most part too small and infertile to be of much use to the mass of Mexico's peasants. But Cárdenas began an extensive program of land reform, under which he distributed millions of acres of land (taken mostly from enormous haciendas) to the peasants. The communal management of this appropriated land was organized around the old *ejidos*, for the purpose of "the production of commercial crops on a profit-sharing basis." [25] Financial administration of the rejuvenated and expanded *ejidos* was handled through the *Banco Nacional de Crédito y Ejidal*. As Lowry describes it in "Garden of Etla," this bank differed from another bank in that

> instead of your going to it, it went to you—if you were a remote Oaxaquenian village—largely on horseback on those days, and across wildly dangerous mountainous terrain.

Carrying money from the central bank out to its branches in the *pueblos* in the mountains and deserts was done by horsemen, who encountered danger not only from the wildness of the terrain, but also from the enraged owners of the haciendas, who employed their own bands of brigands to harass—and often, where possible, to

25. Henry Bamford Parkes, *A History of Mexico* (Boston, 1950), 403. I am grateful to Professor Dale Edmonds for directing me to this work.

kill—these riders. This was the fate of the peon who dies by the side of the road in *Under the Volcano:* he had been a rider for the *Banco Ejidal*, and had been mortally wounded either by some *hacendado's* goon squad, or by members of the fascistic militia. Such a rider was Juan Fernando Márquez, and he gloried in the job: for its rigors, and for the ways in which it allowed him to help his people. According to Lowry, his friend had often to act not only as horseman, but also as doctor, and translator: fourteen different languages are spoken in the state of Oaxaca, and Juan Fernando spoke them all, "including Chinanteco, Popaloco, and Zoque, and the mournfully majestic old Spanish of the Conquistadors, such as is still used in San Lorenzo Abarrotes. In addition he spoke Italian and French fluently and had mastered English, though in speech he had a haunting habit of putting prepositions ('I like to work them with') at the end of a phrase" ("Garden of Etla," p.47).

According to Lowry (*Dark as the Grave*, p. 216) he met this remarkable Zapotecan in the Covadonga Bar in Oaxaca. Before long they were spending their mornings fencing at the *Banco Ejidal*, and their afternoons drinking at the cantina that Lowry was always in his writings to call the Farolito (though in *Under the Volcano* he was to move it to the pueblo of Parián, to serve as the setting for the humiliation and murder of Geoffrey Firmin, the Consul). Apparently Juan Fernando was, in addition to being an adventurer, chemist, and linguist, a drinker. (In *Dark as the Grave* he announces mournfully to Sigbjørn Wilderness on the day of their first meeting that he is a drunk.)

At least once during the winter of 1937, Juan Fernando took Lowry with him on one of his excursions. Lowry recalled this journey in the "Garden of Etla" essay:

> I once had the privilege of being invited on one of his more hazardous journeys, in fact from Cuicuitlan to Nochixtlan, via Parián, where at that time there was no road. On the way (this was 1937) we ran short of a horse and rather than wait longer for another, Fernando insisted I use his while he ran. A mere matter of twenty miles, mostly slightly uphill. Moreover every time I prepared to dismount he would urge

his horse, who was enjoying the whole thing after a rest, to canter once more, and when I would inquire if he were not getting tired, Fernando would laugh, and had the breath to do so uproariously. He liked, he said, to run his horse with.

He was off on this adventure with Juan Fernando long enough to write back to Antonio, manager of the Hotel Francia in Oaxaca, to complain about having been spied upon there, and to ask that Antonio "conserve carefully even down to the most crushed piece of newspaper" everything in his room. He was, presumably, concerned lest the "spies" steal his manuscripts, or perhaps even his passport, which he had left in a desk drawer.[26]

Before the end of the year Juan Fernando was transferred to the branch of the *Banco Ejidal* in Cuicuitlan, and Lowry returned to the Hotel Francia and his paranoia. They never saw one another again, but they corresponded. One letter, written from a cantina operated by one José Cervantes, begs Juan Fernando to return and help him with his financial and drinking problems. Another, published in *Selected Letters*, appears also to be written from a bar. It begins, "I am here because there is much hostility in my hotel," and continues with the sort of complaint of which we have already seen several instances:

> I am trying to do some work here but my life is so circumscribed by your detectives who walk up and down the street and stand at the street corner as though there were nothing better to do than to spy on a man who is unable to do anything anyway and never had intentions of doing anything but be good and love and help where help was necessary that I am rapidly losing my mind. It is not drink that does this but Oaxaca. . . . If I do not drink now a certain amount there seems no possible doubt that I shall have a nervous breakdown. If I have that, equally I shall find myself in that Goddamn jail to which I seem to be progressing almost geometrically, and as you know, when one goes there sober, one comes out drunk.

26. This letter is on file in the Special Collections Division, University of British Columbia Library, as is the letter to Juan Fernando mentioned in the following paragraph.

Juan Fernando answered Lowry, in a letter dated January 6, 1938. Lowry preserved it, and later incorporated most of it in *Dark as the Grave* (p. 60). In the letter, Juan Fernando says to Lowry that "Now, at this time, I am not able to go and have a talk with you, so if you are so kind write me a note and send it to me. Tell me your tragedies of this day and also tell me if you are drunk. . . . Did you keep out of drinking today to give that present to your wife on your wedding day? Is there no more remedy than cut out our friendship if you are continuing on drinking?"

Lowry's visit to Oaxaca was, then, crowded: during the time when he was writing of being spied upon as he drank in one cantina or another, he was spending time in town with Juan Fernando, and then was off with his friends for trips to the towns in the hill country in the northern part of the state. During Christmas, probably, and possibly New Year's as well, he was in jail, for whatever reason. By the time of his wedding anniversary, he was writing letters of complaint again, this time to Aiken and to Juan Fernando. How, or precisely when, his visit to Oaxaca ended, we do not know. The letter to the manager of his hotel, written certainly in December, asks that the following month's mail be sent to him care of Wells, Fargo, Ltd., Avenida Madero, Mexico City; so it is reasonable to assume that Lowry intended to be there sometime around the end of January or the beginning of February.[27] Paranoia or not, he was wise to want to get away from Oaxaca. Lowry almost certainly exaggerated the extent of his persecution, and contrived the business about playing Sidney Carton for a fugitive communist; but the political situation in Mexico was rapidly worsening, and—especially in provincial cities—any aliens whose behavior made them conspicuous were often subjected to various kinds of official and quasi-

27. In the Special Collections Division of the University of British Columbia Library is a letter to Lowry from Ann Watkins, a literary agent, sent to the Hotel Francia, and dated January 31, 1938. Miss Watkins had obviously been given parts of *Under the Volcano* to read (possibly by Davenport) and she here expresses her enthusiasm for what she has read. She asks that Lowry make her his agent, and concludes by remarking that publishers often question her about his work. It is possible that it was this heartening letter that made Lowry decide to leave Mexico; and the date of the letter suggests that Lowry left Oaxaca in February.

official harassment. And Lowry's drinking habits must certainly have made him conspicuous, to say the least.

President Cárdenas, an extremely idealistic and altruistic socialist, had a large following among the labor unions and the *peones;* but he was, predictably, hated by the landowners and industrialists of Mexico. By the mid-Thirties rightist opposition to Cárdenas was strong enough to make Nazi Germany think that there might be a real possibility of overthrowing his government, and installing one that would provide them with an active ally in America. By 1938, moreover, Franco's army was doing so well in Spain that the Spanish Fascist organization, the Falange, could begin turning some of its attention to the support of like-minded Central and South Americans. Soon there were springing up in Mexico paramilitary forces of some strength, all eager to help destroy the country's benevolent and progressive leftist government. German and Spanish agents were everywhere, often acting as "advisors" to police forces and military garrisons in provincial towns and cities. It was not a good time to be an Englishman in Mexico, especially if one were a very vulnerable drunk with no influential friends—indeed, with only one friend, and he a member of the *Banco Ejidal,* a prime target of Fascist sabotage and terrorism. Mexico City in 1938 was a safer place for Lowry than Oaxaca.

By April 1938, however, he had left the capital and gone to Acapulco. The political situation by now was such that leaving the country entirely would have been distinctly indicated. In March Cárdenas had ordered the expropriation of all foreign oil companies. Great Britain promptly protested this, to no avail; and in April, diplomatic relations between the two countries ended.

All this turmoil seems to have gone right over Lowry's head. All we know of what he did in Acapulco during the spring and early summer of 1938 comes from Margerie Lowry's recollections of what he told her over the years, and one senses in most of this a fair amount of fabulating on his part. He told Margerie, for instance, that during one part of his stay in Acapulco he was, with his father's allowance, supporting the film actress Gilda Gray and her lover, who had fallen on hard times in Mexico. One day, tired of the responsibility of providing for them, and fed up with life in general, he had decided to kill himself by swimming out to sea until, overcome by fatigue, he drowned. The beach he chose for this was the Playa de Hornos, the one used in the afternoons by bathers (the beach for mornings was La Caleta, on a neighboring bay). The attempted suicide ended in failure when he reached the open water outside the bay, was attacked by a barracuda, escaped by racing to Roqueta Island, nearby—from which he was rescued by Gilda Gray, in a motorboat.

More believable than the Gilda Gray story, however, is Lowry's very circumspect and almost unwilling recollection of having known in Acapulco a man named Bousfield. This person, an American whom Lowry later portrayed in *Dark as the Grave* as "John Stanford," was for the rest of Lowry's life to signify real human evil. We know about the shadowy Bousfield only that he and Lowry got into several scrapes of which Lowry was truly ashamed, and which he—normally the most open and indiscreet of men—would never discuss with anyone. He *did* tell Margerie only one thing about Bousfield: that when the American Consul in Acapulco borrowed the manuscripts of *In Ballast to the White Sea* and *Under the Volcano* to read, and then left Acapulco without returning them, Bousfield very casually broke into the consul's home at night and stole them back for Lowry.

In late June Lowry went back up to Mexico City (accompanied by Bousfield, if Lowry is working from fact in *Dark as the Grave*, p. 233), where his father's agents succeeded in reaching him at the Carleton Hotel. John Davenport, in his unpublished preface to *Ultramarine*, claims that in September 1938, Lowry was deported from Mexico as an "undesirable alien." This can scarcely be true, however. For one thing, Lowry wrote to A. Ronald Button, in the 1946 letter already cited, that he left Mexico in July 1938, "and was admitted to America at Nogales" (*Selected Letters*, p. 94). For reasons I have already mentioned, Lowry would certainly have been as careful as he could be about facts and dates in this letter; and there is no reason to question his account. According to Lowry, he had gone to Acapulco because he had been wrongly advised that he could have his visa extended only at the place at which he had originally entered the country. He also intended to leave Mexico from Acapulco, via a ship of the Panama Pacific line. He applied for the visa extension, and after the inevitable bureaucratic confusions was told he would have to go to Mexico City in order to procure it. Because his current visa had expired, he had to travel in company with Acapulco's chief of Migración, whose way he had to pay. Eventually, a six-month extension was granted. He was now free in Mexico City, but without money, and in debt—for what, he does not say in his letter to Button. In any case, the problem was soon resolved: "My parents having become anxious about my health put a lawyer at my disposal and my income was paid through him, and before I left Mexico any and all debts were paid in full." When he applied for a visa to re-enter Mexico in 1946, it was immediately granted him—which it almost certainly would not have been if he had been deported as an undesirable alien.

Most likely, Arthur O. Lowry became alarmed by what he heard about his son's difficulties; and stepped in, via his agents, to extricate Lowry from the various webs in which he had enmeshed himself. It is possible that Conrad Aiken, or even Jan, might have written him that his help was needed—though Lowry's own letter to his father from Oaxaca was by itself sufficiently bleak to suggest the need for intercession. Mr. Lowry might also have been disturbed by political conditions in Mexico, especially since he did have business interests in the country, and must have been quite aware of all the ominous activities there. Whatever the reason, he stepped in, and made sure that his lawyers in Mexico City paid his son's bills and put him on the train for Nogales in July.

In Mexico, Lowry had lost his wife, gone further into alcoholism, come close to madness, been mocked, threatened, and—briefly—imprisoned. His disastrous twenty-month's stay ended with his being put on a train as if he were a delinquent adolescent who had misbehaved in school and was being sent home in disgrace.

And yet, eight years later, when beginning his notebooks for *Dark as the Grave* (p. 223), he was to record that "these terrible things were not so terrible in memory. So unimaginably frightful and intense had been his suffering that he looked back upon those days almost as he looked back upon the beauty and health of their Canadian life. They were days as beautiful as vultures circling in high sunlight, as beautiful as death that flies just for the love of flying."

He could take away with him his vision of the terrible beauty of Mexico, of misery in settings of natural majesty, of real gentleness side-by-side with explosive cruelty, of the *barranca* at the base of the volcano. He could take with him his memory of Juan Fernando Márquez, who always was to represent to Lowry the kind of man he would have liked to be: simple, compassionate, daring—a man of such inner peace and strength that drinking only enhanced his pleasure in living. And he was taking with him out of Mexico the embryonic form of *Under the Volcano*—which made all the anguish seem worthwhile.

So far as Arthur O. Lowry was concerned, his youngest son had by
now proven beyond all doubt that he was incapable of managing his
own affairs. "The old man" (as Lowry always called him) resolved
once more that young Malcolm's financial affairs, especially, had to
be directed by other, more responsible hands. So the lawyers who
put him aboard the train in Mexico City provided him with his tick-
ets from there to Nogales, and from Nogales to Los Angeles by
way of Tucson. At the depot in Los Angeles he was met by Benjamin Parks, an attorney who had been retained by the senior Lowry
to serve as his son's guardian and legal agent in that city. (Why Arthur O. Lowry should have chosen Los Angeles as his son's destina-
tion, no one knows—except that Jan was there, and had written
to him about a divorce settlement, and he might have decided that it
would be quicker and cheaper to have one lawyer handle both the
divorce and the day-to-day managing of the prodigal son.) At any
rate, Lowry found on his arrival in Los Angeles that Parks had had
him declared an incompetent. He was registered immediately at the
Normandie Hotel, and given a ridiculously small allowance for
meals and cigarettes; and Jan, through the good offices of Mr.
Parks, was given a sizeable cash settlement by Arthur O. Lowry, in
lieu of alimony. Lowry later told Margerie that Jan took the money
and ran to Santa Barbara, with an old friend from the New York
days. Lowry never saw her again. Two years later, Margerie remembers, Jan wrote Lowry in Dollarton to say that she and her
friend were planning a visit to Vancouver, and suggested that they

all get together—no hard feelings over past troubles, and so on. Lowry threw the letter in the fire, and that was that.

To keep himself occupied in Los Angeles, Lowry worked on *The Last Address*, hired (with his lunch money, presumably) a woman at his hotel to type the current draft of *Under the Volcano*, and began several poems about his Mexican experience. A year later, he wrote about this period to Conrad Aiken that Jan had left him, "a sort of Lear of the Sierras, dying by the glass in the Brown Derby, in Hollywood" [1] ; and one supposes that this statement is a trifle hyperbolic, given his poverty at this time. He will perhaps be pardoned a small lie which he told now, in the 1938 letter to Nordahl Grieg mentioned earlier (*Selected Letters*, p. 15): that he had finished a book of poems, called *The Lighthouse Invites the Storm*, and that he would send a copy to Grieg if he could find one. The implication was that the book had been printed, whereas it had only just begun to be written.

Both John Davenport and Arthur Calder-Marshall had long since returned to England, and Lowry seems during his first eleven months in Hollywood to have made only one friend: J. Garnet Wolsley King, a fellow Englishmen who also was staying at the Normandie. Through his fiancée, Jack King had come to know a former starlet named Margerie Bonner. For some long-forgotten reason, on the evening of June 7, 1939, King, wanting to speak with Margerie, asked Lowry to call her at her home on Beechwood Drive in Hollywood and set up a meeting. Margerie's telephone rang: "Is this Margie?" Lowry asked. "This can't be Jack," she said. "No, it's Malcolm, a friend of Jack's. He wants to see you." Lowry suggested that he and Jack take a bus to the intersection of Western and Hollywood Boulevard, and that she meet them there. Margerie agreed, got in her car, and drove down. She was there first, parked her car, and stood waiting at the bench by the bus stop. A bus ap-

1. Letter to Aiken, dated spring 1940, *Selected Letters*, 18. The date given is incorrect, since Aiken's response to this letter is dated October 29, 1939. It should, then, be dated at probably no later than the middle of October 1939. Mr. Parks has since died, and his records are not accessible; so there seems to be no way at this time to discover the precise terms either of Jan's settlement or of Lowry's allowance.

peared, stopped. Lowry, alone, dismounted and walked straight up to her. "Margie," he said. "Malcolm," she replied. They threw their arms around each other. Minutes later, Jack King—who had been detained—arrived, and found them still embracing. If there is such a thing as love at first sight, this was it.[2] And if it sounds melodramatic, so be it: both Lowry and Margerie turned out to be people who thought of domestic life in melodramatic terms. Their happy times together were full of billings and cooings, private signs and words, secret jokes and games, small tendernesses that invariably sound cloying to the outsider. Their battles were as if directed according to the formulae of soap-opera: bravura gestures, gnashed teeth, stalkings from rooms, tossings of heads, brooding silences, and so on. But this was how they chose to conduct their marriage; and, when one considers what storms they survived together, to scoff becomes rather more difficult. We should not, most especially, be too ready to think of their married years as a modern-day Daphnis and Chloë idyll, for those years were far too full of frustration and confusion and—sometimes—resentment. Lowry, moreover, was much too much of an ironist to be unaware of how faintly ludicrous he looked as lovesick swain; and Margerie was, in her own way, just as tough and relentless as Jan had been.

Margerie Bonner was born on July 18, 1905, in Adrian, Michigan. Her father, John Stuart Bonner, was a diplomat, newspaperman, foreign manager of the Page Woven Wire Fence Company (Adrian's only industry), and lieutenant colonel in the AEF. During the Great War he somehow lost the family's money, so that Margerie's elder sister, Priscilla, had to leave finishing school and go to work. The work her mother chose for her was in Hollywood, as an ingénue. Priscilla was sent to stay with friends in Los Angeles, while Mrs. Bonner remained in Chicago to see Margerie through her first (and only) year of high school.

---

2. For most of the rest of this book, accounts of Lowry's day-to-day life come from countless interviews, in person and by correspondence, with Margerie Lowry. The reader can therefore assume that, unless material is specifically cited as coming from another source, the information being used derives from Margerie Lowry's generally meticulous recollections.

In two months Priscilla, at eighteen, had become the leading woman of one Charlie Ray. In 1919, impressed with her elder daughter's success (Priscilla was by then starring opposite the comedian Harry Langdon), she decided to see how well Margerie, now fourteen, could do in the same profession.

She did quite well, especially as an adolescent horsewoman in westerns, and had minor roles in dozens of films produced by Universal, Paramount, MGM, and Columbia. For several years she was able to support not only herself, but her mother, father, and sister (whose career had ended suddenly, when her eyes were damaged by Kleig lights) as well. But when talkies came, she was, like so many others, dropped. In 1923, when she was eighteen, Margerie was married briefly, to Jerome Chaffee, whom she describes as having been "wealthy but spoiled rotten." After her divorce in 1925, she worked her way through the next ten years, at first in films, and later at a variety of other jobs, chiefly writing radio scripts and doing work on animations at Walt Disney Studios. In 1939, at the time of her meeting with Lowry, she was a sort of general factotum for the actress Penny Singleton, then starring in the "Blondie" movies. She had also begun writing mystery stories, but had had no luck in publishing them. In 1939 she was a strikingly pretty, tiny, and youthful 34-year-old (curiously like Jan in appearance if not manner, as several of Lowry's friends who knew both women have observed), and the lonely Malcolm Lowry who met her at the bus stop must have seen in her his best hope for the future—which perhaps she was.

At any rate, Lowry and Margerie took up with one another immediately and uxoriously for the rest of the time he was in Hollywood—not a long time, as it turned out. In July, a few days before Lowry's thirtieth birthday, Benjamin Parks decided that Lowry would have to leave the United States. The reason he gave to Lowry was that it was time for a renewal of his visa, and that this could be accomplished only by his leaving the country and reapplying for admission. Mexico was nearer than Canada, but inadvisable for a number of reasons, not the least of them being Arthur O. Lowry's unwillingness to turn his son loose there again; so it was decided that Lowry should go up to Vancouver, stay there for the required amount of time, then return to California. Since, however, it was not necessary to go through all of this traveling about in order to renew one's visa—Lowry could have done it without leaving Los Angeles—one must suppose that Parks had his reasons for wanting Lowry out of the way, at least temporarily. Arthur O. Lowry, stung by the loss of the money he had settled on Jan, had been grumbling in his letters to his son about the avarice of American women; so perhaps he had complained to Parks as well, prompting the attorney, who knew about his ward's new romance, to take Lowry away from temptation.

And more than temptation—scandal, of precisely, the sort that a man like Lowry's father would have found most distasteful. On July 24, Jan, acting as plaintiff, had Lowry served with a summons to appear within ten days before the Superior Court of the State of California. In her Complaint for Divorce, which she had submitted on July 19, she had stated that "during the married life of the parties hereto defendant has treated plaintiff with extreme cruelty and has been habitually intoxicated, and for more than one year last past has not supported or contributed to the support of the plaintiff." Following the serving of the summons, Lowry was ordered to appear in court on August 19. Probably fearing a loud and revelatory trial, Parks determined to spirit his client out of the country, plead no contest by reason of default, and pay Jan the small sum the court awarded her: $250. He resolved to drive Lowry to Vancouver himself, not trusting Lowry to be able to get there without supervision.

Parks arrived at the Normandie Hotel on the scheduled day of their departure to find Margerie in Lowry's room, helping him to pack. The typist was still down the hall, working on the second draft of *Under the Volcano;* but Parks was in too much of a hurry to permit Lowry to collect the typescript. He assured Lowry that he would pay the typist and forward the draft to him in Vancouver, and fairly shoved Lowry into his automobile. As they drove off, Lowry hung out the window, calling to Margerie, "I'll come back, I'll come back."

Once in Vancouver, Parks turned Lowry over to a Canadian attorney, A. B. Carey, who, as an Oxford Grouper, would have seemed a suitable guardian to "the old man." The arrangement with Carey was to be the same as it had been with Parks: Carey was to receive all of Lowry's monthly allowance (which amounted to around $100), to pay for Lowry's room out of this, and to permit him a very small sum for meals and incidentals. He found Lowry a room, and appears to have done little else to supervise his charge.

Lowry remained quite docile for a month, spending his money only on telephone calls, wires, and daily air mail letters to Margerie. Finally he decided that he must go back to Los Angeles. He bought a bus ticket and set out, quite drunk, for California. He was intercepted at Blaine, Washington, reeling and incoherent, and was refused entrance to the United States. Practically speaking, this meant that he would now have to wait another year before reapplying; psychically speaking, the damage was even greater: Lowry, always terrified of anyone in authority—especially in *uniformed* authority—from now on added "Turned Back at the Border" to his litany of fears and woes, and always hereafter commenced sweating and trembling days before he had to pass through the Customs of any country. He sobered up, and then sent a cry of anguish to Margerie: if he could not get to her, then she must come to him. Margerie promptly quit her job with Penny Singleton, collected the few hundred dollars she had saved, got a statement from her mother indicating that her daughter was in fact an American citizen, and set off on August 29, 1939, to rejoin Lowry.

When she reached Vancouver she found that Lowry had managed to become involved with a cockney taxidriver and a person named Maurice Carey, who were now taking care of him. The cabbie soon disappeared, but they were to be for some time in the care of Carey, a retired sergeant-major in the Canadian army who lived with his wife, a teenage son, and a set of infant twins in a seedy section of West Vancouver. Lowry had somehow made Carey's acquaintance, and told him his troubles—including the information that Margerie would soon be arriving, and that she would certainly be staying with him. Carey assured Lowry that he would be happy to have him and Margerie as paying guests in his house on West 19th Avenue, and that he would be able to arrange the whole business with the *other* Carey, Lowry's guardian. A. B. Carey was apparently happy to have the retired soldier take Lowry off his hands, and agreed to turn over most of Lowry's allowance to him each month, in payment for room and board. (Maurice Carey charged Lowry $125 per month, $25 more than his father was sending from England; but Carey knew that Margerie would be able to make up the difference.)[3]

When Margerie arrived in Vancouver they went to Carey's house, where he rented them a single room in the attic. He announced then that he would be able to let Lowry have only $2 each week as his personal allowance, food costs being what they were. Lowry and Margerie spent most of their time huddled in their attic room, hiding from Carey and his ménage, which he described to Conrad Aiken as "a family of six, including a loud-speaker, a howling wind which rages through the house all day, twins, and a nurse. I forgot the dog, the canary, and a Hindoo timber merchant, educated at Corpus Christi —you can't get away from Oxford—who sleeps in the woodpile in the basement, hoping, with his fine Oriental calm, that one day he'll be paid for the wood" (*Selected Letters*, p. 20). In this same letter, Lowry says that he is "very near a mental and nervous collapse, though cheerfulness is always breaking in." It was obvious that they would have to find work, but since neither could secure a permit, this was impossible—unless, as he wrote James Stern, Lowry were able to become "a scab lavatory attendant in Saskatchewan" (*Selected Letters*, p. 31). Finally he grew desperate enough, after a month in the cold attic, to write John Buchan, Lord Tweedsmuir, who was Governor General of Canada, to say (as one writer to another) that he was stranded in Vancouver, and to ask whether there were not any sort of writing work he could do. Buchan promptly sent him a check for $50, as well as a letter of introduc-

---

3. Maurice Carey's own description of his relationship with Lowry can be found in his article, "Life with Malcolm Lowry," in *Malcolm Lowry: The Man and His Work*, ed. George Woodcock (Vancouver, 1971), 163–70.

tion to the managing editor of the Vancouver Daily Province. Lowry did in fact write a couple of short pieces for the newspaper, one of which was on "Mr. Chips" at The Leys, and this brought in a little money.

The check from Lord Tweedsmuir, though, led to one of those unpleasant scenes to which Lowry was so prone. Buoyed up by the prospect of a little money, he decided to go into downtown Vancouver to cash the check. Several hours later, he returned to Carey's house, distraught and barely able to face Margerie. He had, it seems, given the $50 to a bookie, who had put it on what he said was a sure thing at Lansdowne Race Track. But instead of doubling his money, he had lost. Back at Carey's he became more and more despondent, until Margerie, hoping to cheer him up or at least to distract him, suggested that they go for a walk. Lowry agreed, and they went out into the October night. After sixteen blocks, Lowry was no better: he was full of remorse and self-hatred, and beginning to turn on Margerie for all manner of unfounded reasons. Suddenly he began running, tore around a corner, and disappeared. Margerie was shocked—this was the first time she had seen Lowry being anything other than cheerful and tractable—and, after wandering about for a few minutes, she returned to Carey's house. When he had not returned by midnight, she set off after him, in a cold rain. She walked north, until she came to Connaught Bridge, and remembers thinking, "How could I find one man in this city?" By one o'clock she had returned to the corner from which Lowry had bolted. She kept on walking, in the first direction that occurred to her, and eventually came to "a dark, dingy, old house." It was, of course, a whorehouse; and Lowry was, of course, there. She found him very nearly passed out, wearing only his undershorts, lying in a filthy bed. He had sold his clothes to buy a bottle of gin, which he had mostly emptied. Margerie says that she climbed in bed with him to keep him warm, and stayed with him until he awoke in the morning. If he had been remorseful after losing the $50, now he was on the edge of despair, crying out, "What can I do? I'm finished!" Margerie, who was to become very expert at handling this sort of unpleasantness, reassured him, woke up the proprietor of the house and told him that if Lowry were not immediately given something to wear, she would call the police. The proprietor quickly located an old suit and a pair of shoes. They left, Lowry doubled over with shame and hangover. After walking for perhaps a block toward Carey's house, he stopped, and said he could go no further without a beer. Margerie had no money, so Lowry stood on a street-corner and begged passersby for the ten cents a draft beer would cost him. After he had drunk his beer, Margerie guided him back to the Carey's, and put him to bed in the attic room.

When he had recovered enough to write again, he began composing the long and urgent letter to Conrad Aiken mentioned earlier, describing their plight and suggesting that Aiken get in touch with Arthur O. Lowry (who apparently at this time was refusing to correspond with his son, or at least refusing to acknowledge Lowry's pleas for compassion). Aiken should convince him that his son was not the moral abomination he supposed, and suggest that he, Aiken, resume his duties as Lowry's guardian. Lowry, who somewhat understandably regarded Vancouver as "the most hopeless of all cities of the lost," wanted badly to escape from British Columbia and come East—to Toronto, or Montreal preferably, since he could not hope to return to the United States until the fall of 1940. He had even toyed with the idea of returning to England in order to enlist, and did in fact during the first month after war was declared stop briefly by the recruiting office in Vancouver. The medical examiner found several immediate reasons for rejecting him, and he was turned down flatly and emphatically. Lowry could not have been too disappointed, for he says to Aiken that "eventually I shall probably have to join up and fight for the forces of reason but at the moment I am more concerned with preserving my own, which I consider no less valuable and certainly as remarkable as Hitler's."

His advice to Aiken on how to engineer his protégé's escape from his bondage in Vancouver is detailed and ingenious: he offers a twelve-point program, all centering on the basic assumptions that he is miserable, exploited, deceived, maligned, and unable to work in Vancouver; and that the money he is receiving from his father is not sufficient to keep him alive. In eastern Canada he would be accessible to New York publishers, in a healthier climate, under the more understanding care of Aiken, and—in an appeal to A. O. Lowry's patriotic spirit—better able eventually to reach England and join the fighting. However Aiken made his plea, though, he was under no circumstances to mention Margerie to his father, who "would not take kindly to my marrying again so soon after one marital disaster." Aiken did write Lowry's father, telling him that he had "hatched a genius," and that he and his wife would undertake to look after Lowry if he should be able to come to Massachusetts—which, of course, he could not do. Aiken could only reply to Lowry, as he did on October 29, 1939, that he could lend him no money, being himself deep in debt; but that he would alert his agent, Bernice Baumgarten, to Lowry's existence, and ask her to read whatever could be sent her from Vancouver. Perhaps if she were able to interest a publisher in what Lowry had written, then he could be as it were *summoned* to New York for "professional conferences"—the sort of command that neither a businessman father nor a Customs official would be likely to discount.

Lowry did send what he had available (*In Ballast to the White Sea*, *The Last Address*, and a couple of stories) to Bernice Baumgarten, but she reported to Lowry that she found it all "too cerebral and unsaleable." Fortunately, before Lowry had time to feel too depressed about this judgment, he received some good news: Jan had definitely gone through with her plans for divorcing him, and on October 11 had been granted an interlocutory judgment. This meant that the divorce would become final one year from that time, thus making Lowry free to marry Margerie. And arriving almost simultaneously with this news came a package containing the typed second draft of *Under the Volcano*. He promptly sat down and, almost daily for the next nine months, worked on a third draft.

The second draft was 360 pages long, divided into twelve chapters. In Chapter One, we find a French film producer, Jacques Laruelle (his name had originally been "Lacretelle," but is changed here, in Margerie's handwriting, to what it was to remain in further drafts), talking to a Mexican friend, Dr. Vigil. It is the Day of the

Dead, possibly in 1937, and as they sit chatting on the sundeck of the Hotel Casino de la Selva above Quauhnahuac, preparations for the fiesta are going on in the town below them. The two men are discussing their late friend, the Consul; his wife, Priscilla (originally "Enid," but again changed by Margerie); Hugh, a young man who hadn't gone to the Civil War in Spain after planning to do so; and Yvonne, the Consul's daughter. Lowry wastes no time in establishing the symbolic importance of this Consul: Laruelle exclaims on page four to Vigil, "My God, if I only had the time to put a character like the Consul into a film!"

> "Yes, supposing, Doctor, that all the suffering and chaos and conflict of the present were suddenly to take human form. And to become conscious of itself! That is the impression I would want to give of my man: a man to whom, like Jesus, the great betrayal of the human spirit would appear in the guise of a private, anguishing betrayal. And you would realize somehow too that this character of mine was yet aware of all the agonies with which the human lot would become presently involved. And, my word, now that I think of it, Doctor, it *does* almost seem possible that it already happened! Supposing that all these horrors of today before they became part of our lives had suddenly convulsed upon themselves to create a soul, and then that soul had sought a body, and the only body it had found sufficiently photophobic for its purpose was the Consul's." He paused. "If I could only convey the effect of a man who was the very shape and motion of the world's doom," he went on, "But at the same time the living prophecy of its hope!"

They discuss this Promethean figure for some time, and then Laruelle leaves for town, walking across a bridge over the "terrific drop" into the *barranca* that cleaves Quauhnahuac, passing the decaying palace of Maximilian and Carlotta (Lowry does a fair amount of re-arranging of Cuernavaca's geographical and architectural details throughout), and stopping in the entrance to a cinema as an autumn thunderstorm breaks—as one had broken on the night of the Day of the Dead, the year before. He slips into a *cervecería* next door for a drink, where the manager hands him a small

The *barranca*, Cuernavaca.

book of Elizabethan plays that had belonged to the Consul. In it is a
letter the Consul had partially written to Priscilla, who had deserted
him, commenting on her infidelity. (She had, it soon develops, most
recently cuckolded him with Laruelle, here in Quauhnahuac.) Laruelle lapses into a semi-awake state in which he dreams vaguely
about a quarrel between Hugh and Yvonne, a conversation he had
once—perhaps—had with Priscilla, and a bus-ride Hugh had
told him about, during which he and Yvonne had seen an injured

peon lying by the side of the road. As Laruelle thinks of appropriate lines from Marlowe's *Dr. Faustus* and Shelley's *Alastor*, the
chapter ends.

Chapter Two opens precisely one year and a day earlier than the
time of the first chapter, with Yvonne Ames, the 24-year-old
daughter of the Consul and Priscilla, in her hotel room in Acapulco.
She has just arrived from California aboard the *S.S. Pennsylvania*,
and intends to head inland to Quauhnahuac shortly. She stares at
herself in the mirror, and is displeased with the cover-girl prettiness
of the blonde who stares back at her. She broods, and broods, and
broods: all of the characters in this novel are—at least inwardly
—very articulate, and given to long periods of morose reminiscences and semi-organized philosophizings. She broods about her unsatisfactory education at Girton College, Cambridge, with abortions
on every vacation; her depressing love-affairs; and her drunken
father. She thinks of Hugh Fernhead, a Stanford post-graduate
student she had known first in Spain (they had met at the Alhambra) and then later in Paris. Hugh seems to have been unique, in
that she did *not* sleep with him. As she is thinking of these things, a
constant racket is going on outside her window: a passing English
sailor is telling someone the story of the captive pigeon from *Ultramarine;* and an American in the next room is talking loudly about
Alabama farmers. (Lowry and the Aiken montage-effect, again.)

Yvonne walks out of the hotel that evening, and runs into none
other than Hugh, who has dropped out of Stanford and is now
traveling aimlessly around, perhaps on his way to fight for the Loy-
alists in Spain. He suggests that they go together to Quauhnahuac,
which they do, in a plane flown by the American whom she had
overheard earlier, and whom Hugh identifies as a right-wing rab-
ble-rouser, down to help foment a Fascist revolution in Mexico.

In the third chapter, Hugh and Yvonne walk through Quauhnahuac the next morning looking for her father, whom they find sitting in the bar of the Hotel Bella Vista, gray-haired and rather
distinguished looking, with his neatly trimmed beard and his evening clothes which he is wearing because he had been, the evening
before, to a charity ball, and has not yet returned home. He looks,

Hugh thinks, like "King Lear in full face, Hamlet in profile," and manages somehow to convey the impression, while sitting perfectly still, of being "at least fifteen times drunker than anybody he had ever met." Yvonne is struck by the curious glare in his eyes, as though he "saw into hell." The two young people take the Consul back to his house, which seems almost exactly like Lowry's cottage on the Calle de Humboldt. The Consul and Yvonne talk unhappily, in Yvonne's bedroom, about the Consul's failed marriage, and especially about how unhappy his drinking had made Priscilla, who is now in California arranging a divorce. Yvonne asks him why he drinks, and is annoyed by his answer: "Because I must get a lot of fun out of it after all."

Chapter Four has to do chiefly with Hugh and Yvonne, who saunter about the lawn, inspect the *barranca*, and find a stable nearby. They rent a pair of horses, and ride out into the plain that lies between Quauhnahuac and the foothills of the Sierra Madre. A woolly black dog and a small group of foals accompany them as they ride. We learn, among other things, that Yvonne had left France for America in order to have an abortion, and that the Consul had at one time been something of a scholar: he had taken his degree in languages at Liverpool, lectured at the University of Helsingfors on zoology, speaks Finnish and Hungarian, and had taught for a time also in Lithuania. On their way back, Hugh and Yvonne stop briefly at the ruins of the Borda Gardens, and meditate about the sad fate of Maximilian and Carlotta, doomed lovers of an earlier time.

In Chapter Five the Consul, waking to find Hugh and Yvonne gone, wanders down into the ruins of *his* garden, and stops to speak with Mr. Quincey, his American neighbor. Quincey is amiably courteous, and slightly obtuse: the Consul is being his most allusive, and it all goes over Quincey's head. Dr. Vigil appears, as hungover from the charity ball as the Consul himself, and they speak about drunkenness. Hugh and Yvonne return, and they decide to travel to Chapultepec to see a bull-throwing (a sort of *corrida* and rodeo combined) which is to take place there that afternoon.

Slightly later (we are in Chapter Six, now) Hugh lies on the day-bed on the porch and thinks about his wasted youth (though he cannot be more than twenty-five) in America and Europe, and listens on his radio to an American station playing a jazz record featuring Joe Venuti and his Hot Five. The Consul, in the next room, doesn't like the music, and is annoyed at Yvonne, who is bathing as she harangues him still about his various failures. Then, in what is probably the most successful scene in this draft, the Consul, who is shaking too badly to shave himself, asks Hugh to do the job for him. Hugh does so, and he and the Consul become for the moment great friends—even conspirators, against the petulant Yvonne, who is making disgusted sounds as she dresses nearby. The Consul tries taking a swig of bay rum to calm his nerves, vomits, and then feels marvelously well. Hugh is amazed, in fact, to see how healthy the bathed and shaved Consul looks, and how young:

> It was as though the passionate narcissism which drinking and his almost purely oral response to life entailed had fixed his age at some time in the past, at that unidentifiable moment, perhaps, when his persistent objective self, weary of standing askance and watching his downfall, had silently withdrawn from him altogether, like a ship secretly leaving harbour at night.

At the last moment, with all three dressed and standing on the porch, they cannot decide what to do. Where shall they go? Or shall they not go at all? Is Yvonne's hat suitable, or should she change it? Ought they to have one last drink? (The Consul does so.) As the Consul is delivering one of his rather pompous lectures on flora and fauna—this one is about the suicidal tendencies of scorpions—Hugh begins laughing at their sudden inertness, "although another self warned him that this doldrums in which they found themselves was a reflection of something else not so funny: a reflection of a common state of mind of people everywhere waiting like this, waiting under the volcano, for the order to kill, for the word to change, for the permission to begin to accomplish everything at once, for the license to continue to do nothing forever." (Such reflections as these are frequent in this version, and seem,

Laruelle's house in Cuernavaca, 1946.

whatever their eloquence, to serve chiefly as a means whereby
Lowry could explain his book to himself, and to his hypothetical
readers as well. One enjoys them, but one understands why most of
them were excised somewhere along the way toward the publisher's
acceptance of the final draft of the novel.)

In the following chapter they finally do set off for Chapultepec,
but their way takes them past Laruelle, who insists that they stop
by his place for a drink. His house, which looks as if it comes from
"some stills of *The Cabinet of Dr. Caligari*," has windows which
"are set in the wall like the separated halves of a chevron," and is
really composed of two towers, "on the top of each of which was a
minaret." On the wall nearest the street is an inscription in gold
leaf: "No se puede vivir sin amar"—one can't live without loving. The words come from Fray Luis de Leon, the sixteenth-cen-

tury Spanish ascetic poet-priest who was executed by the Inquisition for translating into Spanish *The Song of Songs*, but the Consul maintains that someone with a taste for Somerset Maugham must have done the inscription on Laruelle's wall. It was here that Priscilla had slept with Laruelle, and the Consul, recalling this, grows quite surly. (And he has just the minute before received a postcard from Priscilla, written months before, expressing hope in a reconciliation.) They sit for a time in Laruelle's house, then Hugh and Yvonne leave to walk around the *zócalo*, watching the fiesta until the time to take the bus. The Consul and Laruelle follow them shortly afterwards, and an almost violent quarrel breaks out when Laruelle tries to talk the Consul into behaving better. The Consul becomes enraged, says to Laruelle, "You have my full permission to go and shit in your sombrero," and calls his erstwhile friend a "mingitorio [urinal]Cellini" and a "dungcart." Laruelle disappears, and the Consul climbs aboard a loop-the-loop ride called *La Machine Infernale* (in this draft Lowry kept the French; later the ride got its Spanish title), which takes him up above the crowded park, and for a moment holds him dangling there, upside down, as all his money, his passport, and his pipe drop from his pockets. When all of these are returned to him by surprisingly courteous children, the Consul goes into the Cantina Terminál, and orders a tequila and a marijuana cigarette from Senora Gregorio, the proprietress.

Chapter Eight is essentially a minor revision of the story "Under the Volcano," with the diction and imagery considerably tightened, and—as is the case throughout this second draft—the political element stressed: Lowry, surprisingly, was not only aware of what was going on in Spain and Mexico, but actually rather well informed, and very nearly a gifted prophet about, say, what a victory for Fascism in Spain would do to the cultural life of that country. Here, the *pelado* is clearly identified as a Spanish Fascist, and the murder and robbery of the *Ejidal* horseman takes on all sorts of political attributes:

> The Consul saw that this was not only a man dying, it was a
> nation, it was mankind. And he saw too that these were not

merely men talking, they too were nations, nations that argued over trivialities while mankind perished from the face of the earth.

The startling, but obscure, conclusion of the short story—the old man carrying the still older man on his back—is taken from this chapter, and made the conclusion of the next, where it is an appropriate summation of a great many instances of the grotesque and obscene.

This ninth chapter, focusing chiefly on the bull-throwing at Chapultepec, was intended by Lowry to do two things: to allow for a display of heroics by Hugh, while the Consul's jealousy begins to be noticeable; and to provide Yvonne with another opportunity to brood. The first is successful; the second is not. Lowry was never to be able to imagine or portray with any credibility what went on in the mind of his fictional women, and generally he knew better than to try very much of this sort of thing; but here we have again Yvonne with her depressing past—the number of abortions she has had seems to grow with each chapter—and most of this was judiciously excised.

Chapter Ten begins comically, as they laugh at the absurd English menu of Señor Cervantes at his Salón Ofélia. Then Hugh, who is slightly humorless, does not notice that the Consul is becoming surly again, and tries to engage him in a reasonable political conversation. But the Consul is eloquent in his contempt for such "indoor Marxmen" as Hugh, and shouts his detestation of everyone who "has ideas," and who tries to impose those ideas on others. But he has had too much to drink, and becomes confused: suddenly it seems that "Yvonne *was* her mother, his own Priscilla, Hugh a rival, a Laruelle, to be dispatched." He goes after Hugh savagely; but Hugh beats him at his own game of allusions, by showing that he knows his Tolstoy better than the Consul; and the Consul, having lost face before Yvonne (for whom he has somehow been competing), can only counter-attack, in the cruellest way that he knows: in one of the harshest, ugliest passages in modern fiction, he attempts to humiliate them both. He taunts Yvonne for having had her abortions, and calls her a whore; then he turns on Hugh and mocks his naïveté, attacks the sanctimonious attitude of the United States, and tears into all the leftist idealists who see in Spain a real and just cause:

> To the front line with all of you! And all your poets who (in three years or so) will be preaching war, while at night they furtively burn their great poems about men living in peace like brothers, on which they've been working for the past decade (but which nobody has seen). Yes, all those who will mysteriously discover another sort of courage overnight. Au Rancart! To the tumbril of war with them. And with you too! First!

Hugh can only stand in hopeless rage—he cannot bring himself to strike Yvonne's father—and cry out, "Cockeyed old necrophile!" and "insulting old corpse!" The Consul, his tirade ended, pays the bill and limps out, toward the dark forest.

The eleventh chapter concerns Hugh and Yvonne, and it is easily the weakest in the entire draft. They think of following the Consul, to protect him from himself, but seem to forget this good intention in favor of wandering aimlessly about in the forest, having one of the most improbable "intellectual" conversations in all literary history. Within the space of a very few pages, they manage quickly to drop no fewer than 37 names, of which the following list is a sample: Plato, Nietzsche, Schopenhauer, Chaucer, Donne, Beethoven, Kafka, D. H. Lawrence, Rilke, Lorca, Rabelais, Shakespeare, Mozart, Stendhal, Proust, Hart Crane, and Walt Disney. Not bad, one reflects, for two people who have drunk a great deal and who have just been through an extremely traumatic scene with the Consul. But all this intellectual muscle-flexing (on the part of Lowry, of course, trying to get it all in before the end of the book) leads them, not to the Consul, nor to any illumination other than that which comes to them when they lie down together in the undergrowth, and, as the chapter ends, begin to make love. In the published version Lowry retained something of the final paragraph, although Yvonne's fate was entirely different:

> She saw the waves again coming in that morning in Acapulco, each one a little higher on the beach than the last, and somehow all the weight of the laboring world with its journeys and injustices and sadness was being lifted from her soul, until she was unconscious of any burden, or of her own body, or of thought, knowing only that she was being borne upwards, irresistably, towards a haven swarming with golden moons and wandering lights.

The final chapter is, intentionally, chaotic. The Consul crawls and stumbles through the forest until he comes to the town of Parián, home of a group of fascist militiamen, and site of the forbidding cantina, El Farolito. Upon entering the cantina the Consul is handed a packet of old letters from Priscilla which the proprietor, Diosdado, has been saving for him. He takes his drink to a table at which a German named Bunge is sitting, and begins to read through the letters, which are utterly convincing in their expressions of love for the Consul. Shaken by them, the Consul rises and withdraws further into the dark recesses of the cantina, where he is accosted by Maria, a prostitute. He goes to her room, where, "kneeling on the bed grimed with footmarks, he felt his passion wavering." To distract himself, he tries reading off the saint's days for each day of December on the calendar hanging on the wall before him. But it is no good: "he had arrived at his feeble crisis, a crisis without possession, almost without pleasure. As with a shamed grimace, he gave Maria, who was laughing at him, her few pesos, a knowledge of what hell really was blazed on his soul."

Back in the forward part of the bar, the Consul is not long in encountering another sort of hell: a small group of militiamen in the crowded, noisy room begin to pick on him. Their leader seems to be the Jefe de Jardineros (improbably, the Chief of Gardeners), who demands to see the Consul's passport, which identifies him as William Ames. Since he has already a few minutes earlier identified himself to this chief (here named Fructuosa Badrona) as "William Blackstone, the man who went to live among the Indians," he is in trouble. Badrona accuses him of being a spy: "You say you a wrider. You are no wrider, you are de espider and we shoot de spiders

El Farolito.

in Mexico." (Lowry always insisted that the Spanish word for
"spy" was "espider," not "espía.") Suddenly Badrona comes to represent for the hysterical Consul everything that has in his lifetime
contrived to humiliate him, and he swings at the man. Then, as he is
pummelled and pushed toward the door of the cantina, he delivers a
long denunciation of everyone, himself included. Outside, he ac-

cuses Badrona of murdering the *Ejidal* rider and stealing his horse (which, with the number seven branded on its rump, is tethered outside the bar); and Badrona draws his revolver and fires it at the Consul. He falls to the ground, dying, but thinking and amalgamating disparate experience to the end. He sees himself as another sort of *pelado*, as another St. Dismas, and thinks of appropriate music by Mozart, Gluck, and Bach. Then, consciousness finally fading, he dreams of ascending Popocatepetl, and dies. He is thrown into the nearby *barranca*, and a dead pariah dog is tossed in after him.

Anyone who knows the published *Under the Volcano* at all well will recognize it from this description of its earliest surviving full-length version. The basic content of each chapter is the same, from 1938–39 to 1947. Descriptions and dialogue are often identical. The chief differences lie in character definition, allusive content, importance of political reference, amount of generalizing explanation, and—in the case of Yvonne, at least—in the outcome. The most extensive single change was in doing away with Priscilla, changing the Consul and Yvonne from father and daughter into husband and wife, and making Hugh the Consul's half-brother. But an alteration more important, even, than this identity-revision, took place in the *texture* of the novel, as Lowry's mythopoeic bent led him into ever-increasing intricacy of allusion. Many of the important images were already there, in very nearly their final form; but dozens more were to be added—signs, natural phenomena, snatches of poems and songs, pictures, remembered books and films, shadowy figures appearing, disappearing, and reappearing—until *Under the Volcano* finally became not a novel at all but a kind of monument to prodigality of vision. In 1939 it was on its way, but it was still very clumsy, talky, even boring and pretentious.

One ought to make a final observation about this draft before moving on, as to the evidence it provides us of Margerie's participation in Lowry's writing. In a letter he wrote on October 19, 1939, to Margerie's mother in Los Angeles, he says that "we are working together on a book" (*Selected Letters*, p. 18), and his use of the pronoun is precise. Margerie's emendations were not limited to changing the names of characters. Before one is very many pages into this draft he begins noticing her revision not just of occasional words, but of phrases, too—candle flames which originally "began to blow hesitantly" were made instead to "waver incessantly," for instance. She inserted whole sentences, usually having to do with natural description ("Toward the east the stars were fading where the sky was green"), and gave marginal warnings to Lowry about over-use of certain words: "watch 'ghastly,' boy." One can usually see that her revision is in the direction of smoothness. Whether or not one regards this as an improvement in a writer in whom smoothness was not necessarily a virtue, is another question. In any case, Lowry came more and more to rely on Margerie for this sort of editorial work as the years went on. He would often hand her a page he had just written and say, "Margie, kindly tell me what the hell I'm talking about here." Margerie would take the page, and type from it her "Margie-version," which the two of them would then compare with Lowry's initial version. From this Lowry would write a third version, presumably more coherent (and always smoother) than the first.

As the winter of 1939–40 dragged on, Lowry and Margerie sat in Maurice Carey's attic, working first at cleaning up the second draft, and then moving on to a third, which they did not complete until late spring. Basically, this text was not significantly different from the previous one. It was longer (404 pages), chiefly because of the accretion of surface detail, but the characters and their situations remained largely as they had been. Jacques still dreamed his expository dreams in the first chapter; Yvonne still was allowed so unnecessarily to mope in Acapulco in the second, and was once more permitted to nag the Consul in the third and sixth. In the fourth chapter it began to become apparent that Lowry was now taking Hugh more seriously, as an important member of the configuration that was ultimately to become quadrate (the other members being the Consul, Yvonne, and Laruelle). In the second draft he had been intelligent, but rather bland and vacillating. Now Lowry places more emphasis on Hugh's experiences at sea, and adds to his past several items that came from Lowry's own life, real or imagined. Hugh was still American, and very young, but there are more than a few signs that Lowry was beginning to think of him as perhaps even a brother.

Later, in the sixth chapter, we see Margerie's hand changing Yvonne from daughter to wife, and Hugh from friend of Yvonne to brother of the Consul. (Since Priscilla still exists, in the wings, it is probable that this emendation was made after the novel had been returned from Lowry's agent in 1941, and not at the time of original revision of the second draft.) For the rest of the chapter, there are a number of inserted pages, all having to do with the changes in relationships. They were clearly done on a different typewriter from the one Margerie used in typing the basic third draft, which helps to confirm one's suspicions that these emendations were made some time after the draft itself. For the rest of the draft, we see—always in Margerie's hand—more and more evidence of the metamorphosis. On a page inserted into Chapter Six, Yvonne calls the Consul "Jeffrey," and this name, or "Jeff," appears written in with consistency from that time on. Near the end of the chapter, when Hugh marvels at how young the Consul looks, Margerie adds a sentence: "Well, why shouldn't he! After all, he was only ten years older than Hugh himself." It is entirely possible, one must conclude, that this rather radical alteration of the novel was Margerie's idea. One can in any case say with certainty that it was Margerie who executed the changes.

In the seventh chapter, as the Consul hangs in inverted helplessness over the fiesta when the infernal machine temporarily stops, we find Lowry's first direct reference to the occult. The Consul "stopped, imagining himself hanging head downward from the crippled maple tree in the front garden, upside down like the clown in the Tarot Pack, in the branches condors brooding like bishops." One should not, however, assume from this single allusion that Lowry had by this time already set about making himself an adept in the Tarot, let alone the Cabbala, the I Ching, Rosicrucianism, or whatever: anyone of his student generation who had gone to Oxford or Cambridge without coming up against *The Waste Land* must have been totally without interest in literature.[4]

4. Lowry had, however, since undergraduate days been a fan of J. W. Dunne, P.D. Ouspensky, and Charles Fort. In a letter to Margerie's mother of April 16, 1940, he recommends Dunne's *An Experiment with Time*, Ouspensky's *A New Model of*

By the beginning of the ninth chapter the relationship-changes have ceased, and Yvonne is once more daughter, Hugh suitor, and the Consul (no longer "Jeffry") is once again the doomed *senex iratus*, just as he had been in the second draft. This would suggest that after trying for eight chapters to see whether the third draft could be improved simply by the insertion of occasional new pages, and by frequent marginal corrections, Lowry and Margerie realized that they would have to write an entirely fresh draft. Before he put the third draft aside, however, Lowry made one curious and unfortunate excision. In the twelfth chapter, as Geoffrey stands at the bar in the Farolito, he ponders over the antithetical natures of real life and symbolic life:

> Life was a forest of symbols, was it, Baudelaire had said? But, it occurred to him, even before the forest, if there were such a thing as "before," were there not still the symbols? Yes, before! Before you knew anything about life, you had the symbols. It was with symbols that you started. From them you progressed to something else. Life was indeed what you made of the symbols and, the less you made of life the more symbols you got. And the more you tried to comprehend them, confusing what life was, with the necessity for this comprehension, the more they multiplied. And the more they multiplied, that is, disintegrated into still more and more symbols which in the first place never had the slightest intention of meaning anything, let alone of being understood, just like human beings in short, the more they liked it, until, in the end, life itself . . . fluttered away abruptly, leaving an abstraction behind.

One begins by seeking symbols, connections, in order to understand life. But if one is not wary, he is caught up in the symbols themselves, which, after all, obscure life more than they illuminate it. And the more one is caught up in them, the more the symbols proliferate, until life is totally gone, leaving behind it a fantastically

---

the *Universe* and *Tertium Organum*, and Fort's *Lo!*, *The Book of the Damned* and *Wild Talents*. These are not, strictly speaking, studies in occultism, but they would certainly have been provocative to one who did not find the mortal world enough—as Lowry never did.

spun-out web of symbols, beautiful perhaps, but after all only a network of empty abstractions. The deleted passage takes on real poignance when one realizes how precisely it describes not only the Consul's, but also Lowry's, intellectual malaise. Lowry, like Dana Hilliot and Bill Plantagenet, longed for a life lived simply, with order and symmetry; and yet the life he conjured up for himself and his protagonists had increasingly to be read like a cryptogram, until it was no life at all. He was drawn to the poetry of Rilke, but he could never understand what Rilke meant by his celebration of *die Dinge*, the small things, rocks, trees, vines, plates, the authentic simple forms, which had all their own meaning inside themselves —or no meaning at all. Lowry had no gift for simplicity. He admired Lorca, but he would not have known what to make of the absolute self-sufficiency of such a statement as "I used to believe that the world was a place where bells were always ringing, and that white inns were along all the roads, with blonde serving girls in them, sleeves rolled up to the elbows."[5] He had in him that which prohibited him from stopping at the thing in itself; the thing had to *mean*, had to relate to another thing, and so on until order and symmetry were lost in a maze of arcane correspondences and brilliant conceits. One must begin to speculate that perhaps Lowry might have used alcohol as, among other things, a mental anesthetic: a means of stopping or at least slowing down this beautiful but ruinous construction of labyrinths.

In addition to turning *Under the Volcano* into a forest of symbols, Lowry occupied himself during these months with the composing of eloquent appeals to his father for release from his bondage in Vancouver. Arthur O. Lowry wanted to see his son grovel; and the son was more than willing to do so if only grovelling would get him out of his penury, and from the shame of being a thirty-year-old man with the legal rights of an infant. In one letter written on April 22, 1940, Lowry summarizes the shortcomings of his Cana-

5. Federico Garcia Lorca, *Los Titeres de Cachiporra, Cuadro IV, Obras Completas* (Buenos Aires, 1965), 753. ["*Yo me creía que por el mundo estaban siempre repicando las campanas y que en los caminos había blancos paradores, con rubias muchachas remangadas hasta los codos.*"]

dian guardians, hinting at difficulties with them which he must, "being a gentleman, keep dark." He has reformed: "I have kept my head, shut my door, not drunk, worked like the very devil himself." He is determined to prove himself to his parents, during the few short months he has left him before the war claims him. He *must* write during the time that remains, and he must get away from Vancouver in order to do so—preferably to Conrad Aiken, who can best help him with his progress on the major work which he proposes to dedicate to his father. He concludes:

> I would write, keep you informed of my doings, and we could, even though at a distance, somehow, if we can bury the past, re-establish all our relationships on the sincere, decent happy plane on which I have brought low through my inexperience and folly. And this would make mother happy! Which I want, yes, sincerely, above all! I am yelling at you over a thousand miles of mine-infested Atlantic and 4 thousand miles of land. *I am cooperating with you. Will you help? Drink, follies, are a thing of the past. This is the last chance.*

Arthur O. Lowry answered this on May 7 with a short and deflating letter which begins, "I thank you for your long and interesting letter of 22 April," and which continues, "The main issue in my mind is that you now shew some contrition for your past treatment of your father and mother and if this is maintained it will I hope lead to happier relations between us than your conduct has formerly made possible." The Treasury's restrictions on the sending of money out of England are such that, even if he wished to do so, he cannot make the necessary arrangements for a change of residence for Lowry. If, however, Lowry were able to convince him that he were now able at least partially to manage his own affairs, then perhaps he would be able somehow to arrange for the monthly remittance of $100 to be resumed.

Lowry answered this piece of parental blackmail by saying that he understood his father's difficult position, and would be grateful for whatever small favors could be done for him. On May 31, "the old man" replied that there now was very little he could do, the

Treasury situation being as it was. "However," he concludes, "the self-reliant tone of your letter makes me feel you won't take this news too badly, and you may be sure that your determination to look after yourself will not weaken my own willingness to help you when I can."

When the money from England stopped coming in, A. B. Carey gave Lowry what was left in his account (about $200), and, with no money coming in for rent, Lowry had to vacate his attic lodgings. He had now to find another apartment, one which would be acceptable to the pious A. B. Carey, and yet would be the sort of place which would permit him and Margerie to live in what all of Vancouver would have regarded as a state of sin. Luckier than usual, he found such a place in mid-April. It was in a home on West 11th Street owned by an Englishman named Smith, a member of the British Israelites (a group who believed themselves to be descendants of one of the lost tribes of Israel). Lowry told Smith and his wife that he and Margerie were married, but that his father disapproved of her, and would send him his allowance only if he lived apart from his wife. To the Smiths this sounded monstrous (as indeed it would have been, if true), and they took Lowry and Margerie in, giving them a comfortable suite composed of bedroom, bath, and kitchenette. Fortunately, a door in the bedroom led to the cellar of the house. A. B. Carey had to give his approval to the arrangement before Lowry could officially move in, so he came to inspect one day near the end of April, having given Lowry only a few minutes' warning that he was coming. Margerie hurriedly packed her suitcase and ran with it into the cellar, where she hid while Lowry showed Carey around.

The Smiths were very kind to them, and gave them enough quiet and privacy to complete the third draft of *Under the Volcano*, which Lowry sent off on July 27, 1940, to Harold Matson, whom he had met in 1936, and who was now Lowry's agent in New York. This done, Lowry wanted a vacation "by the seaside." When Margerie suggested that they were perhaps not in any financial position to afford such a spree, Lowry looked through the classified section of the Vancouver *Sun*, and found an advertisement for a cottage on the shore of Burrard Inlet and Indian Arm, in the small hamlet of Dollarton. The rent was $15 a month. Margerie went out that afternoon by bus, and was met at the Dollarton stop by Percy Cummins, who ran the general store there. The setting was magnificent: behind them rose Seymour Mountain; around them was thick pine forest, obviously full of wildlife; and a hundred yards or so down a path through the forest were the rocky shore and the clear, glacier-fed water of the inlet. The only flaw in this Edenic scene was the fisherman's shack that Cummins showed Margerie: it was about to collapse, and filthy to boot. Discouraged, Margerie returned to Vancouver. Two days later Cummins called: he had found just the place for them. It was a cottage nearby, owned by a group of Scotsmen who used it only on occasional fishing vacations. They went out, looked, and took it immediately. The rent here, too, was $15. All of this wooded point was owned by Vancouver's Harbour Board, which had for some time allowed squatters to build small cottages there without charging them anything for the land they used; so that the squatters could afford to rent their cottages to others for next to nothing.

Their "shack," as Lowry called it, was neat, clean, and well-painted. It consisted of two rooms, the larger of which had windows on three sides, with a porch across the front. In this room was a cook-stove, and a table, with two chairs, placed against the shore-side windows. The smaller room contained a small double-bed, a sink, and a certain amount of storage area. Thirty feet uphill toward the Dollarton Road was an outhouse. On August 15 they began what they thought was to be a month's vacation in Dollarton, but which actually became a qualified, Lowryan sort of idyll which did not end until they left for the last time in August 1954.

There were perhaps ten or fifteen such "shacks" on the shore at Dollarton, most of them used only by summer vacationers. The other inhabitants were fishermen, who usually stayed on over the winter months. For the rest of August and half of September, Lowry and Margerie went on picnics, explored the woods, read, and generally recuperated from the effects of their depressing months in Vancouver. After Labor Day all the vacationers departed, leaving the point to the few fishermen. Lowry was reluctant to return to Vancouver, and suggested to Margerie that they stay on in Dollarton over the winter. She, who was only just beginning to understand the mysteries of the cook-stove, was at first reluctant; but he persuaded her, got in touch with the Scots owners and arranged an off-season monthly rent of $7.50, and brought the rest of their belongings, which consisted of not very much but a few thousand pages of manuscripts and Margerie's typewriter. They went back into Dollarton and spent most of their remaining money on wool trousers, flannel shirts, green and white lumbermen's jackets, wool socks, and thick-soled boots.

Lowry passed the waning days of fall swimming whenever the water of Burrard Inlet was not too icy. Their shack was built partially on piles, and sat above the shoreline, so that when the sixteen-foot tide was in, Lowry could dive off the porch into the water. The Scotsmen had left behind a small, sturdy rowboat, and Lowry delighted in taking Margerie for brief cruises which before long were not too brief: one morning in late fall he rowed her ten miles up Indian Arm, ate a picnic lunch with her on a small island in the middle of the water, and rowed her ten miles back to the shack for supper. He was hardly drinking at all, now—just the odd beer during the day—and his remarkable constitution, given this sort of exercise, quickly brought him into splendid physical condition.

When the first winter fog came, it turned out to be what Canadians call a "freezing fall": the whole forest turned to crystal, and the windows of the shack were completely frozen over. It occurred to Lowry that they would need wood for the stove (especially since it was their only source of heat), and that he did not have the slightest idea of how to chop wood. Luckily, one of their few neighbors was an old fisherman, known to them only as "Sam," who took them in hand before they froze, and showed Lowry how to gather kindling (Lowry did not know what kindling was) and use an ax. Having once discovered the pleasure of chopping wood, he was hard to stop: Margerie remembers an enormous pile of pine logs nearby, which grew larger daily until she found other tasks for Lowry—like washing windows, which he loved doing ("It makes

Lowry at Burrard Inlet, Dollarton.

Margerie, Dollarton, August 1942.

Sam the Fisherman, November 1946.

me feel like a god," he said); or walking up the path to get water from the pump at Percy Cummins' garage, which Lowry did not enjoy so much, as it entailed contact with the world beyond the forest.

In a gesture of welcome, old Sam appeared one stormy night bearing a large basket of live giant crabs. They thanked Sam profusely, and as soon as he had left began frenziedly to kick, push, and sweep the scrabbling dozens of crabs out onto the porch, and then down to the beach. Unfortunately, the tide was out, and they had to chase the crabs across the rocky beach to get them to water. Sam undoubtedly heard (and probably saw, with delight) this noisy spectacle, and thenceforth brought his new neighbors only cooked crabs. Since by May the English Treasury was allowing no currency at all to leave Great Britain, and Lowry's small capital was growing smaller with every trip up to the general store for provisions, such gifts from Sam must have been more than welcome.

When he was not learning to cope with wilderness life (and Dollarton *was*, however near Vancouver, still wilderness: their woods were full of deer, foxes, and raccoons; and occasionally even bears and cougars wandered through), or taking lessons in birdwatching and astronomy from Margerie, Lowry was waiting optimistically for word from Harold Matson about *Under the Volcano*, and concentrating on writing a number of poems for the projected volume, *The Lighthouse Invites the Storm*. This work, which has not been published, and probably ought not to be, ultimately contained 170 poems, and is divided into seven sections. The first, "The Roar of the Sea and the Darkness," seems to consist chiefly of sea poems, and to draw mostly on Lowry's early voyages for their material. The second and third sections, "Thunder Beyond Popocatepetl" and "The Cantinas," represent the Mexican experience. The next three, "Venus," "The Comedian," and "Songs from the Beach: Eridanus," deal primarily with their life in Dollarton. And the final section, "The Language of Man's Woe," presumably is drawn from the last three years of travel, and the final months in Sussex.[6] The divisions are not, however, precise; neither are they chronological. It is often impossible to determine the date of composition of a Lowry poem: whenever he wrote one, Margerie typed it and added it to the stack of pages that grew slowly over the years, without any indication of when it had been written. So, though one knows that, say, "Xochitepec" was clearly not written *before* Lowry went to Mexico, one cannot say with any pretense of accuracy when *after* the Mexican period it was composed. Except for scholarly interests, this hardly matters. Though Lowry thought of himself as a poet primarily, and always claimed that he intended eventually to cease writing prose, and to spend his declining years at his true vo-

6. Only four of these subtitles (the first, third, fifth, and sixth) were Lowry's own. The others, and the ordering of the poems within the divisions, are the inventions of Lowry's friend, Earle Birney—who, with Margerie's assistance, edited in 1962 a volume called *Selected Poems of Malcolm Lowry* which was published by San Francisco's City Lights Books. This edition contains seventy poems from *The Lighthouse Invites the Storm*, and probably shows Lowry at his best as a poet.

cation as poet, it is all too obvious to the reader of *The Lighthouse Invites the Storm* that, though Lowry's prose could be majestically poetic, his poetry is prosaic in the extreme: leaden, in fact, when it turns from doggerel to high seriousness. The best one can say for it is that it is, indeed, confessional: it is clearly Malcolm Lowry speaking with absolute openness in his own voice. But the characteristic diction of all but the best of his poems is so archaic, and the rhythms so stiff, that any sense of urgency or turmoil—or life—in the confessions is lost. In "The Days Like Smitten Cymbals of Brass," for instance, a poem from the first section, we have

> When I was young, the mildew on my soul,
> like it chanced to me,
> or Melville's Redburn, to take that soul to sea
> And have it scoured.
> Ah! the days like rust smitten from iron decks
> were beaten into one deafening roar
> of sunlight and monotony.

But this is an early poem. So, one hopes, is "Reflection to Windward," which begins

> A grey day of high tempestuous seas
> As homeward rolls the *Dimitrios N. Bogliazides*,
> Each weary hand a sweat-ragged Ulysses.

Typical of all but the very few good poems is one from the third section, called "Self-Pity":

> Pity the blind and half but yet pity
> The man at the bank in the pitiless city,
> The man at the bank who can't sign his own name—
> Though he call on his courage and posthumous fame—
> This man with the terrible shakes far from home.
> Ah pity this man with his pitiful income
> Arrived now from far, from far sources of shame,
> For a man at a bank who can't sign his own name,

Though he sweat till the ultimate Manager came
—Pity the blind, and pity the lame,
But pity the man who can't sign his own name!

Sometimes Lowry manages in his poetry to touch the grandeur of *Under the Volcano*'s language and imagery—most often, appropriately enough, in his Mexican poems—and when he does so he can produce a brooding sort of loftiness, as in "Thunder Beyond Popocatepetl":

Black thunder clouds mass up against the wind,
High-piked beyond Popocatepetl;
So with force, against whose swollen metal
The wind of reason has the heart pinned
Till overbulged by madness, splitting mind . . .
Or, drifting without reason, see mind's petal
Torn from a good tree, but where shall it settle
But in the last darkness and at the end?
Who take no arms as the good wind's defender
You psalmists of despair, of man's approval lease,
Reason remains although your mind forsakes
It; and white birds higher fly against the thunder
Than ever flew yours, where Tchechov said was peace,
When the heart changes and the thunder breaks.

He does this in "The Volcano is Dark," too, even though the central vision is clumsily executed:

The volcano is dark, and suddenly thunder
Engulfs the haciendas.
In this darkness, I think of men in the act of procreating,
Winged, stooping, kneeling, sitting down, standing up, sprawling,
Millions of trillions of billions of men moaning,
And the hand of eternal woman flung aside.
I see their organ frozen into a gigantic rock,
Shattered now. . . .
And the cries which might be the groans of dying
Or the groans of love—

On the whole, though, one must conclude that, while Lowry could parody Eliot ("Mr. Lowry's Good Friday Under a Real Cactus") and offer poems up to Rilke and Yeats:

> Help me to write,
> Show me the gates
> Where the orders are,
> And the cage
> My soul stares at,
> Where my courage
> Roars through the grates . . .

his own poetic voice most often echoes those of William Ernest Henley, John Masefield, or Rudyard Kipling. It is too bad that Lowry could not have learned from Conrad Aiken more about the writing of poetry, and less about the writing of prose. More even than his least successful fiction, Lowry's poems have the air of being unfinished—of having emerged only part way from the notebooks and scraps of paper on which he first jotted them down. To his credit, Lowry knew this: it was only with great difficulty that Margerie and Earle Birney could get him, in 1947, to begin sending them out to magazines. He knew they were unfinished, and that (as was in fact the case) they would be accepted and published mainly because the man who had written them had also written *Under the Volcano*.

Lowry was only marking time, anyway, during this first autumn in Dollarton, waiting until word should come from Harold Matson; and waiting until his divorce from Jan became final. On November 1 he heard from Los Angeles that he was free to marry Margerie, and on December 2 he did so. They went into Vancouver, to a Unitarian minister, who brought in the janitor and his wife to act as witnesses. After the ceremony, they stood about for a few minutes, drinking one another's health with carrot juice; and then the Lowrys went back to their shack, respectable at last (though Lowry could still not bring himself to tell his parents about Margerie's existence).

Almost exactly one month later they heard from Matson: *Under the Volcano* had been rejected by four publishers, as being too cerebral, too depressing, too uncoordinated, too confusing. On January 6, 1941, they co-signed a letter to Matson (*Selected Letters*, p. 37) thanking him for his help, and, while still expressing confidence in *Under the Volcano*, agreeing that in its present form it was too flawed to succeed:

> In thinking the book was so good when we sent it to you, perhaps we confused a spiritual victory with an aesthetic one, since it is impossible to convey to you the difficulties under which it was completed—which is, of course, no substitute for actual merit. But we know that within its matrix there *is* a novel which is not only truly good but saleable, and we only feel a relief and a sort of gratitude that by some fluke it was not sold in its present form.

They were (as we are) fortunate indeed that *Volcano* was not accepted in 1940; but they were nowhere near as stout-hearted when Margerie wrote this letter (Lowry only managed to scrawl his signature after hers at the bottom of the last page) as the letter would have led Matson to believe. Lowry was literally prostrated with disappointment. For days he lay on his side of the bed, his face turned to the wall, while Margerie tried to console him. He would not speak, nor eat—nor even drink. Finally Margerie hit upon the remedy: she herself began to write—a mystery novel, to be called *The Shapes that Creep*. For a day or so she worked away at the table in the larger room, listening for signs of activity from her husband. Hearing none, she began calling to him now and then for help with the writing: how might one best express this or that? how ought such-and-such a character to behave? It worked: finally, a morose and "utterly tragic" Lowry shuffled out of the bedroom to peer down over her shoulder and look at what she had been writing.

The recovery was swift, after that. Before he himself began working again, however, Lowry had to spend a considerable

The second shack, Dollarton.

amount of time on a non-literary concern. In late March Sam the fisherman came by to tell them of a nearby cottage that was for sale for $100. They walked over to look at it, and found it to be an appealing but run-down place, with a shingled roof (which needed new shingles), two rooms again, with the long, rectangular living room toward Burrard Inlet, and a porch over the shore. In the living room were a sink and a stove. In the bed-room was a card table, which Lowry claimed as his desk. With the rest of the money in his account, as well as most of what cash of hers Margerie had managed to save, they bought the new "shack" on April 1, 1941.

The next month was given over to cleaning, painting, and furnishing. Since no one had lived in the shack for some time, the cleaning was a real chore. While Margerie was doing this, Lowry (with Sam's occasional help) was re-shingling the roof. In a burst of exuberance, they painted the door red, and the window frames yellow. From Vancouver they brought the necessary second-hand furniture, which they trundled down to the shack in a wheelbarrow. Lowry kept the card table, and for Margerie they made a desk out of planks and a pair of orange crates. On May 1, they moved into their own home, and began what must surely have been the happiest three-and-a-half years of Lowry's life.

As their first act, once settled in, they began building the pier that was to mean so much to Lowry. Aided by Sam and Jimmie Craige, a tiny, blue-eyed old Manx boatwright, they drove pilings down into the offshore hard pan, then constructed a walkway of two-by-fours. For railing, they strung a length of thin rope along the edge of the platform. The effect was one of jaunty flimsiness, and no one—not even the Lowrys—believed that the pier would last through one real storm, let alone one Canadian winter. But it rode out gales and tides that pulled down more than a few sturdier-looking piers along the beachline, and—as I noted in Chapter One—Lowry came to feel for his pier a very special sort of tenderness: that such apparent frailty could endure great hardship seemed the best sort of augury to him. The pier did eventually collapse, of course, and Lowry—soon to die, himself—was immeasurably saddened by its loss.

Margerie remembers when she first met Lowry, and for almost two years afterwards, he was given to frequent and unforeseeable rages: "black moods, childish tantrums, always over trivial things, like why didn't I do something about the dark circles under my eyes the way other women did." It often seemed that he would wait, watching carefully, until she was in a relaxed mood, and then stun her with some gratuitous insult. "He didn't trust me," recalls Margerie, "probably because he'd been hurt so much in the past; and though he often hurt me, he didn't really want to, and was always full of remorse and apologies. His character wasn't formed yet, I think." Once they were settled into the new shack, however, most of these manifestations of instability vanished, and Lowry's many defensive stances gave way to a prevailing mood of relaxed good humor. He didn't stop drinking, but now and for some time to come there were neither the day-to-day soddenness of Mexico, nor the disastrous binges of Vancouver. There were instead the few daily beers, and the occasional evening spent with friends over gin and orange juice; and we must believe Lowry when he wrote to Juan Fernando Márquez now that "You will be glad to know that I gave up drinking to the point only of the necessary drink, that I am well and strong and have thrown away that part of my mind that should be thrown away." And, perhaps, for the first time in his life there was sexual fulfillment. So he told Margerie, at any rate; and there is no reason to doubt him, here.

The daily life of the Lowrys was as close as possible to the utter simplicity which Lowry required for the achieving of a state of equilibrium. Before their savings were completely gone, the Treasury began again to allow British currency to enter Canada, and Arthur O. Lowry renewed his monthly remittance—thus taking from his son his single greatest anxiety. They were not exactly financially secure, now; but they had enough not to have to worry about starving. Scribner's, moreover, accepted Margerie's *The Shapes that Creep* in June 1941, and it seemed to them that it would be very easy from now on for Margerie to whip off a mystery novel whenever they needed extra cash.

In summer there was, of course, swimming and rowboating in

Dollarton, Summer 1946.

Burrard Inlet, and hiking through the forest around them. A few hundred yards down from them ran a little fresh stream, on the banks of which grew dozens of varieties of wildflowers; and Margerie added botany lessons to those she was already giving Lowry in astronomy and birdwatching. He was an eager student, though with the flowers he was always more responsive to the names than the appearance: the contorted lousewort was his favorite, though the wild bleeding heart was a close second. The woods were full of blueberries, and the Lowrys often encountered small brown bears that had come down from Seymour Mountain to eat the blueberries. There were many deer wandering through the forest, and in spring the Lowrys could sit on their porch and watch groups of does taking their fawns down to the water and then nudging them across the inlet. Often they would have to step off the path near the shack in order to allow three or four does, with a stag racing behind them, to gallop past. On clear winter nights they could often hear wolves howling in the highlands behind them, and twice during one very cold winter a cougar came down to forage through the squatter's area. As Margerie remembers, "it ate Percy Cummins's dog and our cat, poor thing, and Malc and I went racing through the forest at night, me carrying a flashlight and Malc a stick of wood, searching for our little cat we loved with the cougar at large. I don't know why we did such a silly thing or why we weren't frightened."

Their chief delight was the bird population, which was enormous. There were the seabirds that swam right under the window of the shack, changing with the seasons from high plumage to winter plumage. Some migrated and returned, and some were only winter visitors, but Margerie and Lowry knew them all. For the songbirds Margerie would put out food during snowy or cold winters, and many of them became so tame that they would light on Margerie's shoulders, hands, and head to take the food. Lowry would stand nearby watching, very moved by the scene. And there were pet seagulls, that came for food every day, banging with their beaks on the windows of the shack if no food had been set out for them.

Very nearly their only friends during this period were Sam, the

Lowry with Jimmie Craige, March 1947.

Jersey Island fisherman who had befriended them earlier; Whitey, a gruff old Dane who, like Sam, would take his little boat up to Alaska every summer for the season's fishing, and not return until fall; and Jimmie Craige, who lived and worked a few hundred yards down from the Lowrys.

Each spring Lowry and Margerie would help Sam and Whitey caulk their boats, then see them off for Alaska. When fall came, and the Lowrys knew it was time for Sam and Whitey to return, they would begin worrying and looking down the inlet for their boats. They would eventually appear, and would come immediately to the Lowrys' shack, bringing gifts of fresh red salmon and crabs, which they showed Margerie how to preserve. Whitey, Margerie remembers, was a little standoffish at first, and decided she was worth talking to only after silently watching her sewing buttons on one of Lowry's shirts, and concluding that she was worth at least minimal recognition. Once they all became friends, they would often gather during winter evenings at the Lowrys' shack; where, over tea, Sam would sing sea shanties, all very sad, and none obscene, and Whitey would tell ghost stories, always of events he himself had witnessed.

It was Jimmie Craige who was their closest friend, and whom they saw most often during the war years in Dollarton. He had two fisherman sons, and had built their boats for them. (His daughter, Marjorie, was married to a local schoolteacher named Downie Kirk, later to become a good friend of Lowry's; but they did not meet her at this time.) Without Jimmie's help, Margerie says, she and Lowry could never have lived in Dollarton. He gave Lowry almost daily lessons in carpentry and was able eventually to tell him that he was "a good man with a nail," which puffed Lowry up so that he was almost unbearable for days. He showed Margerie how to preserve blueberries and blackberries for the winter months; and generally he shared all their sorrows and triumphs like a father. Whenever the Lowrys went away, then or later, Jimmie Craige took care of their shack, and when they returned he was there to greet them, with a fire going in the stove, and hot bricks in the bed to dry out and warm the sheets, and a bottle and some food all ready. He and Lowry spent many evenings sipping gin and harmonizing over old ballads, while Lowry strummed his taropatch. Once, Jimmie Craige found an eagle's feather in the forest, and made a pen of it for Lowry, who loved it, and kept it for signing contracts and any sufficiently important letters.

Aside from these three, George Stevenson (the local game warden), and Percy Cummins and his wife, the Lowrys made only one other friend during these years, and a most curious friend he was. One day, in the spring of 1942, as he was working on *Under the Volcano*, Lowry called to Margerie that he had just realized that the Consul was a sort of black magician, or a white magician gone bad, and that Margerie would have to bring from the public library in Vancouver whatever she could find on alchemy and sorcery. He had dipped long before now into Swedenborg and Böhme; had had his interest in magic sharpened by Marlowe and Goethe; and knew from reading Yeats during his Cambridge years (and from T. R. Henn's conversations about Yeats's fascination with the occult) something about MacGregor Mathers, Eliphas Lévi, and Madame Blavatsky. For philosophical background he kept William James's *Varieties of Religious Experience* by his bed. But he needed practical information about how one went about being a magician, white or black; and one doubts somehow that the Vancouver Public Library could have helped him much in this area. Two days after Lowry announced his discovery about the Consul to Margerie, however, they received a visit from a stranger: a tall, cadaverous Welshman who introduced himself as Charles Stansfeld-Jones. He had come, he announced, as a census-taker for voter registration. Lowry invited him in for tea, during which Stansfeld-Jones remarked that census-taking was not his real vocation. He was *really* Frater Achad, an adept in the Cabbala, a former member of the Hermetic Students of the Golden Dawn, the mystical child of the infamous Aleister Crowley, with whom he had for a time edited *Equinox* magazine, founder of a group of Chicagoans who called themselves the *Colegium ad Spiritum Sanctum,* and author of two privately printed Cabbalistic texts, *The Reception of the Bride* and *The Anatomy of the Body of God.*[7] Lowry was dazzled: here was precisely the person he needed, just when he was needed most.

Enthusiastic over having come upon a possible convert in such an unlikely place as Dollarton, Stansfeld-Jones returned to Lowry's shack the next day, bringing with him a giant chart depicting the Sephirotic Tree, and a copy of the Hebrew alphabet. The tree, with its three triads and ten emanations from the mystical body of God, was ultimately to become for the Consul of *Under the Volcano* the

---

7. *The Anatomy of the Body of God* was published in 1925 by Frater Achad's *Colegium* in Chicago, and is full of obscure and fugitive learning, interspersed with illustrations of amazingly intricate geometric patterns which presumably indicate the author's awareness of divine cosmic complexity. I have not been able to locate a copy of *The Reception of the Bride.*

"rigging of the Cabbala" in which he could dodge about "like a St. Jago's monkey." When Lowry had absorbed this first lesson, Stansfeld-Jones brought him copies of his own two books, expressing a doctrine which Perle Epstein classifies as a "corruption" of the original Cabbala—which meant that what Lowry was learning was not the "legitimate" Cabbala of Hebraic scholars, deriving from the eighth-century *Sefer Zohar* or the thirteenth-century *Sefer Yetzirah*, but a mongrelized version full of *fin de siècle* posturings about the Tarot, alchemy, Rosicrucianism, astral journeys—in other words, precisely the sort of hothouse arcana that had so beguiled Yeats fifty years earlier.[8] Before long, Lowry and Margerie were spending evenings in Deep Cove with Stansfeld-Jones and his wife, Ruby, taking astral journeys to Venus, casting sticks about in the manner prescribed by the *I Ching*, practicing Yoga exercises, and climbing about in the Sephirotic Tree. Stansfeld-Jones owned a large library of occultism, and Lowry read hungrily about in it for several months, taking what he needed for *Under the Volcano*. He probably saw here most, if not all, of the works Hugh notices on the Consul's bookshelf in Chapter Six of *Under the Volcano* (p. 185), but he paid particular attention to two works of translation by MacGregor Mathers, *The Kabbala Unveiled* and *The Book of the Sacred Magic of Abra-Melin, The Mage*. He seems also to have read some, at least, of Mathers's translated condensation of the *Zohar*. Within a matter of weeks, Lowry either tired of the magical experiments, or became afraid of them—afraid, as Margerie puts it, "of opening doors which should remain closed." But his visits to Frater Achad's library did not stop until 1944, and in the course of this time the Consul of *Under the Volcano* was becoming, among fifteen or twenty other things, a Cabbalistic adept, a black magician

8. Perle Epstein, *The Private Labyrinth of Malcolm Lowry:* Under the Volcano *and the Cabbala* (New York, 1969). I shall have more to say about Lowry and occultism in my own discussion of *Under the Volcano*, but the reader who desires a good brief description of the Cabbala should consult Epstein's book. Let him beware, however, of her ingenious yet persistently wrong-headed and reductive interpretation of the novel: Lowry may have been interested in the Cabbala, but he was interested in a great many other things, too—and Epstein does not see this. (Or perhaps I should say that she *chooses* not to see this, since elsewhere she has shown herself to be among the most astute of Lowry's critics.)

condemned to be hurled from the Sephirotic Tree down through the abyss, to suffer eternal torment in Qliphoth, the Land of Husks and Demons, presided over by Beelzebub, God of Flies.

All the while, of course, Lowry *was* working on his revision of *Under the Volcano*, in spite of the diversion provided by flora and fauna, friends, and the Cabbala. He was not even particularly disturbed when Harold Matson wrote him on September 25, 1941, that the third draft of the novel had now been rejected by thirteen publishers,[9] and that he had regretfully come to the conclusion that he was not going to find a publisher at all. By then Lowry was already well into the fourth draft, and had long since ceased worrying about the failure of earlier versions.

He was not even particularly disturbed when Arthur O. Lowry, on April 22, 1942, fired another pompous salvo at him. His son, he decided, had not been sufficiently repentant in his letters from Canada, and had instead been guilty of self-justification.

> I aspire to no literary effort in this letter but just to simple plain facts.
> 1st, Cambridge, London and France left deep scars on my heart.
> 2nd, Mexico and subsequent events deepened these wounds. Read the Bible story of the Prodigal Son leading up to where he says *"When I came to myself."* He didn't try to justify himself in his father's eyes, but said "I will arise . . . and say to my father, 'I have sinned,' " and his father met him half way & *forgave* him.

What he now requires from his youngest son is

> 1. A frank statement as to your having seen the grave error of your ways, an expression of sorrow for the harrowing and heart-breaking agony you caused your father and mother, and—like in the illustration I have cited—full assurance that you have turned your back upon those

9. The thirteen were Farrar & Rinehart; Harcourt, Brace; Houghton Mifflin; Alfred Knopf; J. B. Lippincott; Little, Brown; Random House; Reynal and Hitchcock (where Albert Erskine was not yet editor); Scribner's; Simon and Schuster; Duell, Sloan & Pearce; Dial Press; and Story Press.

dark happenings and (figuratively) have turned to your father and mother, and have sought forgiveness.

2. That your divorce has been made *absolute* & that there has been no turning back in that respect.
3. Under what conditions are you living?
4. What are you earning?
5. What is your daily occupation & so on.

If Lowry can reply to all of these requirements and queries satisfactorily, then, his father says, he "will receive our forgiveness." He concludes the letter with a postscript in which he tells Lowry of a motoring accident that had occurred four months earlier, in which he had braked on an icy road, skidded, and slammed sideways into a motor lorry heavily loaded with cheese. In the accident, Lowry's mother had received "a nasty cut on the head which bled profusely." Arthur O. Lowry manages to suggest pointedly that there had been a direct relationship between Lowry's derelictions and his mother's wounding.

Lowry was once again properly contrite. On May 26 he replied, saying that he was sorry for the accident, and that he was "dreadfully and passionately sorry" for the suffering he had caused his parents. He is, he says, "often filled with loathing and despair" for having behaved so badly, and that he has no intention of trying to justify his past conduct. Moreover, he could not do so, even if he were to try:

> And you must agree that at this time and distance it is impossible to trace in detail the events and actions that led one to that absolute, black, horrible, lonely midnight of a Gethesemane [sic] I am aware I invited you both awfully to enter too.

Having foresworn the urge to justify himself, Lowry goes on to suggest that his behavior in Mexico had been perhaps caused—or at least exacerbated—by "infantile paralysis in a modified form," and that exhaustive tests by highly qualified physicians in Vancouver have shown him to have been suffering for some years from "a multiple infection of the glands, largely sprinkled with the streptococci." He is coming around now, under treatment, and may be his old self in six month's time. He ends by tersely describing his life in Dollarton, never mentioning Margerie's existence. He received no answer to this letter, nor to others he wrote on June 30 and August 7, until his father wrote on November 25, 1942, to say that, while his love for his son had "never changed fundamentally," he had had a long struggle to regain the "whole hearted confidence" in Lowry that he had lost. But the struggle was over: his faith in his son's basic goodness had been restored. And his money would continue coming.

Through all this the Prodigal Son worked daily, leaning for hours over his makeshift desk, staring down at *Under the Volcano* and slowly developing it into what it was to become. He would start off each morning, standing up at his desk, braced on his left hand (always held palm upward, ape-fashion), and scribbling out his almost unreadable script with his right. During the first hour, say, Margerie had to sit absolutely still in the next room. There she would hear deep sighs and groans. Then dead silence. Then a few excited little sniffs, and off he would go, totally oblivious to any sort of noise she might make. This was the routine for every day, though he worked for a varying number of hours. He seldom wrote in the evening, keeping this time for walking with Margerie, or reading, or seeing their few friends, or, on Saturday nights, for bathing in the large tin tub Margerie had bought in Vancouver.

Between February 1941, when he began his revision of the third draft, and Christmas Eve 1944, when he completed it, he produced not only a fourth draft, but also more than 1100 pages of "working notes" that led up to that draft. Each of the twelve chapters went through at least four more revisions, from holograph manuscript to Margerie's rough typescript to a second holograph revision, and finally to a finished typescript, at which point the chapter was ready to be incorporated in the overall draft of the novel. In the course of these reworkings, the relationship-changes in the main characters were completed, and Yvonne and Hugh were given new backgrounds. There were hundreds of new sub-motifs added, plucked by Lowry from the Cabbala, the *Mahabarata*, the *Tibetan Book of the Dead*, Agrippa's *The Philosophy of Natural Magic*, Lewis

Spence's *The Myths of Mexico and Peru,* and the writings of Paracelsus, Blake, Marvell, Shelley, and so on and on. As sources, Goethe, Marlowe, and Dante remained paramount; but their dominance was not nearly so obvious as it had been. Canada entered the novel now, too: as a possible land of salvation for the Consul (whose name had become Geoffrey Firmin—the surname borrowed from the protagonist of the early Lowry story, "June 30th, 1934") and Yvonne. Quincey, the American neighbor, gradually lost his pleasant disposition, Laruelle's childhood friendship with the Consul was constructed, and Yvonne was killed: Lowry, in revising Chapter Eleven, suddenly realized that he had left Hugh and Yvonne wandering about in the forest below Parián, and asked Margerie what should become of his heroine. It was Margerie's immediate notion, she recalls, to have the horse with the number seven on its rump trample her to death. Lowry enthusiastically agreed to this, and Yvonne was doomed.

A study of these working notes will one day soon no doubt provide a splendid subject for some doctoral candidate with good eyesight and the patience of Job. Let us say here only that they show Lowry as a skilled reviser of his own work, always in the direction of amplification: when faced with a particular piece of clumsiness or unwanted obscurity, he modified almost always by expanding, almost never by contracting. If one detail did not make a subject clear, perhaps three details might. This is not to say that *Under the Volcano* became longer: it did not. It became denser, as he applied quick, small pieces of information and insight here and there, in masterfully controlled profusion. Dialogue was pared down, as were the long, explanatory passages that gave an occasional sense of *longueurs* to the earlier drafts. *Under the Volcano* was becoming, slowly, an extremely sensuous novel, almost insupportably full of noises, words (spoken and unspoken), visions,—a welter that was to fatigue many readers, and to dazzle others. It was becoming, moreover, not simply metaphysical, but magical as well. And funny, too, in ways that most critics have ignored. Lowry meant for his Consul to be a figure of tragic grandeur; but he wanted Geoffrey Firmin also to be a bit of a clown—as his creator was. No one should take the Consul *too* seriously, anymore than he should take Marlowe's Dr. Faustus or Goethe's Faust *too* seriously. And we ought not always to take Malcolm Lowry solely as tragic victim: he was, after all, a bit of a buffoon, too.

He seems to have become almost totally dependent on Margerie by now, and reluctant to be without her for any time at all. Regularly throughout this period Margerie would go into Vancouver to get books from the library; and each time she returned, she would be met at the bus stop at Percy Cummins's store by a frantic Lowry, who was convinced she had come to grief somehow during her trip. Their life was going so well that he could not but believe that some sort of catastrophe was imminent. So it was, but not owing to any absence on Margerie's part.

On the morning of June 7, 1944, Lowry got up to make coffee, smelled smoke, and heard a crackling noise. He dashed outside, and saw flames pouring from the small crawl-space under the roof of the shack. The tide was out, and they had no pump or hose. He ran up through the forest to call for the Dollarton fire truck, which turned out to be an antiquated old contraption incapable of putting out any but the smallest of fires. Margerie in the meantime had rescued the manuscript of *Under the Volcano* and dozens of poems. She knew that *In Ballast to the White Sea* was only six feet inside the door of the shack, but members of the small crowd that had gathered would not let her go in. Lowry, beside himself over what he was losing, raced inside, to be struck immediately on the shoulder by a burning beam that fell from the rafters. He staggered out, leaving *In Ballast* to the flames, and collapsed. Aside from *Under the Volcano* and the poems, they saved only a few clothes. The shack was totally destroyed.

Lowry and Margerie wandered about in a daze. Percy Cummins's wife, Ethel, gave them tea and banana sandwiches. Later in the day, Charles Stansfeld-Jones and his wife brought them up to their house, gave Lowry first-aid treatment for his burn, and then put them both to bed. The next morning, Stansfeld-Jones took Lowry into a hospital in Vancouver, where his injured shoulder was properly dressed. George Stevenson, the game warden, took them in next, for a few days, until their shock began to lessen. Then Downie Kirk, Jimmie Craige's schoolteacher son-in-law, let them have his cottage on the inlet, where they sat mutely for perhaps two weeks. Staying in Dollarton seemed for the moment to be impossible. They wrote Gerald Noxon, Lowry's old Cambridge friend, who was now living near Toronto and working as a producer-writer-newscaster for the Canadian Broadcasting Corporation, and Noxon wired them train fare from Vancouver to Toronto, saying, "Come East and stay with me." Margerie's brother-in-law, Dr. E. B. Woolfan, sent them $100. In early July 1944, they boarded an east-bound train crammed with soldiers, with Lowry still semi-hysterical, crying out to anyone who would listen to him. "My house burned down, my house burned down." It was, Margerie recalls, a long trip. She carried *Under the Volcano* with her in a small suitcase, and Lowry would not let her put it down.

Gerald Noxon and his wife, Betty, lived in a large old house surrounded by trees, in Oakville, on the edge of Lake Ontario. Here Lowry finally began to recover, and eventually even to continue with the revision of his novel, but the shock was with them for a long time. In the fall of 1945 Lowry wrote to Conrad Aiken that he did not know how the Noxons bore with him during these days:

> Actually the business of the fire seemed to drive us both slightly cuckoo. Its traumatic effect alone was shattering. We had to live through the bloody fire all over again every night. I would wake to find Margie screaming or she would wake to find me yelling and gnashing my teeth. (*Selected Letters*, p. 48)

After they had been in Oakville for two or three weeks, they took a fancy to a small house nearby, because it reminded them of the Dollarton shack, and began to talk of renting it for the winter. Betty Noxon had painted a picture of the house, and kept the picture in her attic. One day, when everyone was out, Lowry climbed up to the attic and sat looking at the painting. In his imagination, the house kept bursting into flames. Two weeks later (he reported to Aiken) the house did precisely that: and "they couldn't get the fire engines through the woods, nothing of the kind had happened for fifty years in that rural route, and there was a terrific to-do, through all of which Margerie and I, for once, calmly slept." Understandably, this all did little to restore Lowry's equilibrium.

In the end of July the Noxons bought a house in Niagara-on-the-Lake. Since their lease on the Oakville house ran until the end of September, and they had already paid the rent for it, they suggested that the Lowrys stay on there. Lowry continued working during the day on *Under the Volcano*, and all went well enough until one evening when he announced that he wanted to walk into Oakville for a beer. Since they were only three-quarters of a mile from town, Margerie began to worry when there was no sign of her husband after four hours. Finally he appeared, perfectly well but quite drunk, arm-in-arm with an Indian whom he introduced to Margerie as the "Chief of all the Mohawks," and who was at least as drunk as Lowry. The Chief pointed at Margerie and said, "Squaw get into kitchen." Lowry laughed and agreed with the order. Margerie went into the kitchen and sat there until Lowry and the Chief, beginning to grow cold, called for her to come out and build them a fire. This she did, and did well, so that the Chief was moved to allow her to sit in a corner of the living room instead of returning to the kitchen. He even gave her a drink of the liquor they had bought from an Oakville bootlegger. Then, well after midnight, the Chief began to teach Lowry the Mohawk war dance. Margerie, rather annoyed by now at her husband's capers, went into the kitchen for a moment, and returned to find Lowry gone, and the Chief stumbling about by himself. He hadn't missed Lowry, and had no idea where he had gone; but he was having such a good time that he intended now to return to Oakville, collect more liquor and a few of his braves, and come back for more dancing. As soon as he had gone, Margerie ran outside to look for Lowry. She found him in the woods, curled up fast asleep at the foot of a large tree. Unable to wake him, she returned to the house, locked all the doors and windows, and sat terrified in the living room for the rest of the night, awaiting the return of the Mohawks. They did not arrive, but a rather devastated Lowry did, shortly after dawn.

Before the end of September the Noxons called to say that they had found a very pleasant cottage for rent in Niagara-on-the-Lake. On October 1 the Lowrys moved into it, and spent four months of relative happiness there. Their one bad moment came as the result of yet another fire. One night they were dining at the Noxon's when they heard shouts and bells, and saw a red glow in the sky in the direction of their cottage. They raced over, to find that it was not theirs, but the house next door that had gone up in flames. Lowry began to believe that his playing about with the occult in Stansfeld-Jones's house had put him in bad repute with certain demonic forces, and that it was his destiny to be pursued by the element of fire. Being Lowry, he began thinking also that quite a novel could be made of this, and started taking notes for what was eventually to become *October Ferry to Gabriola*.

Except for this one fright, there was little that occurred during their stay in Niagara-on-the-Lake to take Lowry away from his revision of *Under the Volcano*. He and Margerie did hitchhike one weekend to Niagara Falls, and went through the whole honeymooner routine, with rides on the *Maid of the Mist* and trips to the Cave of the Winds; but this was no real distraction. Finally on Christmas Eve 1944, the work was completed. It was a freezing day, full of snow and wind; and Lowry, after working for hours, wanted a beer. He and Margerie walked, carrying *Under the Volcano* with them, to the Riverside Inn, an old pub right on the Niagara River where it meets Lake Ontario. Lowry drank his beer, made a few marginal notations in the pages of Chapter Twelve, then put his pencil down and said, "I've finished it." They carried the novel back to the Noxons. After dinner, Lowry read them the final chapter. When he had finished, Gerald Noxon said, "I have a feeling of exultation." If we except *Ultramarine*, it was the only time in his life in which Lowry was to complete a long work of prose. Margerie typed the chapter the following day, and Lowry gave Gerald Noxon the holograph manuscript of the fourth draft.

So that they could have a little income beyond Lowry's monthly remittance, Margerie had, with Noxon's help, found work during this time, writing radio scripts for Toronto programs. She was quite good at this, and in a very few weeks had done several scripts for CBC's broadcasts to schools, as well as a story about beavers by Stephen Leacock, and a dramatization of Louis Hémon's Canadian novel, *Marie Chapdelaine*. CBC offered her a contract, but she and Lowry thought only of going back to Dollarton, and she was working only long enough to earn their train fare and a little extra for rebuilding their shack. In February 1945, they took a train back to Vancouver, and were met by Jimmie Craige. He brought them out to Dollarton, and—after helping them unload their luggage at Whitey's cottage, where they were to spend their first few nights —took them down to look at the ruins of their old shack. Only their pier remained. To their dismay, they had new neighbors. As Lowry described the depressing scene to Conrad Aiken:

> When we arrived back here too it was to find that someone, strangers and vultures, had disregarded our burned stakes and notices and built smack on half our old site, blocking our southerly view, a great tall ugly creation to be full in the summer of rackety rickety children and hysterical fat women who meantime had pulled down the flags we had left— perhaps too dramatically—flying on our poor old ruin, thrown dead mice down our well, and shat—even on the walls—all over our toilet. (*Selected Letters*, p. 49)

Whitey took them in, rigged a curtain around his bed and gave it to them to sleep in, while he slept on the floor. During their first week at Whitey's, they received news of the death of Arthur O. Lowry, from—of all things, given his abstemiousness—cirrhosis of the liver. As noted earlier, Lowry said nothing, but went for a long swim in the freezing waters of Burrard Inlet. It is odd to reflect that "the old man" died without having known anything of Margerie's existence—or, at least, without ever having acknowledged her existence, if he did know of it.

When the Lowrys decided definitely to rebuild their cottage, in spite of their unsavory neighbors, they re-rented from the Scotsmen the cottage they had first lived in at Dollarton, and began looking about for materials—wood, nails, shingles, and pilings: they were resolved to do the whole job themselves, with help only from Whitey, Old Sam, and Jimmie Craige. Two weeks later they were sinking the pilings into the hardpan on the shore, a job requiring considerable strength and tenacity. From a recently abandoned sawmill they bought all the lumber they needed, and Jimmie Craige brought them nails. By the end of March they had four walls and a roof constructed, and were at work laying the red linoleum tiles that were to constitute the floor. As they were building the adjoining woodshed, Margerie stepped on a four-inch spike and ran it through her foot. She sat down, pulled out the spike, and called over to Lowry, who was sawing nearby. He carried her back to the Scotsmen's cottage and helped her soak the injured foot. But in the night she became delirious and Lowry had to run over to George Stevenson's for help. Stevenson brought his car to the edge of the forest, and Lowry carried Margerie up to meet it. They drove in to the North Vancouver Hospital, where Margerie went through a very bad several days. There was for a time, she remembers, some question of amputation, but eventually she was released, and returned, hobbling about on a cane, to oversee the reconstruction of their shack.

It was summer by now, and the new shack was, if not completed—the inside walls had still to be constructed—at least habitable. It was not so attractive as their second home in Dollarton, but it was more comfortable inside. There were large windows on three sides, and the two rooms were larger than they had been in the previous shack. Margerie made monk's-cloth curtains for the windows, and brightened up their drab sofa by throwing an Indian blanket over it. Lowry built bookcases and desks for them both; and in June, 1945, they moved in. No sooner had they done so than Lowry sent *Under the Volcano* to Harold Matson. He had been holding onto it since Niagara-on-the-Lake, making dozens of last-minute changes, until finally even he could think of nothing more to do to it.

No sooner had they settled into their new home when they received a notice from the Harbour Board: the city of Vancouver had decided that in the very near future it was going to tear down all

The third shack, the one built by the Lowrys, showing the pier.

the squatters' shacks and the forest around them, in order to erect
"autocamps of the better class." But almost before the Lowrys
could react to this latest emotional affront, a reprieve came: nothing
would be done about eviction for at least three years, and the squatters could continue to live on, rent-free; and then would be given
the opportunity to buy the land on which they were living. They
still had no inside walls, but the roof did not leak, even in the rains
of early fall. For the time being, the shack was adequate shelter; but
it would not do as a winter home.

Then, in late September, they received word from England that
Arthur O. Lowry's estate had been settled, and that they would
shortly be sent a check for several thousand dollars. Since it was too
late in the year to complete the winter-proofing of their shack,
Lowry decided they ought to take a trip—to Mexico, where he
could see Juan Fernando Márquez, show Margerie the land she had

come to know so well from her work on *Under the Volcano*, and, perhaps, prove to himself that this time he would be strong enough to overcome the dangers of his own personal Inferno. On November 28, then, he and Margerie flew from Vancouver to Los Angeles, on their way to Mexico City, Cuernavaca, and Oaxaca—Lowry's City of Dreadful Night.

Though Lowry had corresponded often with Margerie's family in Los Angeles, he had never met them until he and Margerie arrived in California on the first leg of their flight down to Mexico. Lowry had some reason for tension, now, even though settlement of his father's estate had left him financially secure—more or less—for the first time in his life. For one thing, Harold Matson had written him almost five months earlier to say that he was not entirely satisfied with the fourth version of *Under the Volcano:*

> Your novel has for me a peculiar fascination, sometimes aggravatingly. It is full of wonderful potentialities, in my judgment, but it needs a great deal of work to bring it down to size and proportion within the limits of its own worth. Perhaps I have become impatient with it and that may be the reason why this novel is much too long, and much too full of talk—for me.
>
> *(Selected Letters,* p. 420)

Matson added that the editor at Duell, Sloan, and Pearce had felt the same way, but said that he, Matson, still intended to continue sending the novel around to New York publishers. Margerie had sent off a very patient response to Matson, suggesting that he perhaps had read *Under the Volcano* too hastily to comprehend the complexity of the book; but there is no reason to suppose that Lowry had much reason to be optimistic at this time about his chances for success. He had, moveover, also sent a copy of the novel to his friend Innes Rose at J. Farquharson and Company in London, who had forwarded it on to Jonathan Cape; and Cape had so far said nothing definite. (He had written on October 15 to say that he had begun to read *Under the Volcano* with hope and expectation, and that he would shortly send a cable to Lowry. But no cable came.) It looked, in fact, as if the fourth version were on its way to the same dreary round of refusals that its predecessor had encountered almost four years earlier.

Perhaps because of his anxiety over his novel's fate, Lowry had begun in the fall of 1945 to drink again: no startling alcoholic pyrotechnics; just steady, quiet boozing. Margerie, still not wholly recovered from the infection in her foot, had begun for the first time to lose patience with her husband. She now would sometimes match him drink for drink, and there were increasingly frequent quarrels. They were—especially to outsiders—still a conspicuously devoted couple; but Lowry did feel that their marriage had somehow slipped a notch or two—as well it might have done, given the stresses to which it had recently been subjected.

In spite of whatever tension he may have felt, Lowry impressed Margerie's mother, Mrs. John Stuart Bonner, and Priscilla and her husband, Dr. E. B. Woolfan, during his weeklong stay at their home in Hollywood Hills. He wore his best Cambridge manners (which, in fact, he almost always did), drank moderately, and seemed genuinely to relish the company of his in-laws. Priscilla especially was taken with him: by his handsomeness, by his beautiful, rather formal, manners, and by his obvious pleasure at "belonging" to a real family. He would follow her about as she went through her housewifery, and ask her if he might keep her company in the kitchen as she cooked supper.

The Woolfans often went to the director Preston Sturges' weekly Sunday night dinners in Beverly Hills, and they took the Lowrys along with them on December 2, so that Lowry could see something of real Hollywood people. He was seated next to a man who had just worked as the photographer for the filming of Charles Jackson's recent bestseller, *The Lost Weekend*. The photographer was quite enthusiastic about both the novel and the film—which must have put Lowry's good manners to something of a test, since he had been after one quick reading convinced that Jackson's novel about a drunk had quite stolen the wind from the sails of *Under the Volcano*. He recovered enough to beat all after-dinner challengers at ping-pong (a game which he had mastered at Jeake's House years before), in spite of the pain which varicose veins in his legs were causing him.

Early the following week Dr. Woolfan gave Lowry a series of injections which helped his legs somewhat; and on December 11 he and Margerie left Los Angeles on American Airlines for Mexico City via Phoenix, El Paso, and Monterrey.[1] Throughout the trip, Lowry was assailed by all sorts of well-justified anxieties. What if he had troubles getting through Customs? What if he should fail Margerie, as either tour-guide or husband? What would he do when confronted once again with tequila and mescal? What if he were to continue to fail as a writer? Margerie, beside him in their rear-row seats (he insisted on sitting as far aft as possible, so as to be observable by a minimum number of strangers), chattered on happily about the sights they were to see in exotic old Mexico, but Lowry slumped in his seat, his right leg propped for circulation's sake on the seat in front of them, and tormented himself with thoughts of his manifold inadequacies. It seemed to him that only he, among all contemporary writers, was alienated, incompetent:

> On the face of it, you would think they—and by "they" he meant all the better writers of his own language he could think of at the moment—were the kind of people who rose early and shot pheasants boisterously out of the sky, were capable of gigantic feats of farming or engineering or even stone masonry, had muscles like barbellmen, hurtled through Belgium on motorcycles, fought in wars like young Charle-

1. This flight is described in great detail in chapters one, two, and three of *Dark as the Grave Wherein My Friend Is Laid*. Most, but not all, of the material in this novel comes directly from the journals which Lowry kept at this time; a small amount comes from invention on his part. Since I have not been able to determine in every case precisely what really happened, and what Lowry may have imagined to have happened, I shall adhere closely to the factual bare bones of the trip. For fleshing out, let the reader consult *Dark as the Grave*.

> magnes, were traitors, or became heroes of the people, like
> Erikson [Nordahl Grieg], with equal zest, and even when
> they were geniuses, like Daniel [Conrad Aiken], turned out
> their work as easily as if it came out of some celestial sausage
> machine. And they had one thing in common: with very few
> exceptions, they all seemed, at bottom, to be incorrigible op-
> timists, even when their works were most despairing. . . .
> Such people might go into exile, forcibly or as a protest, but
> you could never think of them being turned back from a
> border as a person likely to be a public charge.
>
> (*Dark as the Grave*, p. 12)

And here he, Malcolm Lowry, was: a man who drank, who let his
houses burn to the ground, who had done nothing in the war, who
had labored for eight years to produce a novel which even his agent
felt still needed "a great deal of work," who was (in spite of cheer-
fulness always breaking through) very far from being an optimist
—and who was, he was sure, about to be denounced at any moment by officials at the border—any border.

Why, one might ask, should such a man have wanted to carry
this heavy burden of anxieties back to the settings of his greatest un-
happinesses? There were several reasons: he wanted, he said, to correct the Spanish colloquialisms in his novel, and a return to Mexico
seemed the best way to do this. He had in mind a sequel to the
book, he told friends; and, having gone to Mexico to write *Under
the Volcano*, he had no choice but to return if he were to write
Under Under the Volcano. Less facetiously, there was the fact that
Margerie had never been to Mexico, and wanted very much to see
the land where the novel with which she had spent so much time
over the past six years had been written. Lowry, moreover, looked
on the journey as an opportunity for some sort of exorcism of bad
memories: they would make a pilgrimage to every hotel, every cantina he had known in the Thirties; and, by seeing them now as it
were in the light of relative happiness and sanity, prove that they
were not such nightmarish places as they had once seemed.

> Was it that he wanted to return there, as if to gloat over the
> conquest of these things, as he might have looked down from

the mountains upon the valley, upon the narrow-gauge railway line . . . that had carried him on his first, his second, his
third, last, and disastrous trip to Oaxaca, with a feeling of
pride, thinking that all this had been transcended? How
much better I am now! . . . Had he really transcended it?
Was he coming here with a pride of accomplishment with
[Margerie], and a gesture of defiance, to fling his gage in the
face of fate and say (and say moreover in clichés), Look, I
have succeeded, I have transformed, single-handed, my life-
in-death into life, nay what is more I am going to make that
life-in-death pay for the future, in hard cash, I have come
back to show you that not an hour, not a moment of my
drunkenness, my continual death, was not worth it: there is
no dross of even the worst of those hours, not a drop of mescal that I have not turned into pure gold, not a drink I have
not made sing.

(*Dark as the Grave*, pp. 210–11)

Brave, and perhaps even true words, but sadly naïve, too; for what
Lowry had not reckoned with was the peculiar force that resides in
places to which unhappy memories are attached. It was possibly
courageous of him to take Margerie, once they had landed in Mexico City and gone through the ritual fleecing at the hands of bell-
hops, cab drivers, and doormen, directly to the Hotel Canada,
where he and Jan had spent their last unhappy nights together in
1938; and then to lead her on a tour of all the cantinas he and Jan,
or he and Bousfield, had visited then. But it was not many days before the weight of all these *recherches du temps perdu* began op-
pressing him. He suggested to Margerie that they consider returning to Canada; but she, entranced by the beauty of Mexico, and
intrigued by their original, simplistic notions of exorcism, insisted
that they stay. They had to see Cuernavaca and its *barrancas;* they
had to visit Oaxaca, to see the Farolito. And, of course, there was
Lowry's good angel, Juan Fernando Márquez, who was presumably
still somewhere in the Oaxaqueñan countryside; and they could not
very well leave Mexico before they had seen *him.*

So, after a week in Mexico City, they took the old Flecha Roja
bus down to Cuernavaca, and went straight to the Café Bahía,
where Lowry had once heard much of the dialogue that was even-

Calle de Humboldt, Cuernavaca, which became the Calle Nicaragua in *Under the Volcano.*

tually to go into Chapter Twelve of *Under the Volcano.* They struck up a conversation with the proprietor, Eduardo Ford, whom Lowry had known slightly in 1937. Ford, it developed, knew of an apartment on the Calle de Humboldt. As he began describing it, Lowry realized with a shock that the apartment was in the very house—Number 24—that he had made the home of Jacques Laruelle in his novel. Margerie walked down with Ford to look at it, and to meet its owner, Señora María Luisa Blanco de Arriola; and returned shortly to report to the stunned Lowry that, though there was no inscription on its street-side wall, Laruelle's house still had its chevron-shaped windows and its grotesque towers and parapets. They took the vacant apartment, in spite of Lowry's misgivings: it seemed to him that he was in grave danger of being taken over by his own fiction, of becoming a character in his own novel.

The idea was fascinating, but terrifying. What, he began to wonder (and to note in his journals) if he were coming back to Mexico not to assert his rejuvenation, but to seek the death that had eluded him there eight years earlier? What if he had invented that death in the final chapter of *Under the Volcano*, and now had returned to claim it as his own?

These morbid speculations were not dissipated by Margerie's insistence, as soon as they had unpacked, that they walk down the garden path that led from Laruelle's house, to peer into the *barranca* that lay at its end. The day was ending, now, and as they turned to walk back to the house they saw the moon rise over Popocatepetl's neighboring volcano, Ixtaccihuatl. They ate dinner, then went for a walk toward the *zócalo*. As they were returning, they discovered that they were watching a lunar eclipse in progress. Very quickly the night became quite dark, and they had trouble negotiating the last few blocks. Back in their apartment, they stood on the balcony and watched the moon emerge from the earth's shadow and go "sliding down a wide sapphire night sky into a kind of white ocean of fleece" (*Selected Letters*, p. 54). It was all highly portentous, Lowry was sure; but whether the eclipse signified life or death, he could not say.

The next twelve days, in any case, were a kind of death-in-life, as they anxiously watched their mailbox for some word from agents or publishers about the novel. Lowry thought of himself as a latter-day Tristan, languishing in a foreign land, hoping for some word of hope from his own Isolde, Jonathan Cape. But "No mail, no sail," he wrote in his journal. He took Margerie to Cortés's palace, and to the Borda Gardens. They swam in the pool in the patio of Laruelle's house. Mostly, though, they sat on their balcony, looking down at the mailbox. Finally, on New Year's Eve, a letter came.

It was from Cape, and was dated November 29, 1945.[2] He began by recalling what Lowry had written from the preceding August about how nearly impossible it would be to revise the novel yet another time:

2. An abridgement of this letter is in Appendix 3 of *Selected Letters* (p. 424).

Lowry in the Borda Gardens, 1945.

> But it would be heart-breaking to be told, when so much has
> been taken into account, that it should be couched in sharper
> or more dramatic form or something of that nature: it was
> created on many planes and everything in it, right down to
> the precise number of chapters, is there for a perfectly good
> reason.

Cape went on to say that he, along with two of his readers, had
gone over *Under the Volcano* carefully, and that he was including a
copy of one reader's report, which seemed to "crystallize most
effectively and exactly" what the three of them thought about it.
The report called for revisions, and Cape wanted to know whether
Lowry were still as adamant about this as he had been at the time of
his August letter, or whether he might consider making the revi-

sions. Cape did not say that he would not publish the novel if there were no further revision; but he *did* guarantee to publish it if Lowry *did* revise the book again. He concluded by saying that "We feel here the book has integrity and importance, but it would be a pity for it to go out as it stands, believing as we do that its favourable reception will be helped tremendously by the alterations," and that "At the same time we believe that it would be considerably improved aesthetically" if the suggestions included in the report were carried out.

The reader's report does not seem to us today particularly startling. *Under the Volcano* either excites its readers, or it does not. The reader for Cape was not excited. He says that he found the first quarter or third of the book "extremely slow," but gradually became more interested. He jots down a brief outline of the plot:

> It is a novel, but a novel of situation rather than action. The time is 1938, the setting Mexico, and the action, such as it is, occupies only one day. The situation is that an Englishman, Geoffrey Firmin, with a sinecure as English Consul in a Mexican town, is a hopeless drunkard divorced from his American wife, Yvonne. He has not ceased to yearn, boozily, for her; and she has felt impelled to return to him, with the hope of reforming him by starting life anew—the simple life, in British Columbia. Also present, Geoffrey's younger brother, Hugh, an athletic Communist rolling stone; and a stray Frenchman, Jacques Laruelle, a lifelong friend of Geoffrey's who has in the past slept with Yvonne.
>
> All that *happens* is that Geoffrey, Hugh and Yvonne spend the day roaming about, riding in a bus, visiting a fair, etc.; Hugh and Yvonne being mostly together and Geoffrey largely on his own. Eventually they lose him, he drifts into yet another cantina to booze, and in the end gets shot by a local thug.

All of this situation, continues the reader, is "enormously elaborated" by (a) "flashbacks of the characters' past lives and past and present thoughts and emotions"; (b) "Mexican local colour heaped on in shovelfuls"; and (c) "the mescal-inspired phantasmagoria, or heebie-jeebies, to which Geoffrey has succumbed." The first of these he finds "tedious and unconvincing"; the second is very well done; and the third is, though impressive, "too long, wayward, and elaborate"—and (what must have hurt Lowry most) evocative of "the recent novel and film, *The Lost Weekend.*"

Thus, though he likes the "vivid and well-observed picture of Mexico" and the "equally vivid and mostly impressive exploration of the tormented weakness of the drunken Geoffrey," the reader objects to the book's long initial tedium, the weakness of the characterization, and the excessive length of the novel: "The book is *much too long* and over-elaborate for its content, and could have been more effective if only half or two-thirds its present length." He concludes that "the author has over-reached himself, and is given to eccentric word-spinning and too much stream-of-consciousness stuff," and suggests that a great many cuts could profitably be made in these "more rambling" passages, as well as in such "straight" sections as that dealing with Hugh's past life: "Everything should be concentrated on the drunk's inability to rise to the occasion of Yvonne's return, on his delirious consciousness (which is very well done); and on the local colour, which is excellent throughout."

The report was a remarkable one: with surprising consistency it condemned exactly what supporters of *Under the Volcano* have found great in it; and praised the work for those qualities which, while perhaps not insignificant to Lowry, were certainly not of paramount importance, either to him or to his followers. Lowry was shattered: he was being asked to cut his novel almost in half, and to excise that which he felt was best in it. Fortunately, he took the letter from Cape in the best possible way: as a challenge. Cape, he felt was asking him to defend his book, to say why it should be left as it was. Bravely and calmly he sat down on January 2 and began a sustained and brilliant defense of *Under the Volcano*. It could not have been easy to write, and he broke down briefly midway through its composition; but by the time he mailed it to Cape on January 15, it had become a document absolutely unique in literary history: a thirty-one page exegesis which demonstrated on every page that Lowry knew precisely what was going on in every chapter in his novel, why it was all there as it was, and what it all meant.

He begins by making a few concessions to Cape's reader. The main defect of the novel, he admits, from which the others spring, "comes from something irremediable. It is that the author's equipment, such as it is, is subjective rather than objective, a better equipment, in short, for a certain kind of poet than a novelist." [3] The conception, therefore, is poetic rather than novelistic—which means, among other things, that the work will, like a good poem, have to be read several times before its "full meaning will reveal itself, explode in the mind." (If this seems an unreasonable attitude on Lowry's part, let us recall James Joyce's assertion that, since he had taken eighteen years to write *Finnegans Wake*, he saw no reason why it should not take eighteen years to read.) The first chapter is admittedly long and slow, but deliberately so: it sets the mood and tone of the book as well as "the slow melancholy tragic rhythm of Mexico itself—its sadness—and above all it establishes the *terrain*." And he agrees that the reader's criticism of the weakness of the character drawing is valid: in fact, he admits that the character drawing is "not only weak but virtually nonexistent, save with certain minor characters." But, for one thing, there had simply been not enough *room* for good old E. M. Forsterish "round" characters; and for another, the four main characters are not individuals, anyway, but "aspects of the same man, or of the human spirit." Furthermore, is characterization necessarily so important? "There are," he says, "a thousand writers who can draw adequate characters till all is blue for one who can tell you anything new about hell fire. And I am telling you something new about hell fire." He insists that what appears to the publisher's reader to be "eccentric word-spinning and too much stream-of-consciousness stuff" is all vital, not only to the poetic quality of the book, but to its exposition as well. And he objects to his evocation of place described as being "Mexican local colour heaped on in shovelfuls," even though the reader seems to have approved of this aspect of the work. The setting is not there for reasons of mere "local colour," nor is it "heaped on": it is all, like the often febrile diction, there for a reason. In other

3. The entire letter to Cape is in *Selected Letters*, pp. 57–88.

words, Lowry is arguing for the organic wholeness of his book, and insisting that, if Cape were to cut one apparent excrescence in, say, Chapter One, he would very probably be destroying a necessary effect that is not realized until, say, Chapter Eleven. He mentions, in passing, the esoteric element: there *must* be twelve chapters, no matter what, not only because "each chapter is a unity in itself and all are related," but also because twelve is a universal unit: there are twelve hours in the course of the novel's single day; there are twelve months in the year that elapses between the end of Chapter Twelve and the beginning of Chapter One;

> while the deeply buried layer of the novel or poem that attaches itself to myth, does so to the Jewish Cabbala where the number 12 is of the highest symbolic importance. The Cabbala is used for poetical purposes because it represents man's spiritual aspirations. The Tree of Life, which is its emblem, is a kind of complicated ladder with Kether, or Light, at the top and an extremely unpleasant abyss some way above the middle. The Consul's spiritual domain in this regard is probably the Qliphoth, the world of shells and demons, represented by the Tree of Life upside down—all this is not important at all to the understanding of the book; I just mention it in passing to hint that, as Henry James says, "There are depths."

The inclusion of various kinds of arcana is, not, then, for the purpose of ornamental or pretentious complication, but to add resonance. The book is intended to exist on numerous planes, but not so as to baffle or confuse, but to simplify, to make the work accessible to any kind of reader. Something for everyone, from Joyce's ideal reader (the author himself) down to the least perceptive of publisher's readers.

> The novel can be read simply as a story which you can skip if you want. It can be read as a story you will get more out of if you don't skip. It can be regarded as a kind of symphony, or in another way as a kind of opera—or even a horse opera. It is hot music, a poem, a song, a tragedy, a comedy, a farce, and so forth. It is superficial, profound, entertaining and boring, according to taste. It is a prophecy, a

political warning, a cryptogram, a preposterous movie, and a writing on the wall. It can even be regarded as a sort of machine: it works, too, believe me, as I have found out. In case you think I mean it to be everything but a novel I better say that after all it is intended to be and, though I say so myself, a deeply serious one too.

The principal concern of the work is with "the forces in man which cause him to be terrified of himself." [4] It is also concerned, Lowry says, "with the guilt of man, with his remorse, with his ceaseless struggling toward the light under the weight of the past, and with his doom." The allegorical basis is that of the Garden of Eden, with the Garden representing the world; and the drunkenness of the Consul "is used on one plane to symbolize the universal drunkenness of mankind during the war, or during the period immediately preceding it . . . and what profundity and final meaning there is in his fate should be seen also in its universal relationship to the fate of mankind."

The remainder of the letter consists of a summary of *Under the Volcano*, chapter by chapter, as Lowry patiently leads Cape through his Baudelairean forest of symbols, explaining Mexico here ("It is paradisal; it is unquestionably infernal"), the Cabbala there; reminding him of certain broad political implications; illustrating how he goes about effecting alterations in mood and tone; and summing up characters (Hugh, for instance, is "Everyman tightened up a screw, for he is just beyond being mediocre"). Most importantly he underlines the book's important themes: the desire on the part of

---

4. Lowry cites as his source for this clause an essay on Gogol by Edmund Wilson. So far as I have been able to discover, Lowry must have been recalling a piece by Wilson published in *The New Yorker* on May 27, 1944, called "A Treatise on Tales of Horror." Lowry did not have this treatise with him in Mexico, and so his words here are really his own, and not Wilson's. What the treatise *does* say, speaking of Hawthorne, Poe, Melville, and Gogol, is that "All four of these authors wrote stories that were at the same time tales of horror and psychological or moral fables. They were not interested in spooks for their own sake; they knew that their demons were symbols, and they knew what they were doing with these symbols" (as reprinted in Wilson's *A Literary Chronicle: 1920–1950*, New York, 1952). Lowry, I suspect, would have put himself in just this category of psychological horror writer.

the characters for *goodness;* and the concepts of individual guilt and responsibility, epitomized by the ubiquitous sign appearing in the gardens of Quauhnahuac: ¿LE GUSTA ESTE JARDÍN QUE ES SUYO? ¡EVITE QUE SUS HIJOS LO DESTRUYAN! which means "Do you like this garden which is yours? Don't let your children destroy it!" but which the Consul appropriately mistranslates as "You like this garden? Why is it yours? We evict those who destroy!"

Finally, the twelfth chapter is the one in which "All the strands of the book, political, esoteric, tragic, comical, religious, and what not are here gathered together"; but Cape is warned that he ought not to stop reading at the end of the chapter:

> No. The book should be seen as essentially *trochal,* I repeat, the form of it as a wheel so that, when you get to the end, if you have read carefully, you should want to turn back to the beginning again, where it is not impossible, too, that your eye might alight once more upon Sophocles' *Wonders are many, and none is more wonderful than man*—just to cheer you up.

Lowry may, as he claims in his letter to Jonathan Cape, have thought of the process by which he wrote and rewrote *Under the Volcano* as one of simplification; but the fact remains that his novel has seemed to almost every reader an enormously complex, even obscurantist, piece of fiction. It is not surprising then, that, instead of essays which explore the novel as *Gestalt,* critics have so far concentrated almost without exception on one or two of the many strands which woven together produce the whole work. Thus we have seen articles on *Under the Volcano* and Faust, and the Cabbala, and (implausibly and unconvincingly) Sisyphus, and jazz. There has been a description of the sea metaphor in the novel. There has been a plea for the novel as comedy (Lowry was always hurt when no one noticed how funny his work often was). Lowry's old friend David Markson wrote an ambitious and necessarily fragmentary piece on "Myth in *Under the Volcano.*" (One might note here that Markson's unpublished M.A. thesis for Columbia University, written in 1952, is still the best study of the novel's symbolism.) There have been a few source studies, having mostly to do with Conrad Aiken and James Joyce (nothing so far about Poe, Gogol, Melville, or—not so insignificant an influence, one suspects—Julien Green). More usefully, there have been two essays aiming at understandings of *Under the Volcano* considered as spatial form and as static art. At this moment, there is (in addition to Lowry's letter to Cape, and a revised form of the letter printed as a preface to the French edition of the novel),[5] only one published work of criticism which is immediately and unqualifiedly valuable to any reader of the whole novel: Dale Edmonds's "*Under the Volcano:* A Reading of the Immediate Level," [6] which assumes what no one else seems really to have assumed: that the novel "exists powerfully as a story about people," whatever else it may be; and that it is on this immediate level of "people, places, events, and circumstances within a fictional world that most resembles our own" that *Under the Volcano* communicates most affectively. To read Edmonds's essay is to learn that Lowry's novel does indeed respond to a sane, non-Procrustean, non-thesis-pushing analysis. Someday, after we have disposed of *Under the Volcano* and Dante, and Aztec mythology, and Shelley, and Elizabethan poetry and drama, and Swedenborg, and B. Traven, and the expressionist films of Robert Wiene (whose *Orlacs Hände* appears as *Las Manos de Orlac,* throughout the novel, in another of Lowry's meaningful refrains), and Cervantes, and *Peter Rabbit* ("Everything is to be found in Peter Rabbit," Lowry has the Consul proclaim solemnly), we will perhaps see our paths cleared for more fruitful and illuminating studies, and fewer instances of earnest drudgery.

The *Gestalt* reading, when it comes, will do well to pay attention to Lowry's letter to Cape. The whole work is, as he says, a wheel, and a wheel in constant motion. *Under the Volcano* is a highly dynamic work, and one must keep the idea of kinesis always in his mind as he journeys through it. The dynamics are cinematic, dramatic, and most probably have their origins in the play by Jean Cocteau that Lowry saw twice in Paris in May 1934: *La Machine*

5. A translation of this "Preface to a Novel" is in *Canadian Literature,* 9 (Summer 1961), 23–29.
6. In *Tulane Studies in English,* XVI (1968), 63–105.

Infernale. This was Cocteau's version of the Oedipus tragedy. Before the play itself begins, a "Fantome" speaks to the audience of what is about to take place. At the conclusion of this preamble, the Fantome says:

> Spectator, this machine you see here wound up to the full in such a way that the spring will slowly unwind the whole length of a human life, is one of the most perfect constructed by the infernal gods for the mathematical destruction of a human life.[7]

This infernal machine is the universe itself: an ingeniously contrived clock-like mechanism in which every part, every minute, has its function in the machine's diabolical purpose—"the mathematical destruction of a human life." When Lowry wrote to Cape that *Under the Volcano* "can even be regarded as a sort of machine: it works, too, believe me, as I have found out," it was surely of Cocteau's clockwork instrument of execution that he was thinking: which means, among other things, that his novel would be the representation of the destruction, beautifully and horribly worked out, of a human life—that of Geoffrey Firmin, His Majesty's Consul in Quauhnahuac, Mexico. The spring of the machine has been unwinding the whole length of the Consul's life, bringing him inexorably to the morning of November 1, 1938: The Day of the Dead, when the living visit the cemeteries to commune with their departed loved ones.

The spring of the Infernal Machine is, of course, Time. It has taken the Consul forty-two years to prepare himself for his last twelve hours. The infernal gods have contributed to his preparation, by causing his mother to die, then by driving his father north from Srinagar into the Himalayas in search of Himavat, the Magic Mountain of Hindu mythology. They have brought him and his infant half-brother, Hugh, to England, for a series of surrogate parents, a childhood and adolescence of loneliness and vulnerability.

---

7. "*Regarde, spectateur, remontée à bloc, de telle sorte que le ressort se déroule avec lenteur tout le long d'une vie humaine, une des plus parfaites machines construites par les dieux infernaux pour l'anéantissement mathématique d'un mortel.*"

They have turned Geoffrey into a poet, a scholar, a war hero (and killer), and a drunkard; and they have caused young Hugh to become a drifter, an ordinary sort of musician, a failed sailor, a petty plagiarist, and a would-be heroic and virtuous Communist. (Obviously, these *Doppelgänger* represented for Lowry the two aspects which he fancied were warring in himself: the contemplative, scholarly man, and the swashbuckling man of action; but he was self-aware—and humble—enough to depict them each as flawed in very much the same ways as he himself was flawed.) Somewhere, Geoffrey has conceived an enthusiasm for the occult; and how those infernal gods must have welcomed his posturings as magus, as Cabbalistic adept, as black magician. If he had ever possessed any magical powers, ever hoped for any real ascent up the Sephirotic Tree of Life, then alcohol soon ruins it all: the Holy Cabbala demands abstemiousness, and the infernal gods had determined that they would make the Consul's drunkenness the visible manifestation of their machinations. They provide the Consul, in his thirty-ninth year, with a lovely wife, Yvonne, and then cause him to neglect and humiliate her through his drunkenness until she turns for momentary consolation to Hugh, an athletic type of her own age and slightly ordinary intellectual power.

To Mexico they all are brought: Geoffrey and Yvonne first, and then, eighteen months later, Hugh—who arrives just before Yvonne (who had deserted the Consul and divorced him) returns to Quauhnahuac to try to renew their marriage. On the day Yvonne returns, the spring unwinds all the way, and the Consul and Yvonne die with stunning poetic efficiency: the machine works. With two notable exceptions, however: Hugh is left rattling about in the dark forest east of Quauhnahuac, lost in the middle of the road of his life, drunk, unbrave but wanting to be brave, unloving but hoping to love, banging out songs of martial brotherhood on a cheap guitar as his half-brother and Yvonne are destroyed only yards from where he stands. And Jacques Laruelle, the fourth element of the single human who is the subject of the book, a childhood friend of the Consul, a French film producer who has come to Quauhnahuac for no purpose other than to add another humiliation to Geoffrey's burden, is left with nowhere to go, nothing to do: he sits in his grotesque villa, comforted by a quarreling mistress and a roomful of expensive Mayan statuettes he would never be allowed to take with him out of Mexico. Whom the infernal gods do not destroy, they humiliate.

The novel is about damnation. The three epigraphs with which Lowry begins—one from Sophocles, one from Bunyan, and one from Goethe—tell us, in effect, that man is magnificent ("Wonders are many, and none is more wonderful than man. . . . only against Death shall he call for aid in vain; but from baffling maladies he hath devised escapes"); that he must actively desire his salvation if he is to achieve it; and that one's own effort *can* bring about that salvation (*"Wer immer strebend sich bemüht, den können wir erlösen"*). Or, put more negatively: Man is marvelous. If he wants salvation, he can be saved. But sometimes he may not want it. This much, the epigraphs say; it is the function of the rest of the novel to show one marvelous man turning his back on salvation, not wanting it, not only refusing to strive upward but rushing instead headlong into hell, into the arms of the infernal gods.

That Lowry is about cosmic business is evident in the first paragraph of the novel, as he hurtles us down from the stratosphere, down onto the spinning world until we stop at the mountain town of Quauhnahuac. His cinematic eye pans over the city, picking up details—pools, walls, roads, a golf course—until it reaches the Casino de la Selva, on a hill above the town, where two men in white sit talking. They are Jacques Laruelle and Dr. Arturo Díaz Vigil, they have been playing tennis, and they are—of course—discussing their departed friend, the Consul. It is the Day of the Dead in 1939, the first anniversary of his death, and his friends are apparently in some kind of shock. Vigil, whose speech and mannerisms are those of Juan Fernando Márquez, remarks to Laruelle that the Consul had been sick not only in body, "but in that part used to be call: soul. Poor your friend, he spend his money on earth in such continuous tragedies." It is the thing that "used to be call: soul" that interests Lowry; and one of the most important lessons to learn about *Under the Volcano* is that for its author the concept of the soul still meant something: for him, to speak of salvation or damnation was not to speak metaphysically, but to speak of realities. Like his hero, Rimbaud, he felt that *"La théologie est sérieuse, l'enfer est certainement en bas,—et le ciel en haut."* ("Theology is serious, hell is certainly *down below*,—and heaven on high.") [8] If Lowry's novel has any claim to being called tragedy, that claim must base itself in Lowry's almost Elizabethan concept of man and the universe that surrounds him. For Lowry, and the Consul, there *is* heaven; there *is* hell; and between the two there is (to crib from Pascal) only life, the most fragile thing in the world. The tragic quality of the novel derives from this: that the Consul, like Faust, courts damnation, toys with it, and learns too late that it is real—and learns also that hope of heaven would not have been a prerequisite for being saved: that simply loving in the real and fragile world would have sufficed.

Such an antique world-view calls for a response to teleological questions that is passionate, in a way that is quite alien to our disbelieving time. Thus *Under the Volcano* seems to many to be overwrought, melodramatic rather than tragic. We are, after all, watching merely a drunkard's death; and it is sad, and sloppy, and unfortunate—but after all, what is the death of one man, especially so flawed a man? Lowry's answer would be that the death of one man, especially such a man as Geoffrey Firmin, is vitally, crucially important. Not just because he is a brilliant, potentially powerful man (or because he is, partially, Malcolm Lowry), but also because he is, in a way, Lowry's representative of the human spirit, of all mankind: and his peril is our peril, his death our death.

Under the Volcano is, then, a deeply moral work. To say that it advances its cause on several levels at once is to state the obvious —but the obvious is necessary, here. I can, still foreseeing the eventual *Gestalt* approach to the novel, discern at the moment five such levels, all in motion, all interdependent, all pointing toward the inevitable conclusion.

---

8. *"Nuit de L'Enfer," Une Saison en Enfer.* One almost wishes that Lowry had placed at the end of his novel another quotation from the same poem: *"Pourtant, aujourd'hui, je crois avoir fini la relation de mon enfer. C'était bien l'enfer; l'ancien, celui dont le fils de l'homme ouvrit les portes."* ("However, I think I have finished today the story of my hell. It was really hell: the old hell, the one whose doors were opened by the son of man.")

The first of these is that which we might label *chthonic:* the earthbound level, composed of natural elements either on or beneath the earth and (for purposes of neatness in classification) man-made elements which are made to function in accord with Lowry's chthonic grand scheme. Here also belong all subhuman living creatures. Above all, of course, is the great volcano, Popocatepetl, the Smoking Warrior, standing guard over his sleeping mate, Ixtaccihuatl, and serving as representative of all the world's magic mountains: the real ones of Hawaii, Yvonne's birthplace, and of Karakoram and the Hindu Kush, looming in the far north of Geoffrey's native Kashmir; and the mythic or literary ones of the *Divine Comedy,* the *Mahabarata,* and the Hellenic Mount Erebus. In Lowry's novel the conventional salvific notions about ascent of the magic mountain are employed only ironically, negatively; what really concerns him is what, after all, is *under* the volcano: the frightening realm of Tartarus, the infernal abyss below Hades. His characters may walk on the surface of the earth, but they are constantly being reminded of what is below them: the treacherous and fetid *barranca* winds through Quauhnahuac, and yawns also behind the Farolito in Parían, waiting to receive the body of the Consul. "Quauhnahuac was like the times in this respect," Jacques Laruelle reflects in Chapter One, "wherever you turned the abyss was waiting for you round the corner." And there are caves beneath Quauhnahuac, where silver and iron have been pulled for centuries from the earth. In addition to possessing their existential reality, these abyssal images constantly thrust themselves outward until they function as Dante's Malebolge, the eighth ring of the Inferno; the dwelling place of Prometheus, where he is tormented daily by his attendant vulture; of Ixion, tied for all eternity to his spinning infernal wheel; and of Shelley's Alastor, "the dark magician in his visioned cave."

For water, there is the distant sea, serving here chiefly to isolate the action from the rest of the world, and to concentrate it on the "earthly paradise" of Mexico. The sea has been, in the past, the scene of shameful experiences, both minor (Hugh's routine humiliations during his travels aboard the *Philoctetes* and the *Oedipus Tyrannus*) and major (Geoffrey's having been—indirectly, perhaps

—responsible for the immolation in his ship's furnaces of several German U-boat officers); but now it acts either as separator or as an element possible to be known in the future: with luck, Geoffrey and Yvonne might have gone to live at the edge of the sea in British Columbia; and Hugh might or might not after the Day of the Dead in 1939 have gone to sea on a ship futilely and quixotically carrying munitions to the doomed Republican army in Spain.

There are Quauhnahuac's 400 swimming pools, one of which belongs to Geoffrey Firmin; and Hugh and Yvonne do swim twice during the day. But the only water of significance in the novel is conspicuous by its absence: the cleansing, revivifying fountain, represented throughout by the Consul's recollection of a refrain from Marvell's "Clorinda and Damon": "Might a soul bathe there and be clean or slake its draught?" No, of course, here it might not: no water comes even from the shower under which, fully clothed, the Consul stands. Instead of water, we have alcohol, more of it than one would have believed possible to pour into a mere twelve chapters: pulque, beer, Scotch and Irish whiskey, tequila, and the dread mescal.

In the earthly paradise, there are, naturally, gardens; but they are ruined, overgrown, rotted. The once-magnificent Borda gardens of Maximilian and Carlotta have long since been allowed to deteriorate, and in the year of Yvonne's absence from Mexico Geoffrey has allowed their own garden to fall into a dry, obscene, phallic mockery of fruition: in the front yard are "tall, exotic plants, livid and crepuscular . . . perishing on every hand of unnecessary thirst, staggering, it almost appeared, against one another, yet struggling like dying voluptuaries in a vision to maintain some final attitude of potency, or of a collective desolate fecundity." And the main garden, behind the cottage, has become so overgrown that the Consul almost expects *le douanier* Rousseau to "come riding out of it any moment on a tiger."

All around the town is the forest, which exists not to provide shade or coolness, but to obscure and confuse. Through it run dark and twisted paths, leading to no happy end. It is the forest of which Dante speaks in the first canto of his *Inferno:*

Nel mezzo del cammin di nostra vita
    mi ritrovai per una selva oscura
    che la diritta via era smarrita.
A h quanto a dir qual era è cosa dura
    esta selva selvaggia e aspra e forte
    che nel pensier rinova la paura!
[In the middle of the road of our life
I came to myself in a dark wood
Where the straight way was lost.
Ah, how hard a thing it is to tell
Of that wood, savage and harsh and dense,
The thought of which renews my fear!]

This is the forest through which Geoffrey will crawl to reach the Farolito; in which Yvonne will die; and in which Hugh is left, lost, singing, and drunk, at the novel's conclusion.

There are many other aspects of the natural world in Lowry's novel; but they are used either semiotically, like the cleft rock in Chapter Two, which signifies to Yvonne the sundering of her marriage with Geoffrey; or as atypical and taunting instances of affirmation, like the halcyon terrain of Chapter Four, in which Hugh and Yvonne ride through gently sloping fields across a cool stream to reach a tranquil and orderly park. Such beauty cannot be real, Hugh knows; it is only as if he and Yvonne "have been allowed for one hour a glimpse of what never was at all": because this is the day when the dead come to life, they have been allowed a glimpse of the way things might have been had Man not fallen. Much the same thing might be said of the paradisal vision of life in British Columbia which Hugh conjures up for Yvonne in Chapter Four. It is beautiful, but totally impossible, given the fallen state of those who long for it most.

The chthonic imagery is, clearly, archetypally demonic in nature: [9] that is, it employs the traditional affirmative apocalyptic

9. The terminology here derives from Northrop Frye's already cited *Anatomy of Criticism*, most especially from the third essay in this volume, "Archetypal Criticism: Theory of Myths." Also in the background of this discussion is Paul Ricoeur's *The Symbolism of Evil* (New York, 1967).

images of the Mount of Perfection, the fertile valley, the cleansing stream or fountain, and the blossoming garden, but employs them in an inverted, ironic form. What had indicated fruition, now indicates sterility; what had represented cleansing, now represents corruption, and what had symbolized the soul's striving upward toward salvation, now symbolizes the descent into damnation. It is of a world turned upside down that Lowry writes.

He does this also, still on the chthonic level, when he turns to man-made objects. What in an affirmative apocalyptic vision would have been the celestial city is now the seedy, sordid town of Quauhnahuac, presided over by the palace of Cortés, the exploiter of a culture older and more benign than his own; and by the once-beautiful summer estate of Maximilian and Carlotta, now an architectural obscenity:

> The broken pink pillars, in the half-light, might have been waiting to fall down on [Jacques]: the pool, covered with green scum, its steps torn away and hanging by one rotting clamp, to close over his head. The shattered evil-smelling chapel, overgrown with weeds, the crumbling walls, splashed with urine, on which scorpions lurked—wrecked entablature, sad archivolt, slippery stones covered with excreta—this place, where love had once brooded, seemed part of a nightmare.
>
> (*Under the Volcano*, p. 14)

And there are the cantinas, some named with naïve facetiousness (the "Todos Contentos y yo También," the "Amor de les Amores,") some ominously ("La Sepultura"), and one—the worst—called, with supreme irony, "El Farolito"—the Little Lighthouse, the place that the Consul calls "the paradise of his despair." Lowry makes very certain that we catch the significance of its name when, in Chapter Seven, he causes Geoffrey Firmin to cry out, "Could one be faithful to Yvonne and the Farolito both?—Christ, oh pharos of the world, how, and with what blind faith, could one find one's way back, now, through the tumultuous horrors of five thousand shattering awakenings, each more frightful than the last, from a place where even love could not penetrate, and save in the thickest flames there was no courage?" Here is demonic irony at its most savage: the beacon that is meant to represent Christ, the Pharos, is instead a filthy and fatally dangerous cantina, constructed not like a lighthouse but a labyrinth, "really composed of little rooms, each smaller and darker than the last, opening one into another, the last and darkest of all being no larger than a cell." Mythically speaking, the Farolito is a path into the Underworld (the Consul himself notes that it is directly beneath the volcano, Popocatepetl); and, this being a modern, or "displaced," myth, we are not surprised to find in its innermost, cloacal room, not a minotaur, but an obscene dwarf, sitting hunched in a corner on a lavatory seat, "so short his trousered feet didn't reach the littered, befouled floor."

These very potent images all have their appropriately sinister attendants from the insect and animal worlds. The novel swarms with scorpions, spiders, vultures, armadillos, hideous and starving pariah dogs, and horses straight from the Apocalypse. When more benign creatures appear, they do so almost always in sequences like the horseback ride in Chapter Four, when Hugh and Yvonne are accompanied by a pair of foals and a frisky, healthy, and woolly white dog. Other than the ever-present pariah dogs, the animal Geoffrey Firmin sees most often is probably the figure on the label of bottles of Anís del Mono: a red and grinning monkey, brandishing a pitchfork and wagging his barbed tail.

These are the paramount images on the chthonic level of the novel. There are others that the ultimate *Gestalt* interpretation must encompass: the signs, posters, and illustrations along the way, some highly portentous ("*No se puede vivir sin amar,*" "*¿Le gusta este Jardín . . . ?,* *Las Manos de Orlac*), some as mere distractions, used to indicate that the senses of the central characters are constantly being assailed by one appeal after another; until, surrealistically, the gratuitous signs come to seem as momentous as the crucial ones. There are the twisted railway tracks and roads: a grand American-style highway, for instance, enters Quauhnahuac from the north, but becomes lost in the narrow streets of the town and emerges from the south end as a goat track. And, of no small importance, there are the two chief attractions of the carnival that is taking place in Quauhnahuac: the Máquina Infernal, by now surely familiar to us, and the Ferris wheel, looming above the town, and carrying all the symbolic weight Lowry can give it:

> This wheel is of course the Ferris wheel in the square, but it is, if you like, also many other things: it is Buddha's wheel of the law . . . it is eternity, it is the instrument of eternal recurrence, the eternal return, and it is the form of the book; or superficially it can be seen simply in an obvious movie sense as the wheel of time whirling backwards. . . .
>
> (*Selected Letters*, pp. 71–72)

The main point to understand about all of this chthonic imagery is that it is the very opposite of static. Even the volcano seems to be in constant motion, brooding ominously one moment, smoking benignly in the distance the next. The *barranca* fairly snakes along through the countryside, sentient, scheming. The ruined gardens reek of rot and thwarted sensuality; and the cantinas (especially the Farolito) are not safe, snug caves in which the Consul can hide and slake his draught: they are, like the *barranca*, abysses opening into hell. (That the Consul considers them happy and attractive places is a problem shortly to be discussed.) The signs are constantly flashing by one's eyes, and the machines at the carnival either sit silently, menacing and insect-like; or they are in frightening motion, going about their Cocteauvian business of grinding up human lives. Far from being simply "Mexican local colour heaped on in shovelfuls," the natural and man-made setting for the novel is quite possibly the most vital element in it, and as expressive of the "meaning" of *Under the Volcano* as any of its other thematic levels. It is this chthonic level that gives the work its extraordinary textural density, its oppressiveness which is sometimes almost insupportable. Everything in nature is rendered alive and febrile, as in a woodcut by Munch or an oil by Ryder. Such vitality is initially exhilarating, but—like a fever—ultimately exhausting.

Fortunately, there are other levels than the chthonic in *Under the Volcano*. Sometimes they intensify the fever, but occasionally they

332

distract us from it. The second, or *human*, level does both. The background figures seem for the most part to have been suggested by Breughel, or perhaps drawn from Buñuel or Eisenstein films set in Mexico: there are noseless peons, legless beggars, exalted madmen, loathsome old crones, brutal, mustachioed policemen—and, of course, the *pelado* aboard the bus in Chapter Eight, and the laughing dwarf in the *mingitorio* of the Farolito. These extras are really part of the setting, and scarcely function as characters. But there are minor figures who do indeed come across as recognizably human. Dr. Vigil, for instance, is a small triumph: he is not only two kinds of physician, advertising himself publicly as a specialist in illnesses of childhood and nervous indispositions, and privately— in men's rooms—as a clinician for all manner of sexual disorders; he is also a sportsman, a gentleman, and almost as great a drunk as his friend the Consul. Through precise and deft descriptions of a few of his mannerisms (the quick flick of his wrist, say, as he whips his cigarette lighter from his pocket), Lowry conveys to us exactly what sort of person the agreeable Dr. Vigil is: concerned, elegant, intelligent, but perhaps too much of a playboy to take himself or his profession very seriously—a well-meaning but finally rather inadequate Virgil to the Consul's Dante.

The only purely malevolent character in the novel is the mysterious Fructuoso Sanabria (Lowry had toyed with his name for some time before coming up with this suitably ironic final version, which signifies—approximately—"fruitful well-being"), the Chief of Gardeners in Quauhnahuac. It is Sanabria, presumably, who has caused the menacing signs to be placed in all the town's gardens; and it is he who decides the Consul's fate in the last chapter. Sanabria's title is deceptive; as drunk as the Consul is at the Farolito, he can tell that Sanabria is no gardener, but in fact a very important Castilian who has come to Mexico as part of Franco's aid to the rightist revolutionaries there. Sanabria is tall and slim, wears well-cut American tweeds, and has long, beautiful hands, murderer's hands. It is certainly no accident, incidentally, that Lowry also describes Hugh Firmin's hands as "beautiful"; and that both Jacques Laruelle and Yvonne are somewhat vain about their hands. In this novel, only Geoffrey Firmin, like Dana Hilliot in *Ultramarine* and Bill Plantagenet in *Lunar Caustic*, has small, clumsy hands. Sanabria's hard, sombre face seems curiously familiar to the Consul, who has none the less never seen him before this night. After some minutes, the Consul makes the connection: the Chief of Gardeners "might have been the image of himself when, lean, bronzed, serious, beardless, and at the crossroads of his career, he had assumed the Vice Consulship in Granada." Here, then, is yet another destructive alter-ego for the Consul. Sanabria never speaks to him, but judges him guilty, and gives the nod to the man who hurls the Consul into the street and shoots him.

There are several characters who, like the American Fascist Weber, exist primarily to provide the same sort of counterpoint in dialogue that Lowry had experimented with in *Ultramarine;* and there are those who exist to listen to the Consul, and to react sympathetically (like Señora Gregorio, who runs the Terminál Cantina el Bosque) or unsympathetically (like Diosdado, the elephantine proprietor of the Farolito). A few, like Señor Cervantes of the Salon Ofélia, are present for comic relief. And one, at least, is invisible throughout: Juan Cerillo (modelled, like Dr. Vigil, on Juan Fernando Márquez), who has been a friend and mentor of Hugh Firmin in the past, and who now is working near Oaxaca as a rider for the Banco Ejidal. We never see Cerillo; for Hugh he is only a friendly ghost, a good man he ought to visit while in Mexico, but does not.

The emphasis on the human level of *Under the Volcano* is of course on the four chief characters. Since this is Dale Edmonds' "immediate level," let us assume that it is these four who bear the burden of realistic delineation in the novel. Geoffrey Firmin, then, may be any number of extraordinary things, but he is first of all a man, and a man of definable qualities. He has been a very vulnerable and touching kind of orphan, a champion boy golfer, an eccentric sort of scholar, a naval hero, a diplomat. He has for years been engaged in writing a book on "Secret Knowledge," which shows no signs of being completed. He has been, for probably not more than four or five years, a serious drinker. This has ruined both his career and his marriage to Yvonne. He has been in Quauhnahuac as His Majesty's Consul since the spring of 1937; and, now that England has recalled its diplomatic corps from Mexico, is without a job of any kind. (Edmonds makes something of a case for Geoffrey Firmin's being a kind of counter-spy, kept on in Quauhnahuac to look into right-wing activities there; but I am still unconvinced. Since we are operating on a more or less mimetic level, now, it seems appropriate to observe that a hopeless drunk would not really be the sort of man any intelligence service would be likely to employ.)

That he is unemployed does not appear to bother the Consul greatly; for, since Yvonne's departure from Mexico eleven months earlier, he has been able to devote himself wholeheartedly to drinking and to paranoid fantasies. The author of *Under the Volcano* kept as one of his bedside books William James's *Varieties of Religious Experience*, and one suspects that such passages as the following might have had a great deal to do with the conception of Geoffrey Firmin's personality:

> In delusional insanity, paranoia, as they sometimes call it, we may have a diabolical mysticism, a sort of religious mysticism turned upside down. The same sense of ineffable importance in the smallest events, the same texts and words coming with new meanings, the same voices and visions and leadings and missions, the same controlling by extraneous powers; only this time the emotion is pessimistic: instead of consolations we have desolations; the meanings are dreadful; and the powers are enemies to life.[10]

Though his alcoholism is bad indeed, it is not the worst of the Consul's problems—is, in fact, only a symptom of something far more dangerous. He is mad, in the manner described by James; and, though Lowry does not give us very much in the way of early biography to go on, we can nevertheless seize on a few instances of his Consul's life as contributing to this madness. His mother, we know, had died when he was an infant. His father had remarried,

10. William James, *The Varieties of Religious Experience* (New York, 1961 [orig. written 1901–1902]), p. 334. The passage cited comes from Chapters 17–18, "Mysticism."

sired Hugh, and then fled north from Srinagar in search of Himavat, driven by some kind of religious exaltation. Then Geoffrey's
step-mother had died (though not before he had learned to punish
her for, as he felt, having somehow robbed him of his father and his
real mother), and he and Hugh were sent to England, to be raised
by a series of foster-parents. One of these was the poet Abraham
Taskerson (very loosely modelled on Conrad Aiken), who took him
into his large and noisy household near Leasowe, where Geoffrey
was intimidated by Taskerson's several rough and bibulous sons. It
was here that he learned to drink, and it was here that he was surprised by his friend Jacques Laruelle (also a guest of the Taskersons)
in some fumbling sexual activity with a young girl in a bunker on
the local golf course. During the Great War, Geoffrey had been
acting commanding officer of the *S. S. Samaritan*, a British warship
disguised as a freighter, when it captured a German submarine. He
was decorated for his part in this adventure, but he was also court-
martialled (and acquitted) for having been responsible for his ship at
a time when several of his crewmen shoved the captured German
officers into the engineroom fires. His guilt over this incident was
considerable, though there is some reason to suspect that he over-
does it somewhat in order to excuse his drinking.

In 1935 he met Yvonne Constable in Granada. They married, and
were very happy together for perhaps a year. By the time Hugh
Firmin, then twenty-eight, met them in Paris in 1936, though,
Geoffrey had become a drunk, and the marriage was falling apart.
Hugh did not help matters by sleeping with the distraught Yvonne:
one of Geoffrey's strongest beliefs had been in the sacrament of
marriage; and even though he later forgave Hugh, he was unable to
trust Yvonne, or to allow himself to extend his love wholly to her.
His alcoholism had made him nearly useless to the Diplomatic Service, which now posted him to Quauhnahuac, as a way of kicking
him downstairs to "a position where he was least likely to prove a
nuisance to the Empire." In Quauhnahuac his condition has only
worsened. Jacques Laruelle was there (for no very clear reason),
and—once, at least—provided Yvonne with the same sort of
comfort Hugh had offered her in Paris. In December 1937, Yvonne

left the Consul, and returned to California to begin arrangements for a divorce. Geoffrey stayed on in Quauhnahuac, moping about with Laruelle, who soon caused a rift in their friendship by accusing him of using the *Samaritan* incident as an excuse for self-pity; and took one unhappy trip down to Oaxaca, where he and Yvonne had spent some happy nights when they had first come to Mexico.

By November 2, 1938, he is in very bad shape: life for him has become one long round of cantinas, delirium tremens is a frequent affliction, and his characteristic emotion appears to be one of terror. His researches into occult subjects have fed his growing delusional insanity, until he imagines himself tormented by familiars, *Dibbukim* who love best to pursue hermetic scholars and other hubristic sorts. He fancies that he is a black magician who has, through his drunkenness, lost his magical powers. "Give me back my purity," he prays, "the knowledge of the Mysteries that I have betrayed and lost." But, on some saner level, he knows that what ails him is not possession by demonic forces, but a radical inability to love—or, more accurately, since he does in fact love his wife and his half-brother—to manifest his love. Instead, he can only attack those who care for him, as he had attacked his defenseless step-mother in Srinagar, and do his best to destroy love. If he is an Adam in the earthly paradise of Mexico, then the Fall has occurred and his Eve has departed, leaving him there to suffer in solitude, because of his failure to love. The inscription on Jacques's wall, "No se puede vivir sin amar," taunts him until he can no longer bear to look at it. He writes loving and passionate appeals to Yvonne, begging her to return, but cannot bring himself to post them. When she does return to him, he cannot bring himself to declare his love. They do not quite hold hands, they do not quite kiss. They do not (cannot) make love: the Consul is—as he has been for some time, perhaps since soon after their arrival in Quauhnahuac—impotent. They *almost* embrace; they *almost* speak lovingly. And, when they finally do embrace, the Consul looks over her shoulder, says he loves her, and almost adds, "Only I can never forgive you deeply enough." He can, in fact, hardly restrain himself from lashing out at Yvonne as he had lashed out at his step-mother, and shouting, "I hate you!" at her. He loves, in other words, but ruins his love through simultaneous feelings of hatred. He must demean and attack everyone important to him—including, of course, himself.

Even in the midst of his worst rages, however, he still is aware that he is not really serious, that he does not really mean the cruel and destructive things he says and does. He is crippled by guilt, and his damaged ego cannot allow him to grow away from that guilt. So, to hide from confronting himself, he drinks to shatter his consciousness; and to avoid responsibility, he tries to convince himself that his magical dabblings have doomed him, that he has turned his back on God, and come to long for hell. But he still hears that voice—even as he is only minutes away from his death: in the Farolito, after he has had intercourse with the whore, María, he feels that now surely he is completely damned, and slides into what theologians would recognize as the gaiety of despair. But, even as he is aware of a desire for "complete glutted oblivion," a voice seems to be saying in his ear, "Alas, my poor little child, you do not feel any of those things really, only lost, only homeless." He may think of himself as playing Hephaestus to Yvonne's promiscuous Aphrodite, or Prometheus, or Faust, or the failed Cabbalistic adept, or the guilty warrior; and he may posture about how much pleasure he derives from his torment; but actually—on the human level—he is only pathetic: a good man self-destroyed by his inability to overcome whatever it is that prohibits him from loving.

With the three other principal characters, there is not so much that needs to be said, especially if we take Lowry seriously when, in his letter to Jonathan Cape, he says that all four characters are meant not to be considered as individual entities, but as parts of one larger personality. Since all three men have in fact possessed Yvonne, the four have at least a certain sexual connection; and there are other interesting possibilities if we should choose to assign the four traditional familial roles, so that Geoffrey becomes Father (he calls himself "Papa," as do Yvonne and Hugh, who are both twelve years younger than the Consul), Hugh becomes Son (since Geoffrey has served in a more-or-less parental relationship to him), and Jacques, who is Geoffrey's age and who had been a close childhood friend, becomes Brother, or—let us say, since the song was to become a refrain in *Hear Us O Lord From Heaven Thy Dwelling Place*—Frère Jacques. This leaves Yvonne in the role of *das ewig Weibliche:* the eternal feminine, mother, mate, sister, and daughter, all things to all men. If they are not all the same man, as Lowry claims, they might at least constitute one standard Freudian family.

Certainly they all look to Geoffrey for some sort of leadership, though by the time the novel begins they have come to realize that he can do nothing for anyone, least of all himself. Even when they are angry with him, they rarely lose their deference, from which we may infer that until the past few years he had indeed been something like the masterful Fructuoso Sanabria. Yvonne had married him partly because she was looking for a father-substitute, her own father having been a charming alcoholic failure. Hugh had come to him in Paris for help in ironing out his passport difficulties. And it is entirely possible that Jacques Laruelle, whose career as a film producer had gone sour, had come to Quauhnahuac only because the force of the Consul's personality had drawn him there. They are exasperated with Geoffrey, and are not above mocking him and behaving condescendingly toward him; but they still depend on him. All three are where they are because he is there, and they would have no idea of what to do without him. What becomes of Hugh after the Consul and Yvonne are killed is not given us; but we do know that Laruelle stays on in Quauhnahuac for another year before he can bring himself to leave; and even then no hour passes without his thinking of his friend's fate. (Admittedly, he has loved Yvonne, and is mourning her death as well as Geoffrey's.) Once again, the situation is pathetic: here are three loveless people tied to the man who could, by loving them, allow them to love him and one another. But—though there is a certain sensual tension between Hugh and Yvonne throughout the day—nothing happens.

They cannot help the Consul, but they can—as Edmonds points out—harm him. Here is Yvonne, returned to rescue her husband, discovering within the space of a few minutes that both of the men with whom she has cuckolded Geoffrey are in Quauhnahuac, one of them even living at their house. When Hugh arrives, he recognizes the strain his presence is creating, and knows he ought to leave. But he doesn't. Yvonne does ask Hugh to stay, out of her own uncertainty about what is to happen; but he still knows that he should leave. Then, when they meet Jacques as they are walking from the Consul's house to the *zócalo*, where they will take the bus to Tomalín, he insists that they stop by his house for drinks. Since it is in his house that Yvonne had slept with Jacques, the tension increases rapidly. As the day wears on, Hugh and Yvonne often seem more interested in one another than in the fate of the Consul, who is left to wander from one cantina to another, and even to be caught up in the Máquina Infernal at the carnival in Quauhnahuac. And finally, after Geoffrey has limped out of the Salón Ofélia toward Parián and the Farolito, they do a truly sorry job of looking for him— getting drunk themselves, setting caged eagles free, buying guitars: acting, in short, more like a pair of tourists than people hurrying to save a man's life. And so the Consul dies, and Yvonne dies, and Hugh is left stumbling about in the dark forest in the midst of a wild thunderstorm. Jacques is left to gather up the pieces, and draw such conclusions as he may. If the Consul is weak, they are weaker. Perhaps he does betray them, but one cannot say that they deserve a great deal of loyalty. Like the Consul, finally, they are failures: Jacques will never go back to his film career; Hugh will never be more than an "indoor Marxman," never quite in the right place at the right time to make his heroic gesture of solidarity with the masses; and Yvonne ends up as a poor sort of *das ewig Weibliche*: not only does she fail in drawing her man up to heaven, but she is pulled by his death into oblivion herself. Lowry did leave in the final version of the novel the ecstatic and lyrical conclusion to Chapter Eleven, in which Yvonne feels herself being "gathered upwards and borne towards the stars," and told Cape that he was thinking of Yvonne's death as being like that of Margarete in *Faust*, Part I, in which she is translated to heaven as Faust is sent to hell; but since the passage had existed from the time when, in the early drafts of the novel, Yvonne's ecstasy was caused by sexual intercourse with Hugh, Lowry's Faustian allusion strikes one as after-the-fact, a happy accident.

On the third level of meaning, that which I shall call the *political*, we are still mimetically oriented. Now Mexico becomes the earthly paradise first as ruined by exploiting *conquistadores*, and then as jeopardized by left-versus-right revolutionary activity in the late Thirties of this century. The situation in the novel is close to historical fact as described briefly in the fifth chapter of this book. Mexico's government is leftist, proletarian, and agrarian. The legal government is opposed by most Capitalists, who see Cárdenas rapidly paring away their lands and their incomes. To aid them in their plotting, they import from Nazi Germany and Royalist Spain large numbers of terrorists and organizers, who form bands of paramilitary troops. These, calling themselves *Sinarquistas* and shouting their battle-cry of *¡Viva el Cristo Rey!*, claim they are bringing back to Mexico a reign of law and order under the banner of the Church. Quauhnahuac is not a center for Fascist activity, but nearby Parián is. That the Consul should prefer to drink at the Farolito there, next to a garrison of rightist troops, suggests to Dale Edmonds that he is spying on the militia. Perhaps, but it seems just as likely that the Consul visits the Farolito simply because he desires, without being quite aware of it, to go directly to the most perilous place he can find. And, if Edmonds is correct, the Consul is himself being spied on in Quauhnahuac: wherever he goes he notices strange men in sunglasses dogging his footsteps, peering down at him from balconies and hilltops, and disappearing furtively around corners. I prefer to see all this sort of thing as instances of the sort of paranoia described by William James. They derive from the same fear that causes the Consul to believe the large sunflower outside his back window is watching him, full of hatred.

There can, however, be little dispute about the political significance of the ruined-garden motif. Now the cautionary sign that the Consul sees everywhere applies not just to him, as an Adam who has sullied his paradise, but to mankind at large. Now the earth is a garden, in imminent danger of destruction by the forces of oppression (whether Communist or Fascist); and the reason for worldwide peril is announced by the inscription on Jacques's wall: one can't live without loving. Thus it is not only the Consul who has failed to love, but all of the rest of us hypocrite readers as well. And when the Consul dies, civilization is also perishing:

> the world itself was bursting, bursting into black spouts of villages catapulted into space, with himself falling through it all, through the inconceivable pandemonium of a million tanks, through the blazing of ten million burning bodies, falling, into a forest, falling—
>
> *(Under the Volcano*, p. 375)

In Chapter Ten, Hugh and the Consul have their clumsy political argument. Lowry, as I noted earlier, was recording and not inventing this argument: according to Conrad Aiken, it took place between him and Lowry in 1937 in Cuernavaca, with Lowry taking Hugh's position, and Aiken speaking for the Consul. Lowry, says Aiken, was always of vaguely left-wing sympathies, but was not well enough informed politically to make much of a case for his side. The Consul mocks Hugh and his fellow leftists for their empty-headed idealism, and is angry at the harm they do by rushing off willy-nilly in support of whatever cause is currently fashionable. By November 2, 1938, the last great cause, the Spanish Civil War, was all but lost. The final major Republican offensive, the battle of the Ebro delta, was proving a failure. On November 15 the International Brigades would be recalled from Spain, and the Republic would be doomed. Hugh is tormented by his failure to join in the fighting (Juan Cerillo has fought for the Republic, as have many of Hugh's Cambridge contemporaries), and an inner refrain for him throughout the novel is "They are losing the battle of the Ebro." The Consul, however, believes himself to be above political squabbling. Ideologies bore him, as do "people with ideas." One cause is no better than the next. The signs are speaking to him, but he is as deaf to their political import as he is to their private meaning. He is no samaritan.

Nor is Hugh, though his impulses are somewhat more immediately appealing. When they fail, for whatever reason, to come to the aid of the wounded peon lying by the side of the road to Tomalín, the two men are equally guilty. The dying man groans

"Compañero," but neither chooses to be his comrade. The failure is personal, but the implications are universal: it is not enough to talk about one's duty to one's fellow man; one must act, and act with urgency. When Geoffrey lies dying outside the Farolito, an old peasant leans over him, says "Compañero," and then vanishes. It is only at this moment that the intellectually arrogant Consul begins to realize that he is "after all part of humanity" (as Lowry wrote to Cape)—and, of course, it is too late; just as it is too late for Hugh, who is wandering about in the forest, singing songs of the International Brigades. A year later World War II has begun, Laruelle's native France is imperilled, and Jacques Laruelle can do no better than to think to himself that "He had few emotions about the war, save that it was bad. One side or the other would win. And in either case life would be hard. Though if the Allies lost it would be harder. And in either case one's own battle would go on."

It is on the political level of the novel that the Consul's downfall begins to take on tragic overtones. He alone among the three men *had* been a man of action, and a particularly brave one. He alone had been a man of authority. He alone had been perceptive enough to see what was happening, and powerful enough to do something about it all. And even the well-intentioned but somewhat fatuous Hugh had seen more, and done more, than the Consul. On the political level, Geoffrey is not so much victim as victimizer. Even his violent outburst against the Fascists in the Farolito near the end of Chapter Twelve is ineffectual, for he is drunk, and incoherent—and striking out not, for instance, at Fructuoso Sanabria, but at himself.

The political level bears its relation to the fourth, or *magical* level of the novel. If we choose to take this level seriously (as Lowry pretended to do, but I suspect did not—quite), then we can say that, because every element, every symbol in Under the Volcano is an integral part of that infernal machine, then even the most insignificant details have their share in affecting the downfall of Geoffrey Firmin. Everything, moreover, is related to everything else: Geoffrey's world is a world of occult and total correspondence, one in which there is a vital connection not only between things material and things spiritual, but also in a very mysterious way between all things that have concrete existence. Geoffrey is—or had been, before the gods turned against him—an adept in a number of esoteric cults; he had been a magus, a dark magician who was privy to the innermost secrets of alchemy, Rosicrucianism, Swedenborgianism, and—most importantly—the Cabbala, that ancient brotherhood whose initiates believed themselves to possess the divine wisdom which Jehovah had given to Abraham, which Joseph had communicated to the Egyptian priesthood, which Moses had concealed by symbols in the Pentateuch, which Christ had passed on to Saint John, and which finally had been embodied in the hieratic images of the Book of Revelation.

For a complete explanation of all this, one must go to Perle Epstein's *The Private Labyrinth of Malcolm Lowry*. For our purposes, it is sufficient to say that according to the *Zohar*, the sacred book of the Cabbala, God has manifested His existence in Creation by ten *Sephiroth*, or emanations, which are akin to the Platonic Intelligences, intermediaries between the invisible and the material world. These emanations, arranged hierarchically from spiritual down to physical states in an intricate structure known as the Sephirotic Tree, form for the adept a means of achieving salvation. Before the Fall, man had been able to reach the top of this Tree, which is a triad of *Sephiroth: Kether*, the Crown; *Chochma*, Wisdom; and *Binah*, Understanding. But now, corrupted, he can go no higher (unless he possesses the Cabbalistic secrets) than the second triad: *Chesed*, Mercy; *Geburah*, Power; and *Tipheret*, Worldly Glory, For most men, however, only the lower branches of the Tree—those which belong wholly in the material world of appetites and passions—are accessible.

So long as the adept is chaste and abstemious, the Tree remains upright and he can aspire to salvation; but as soon as he violates the Law, the Tree inverts itself (like the Máquina Infernal) and the sinner's climb toward heaven becomes a slide into *Qliphoth*, the realm of husks and demons. This is precisely what happens to Geoffrey Firmin, as he knows full well, and as he had written to Yvonne six months after she had left him in Mexico:

> Or do you find me between Mercy and Understanding, be-
> tween Chesed and Binah (but still at Chesed)—my equilib-
> rium, and equilibrium is all, precarious—balancing, teeter-
> ing over the awful unbridgeable void, the all-but-untraceable
> path of God's lightning back to God? As if I ever were in
> Chesed! More like the Qliphoth.
>
> *(Under the Volcano,* p. 39)

Once the infernal machine, which takes the shape of the inverted
Sephirotic Tree, has been set in motion, everything in the universe
conspires to drive the Consul, with steadily increasing momentum,
down the tree into the abyss below it.

On the magical plane, then, it is not enough to say simply that
Geoffrey Firmin is a drunk: he is—or had been—a mystic, an
adept in the most esoteric varieties of occultism; and his drunkenness is for him no mere vice, but a depravity of awesome proportions, a sickness of the soul, perhaps even—because he comes to
embrace his depravity, and consciously to seek his destruction—a
perverse way to spiritual enlightenment. Thus his final, suicidal de-
bauchery is more than just that: it is a frenzied and headlong leap
into the abyss, a deliberate and successful attempt at self-damnation.
This failed Consul, this erratic and faintly ludicrous drunk, is nothing less than a modern-day type of the Faustian-Promethean rebel, a
man who turns his back on Grace, and who seeks by doing so to acquire diabolical wisdom and power. He knows, like Rimbaud, Baudelaire, and the rest of the *poètes maudits,* that the way down and
the way up are one and the same; and he, like them, prefers the way
down.

He professes to rejoice in his alcoholism. As he lies drunk in a
chair on his veranda, he looks up at the white clouds passing over
him. They seem to say to him, "Drink all morning . . . drink all
day. This is life." A cantina is a beautiful place, he wants to tell
Yvonne as she sits with him in the bar of the Hotel Bella Vista early
on the morning of her return:

> you misunderstand me if you think it is altogether darkness I
> see, and if you insist on thinking so, how can I tell you why I
> do it? But if you look at that sunlight there, ah, then perhaps

you'll get the answer, see, look at the way it falls through
the window: what beauty can compare to that of a cantina
in the early morning? . . . for not even the gates of heaven,
opened wide to receive me, could fill me with such celestial
complicated and hopeless joy as the iron screen that rolls up
with a crash, as the unpadlocked jostling jalousies which
admit those whose souls tremble with the drinks they carry
unsteadily to their lips.

(Under the Volcano, p. 50)

When he recalls the Farolito in Chapter Seven, he feels the atmosphere of the cantina "enclosing him already with its certainty of
sorrow and evil, and with its certainty of something else too, that
escaped him." That something, he realizes, is *peace.* And when in
Jacques' house he gazes at a crude temperance poster called "Los
Borrachones," showing virtuous and abstemious souls flying palely
and happily toward heaven (and flying in pairs, male and female),
while down into hell, "shrieking among falling bottles and emblems
of broken hopes," plunge the drunkards, selfish and florid-faced, he
identifies, of course, with the drunkards, knows that he too will fall
into hell—and then suddenly senses that his drunken plunge has
already occurred: he is already in hell. This causes him to be possessed by a curious calm. And finally, when he flees from the Salón
Ofélia at the conclusion of Chapter Eleven, knowing that his goal is
the Farolito, he sees his flight as one from the "sober and non-alcoholic paradise" offered by Hugh and Yvonne, to the hell of the cantina. He announces to his friends that he chooses hell because he
likes it. "I love hell," he proclaims, "I can't wait to get back there.
In fact I'm running, I'm almost back there already."

It is obvious, from his extensive occult library and from his constant allusions to the Cabbala, that the Consul finds the notion of
flirting with damnation in order to acquire divine (or infernal) wisdom an appealing one. So, obviously, does Lowry, for he fills the
novel with sly and fleeting symbols that we can, if we choose, relate
to one or another occult system. But the true Cabbalistic adept, as
Lowry knew, seeks not the solitude and emptiness of final depravity, but aspires to achieve Godhead. For the true adept, the way up

and the way down are *not* the same: the way up leads to spiritual perfection and heaven; and the way down to emptiness and hell: and these are radically opposed conditions and places, with precisely *nothing* in common. As I mentioned earlier, once one violates his Cabbalistic vows, the abyss is certain, as the whole universe conspires to hurl the corrupted aspirant to hell. The point is that, at least by the time the novel begins, the Consul is no magus at all, and there is no magic in *Under the Volcano*. The demons that taunt him are not *Dibbukim*, but speaking fragments of his self-loathing. The hallucinations that he sees are only functions of delirium tremens. The Consul may (as he thinks to himself, sitting on the toilet at the Salón Ofélia) feel himself "being shattered by the very forces of the universe," but it is simply his own poor madness, with its attendant fears and frustrations, that is destroying him. He is a major adept only in what he calls the Great Brotherhood of Alcohol. And alcohol does not offer "a perverse way to spiritual enlightenment," or even diabolical wisdom and power. It, and the cantinas in which the Consul drinks, offer only oblivion, forgetfulness, avoidance of human or spiritual commitment.

The Consul's mind sees portents everywhere: a sign bearing the number 666, the mark of the Blasphemous Beast of the Apocalypse; men dressed as devils; the chocolate skulls and skeletons consumed by the children of Mexico on the Day of the Dead; the gnomelike maid, Concepta, who may well have issued from the caverns beneath Quauhnahuac; the Satanic symbol of the black dog; and so on. But because his imagination fastens on these things does not mean that they are meant in the novel to have anything other than existential reality; it simply is an indication of the feverish manner in which the Consul's mind functions. Here, perhaps, the Consul comes closest to being like Lowry. It is important to note that this symbolizing frenzy of the Consul is escapist in nature: as long as he concentrates on such abstractions, he can avoid his real problems; as long as he can feel he is already damned (already, even, in hell), he need not fear salvation. He himself knows, moreover, that he does not really believe most of what he says. As he runs from the Salón Ofélia after hurling his final blasphemies at Hugh and Yvonne, he notes to himself that he "wasn't quite serious." And there is that voice, already noted, saying to him at the Farolito that he does not mean any of this damnation business, that he is "only lost, only homeless." The Consul is terrified of life, terrified of human responsibility, terrified of what he sees in himself. When he prays to Cervantes' little statuette of the Virgin in Chapter Eleven, he says, thinking of Yvonne, "Let us be happy again somewhere, if it's only together, if it's only out of this terrible world. Destroy the world!" Here, he is serious. He wants Yvonne, but can imagine their reunion occurring only in oblivion. The crucial component in Geoffrey Firmin's character is that he lives in continual terror. Not Angst, nor *Weltschmerz*, nor even simple fright: *terror*. All his magical posturing is only a way of hiding first from the world in which he has so signally failed, but chiefly from God, who, Geoffrey Firmin is sure, must hate him.

Which brings us to our fifth, or *religious* level. In the never-posted letter to Yvonne which Jacques Laruelle reads on the anniversary of the Consul's death, the Consul had written: "Love is the only thing which gives meaning to our poor ways on earth: not precisely a discovery, I am afraid." Yet knowing this modest commonplace and believing it are not enough. The Consul is a failure, as we have seen, in his attempts to bring himself to love Yvonne, no matter how he tries, or prays: "Please let me make her happy, deliver me from this dreadful tyranny of self. I have sunk low. Let me sink lower still, that I may know the truth. Teach me to love again." Even as he is trying to make sexual love to her, he alienates her ("he felt her body stiffen, becoming hard and cold") and cannot keep his mind from drifting off to thoughts of cantinas. And in the climactic scene in the bullring at Tomalín, when he and Yvonne at last bring themselves to speak the words of love they have wanted to say, and it seems as if there really might be some hope for them, the moment passes, and the Consul's thoughts turn to the drinks he will shortly have at the Salón Ofélia.

If he fails at *eros*, so he does at *agape* (broadly speaking, love of one's fellow man). As we have seen, the Consul is no more a samaritan than his ship had been in wartime. He is far too wrapped up in himself to feel more than a momentary concern for others. His most compassionate encounter, in fact, is with a starving pariah dog in the cantina run by Señora Gregorio.

It is the Consul's failure to experience love in the sense of *logos* (roughly, devotion to the Divine Word, or to God's authority) that concerns us on the religious level. Like Marlowe's Faustus, Geoffrey Firmin knows that one has only to love God and ask for salvation in order to be saved; and, like Faustus, he cannot love, cannot ask. As he walks with Yvonne through their ruined garden on the morning of her return, he tells himself to "Look up at that niche in the wall over there on the house where Christ is still, suffering, who would help you if you asked him: you cannot ask him." He cannot ask for help for the same reason that Faustus could not: he believes that it is too late. Moreover, he is terrified of God (whom he refers to in his conversation with his neighbor Quincey as "the Old Man"—rather a give-away to anyone who recalls how Lowry referred to his father), and dreads the encounter with Him that being saved would require. He would much prefer the abyss, and tries desperately to convince himself that he is looking forward to hell, and that happiness is possible there. To Jacques he says, "*Je crois que le vautour est doux à Prometheus et que les Ixion se plaisent en Enfer.*" But this is only childish whistling in the dark. He *must* be damned, he believes, because he deserves to be. He is guilty (of what, no matter: he *feels* guilty) and, good Protestant that he is, therefore must be ineligible for salvation. Rather than risk an encounter with the wrathful Old Man, he forces his damnation.

And the Consul *is* damned. One can't live without loving. On the religious level, Fray Luís de Leon's words take on their ultimate meaning: without loving God, one cannot live eternally. *Under the Volcano*, then, gives us an immensely detailed and precise portrait of the failure and self-destruction of a good man who finds truth too simple, and who must complicate his life in order to function at all. The too-simple truth that he cannot bring himself to face, is that in order to survive, he must love his wife, his fellow men, and his God. And if Kierkegaard is correct in saying that love is not an exclusively personal attribute, but an attribute by virtue of which or in which one exists for others, then we can say that Geoffrey Firmin aspires to love, prays for the ability to love, but never succeeds in escaping from what he calls "this dreadful tyranny of self" enough to exist in any real way for others. The Consul is right: he already is in hell, and the hell is himself.

On the night of January 10, 1946, the author of *Under the Volcano*, the greatest religious novel of this century, tried to escape from his own dreadful tyranny of self. Even as he had been struggling bravely and daily to write his letter to Jonathan Cape, he had begun to fall into a depression, and both he and Margerie were spending each evening drinking heavily. He decided on the 9th that they needed at least a day's vacation from Cuernavaca and Jacques Laruelle's house, and proposed that they take a bus north to Zamboala. This they did, but everything went wrong. Zamboala was much farther away than Lowry had thought; their bus connections fell through; they ran into a high wind, cut their feet on broken glass, lost their tempers. Somehow they briefly recovered their good spirits on the return trip; but Lowry made the mistake of going out to buy a bottle of mescal for them. Soon they were quarreling bitterly, and Lowry became drunker than he had been in years. He passed out, and awoke in the middle of the night to find himself on the floor of their living room, with the empty mescal bottle in his hand. Full of remorse, and probably still half-drunk, he stumbled over to a chair and sat down, reaching for his old ukulele. As he played softly, trying not to awaken Margerie, who was asleep in her bed, he began to think of his failures as writer and as husband, of the abortive trip to Zamboala, and of the money they were wasting. He picked up a razor blade to cut one of the strings of the ukulele, then slowly, almost experimentally, began to slice at his left wrist. He made no very deep wound, but produced a great deal of blood. The ukulele fell to the floor, Margerie leaped out of bed, saw what had happened, and ran downstairs to call a doctor. Within half an hour Lowry's wrist was bandaged and he was put to bed, heavily dosed with phenobarbital. This had taken place early on Friday morning. Lowry stayed in bed over the weekend, watched by a private nurse and frequently plied with *ochas*, an infusion of tea and grain alcohol. By Sunday evening he was up and at work on his letter to Cape again. He mailed it off to England on Tuesday morning and, feeling quite fit, resolved to take Margerie down to Oaxaca for the meeting with Juan Fernando Márquez.

They left the next morning, sitting as usual in the back of the bus, Margerie quite cheery and Lowry rather abstracted, but quiescent and tractable. The bus stopped in Cuautla, where they transferred to another which was headed south toward Matamoros. They reached Matamoros after sundown, found a room in a hotel that Lowry swore was a converted brothel, and strolled to a cantina for a few drinks. They left Matamoros the next afternoon, spent a second night on the road—at Huajuapan de León—and continued on the following afternoon, passing roadsigns marked *A Parián* and winding down through the fertile valley of Etla, to reach Oaxaca at dusk. The bus pulled up at the door of Lowry's old Hotel Francia, and within minutes they were walking into his former room, Number Forty, where he had once found a vulture sitting on his washbasin, and where he and Juan Fernando had spent many afternoons drinking tequila and giving each other temperance lectures. Nothing much had changed, except that the glass in the window was now broken. After Margerie had bathed, they set off to find the Banco Ejidal. Unable to find the Avenida de Independencia, where the Banco had been, they returned to the hotel—but not before passing by a municipal garden, and being startled to see a sign that read "*¿Le gusta este jardín que es suyo? ¡Evite que sus hijos lo destruyan!*" (This was, incidentally, the first time that Lowry read the sign correctly. Up until now he had in all the drafts of *Under the Volcano* assumed that the Consul's first, mistaken reading of it was correct.)

At dinner in the hotel, Lowry received another shock: seated at a nearby table was his old friend Bousfield, sharer of his sorry days in Acapulco in 1938. Bousfield, talking to three women who shared his table, did not see Lowry, who made no attempt to call attention to

Near Cuernavaca, February 1946.

himself. As soon as he could, Lowry pulled Margerie from her meal and got them up to their room: Bousfield was one ghost from the past he distinctly did *not* want to raise.

The next morning they found the Avenida de Independencia, walked past the cantina that had been the model for Señor Cervantes' Salón Ofélia, noted that it had been converted into a drugstore, and went in to ask for directions to the Banco Ejidal. It had been moved, they were told, to the Avenida Júarez. Beginning to wonder if they were ever going to locate Juan Fernando, they went back to the hotel for lunch, then decided to spend the afternoon by making an excursion to Monte Albán, seven miles to the southwest. Monte Albán had been the great seat of the Zapotecan kings, and

Lowry felt that a pilgrimage on foot would be most appropriate. But the day was hot, and their path lay uphill across railroad lines and cinder heaps. After they had forded a dry stream-bed and got stones in their shoes, they decided to hail a taxi and forego the romantic approach. Lowry, never one to be very impressed by monuments, found Monte Albán rather tedious, and they were back in Oaxaca by 3 P.M. Soon they were off again, this time to visit an archeological museum to which he and Juan Fernando had donated a petrified Indian head which they had found while wandering about the hillsides near Elta in late 1937. They did succeed in finding the museum, but were unable to tell which among the many petrified heads on display was their discovery.

Lowry was awakened on their second morning in Oaxaca by a knock on the door. It was Bousfield, who had seen Lowry after all, and who wanted to talk over the good old days in Acapulco and Mexico City. Lowry was not anxious to do this, and did not invite Bousfield into the room. After a few minutes of strained conversation Bousfield left, but not before he had depressed Lowry thoroughly by telling him that they were "still *characters* in Acapulco."

After breakfast, he and Margerie asked the manager of the hotel if he could help them locate the Banco Ejidal. He made a telephone call to the Banco, then told them they would find it on the corner of Júarez and Humboldt. Sure enough, it was there. Lowry excitedly enquired at the entrance to the building for Señor Márquez. No one seemed to recognize the name, but they were directed to a pretty young typist seated at a desk in the main room of the Banco. They greeted her, and when Lowry showed her Juan Fernando's name written on a scrap of paper, she smiled in recognition. She spoke rapidly in Spanish, and Lowry got the impression from what she was saying that Juan Fernando had moved to Villahermosa, a distant town in the state of Tabasco, in 1939. It was not until the girl began to cry that Lowry realized that his friend had *died* in Villahermosa, in December 1939. The manager of the Banco, a dignified, mustachioed old man whom Lowry vaguely remembered, came over, to tell Lowry how his friend had died: he had been drunk, crazy-drunk, in a cantina, and had got into an argument with another drunk, who had ended the argument by shooting Juan Fernando to death with a pistol. Lowry, weeping and lamenting incoherently, pulled Margerie out in the street. They walked on a few feet until they came to the dark and dirt-floored little Templo del Carmen. They entered and, kneeling, said a prayer for Lowry's "good angel," he who had served as the model for Hugh Firmin's good man, Juan Cerillo, and for the Consul's cheerful friend, Dr. Vigil.

They spent the next day in a dispirited journey to the ruined city of Mitla, 25 miles southeast of Oaxaca, and, still depressed over their discovery of Juan Fernando's death, went to bed early that night. Long before dawn the next morning Lowry awoke, dressed quietly, drank a tumblerful of wine, crept down the stairs to the deserted lobby of the hotel, and set off up the street. He was headed for the cantina that had been the model for his Farolito, with the intention of discovering whether early-morning drinking were really as glorious as he remembered, and as he had caused his Consul to proclaim it to be. The cantina was there, with its blue strips across its façade and its two low entrances. But the entrances were boarded up, and where the name El Farolito had been was now a hastily scrawled notice that the cantina had moved to another part of the city. Lowry walked on, until he came to the steps of the Iglesia de la Soledad, where he had often taken refuge in former times, and where one might pray to the Virgen de la Soledad, Juan Fernando's "Virgin for them who have nobody with." Lowry entered and said a prayer, then walked back to the Francia and went up to awaken Margerie. At six-thirty, the two of them went out together to retrace the walk that Lowry had just taken, so that Margerie could see at least what the outside of the Farolito had looked like. Then they returned to the hotel, ate breakfast, packed their suitcases, paid their bill, and sat down to wait for the bus that would take them back to Cuernavaca. Temporarily, at any rate, it seemed that the hoped-for exorcism of old ghosts had begun at last to work. Juan Fernando, who had shared Lowry's few happy times in Oaxaca, was dead, which was too bad; but they had seen the Hotel Francia and the Farolito, and had learned (slightly to Lowry's disappointment) that no particular horror inhered in them: they were, simply, places.

Tlaxcala, February 1946.

They sat, for once, near the front of the bus on the trip back to Cuernavaca, which must have represented at least a small sort of victory.

For the next six weeks Lowry and Margerie did little in Cuernavaca except rest, swim, and sun themselves. They did make two more short excurions, one to Puebla and one to Tlaxcala, but in the main this period seems to have been one of the quietest of their lives. By March 1 they had grown a little bored, and were homesick for the shack in Dollarton. Before they returned to Canada, however, Margerie wanted to see Acapulco: after all, there were ghosts there, too, even though they had already encountered, in Bousfield, the most formidable of them. On Friday, March 8, they left Cuernavaca for a projected week's stay in Acapulco. Because they would be in Acapulco for such a short time, Margerie left their passports and visas in the Cuernavaca apartment. They went up to Mexico

City and took an Estrella de Oro bus down to Acapulco, via Taxco and Iguala, arriving there in the evenining of Sunday, March 10.

The ghosts did not wait that long to attack Lowry, however. At Chilpancingo, two drunken Chinese men got aboard the bus and sat down on the rear seat with them. At Tierra Colorada the two drunks climbed out and walked "extremely straight" into the nearest cantina. It was all so much like the scene with the pelado in *Under the Volcano* that Lowry was stunned:

> Suddenly a feeling almost of panic again possessed him, inexplicable, and coming from God knows where: occasionally he was allowed such glimpses to remind himself that he had been a creator, but in the larger pattern of their stay in Mexico—though he had never been aware of it till now —it was as if *he* were the character, being moved about for the purposes of some other novelist and by him, in an unimaginable novel, not of this world, that did not, indeed, exist.[11]

This was not a new idea with Lowry, but it was a persistent one. At this time, especially, Geoffrey Firmin was at least as real to him as Malcolm Lowry. It was very easy for Lowry to imagine that he was not so much writing, as being written about, possibly by some capricious and not necessarily talented *daemon*.

He and Margerie arrived in Acapulco without further incident, and stepped from the bus into a cantina which purported to serve German beer. Some time later they wandered over to the Hotel Monterrey and booked a room. It seemed to Lowry that the desk clerk was staring at him suspiciously, possibly remembering some scandal with which Lowry had been connected. And when, the following morning, they set off to swim at La Caleta Beach, it seemed again to him that he was being spied on. Margerie, however, was

11. This passage comes from page 58 of the typescript of *La Mordida*, on which Lowry worked fitfully from 1947 to 1954. This unfinished novel, which deals with his and Margerie's adventures in Mexico from March to May of 1946, consists of 352 typed pages, as well as hundreds of pages of earlier draft versions, and is on deposit in the Special Collections Division of the University of British Columbia Library. On the following pages I draw material from both *La Mordida* and Lowry's letter to A. Ronald Button (*Selected Letters*, pp. 91–112).

Caleta Beach, Acapulco, March 1946.

delighted with the velvety whiteness of the sand and the clear blue
water at La Caleta, and was very glad they had come. After swimming, they decided to try to find rooms in a hotel on the beach,
rather than having to make the trip out from Acapulco proper.
They went to the Quinta Eugenia, and were shown a vacant room
by an old Indian woman, who was so proud of the hotel's plumbing
that she flushed the toilet to show that it worked. It did not. "What
goes down must come up," Lowry commented sagely. They took
the room anyway, and returned to Acapulco for the clothes, Lowry
chuckling the while about the toilet, and singing softly, "Ah, the
old familiar feces."

Their new room was Number 13, and the always superstitious
Lowry was quite anxious throughout their third day in Acapulco,
which was Wednesday, March 13. But he went to sleep that night,
happy at having avoided any sort of calamity during the day. Early

the next morning Lowry went for a long swim. As he was returning to his room the manager's wife hurried up to him to say that there were "some people" waiting outside his room for him. He raced on up to find a hastily dressed and badly frightened Margerie talking to two men from the Office of Migración. They were polite, but firm: they had come to say that they had in their records an unpaid fine of fifty pesos against Lowry for having overstayed his allowed time in Mexico in 1938 along with a note saying that because he had not paid the fine he was not to be allowed back in Mexico without permission of the Chief of Migración. They demanded to see both his and Margerie's papers. (Naturally enough, they assumed that she was Jan.) Lowry explained that their papers were in Cuernavaca, and offered to go there and bring them back. The men replied that this would be impossible: the Lowrys were not to leave their hotel, except to go swimming. The Office of Migración would wire Mexico City to see what was to be done with them.

This was the moment that any old Mexico hand would have recognized as time for payment of *la mordida*, the "bite": the extortion (usually petty) that officialdom has long practiced on tourists and other vulnerable sorts. Since fifty pesos amounted to not much more than $10.00 then, the Lowrys could probably have saved themselves a great deal of harassment, expense, and even physical danger if they had simply handed the money to the officials, shaken hands all round, and left Acapulco promptly. Unfortunately, this solution did not occur to either of them.

The only thing Lowry could think of after the officials had gone was a drink, which he had, much to Margerie's disgust. She went down to the beach, leaving him with his bottle of *habanero*. When she returned, they had one of the worst quarrels of their marriage thus far, as Lowry continued drinking. The only plan he could come up with was that Margerie should go into Acapulco and plead their case to someone in the Oficina de Turismo. This she did, to no avail, while Lowry sat back at the Quinta Eugenia, waiting for her to return with more *habanero*. When she did, he had another drink, then went for his second swim of the day. He actually felt rather proud of himself, and rationalized his behavior in a novel manner:

what he was doing, he felt, was a difficult thing which could only be attempted by the hardy:

> he was pitting, like Paracelsus, the effects of alcohol against the effects of increased physical exercise . . . to drink through and out the other side of a nervous breakdown, or worse. . . . The symptoms had been arriving for some time. Alcohol was partly the cause of it: but alcohol was also the cure. It was a circle, the dependence on alcohol was there: but the circle was not necessarily vicious. It was damned dangerous: it was perhaps unmoral, and all wrong, but there it was. He had had at one time to have the courage to give up alcohol. Now he had to have the courage to be cowardly enough to give in to it.
>
> (*La Mordida*, p. 235)

Though Lowry himself recognized, even as he was noting this curious therapeutic theory in his journals, how it looked as though he were only deceiving himself, he nevertheless kept for much of the rest of his life to the explanation that he was not drinking himself into, but *through* a breakdown. He could be convincing about it, too: Margerie, at least, believed him—occasionally.

For the next six days they went each day into Acapulco, to try to elicit some sort of response, from either Migración or Mexico City, with no success at all. On Saturday, March 16, Lowry asked the sub-chief of Migración to show him what precisely was against him on his files, which turned out to be, in addition to a notice of the money owed, page after page of Lowry's misconduct in 1938: he had apparently been picked up time and again for drunkenness and misconduct. "Borracho, borracho, borracho," said the sub-chief, slapping the file. "Here is your life." There was not much that Lowry could say to this, neither then nor in the days to come.

At noon on Wednesday, March 20, a man from the Oficina Federal de Hacienda banged on their door. He refused to come in, but stood on the porch and shouted at Lowry that he must pay the fine immediately, or go to jail. Nothing Lowry could say did any good. Finally, however, this official agreed to meet with them again that afternoon in the Oficina de Turismo, where there would be an interpreter to help the Lowrys plead their case. At 4 p.m. they were there, with Lowry sensing his increasing difficulty in coping with reality, to hear the official reiterate his demands. He would not be dissuaded: if the fine were not paid within three days, Lowry would go to prison. At length, however, they persuaded him to allow Margerie to travel to Cuernavaca to pick up their papers and money (they had over $500 in a bank there) and return to Acapulco. He gave her until the following Saturday—four days—to accomplish the journey. She left two hours later, on a second-class bus, while Lowry bought three bottles of tequila and returned to the hotel. It seemed to him a foregone conclusion that with Margerie away he would immediately go to pieces, and the safest course seemed to be for him to get drunk quickly and stay that way until she returned. This he did. By the second night of her absence he was having hallucinations, in one of which Juan Fernando Márquez appeared at the foot of his bed to scold him for his lack of responsibility, and for causing such discomfort to Margerie.

Then, shortly after 2 a.m. Saturday morning, he was awakened by a furious Margerie, who had been traveling almost constantly since Wednesday, who had collected all their papers and money, stopped to see the British Consul General in Mexico City about their plight, and then had taken the bus back to Acapulco, having gone now without sleep for two days and nights. "Get up, you drunken bastard," she said to Lowry. He was so terrified that he forgot to ask her what she had accomplished; he was, in fact, speechless. At eight o'clock, she marched him down to breakfast, then got with him on a bus headed for downtown Acapulco, where they could cash the check she had been given in Cuernavaca. Lowry wanted a drink, insisting that he could not possibly sign his name without at least a steadying beer. Margerie was adamant, pushed him into the bank, put the pen and the check in his hand, and told him to write. He could not move his hand. "You infantile pimp," Margerie said, and took him out for his drink. She had borrowed 50 pesos from an acquaintance in Cuernavaca, and proposed now to give this money to the Authorities so that Lowry would not be taken to prison. (In fact, Lowry was in little danger of imprisonment: the Mexican constitution prohibited imprisonment for debt of any kind. But the Lowrys did not know this.) Together with a man named Hudson, who was to act as their interpreter and witness, they walked to the Oficina Federal de Hacienda, and paid the fine. Everyone was polite and apologetic, until the Lowrys asked if they might now leave Acapulco, return to Cuernavaca to gather up their belongings, and then leave Mexico. No. They had still to hear from Mexico City before they could leave Acapulco.

For ten days they sat at the Quinta Eugenia, with no word. Then on Tuesday, April 2, they heard from the British Consul General that the Mexican government was possibly about to deport Lowry. The next day Lowry called the Consulate in Mexico City and was told that, though he probably would not be deported, he would certainly be asked to leave the country. Then, on Thursday, April 4, the Acapulco Office of Migración decided that Lowry had been there too long, and gave him a letter authorizing his departure. On April 5, having been in Acapulco almost a month, they headed back to Cuernavaca. Shortly before dawn the following day their bus pulled into the *zócalo*, and they walked down to Jacques' house feeling like a pair of escaped convicts.

Lowry slept through the next day, and awakened to find Margerie standing at the foot of his bed, holding a letter in her hand. It was from Cape, accepting *Under the Volcano* as it stood, without a single revision: Lowry's heroic letter had won him over. They were stunned, and still too tired after the trouble in Acapulco to be very excited; but it seemed to them they ought to celebrate somehow, so they walked up to the Café Bahía to ask Eduardo Ford to come down for a drink and a swim. While they were in the pool, the evening mail arrived, brought by the bearded and gnomish postman of *Under the Volcano*. There was another letter, this time from America: Reynal and Hitchcock had also accepted the novel—as is, with no changes asked.

It seemed somehow unlikely that the Mexican government would wish further to trouble Lowry, but this was not the case. On Monday morning they left for Mexico City with Ford, who was to act as their interpreter. They sat all day in the offices of Migración, and were finally told to come back "in a few days." Back they went to Cuernavaca. They returned the following Friday, when they were received by a Señor Corunna, chief of the Oficina de Inspección. Corunna said that though they had paid the fifty-peso fine, he had noticed that they had indicated on their Tourist Cards that they were writers, and so might be presumed to have been working during their stay in Mexico, instead of simply touring. As the consequence of this, they would be deported in three days, unless they each put up a bond of 500 pesos: the *mordida* was continuing, obviously. Ford put up the money for them, and then back they went to Cuernavaca. Lowry was shaking badly again, but had recently learned that he could partially control this affliction with phenobarbital. And Margerie's anger at her husband had not entirely subsided. As they sat in their apartment, she wrote in her own notebook of her despair (Lowry, typically, incorporated her notes in *La Mordida*):

> I am so tired, so tired, so tired, tired, tired, I don't care except for a dull anger that flames and rages now and then. . . . And hatred, and disgust that I'm dragged down myself with trying to drink with him and a hatred of bottles and exhaustion and a sense of my soul slipping away and my whole grip on life. I feel at once that I will *not* be brought to this dismal state, that I will regain my decency and cleanliness and love and at the same time a despair so utter and weariness so that all I want is death. Why don't I kill myself? Is it some vague lingering loyalty to [Malcolm] whom I must still love but now only hate and despise and fear?

But Margerie, like Lowry, had amazing recuperative powers; and within the week the two of them were back in Mexico City, battling it out with Señor Corunna. The British Consulate was being less than helpful: obviously, his countrymen there were as tired of the Lowrys as everyone else, and would have been only too happy to see them deported. Corunna threw one obstacle after another at them: they could not leave until they had airline reservations. But they could not secure reservations until they had received their immigration papers—which they could not have until they had had

Passport photos.

photographs made. Then Eduardo Ford called them to say that the government had cashed in his bond for 1000 pesos, and that if he did not produce the money for the bonding company, he himself would be jailed or his business confiscated. The Lowrys paid him 1000 pesos. This sort of harassment continued until Thursday, May 2, when the Lowrys were sent, with their luggage (which was soon pilfered) to 113 Bucarelli, the least pleasant jail in Mexico City, while Migración decided what more it could do to them. They were put together in a small barred room, where they were held incommunicado until nightfall, when they were driven in a taxi to the train station in the company of a police inspector who belonged to the Oficina de Migración in Acapulco, and whom they (secretly) called "Fatty." They were headed for Nuevo Laredo and deportation.

The trip north was a bad one. Fatty was menacing, they were treated like vicious criminals, and Lowry could keep himself together only by filling himself with phenobarbital and occasional swigs from his bottle of *habanero*. They reached Nuevo Laredo after midnight on May 3, and were taken to the Mexican Immigration Office, near the bridge across the Rio Grande to the United States. There deportation orders were typed, and given them to sign. This they refused to do, until Fatty indicated that he had a pistol, and would be happy to use it on them. They were then allowed to go to a nearby hotel for what remained of the night. At 5:30 a.m. a man came from the Immigration Office to take them back for a last few hours of harassment. Finally at 10 a.m. on Saturday, May 4, they were put in a taxi, rushed through the Mexican Customs, and then taken across the border into America. Once Lowry had been cleared through the U.S. Customs, they were free.

So once again Lowry found himself propelled unceremoniously out of his Mexican earthly paradise. Even though the second visit had ultimately become just as harrowing as the first, and he was now not a possibly resilient 29 but a rather brittle—if muscular—37, he was nevertheless happier at this time than he had been upon his arrival in Nogales after the first expulsion in June 1938. He did, after all, have some place to go now, and some urgent reason for going there: little Jimmie Craige was taking care of the shack in Dollarton for him, but Lowry could not help worrying about what might happen if, say, a floating log should become trapped among the pilings of the shack and its pier during the high spring tides. The inside walls, moreover, would have to be built if they were to be able to spend the next winter there. But even more important than the beloved shack, of course, were two other factors that he counted as vital improvements over his previous condition: he now had Margerie as his mate, guide, and nurse; and he had his novel, with its two letters of acceptance.

He and Margerie flew from Laredo to Los Angeles to spend a week with the Woolfans, then took a bus on May 12 back to Vancouver. Jimmie was waiting for them in Dollarton, and they were happy to see that he had taken meticulous care of their shack. Lowry began almost immediately to construct, with Jimmie's help, the inside walls, and also to begin organizing his journals of the Mexican adventure. In the middle of June he wrote his twenty-one page letter to Ronald Button, a Los Angeles attorney, about their difficulties with "la mordida." He had been advised to do so by Button in case of future trouble with Mexico. (One pauses to wonder what more Mexico could have provided the Lowrys in the way of trouble.)

Then on June 22 he heard for the first time from Albert Erskine, who was to be his editor at Reynal and Hitchcock.[1] Erskine had many queries about specific points in the typescript of *Under the Volcano*, and was hoping that Lowry could help clear them up before the novel went into galley proofs. Since Lowry had left his only copy of the novel in Cuernavaca, he could be of little help. But he answered Erskine promptly, giving him what information he could; and then wrote again on June 30 to say that his carbon copy had arrived from Mexico, and that he was ready to answer any questions. Two weeks after this the galley proofs arrived, and Lowry was almost overcome. Thirteen years had elapsed since the publication of *Ultramarine*, and now here was his second novel, in print of sorts. For several hours he tried to ignore the large package from New York that sat so conspicuously on his writing-table in their living room; then at last he opened it, pawed diffidently at the sheets of proof it contained, and sat down to work. Most authors would have taken two weeks to correct their galley proofs: Lowry took four months. From time to time he would stop revising long enough to write Erskine a letter about what he was up to, or to intercede on Margerie's behalf in her comic-awful struggle with Scribner's over the publication of her second mystery novel, *The Last Twist of the Knife*.[2] But he kept for the most part at his work

1. For a discussion of the long correspondence between Lowry and Erskine, see my article, "Malcolm Lowry: Letters to an Editor," cited in Chapter One.
2. Very briefly, the battle with Scribner's began in 1941, when Margerie submitted to them her mystery novel, *The Shapes that Creep*. In June 1942, the book was accepted. She was sent proofs of the novel some months later. Nothing further was heard about it. Then, in August 1944, Margerie gave Scribner's her *second* novel, *The Last Twist of the Knife*. Like the first, it was accepted (in December 1944) and then ignored. Finally, on January 14, 1946, *The Shapes that Creep* was published (Lowry discovered this when, in February, he came upon a copy of it in a Mexico City bookshop). Then, in May 1946, Margerie received a letter from a worried fan: she had just read *The Last Twist of the Knife*, and had noticed that the last chapter seemed to be missing. Margerie, who had no idea that the book had been published, made enquiries, and found that the fan was correct. Lowry

on the proofs, until Margerie realized that he might very well be on his way to rewriting the whole novel yet another time.

Lowry was distracted again in October, when they heard that the Harbour Control Board was once more considering evicting the Dollarton squatters and turning the whole area into a public park. Feeling that something like this was bound to happen eventually, the Lowrys began casting about for somewhere else to live. Vancouver itself was out of the question: Lowry detested all cities, most especially this one. Now that it seemed they might be, if not rich, at least secure, they thought of buying an island to live on in the summer months, and of spending their winters in traveling. They were rather naïve, here, for, though there are dozens of islands both small and large in the Strait of Georgia between Vancouver Island and the mainland of British Columbia, one would even in 1946 have had to be much richer than the Lowrys to buy an entire island. They found this out themselves as soon as they began looking around in earnest; and were by mid-fall thinking in terms of buying a *piece* of an island, and to put up another shack on it. In October they took the ferry from Vancouver to Victoria, on the southern tip of Vancouver Island, then traveled by bus up to the town of Nanaimo, where they caught a ferry to the island of Gabriola, which was almost seven miles long and two miles wide. There was a small town on the northern shore of the island, but the rest looked like real wilderness, and Lowry stored away in his mind the idea that some day they might buy land there. The daydream slowly began formulating itself in his mind as material for fiction, too; and within a few weeks he had conceived the idea of writing a story called "October Ferry to Gabriola." This story, which—as did so many Lowry stories—gradually expanded into a novella and then into a novel, was to be part of his "work in progress" until his death; and, though never completed, did reach a state at which it could at least be sent out to the pub-

---

dropped work on the galleys of *Under the Volcano* and began a series of polite but firm letters to Maxwell Perkins, editor-in-chief at Scribner's. Perkins was appalled, as was Charles Scribner himself; and both men did everything possible to atone for their firm's mistreatment of Margerie. The whole embarrassing incident is covered in Appendix Four of *Selected Letters*, pp. 426–37.

lishers for their opinion. (Margerie eventually prepared an edition of it for publication, and *October Ferry to Gabriola* was brought out by World in 1970.)

Reynal and Hitchcock proposed to publish *Under the Volcano* in February 1947, and had agreed in the contract to pay Margerie and Lowry's expenses for a trip east at that time, so that they could be in New York for all the social and promotional activities. In mid-November Lowry completed his work on the galley proofs (or, more accurately, Margerie took them from him and mailed them off to Erskine), and set himself to working out an itinerary to New York. When he had done so, it was a typical Malcolm Lowry plan: by plane from Vancouver to Seattle, and then by bus across the United States to New Orleans, by ship to Haiti, thence to Miami and up the east coast to New York.

On November 30, then, Lowry and Margerie left Dollarton for Seattle.[3] They took a midnight bus to Portland, Oregon, huddling under their overcoats in the back seat; and then set off the next morning for Wyoming (where the cowboys in Cheyenne delighted Lowry: "Just like the cinema!"), and eastward to Kansas City and St. Louis; finally, down the Mississippi to Memphis and, at noon on December 6, to New Orleans. Lowry had not been much impressed by the land he had seen. While Margerie, on the bus, had constantly noticed magnificent vistas, splendid sunsets, and picturesque natives, he had as usual filled *his* notebook with observations on slag heaps, automobile accidents, billboards, mens' rooms in bus stations and the graffiti therein, and suchlike instances of civilized nastiness.

They found a room, after a good deal of walking and haggling, in a boarding house at 622 St. Ann Street, in the French Quarter just off Chartres Street. The next few days were spent investigating the bars and cafés of the Quarter, going on walking tours of the Vieux

---

3. My information for the Haitian journey comes from the following sources: interviews with Margerie Lowry; the notebooks she and Lowry kept at this time; letters written along the way, mostly to Albert Erskine and James Stern; a 54-page segment from *La Mordida* called "The Dream: Haitian Notes," which elaborates on the material in the journals; and a letter to me from Edgar D. Brooke, dated December 28, 1971, providing me with his recollections of Lowry's activities in Haiti.

Carré, sauntering up and down Bourbon Street. They took an excursion boat a few miles up the Mississippi; they spent an evening in a cemetery, where Lowry wandered from crypt to crypt copying down inscriptions in his notebook. Then, on December 17, the page proofs for *Under the Volcano* arrived. Margerie and Malcolm went straight from the post office into a bar nearby, where they sat down in a back room and started in to work. The bartender was not happy about this, and refused to admit them when they came back the following morning to resume their editing: "We don't know what kind of a thing it is you're doing, and the boys are asking questions." So they went back to their room, where Lowry scrutinized the proofs, and realized that he had, after all, very little to alter. Not that he regarded *Under the Volcano* as completed: far from it. But it was as good as it could be made for the time being, and he wanted to get the proofs off to Erskine before they sailed for Haiti; so on December 20 he mailed them, and they began securing their visas for the next stage of their journey.

They booked passage on a converted Liberty ship, the *S. S. Donald S. Wright*, which was engaged primarily in bringing bauxite from Venezuela to the United States. Lowry went down to the docks to take a look at the ship, and thoroughly disapproved of what he saw: it was, he noted, "totally unlike any other ship he had been on, with what looked like a great iron perpendicular centipede on top of the foremast, the mainmast looked like a telegraph post, and what seemed to be motorcar headlamps dangled from the mainmast, like the vizored helmeted heads of medieval warriors" ("The Dream," *La Mordida*, p. 163). The *Donald S. Wright* was filthy to boot, from stem to stern; and so was her crew. Lowry's nautical sensibilities were offended. She was supposed to sail on Christmas, but the crew was so drunk that the captain delayed sailing until the following day. Some three hours before departure, Lowry stepped ashore to buy cigarettes. At the last minute he arrived back at the pier in a taxi, too drunk to walk unaided. He was carried aboard and bedded down; and the *Donald S. Wright* lumbered out on its week-long voyage to Haiti.

Lowry awoke the following morning with a truly classic hangover, and was able to record in his journal only that he found the Gulf of Mexico to be the world's most depressing body of water, and that he could see very well why Hart Crane should have wanted to commit suicide while sailing across it; but by the next day he had recovered, and enjoyed the rest of the voyage. While en route he wrote most of the preface to *Under the Volcano* for Jonathan Cape, who had requested one, though it was never used. (There are some indications, in various letters, that it was a severely truncated version of his earlier monumental letter to Cape about the novel, and that it was basically the same preface he gave two years later to Clarisse Francillon for her French translation of the novel.)

The ship reached Port-au-Prince on New Year's Eve, too late for passengers or crew to go ashore. So the Lowrys celebrated in the muggy night by eating nuts, drinking ice water, and watching fireworks displays going off in town. Lowry fancied that he heard drums beating in the hills beyond the port.

Early the next morning he came up on deck and jotted down in his notebook what he saw:

> Port-au-Prince is smack in the sun in the morning from the sea, consequently difficult to make out: strangely beautiful houses of pointed roofs and of seemingly Norwegian design, church spires here and there rise vaguely in the sun giving it a look of Tewksbury, while to the right mist lay in pockets of rolling mysterious mountains like Oaxaca, this truly resembling Mexico, for in Mexico too is that sense of infinite mystery as to who lives up in the mountains—who can possibly live there?—what voodoo, what mysterious rites?

After breakfast he and Margerie watched a boat put out from shore. It was the police boat, bringing medical inspectors to the *Donald S. Wright*. Lowry went through his usual agonies once again: would he be kept from going ashore because of alcoholism? would his hand be shaking so badly that he could not sign the police forms? should he have the necessary, steadying drink before the boat arrived? He passed the examination, managed (barely) to sign his name, and then climbed with Margerie into the boat that was to

On board the *Donald S. Wright*, for Haiti, December 1946.

take them ashore. They had made no plans for a place to stay in Port-au-Prince, so their cab-driver took them to the obvious hotel, the one described in all the travel folders as "the darling of all the theater people and literary set": the Grand Hotel Olaffson, a gingerbread Victorian antique in the hills of Pétionville above the city. Their room was dark, with high ceilings and a balcony from which one could look down on the bay and all of the city—quiet now, but readying itself for the Haitian Independence Day and for the Mardi Gras celebrations. In the room next to them was a New Yorker who sobbed quietly all night because his house had just burned down; and down the hall was a delegation of Dominican dignitaries, complete with murderous-looking bodyguards who slept outside the doors of the diplomats' rooms at night.

Before long the Lowrys were more or less caught up by the small, bizarre groups of Americans and other foreigners visiting or living in Port-au-Prince ("international white trash," one member dubbed the group), and were taken to the Centre d'Art, which was the chief rallying point for those who were or who had some pretense to being on the intellectual side. One member who was especially interested in meeting the Lowrys was Edgar D. Brooke, a stringer for *Time-Life*. He had been told that the Lowrys were a "pair":

> Friends had informed me that Mrs. Lowry had hit Port-au-Prince proclaiming that her husband was a genius and constantly reiterated it, managing to convey that he required and merited special treatment but no handling or strenuous approach, as if he were a rare and fragile object. Conveyed also was the message that he should not be encouraged or invited to drink anything, a message with which he was conspicuously at odds.

Brooke met them at an exhibit of Haitian primitive painting at the Centre d'Art, and observed them with lively interest. Margerie, he remembers, was constantly with Lowry, "hovering about and seemingly over him in a protective fashion." She appeared to Brooke to be "tense, nervous, vigilant—a slender woman in a swirling, vividly-colored dirndl skirt who rarely seemed to be still." In contrast, Lowry was indrawn and stiff, standing rigidly with feet together and arms tight against his sides, his brick-red face expressionless except when a remark compelled a monosyllabic response. He had, recalls Brooke, "the air of wariness of one hoping to be unseen and awaiting the chance to disappear. He appeared to find it painful even to be looked at, as if a glance engaging with his own touched a nerve." A few days later, Brooke happened to encounter Lowry walking alone in a field below the Olaffsen:

> I greeted him, and he flushed to a deeper red, ducked his head, and plunged on desperately. In some curious way, he made me feel that he was anything but hostile; would like to be friendly; but found facing and conversing with another

person more than he could bear. Besides, he gave every indication of having drunk heavily. It made me wonder what kind of torture he was combatting and where it would lead.

It was leading very shortly to a major breakdown, the worst that he had thus far experienced. But, even though in Haiti he began immediately to drink almost without cessation, so that Margerie was herself at the edge of despair, he could still—at first—be something like the outrageously funny Malcolm Lowry that his Cambridge and London friends remember. One afternoon Edgar Brooke was lying beside the pool at the Olaffsen, idly watching a young widow named Sheelagh something-or-other, a "hungry, strapping, man-eating woman," whispering and inching her way toward a semi-hypnotized, handsome, young man reclining near her, and wondering where she would drag him for the kill, when the spell was shattered by a loud hail:

> On the top landing of the long staircase sloping down from the top balcony of the Olaffsen, we saw Malcolm Lowry, weaving and holding a glass. He shouted, "Sheelagh! My love! My heart! Wait! I come!" To our horror, he began to run, stumbling but miraculously not falling, down the long flight of stairs, holding his glass aloft. At that moment, Margerie Lowry ran on to the landing and cried out in anguish, "Malcolm! Stop!" As Lowry staggered up to us, smiling in merry triumph, Sheelagh lurched to her feet in a fury and shouted, "You drunken bastard, why don't you drop dead!" Lowry drew himself up in elegant dignity, exclaimed, "You have killed my heart. I die!" And fully clothed, still holding his almost-full glass, he walked straight into the deep end of the pool, and sank like lead, making no effort to regain the surface. Margerie Lowry screamed piercingly, "You bitch. You have killed him!" And she started running down the steps.
> Someone—I think the young man—dove into the pool, hauled Lowry still clutching his glass to the surface, and several people helped to pull him out. After Lowry had gasped a bit and spit out some water, Margerie Lowry towed the sodden man back into the hotel. But I think that every-

one wondered a bit at Lowry's failure to make any apparent move while under water to save himself. At any rate, that was the end of the swimming party. The group broke up and dispersed.

There were two American women (no one remembers their names) staying at the Olaffsen who befriended the Lowrys, and who were not particularly disturbed by such spectacles. About ten days after the Lowrys arrived in Port-au-Prince, these two women introduced them to Philippe Thoby-Marcelin, a young Haitian novelist and poet. "Phito," as they came to call him, had already achieved some small recognition in France, but was having no luck at all in getting his work translated into English. He and Lowry took to one another immediately, and within a matter of days Phito was escorting them around the island, to places no tourist would normally have seen. One night he even went with them into the least accessible poor section of Port-au-Prince, where they witnessed a Voodoo initiation-by-fire ceremony, complete with sacrificed white rooster, walking through flames, incantations, and drums. Lowry was of course fascinated, and began thinking of himself as a potential Voodoo adept. His conversations became full of references to Baron Samedi, Papa Legba, and Damballah the Snake God.

But in spite of Thoby-Marcelin's distractions, Lowry was going downhill rapidly. Margerie could do nothing with him. When she became too protective, he would take off for a bar of particularly disreputable character in an area of Port-au-Prince considered off-limits for the foreign colony. Before long there was a blow-up in which Lowry was a prime participant. He reportedly did considerable damage by throwing glasses and bottles, and was hauled off to jail by the gendarmerie. Soon after he was released, he disappeared for three days, then walked into the Olaffsen one morning, looking as though he had been on a binge of heroic proportions. Not so, he insisted, smiling enigmatically: he had been up in the hills with a Voodoo high priest, being initiated into the innermost secrets of the religion.

Early in the third week in January, the two American women

Lowry and Philippe Toby-Marcelin, Haiti, February 1947.

rented a house in Pétionville, and—not realizing how bad Lowry's condition was—invited him and Margerie to come stay with
them for the rest of their Haitian visit. Lowry sent Albert Erskine a
letter from the Olaffsen, asking him to do something for Phito
("Please try and help Philippe Thoby-Marcelin—he is a great and
truly good man"), and then they moved into the house of the two
ladies. Two nights later Lowry got into a furious argument with
Phito about no one knows what, and Phito ran off. Margerie, sensing that something bad was about to happen, suggested to the ladies
that perhaps she and Lowry ought to move out. They would have
none of it. That afternoon Lowry drank until he was unconscious,
and sobered up the next day only long enough to read adulatory
letters about *Under the Volcano* written by Alfred Kazin and

James Agee which Erskine had forwarded to him (*Selected Letters,* pp. 438–39).

The following evening Margerie came back from shopping in Port-au-Prince to find the two ladies rushing frantically about on their lawn, exclaiming that Lowry was inside the house having a fit. Margerie told them to get Phito, then ran inside, to find her husband in the bathroom on his hands and knees, banging his head back and forth between the toilet bowl and the wall behind it. He was screaming, and apparently convulsing as well. An ambulance soon came, and he was taken to the Notre Dame hospital in the suburb of Canapé-Vert. There he stayed for a week, until his mind was sufficiently clear for him to be released.

As soon as he regained consciousness in the hospital, Lowry asked for his notebook and a pencil, and began taking notes on the whole experience. What else could he do, as a writer whose only material was himself? He was on a long corridor, he wrote, of tall grey-blue doors with lattice-work at the top. Next to his room was one which contained a man who had been castrated, and whose bloody sheets and dressings lay on the floor of the bathroom he shared with Lowry. When he looked out his window, he saw a tree with horns, and a field of pink grass waving in the breeze. Margerie came to visit, and to talk of the new life they would have: perhaps this time they would win through. Lowry wrote in his notebook that he did not want to win through, nor indeed even to leave the hospital— ever. He spent one day lying in his bed, watching a small spider climb about on the wall of his room. And he wrote: "Frankly I have no gift for writing. I started by being a plagiarist. Then I became a hard worker, as one might say, a novelist. Now I am a drunkard again. But what I always wanted to be was a poet." On the morning of February 12, Phito and Margerie came for him, and took him back to the American ladies' house to pack for the trip to the United States. He found time to write Albert Erskine that he had been in the Notre Dame hospital with a fever and a cough, but was now on the mend, and looking forward to their meeting in New York; then went to bed, and awoke the next morning, February 13, weak but ready for their flight to Miami. They said good-

a last heroic line

Paranomasia: someone was
rights impressive-taste with
damming it on to his heart mechanical elegance
and not a mere outlet of emotion

The psychology + honor of the
shakes. The real horror is in
the hands. All the patient's for
concern is the hands, mental +
physical. Banging but . Have
a sense of buzzing inside your
hands. Some of your who dies
never with present (experience
not inspite or present

Why are shakers sometimes considered
never never present?

Bear hampers
the private lives +
their honored

Psychology of the sense of shame.
Psychology of persecution in
relation to the shakes.

But why should one be
afraid of even of pure of the
laboratory, even of cleaning one's
teeth.

(o link this with Trimalcui.
Evaluate your or her problems
with M. honesty.

(a) Can a writer work
with anything really great,
finally, without a home, a
training but his house where he can
write a great work down have,
a house he is continually
in fear of burning down?

Death of a sense of form.
Death of a sense of humor.
Death of sense.
Death.
How do you recover from this?

What do you fear?
Being found out.
Then why do you (act) (myself) + me.?

What do you want to do?
Hide.
Then why do you not come home + hide with
yourself?

How to conquer the death of the
rebellion against the common ill.
Have you not really selected? Honestly,

What do you seek?
Oblivion.
Then why do you behave in such
a way as will inevitably cause
the most agonizing kind of remembrance
— in such a way in short that you
will even have to stop.
The Dr + el S. Weyses onwards
author — like a steady slow
freight train chugging.

Justification of fear of
what other people think.

Why do you hate lives like I live
Pierces Dark Journey as a big live
like? Leviathan

bye to Phito, who had become nearly as important to Lowry as Juan Fernando Márquez had been, and left Haiti. It did not seem to Margerie (as she recorded in her own journal) that they had much reason for hope now, even if *Under the Volcano* were a great success. Lowry's illness was of a magnitude beyond her imagining, and drunkenness was only its symptom, not its cause.

They landed in Miami, and quickly caught a bus to Charleston. From the Argyle Hotel here he wrote a brief letter to James Stern, to say that he'd been "in hospital in Haiti with a cough," that they were looking forward to seeing him in New York, and that they would need a place to stay when they arrived. They stopped the next day in Richmond, where they visited Poe's home and Lowry took some of the notes which he would use in writing the story "Strange Comfort Afforded by the Profession." [4] On the following morning they sent a wire to Albert Erskine that they would be arriving the next day; and early in the morning of February 19— publication day for *Under the Volcano* in the United States— their bus pulled into the Manhattan terminal. They sat shaking and drinking coffee in the restaurant there until Margerie went to a telephone booth and called Erskine at Reynal and Hitchcock. Erskine had not known when during the day the Lowrys were to arrive, and had been eagerly awaiting some word. When Margerie's call came, he took a cab to the bus terminal and loped over to the Lowrys, trembling as much as they with anticipation. The early reviews of *Under the Volcano*, he told Lowry, were unanimously enthusiastic: it was an instant success, a brilliant explosion on the drab post-war literary scene, a book for the ages. Lowry was a Famous Author. The celebrity stammered something unintelligible, ordered a beer, and buried his nose in it. Erskine had got them a room at the Murray Hill Hotel, on Park Avenue and 41st Street, and he now dropped them off there to recuperate from the trip for an hour or two before the festivities began. He and Frank Taylor (another editor at Reynal and Hitchcock) then took them to lunch, and plied them with wine and reviews of the novel until Lowry was quite overcome.

4. *Hear Us O Lord From Heaven Thy Dwelling Place* (New York: Lippincott, 1961), 99–113.

John Woodburn, in the *Saturday Review of Literature*, February 22, (which had a picture of Lowry on its cover) was very nearly ecstatic: he had not been able to set down what he thought of it after only one reading.[5]

> I was so much within its grasp, so profoundly affected by the tides of its prose, the faltering arc of its tragic design . . . that I said to myself: you are this book's fool, it has stolen you and mastered you by some trickery, and you cannot appraise it tranquilly until it leaves you alone. It has not left me alone. In the street, in my room, where it has set its sorrowful music to the metronome of my clock, in the company of many or only one, it has been with me insistently. I have read it twice, and the second time has bound me to it more tightly than before.

For Woodburn, Lowry was "an apt, not aping pupil" of Joyce; *Under the Volcano* was "better, far better" than *The Sun Also Rises*, and compared favorably with the best work of Thomas Wolfe: "Lowry has Wolfe's wild eloquence and bravura, but more grace and compassion." The novel was, he concluded, magnificent, tragic, compassionate, and beautiful.

H. R. Hayes, writing in the *New York Times Book Review*, February 23, was calmer than Woodburn, but no less approving. For him, *Under the Volcano* was a novel "which achieves a rich variety of meaning on many levels, which is written in a style both virile and poetic, which possesses profundity of insight, which is, in short, literature." And Mark Schorer, in the *New York Herald Tribune Book Review*, February 23, added his praise:

> *Under the Volcano* is ostensibly the story of a man's disintegration and death, but within this appearance is the deeper reality of man's fall from grace, the drama of how we are damned and who shall be saved, the basic contrast in human history of the mind confronted by destiny. One other novelist in this century, James Joyce, has brought to his fiction

5. For an excellent examination of Lowry's treatment by reviewers and critics, see Paul J. Black, "Malcolm Lowry's *Under the Volcano:* A Critical Reception Study," unpublished M.A. thesis, University of Windsor, 1966.

such primary experience, and devised a method whereby the naturalistic surface opens into endlessly amplifying symbolic depths, a style capable of posing these final questions in an aesthetic unity, of holding event and symbol, story and meaning absolutely together, of preventing, that is, allegory. It would be no service to Mr. Lowry to push the comparison further.

For any writer at all (even Joyce, one suspects) such accolades as these would have been strong stuff; but for Malcolm Lowry, who had long since become convinced of his failure as a novelist, they were entirely too much. His only response was to draw almost totally within himself, and to drink. This was, of course, his characteristic reaction when forced to make any real contact with the outside world, and in itself it was not too surprising: anyone who had been in near isolation and almost total obscurity for as long as Lowry had been, would have felt confused and perhaps intimidated by sudden praise and publicity. It was in the *degree* of his reaction that Lowry revealed the woeful fragility of his personality. Pathological shyness does not mean simply extreme timidity: it means real terror in the face of social confrontations. Lowry was, quite literally, struck almost dumb by this fear; and, again characteristically, drinking was his only defense against it. With enough alcohol in him, he could just bring himself to face others; but cordiality (except with old and trusted friends, or with those who—like chance acquaintances in bars—would not be likely to make many demands on his intelligence or stability) was out of the question.

They were scheduled to have lunch with Eugene Reynal, of Reynal and Hitchcock, on the second day of their New York visit. Curtice Hitchcock, who had been the more enthusiastic of the two about *Under the Volcano*, had died some months before; and Lowry was sure that Reynal did not like the book, but wanted to meet its author only out of curiosity. Lowry wanted to forego the luncheon, but Erskine pleaded with him until he agreed. Margerie sent him out in the morning for a shave and a haircut, and told him to be back at the hotel in time to change for the meal. Time passed, and Lowry did not return. Margerie called Erskine, then ran down to the barber shop. Lowry had not been there. Erskine arrived, and he and Margerie set off on a round of the neighborhood bars. No sign of Lowry. The time for the luncheon passed, and the search continued, as far down as Third Avenue, until at 5 P.M. they decided to stop for a drink themselves, and sat down in a bar not far from the hotel. In walked Lowry, swaying slightly. Seeing them, he pulled himself up, struck a pose of outraged innocence, and exclaimed, "My best friend and my wife—drunk, together!" He finally did meet Reynal, a few afternoons later, and—being drunk—managed to be quite rude to him, calling him an "office boy."

James Stern and his wife Tania were still in New York, and had made arrangements with Erskine to give a party for Lowry, at which he could be introduced to the dozens of literary New Yorkers who were curious to see the author of the spectacular new novel. No one who knew Lowry at all well would have predicted any sort of success for such a party, but it had to be done: Lowry had been brought to New York, after all, as part of his publishers' promotion plans, and not simply so that he and Margerie could get away from the Dollarton winter. On the evening of the party, the Sterns had the Lowrys to dinner, along with James Agee and Harvey Breit (the critic and reviewer) and their wives. After dinner, the first 50 guests arrived, and Agee, Breit, and Stern stood guard on either side of Lowry, so that he would not feel deserted (and also, possibly, so that he could not flee). Lowry reacted much as he had at the Centre d'Art in Haiti a month earlier. Breit later recalled

> the entering people coming up to [Lowry], saying sincere words of respect or admiration or congratulations, and Mr. Lowry, feet wide apart as though on the deck of a storm-tossed ship, jawbones working relentlessly, staring out of (we think) very blue eyes, and saying nothing, not one simple, solitary syllable. Then the next person or people or group coming up, shaking hands, greeting him, waiting for his reply—and nothing. And the next, and nothing. And nothing, and nothing.[6]

6. Harvey Breit, "In and Out of Books—Obituary," *New York Times Book Review* (July 14, 1947), 8.

In New York Lowry met W. H. Auden, and Stern introduced him to Djuna Barnes (whose *Nightwood* Lowry admired in spite of what he regarded as its repellent subject-matter). Alfred Kazin, who had written to Albert Erskine such a warm letter of appreciation about *Under the Volcano*, was brought to the Sterns' apartment to meet Lowry, and was appalled to see how heavily he was drinking. The Lowrys also saw something of the writer Dawn Powell—who was present, along with Agee, Erskine, Frank Taylor, and Stern—during one of Lowry's most dramatic deathbed scenes.

One afternoon, during another party in Stern's apartment, Lowry disappeared. Looking about for him, Stern opened the bathroom door. "He was standing in front of the mirror," Stern recalled (BBC "Portrait of Malcolm Lowry"), "snorting blood out of his nose, which he caught in his hands, which he thrust up to the ceiling and all over the wall, so that the whole place was red and white. He was in his singlet, staring at himself and blowing bubbles out of his nose and laughing to himself." Margerie and Stern rushed him to a doctor. The bleeding had stopped, and Lowry seemed quite fit. The doctor made a quick patch test for tuberculosis, which registered positive. This was of course no sure diagnosis, but Lowry was convinced he was about to die. He had Stern and Margerie bring him back to the hotel and put him to bed. Then, propped up on pillows and smiling wanly but bravely (Margerie thought afterwards it was the best thing she'd seen since *Camille*), Lowry received his visitors, who sat solemnly in a circle around the bed. From time to time Lowry would cough weakly and say, "Well, perhaps you'd better get me a drink." Nothing at all was wrong with him, but it was, all agreed, a beautiful scene.

On March 4, 1947, after two weeks in New York, he and Margerie took a train up to Niagara-on-the-Lake to spend a few days with Gerald and Betty Noxon. Margerie, who was exhausted after the New York experience, wanted to return to Dollarton by train from Toronto, which would have taken a little over three days. But Lowry was in a hurry to get home, so he proposed to Margerie that he fly on ahead of her, to get the shack in shape for her return: it was, after all, winter; and the roof would probably need repairing, as would the stove. Margerie was dubious, but too tired to protest very much. On March 10, therefore, Lowry flew alone to Vancouver, and Margerie stayed on at the Noxons'. Two days later a wire reached her: "Little house is ready. Meet you at station." So Margerie caught her train, and arrived in Vancouver on March 17—to be met, not by Lowry, but by Maurice Carey, their old landlord from the unpleasant winter of 1939. Lowry, Carey said, was not out at the shack, but at his, Carey's, house in Vancouver, and had been there for the past week, drinking and raving. He seemed to Carey to be in such bad shape that he might need to be committed somewhere, at least temporarily. When Margerie emphatically refused to consider such a move, Carey shrugged, and then drove her to his house so that she might collect her husband. Lowry was indeed there, and drunk, and quite sullen toward Margerie. He refused to go with her out to the shack. But she packed his bag for him, and called a taxi. Lowry fought and swore, but she got him in the cab and out to Dollarton. It was obvious when they arrived that Lowry had not been there, and that he had not even warned Jimmie Craige that they would be returning, so that the old Manxman could at least have begun to set things right for them. The next few days were bad, but Lowry gradually came around as the solitary life on Burrard Inlet had its therapeutic effect. He was able to write to James Stern on March 23, reassuring him about his complete recovery from his "tuberculosis" attack in New York; and to write to Margerie's mother in Los Angeles about the success of *Under the Volcano:*

> The truth is, the beastly book seemed to go off like a hundred skyrockets at once and I am still trying to dodge the sparks and sticks falling on my head which is, I hope, so far from being swollen that it still has the wit to suggest that such success, if this can indeed be called such, may be the worst possible thing that could happen to any serious author.

Presumably he meant by this primarily that the glare of celebrity is harmful to a writer, who cannot concentrate while he is in it; but he must have also meant that he was already falling prey to those multitudes who batten in one way or another on a successful writer. There were suddenly—over-night, almost—those who had had nothing to do with him before, but who now posed as old friends and early supporters; there were those who hoped to enlist his aid in money-making schemes (he received one telegram from Hollywood which said "This is money and I mean big money, Lowry"); and there was even one woman in Los Angeles whom Lowry had known there in the pre-Margerie months of 1938, who came forward to put in a legal claim for 25 per cent of the profits from *Under the Volcano*, because "he had once jokingly remarked to her that if he ever wrote a successful book at all, which at that moment seemed most unlikely, by crikey he'd give her a quarter of the proceeds." [7] Unfortunately, the woman was able to produce a shakily handwritten statement from Lowry corroborating her claim. This gave Lowry and Margerie some hours of real anxiety, until they realized that Lowry had made his promise to the woman during the period when he had been officially recognized by the courts of California as incompetent, and thus unable to make contractual agreements.

Another, more pleasant distraction came in April, when Lowry heard from Gerald Noxon that he had written a radio dramatization of *Under the Volcano* which Fletcher Markle was about to produce for the Columbia Broadcasting System on their Studio One Series. The program, with Everett Sloan as the Consul, was to be broadcast on the evening of March 29. He and Margerie sat in the shack at the scheduled hour, huddled by their short-wave radio, but heard nothing. Some weeks later Lowry did hear a recording of the broadcast, and was not particularly impressed. Noxon, he supposed, must have been under pressure to complete his script as soon as possible, in order to capitalize on the novel's current publicity, and so had not had time to accomplish well the formidable task of compressing *Under the Volcano* into a one-hour program.

Throughout this spring and summer in Dollarton Lowry was writing long and encouraging letters to Philippe Thoby-Marcelin,

7. Recalled by Lowry in "Elephant and Colosseum," *Hear Us O Lord From Heaven Thy Dwelling Place*, p. 140.

who was still trying in vain to have his novels and poems published in England and America. Lowry was himself rather up in the air now about his own situation with publishers: Albert Erskine and Frank Taylor had both quit Reynal and Hitchcock, which was in the process of selling out to Harcourt, Brace; and Erskine was moving over to Random House, while Taylor was heading for Hollywood to work as a producer for MGM. Lowry wanted very much to keep Erskine as his editor, but was afraid he might be bound by contract to go wherever the company of Reynal and Hitchcock went. This problem was to become exacerbated in the early Fifties, until he had no publisher or editor at all. For the moment, however, he felt no more than mild concern.

By April he had begun work on *La Mordida*, which meant chiefly that he was supervising Margerie's typing out a transcription of the longhand notes he had made in Mexico the preceding year. But there was not really a great deal of time for writing, now. For one thing, both he and Margerie were too excited by the good news that was coming in: the rights to bring out *Under the Volcano* in translation had been bought by five foreign countries (French and Italian translations were already in progress, with German soon to follow); the novel was at the moment reaching toward the best-seller lists; and it had been made an alternate choice for May by the Book of the Month Club. His $3000 advance from Reynal and Hitchcock was mostly spent, and they had so far got nothing from sales; but it seemed to them that the novel was about to become a popular as well as a critical success, so that they felt no particular financial pressure. (In fact, however, *Under the Volcano* was never to become more than a middling sort of popular success, reaching its peak of sales only a few weeks after publication, and then declining slowly, until by the end of the decade it had not passed the 30,000 mark: not bad, certainly; but not good enough to put it in a class with *Forever Amber*, say, or *The Lost Weekend*.)

In mid-April the Lowrys spent a few days at a resort on Saltspring Island, across the Strait of Georgia from Vancouver; and in the last week of the month they stayed at an elegant spa, Harrison Hot Springs, sixty miles inland along the Fraser River. Here they passed

386

Saltspring Island, April 1947.

their mornings reading clippings of book reviews, or answering fan mail, and their afternoons swimming or playing golf. Lowry's only real upset during this period came when he read a distinctly unfavorable review of *Under the Volcano* by Jacques Barzun in the May 1947 issue of *Harper's Magazine*. Calling the novel "fulsome and fictitious," Barzun wrote:

> Mr. Lowry . . . is on the side of good behavior, eager to disgust us with tropical vice. He shows this by a long regurgitation of the materials found in *Ulysses* and *The Sun Also Rises*. But while imitating the tricks of Joyce, Dos Passos, and Sterne, he gives us the mind and heart of Sir Philip Gibbs. His three men and lone woman are desperately dull

even when sober, and despite the impressive authorities against me, so is their creator's language.

> Mr. Lowry has . . . moments borrowed from other styles in fiction—Henry James, Thomas Wolfe, the thought-streamers, the surrealists. His novel can be recommended only as an anthology held together by earnestness.

Barzun was not gentle with Lowry or his book, obviously; and Lowry was hurt enough to reply. On May 6 he wrote Barzun (*Selected Letters*, 143–48), taking him to task for having written "such a horribly unfair criticism," and for having been so insulting in the process. He insisted that Barzun had been wrong in the question of influences ("I have never read *Ulysses* through, of Dos Passos I have read only *Three Soldiers*, and of Sterne I have never been able to read more than one page of *Tristram Shandy*"); accused him of being like those reviewers who attacked, and failed to understand, Wolfe, Faulkner, Melville, and James; and denied that he could have written *Under the Volcano* as he did in order to be fashionable—since, living in the Canadian wilderness, he could hardly hope even to know what the fashionable style was, let alone affect it. Barzun wrote a very courteous reponse (*Selected Letters*, 440), saying that "for an injured author" Lowry had been "extraordinarily forbearing, generous, reasonable." He still found *Under the Volcano* derivative and pretentious, and so could not revise his earlier estimate; but he admitted that he might very well be "entirely wrong in this judgment."

Lowry, somewhat mollified, went back to work on *La Mordida*, and simultaneously on its companion-novel, *Dark as the Grave Wherein My Friend Is Laid*. For the next few months he worked on one or the other of these (though mostly on the latter), and spent some time with the poems for *The Lighthouse Invites the Storm*, as well. On July 23, Margerie wrote to Erskine that Lowry was

> fine, tanned as an Indian, and working hard on *Dark as the Grave*, [of] which he has nearly finished a rough draft; what he will decide to work on, that is, really finish, next I

don't know. I had an idea it might be better for him to publish a combined volume of *Lunar Caustic* and rewritten *Ultramarine* next.

Once again, though, the work was interrupted: the Vancouver press had finally learned that hiding nearby was a famous author, and throughout July the Lowrys were waylaid by reporters and photographers, wandering about the shack with pencils and cameras cocked. On August 1, 1947, an article appeared in the *Vancouver Sun* under the leader, "Wealthy Squatters Find Rent-Free Beach Haven." Predictably, it was a reflection not of civic pride in having the author of *Under the Volcano* living nearby, but of moral outrage that a man who had "struck it rich" should be living so easily and cheaply in their midst. The article began: "A successful novelist who could write a cheque for thousands is 'king' of the beach squatters of Royal Row at Dollarton, 10 miles east of Vancouver." The photographs make the shack appear, if not luxurious, at least too comfortable for non-payers of rent; and Margerie ("a successful writer of 'whodunits' ") looks quite elegant, puttering about with her plants and flowers. The Lowrys did not realize it at the time, but they were providing the citizens of Vancouver with enough righteous indignation for them to renew the struggle to destroy the colony at Dollarton.

Not all Lowry's distractions were so unpleasant. Sybil Hutchinson, of McClelland and Stewart, the Canadian publishing house, suggested to Lowry and Earle Birney of the University of British Columbia that they ought to become acquainted. On May 14 Lowry wrote Birney to suggest that they and their wives meet in the "Ladies and Escorts" section of the pub at the Hotel Vancouver. The meeting took place, and was a great success. In the next few weeks Birney introduced them to two other men who were to be among their closest friends in the area: William McConnell, a young Vancouver lawyer and editor, and Einar Neilson, who lived with his wife, Muriel, in an isolated cottage on Bowen Island, north of Vancouver off Horseshoe Bay. This cottage served more than once as a hideaway for Lowry during the bad days ahead.

Dollarton, August–September 1947.

When he was not being bothered by the press, or making new friends, Lowry continued writing. On August 13 he wrote to Erskine that a first draft of *Dark is the Grave* (as it was called at this time) had been completed; and by October he was getting ready to send installments:

> I write to you, with a scalloped sky outside and clouds like a downswirl of shark's fin, or even the Great Dipper, Van Gogh proved true in grey and winter and against a remote ploughed hurricane, a ramshackle plane flying very slow, and against that, what's more, the mountains showing an obscene sort of serge blue, and an old gasoline can banging under the house, and other purple passages I won't bother you with (to say nothing of the two ravens, making love on Friday the 13th on the gigantic dead fir tree) and just now, a rainbow going up like a rocket.
>
> Well, at all events I am writing because there is news. . . . I am writing what can fairly be described as a good book —I'm not sure, of course, precisely, being a kind of side-street to my own consciousness; however, the report of what is going on from my own point of view would seem to be pretty good, as an objective observer I would like to wander miles to queue up, as a subjective one I would say without any qualification at all that it is tremendo siniestro: at all events, pazienza—you will receive it in driblets, I will have a time to go through before I finish and some of what I send you may seem a little wild. We progress toward equilibrium this time instead of in the opposite direction, and the result is considerably more exciting, if not even more horrible, more inspiring is probably the word.

Lowry sent no installments at this time, however, for he suddenly began now to think of avoiding another Canadian winter by traveling. He had already written to James Stern on September 17 to ask about conditions in Paris: could one get by on $200 per month? was Sylvia Beach still there? at what hotel should they stay? where ought they to eat? On October 31 Margerie, excited at the prospect of her first trip abroad, went to the waterfront area of Vancouver to look for a freighter that might take them to Europe, and found another Liberty ship: the *S.S. Brest*, French 5000 tons, scheduled to sail for Rotterdam, Antwerp, and Le Havre early in December, by way of the Panama Canal. Margerie booked passage for them—the *Brest* did not normally carry passengers, but room could be found for the Lowrys in what had in wartime been the cabin of the Chief Gunner—and returned to Dollarton.

Two days later Lowry received from Jonathan Cape clippings of the first two English reviews of *Under the Volcano:* one favorable, from the *Times Literary Supplement* of September 22, and one moderately unfavorable, by D. S. Savage in the *Spectator*, October 10. He barely had time to read them, and to begin to wonder why his novel was so much more enthusiastically received in America than in his own country, when a wire came from the *Brest*'s shipping company, telling them that the date of departure had been moved ahead, and that they should therefore be aboard and ready to sail on November 7, four days hence. Lowry, who had in the last few days commenced writing on yet another projected work (a novella called *Eridanus*—the Lowrys' name for Dollarton— which was later to be largely incorporated into *October Ferry to Gabriola*) had to decide very quickly which of the several manuscripts he wished to work on while in Europe, so that he could pack it in his luggage. He chose *Dark as the Grave*—not that it mattered, since he made no real effort to work on it during the fourteen months they were gone.

They arrived at the pier in Vancouver just at dusk on November 7, accompanied by Einar Neilson, who had come to help with their luggage, and went aboard the *Brest*. Lowry was depressed at having to leave the shack, when it seemed as if they had just got back to it from the Haiti-New York trip, and wrote in his journal of his sadness.

> This morning, walking through the forest, a moment of intense emotion: the path, sodden, a morass of mud, the sad dripping trees and ocherous fallen leaves; here it all is. I cannot believe I won't be walking down the path tomorrow.[8]

8. Lowry, as was his wont, made extensive use of his journal in constructing a fiction of sorts about this journey. It became "Through the Panama," *Hear Us O Lord from Heaven Thy Dwelling Place* (29–98).

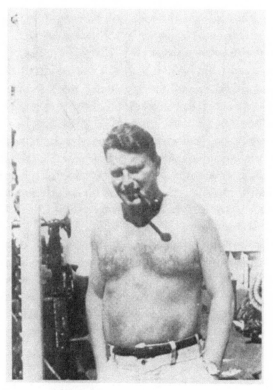

Aboard the *Brest*, November 1947.

He and Margerie sat for hours in their cabin, drinking rum from the
bottle he had providently brought aboard, until they were summoned to the captain's cabin to show their papers to the Immigration officers, and to be given a welcome-aboard cognac by the
captain. The ship finally cast off from the pier at midnight, and
swung round toward Juan de Fuca Strait.

The journey began pleasantly enough. The crew, all Bretons,
were cheery and polite to the Lowrys, and the captain went out of
his way to be courteous. The *Brest* rounded Cape Flattery early on
November 7, and turned south to run down the Pacific Coast. They

put into San Francisco on the night of November 11, and then stopped in Los Angeles overnight. Here Lowry mailed a letter to John Davenport he had written two days earlier, expressing the hope that Davenport and his wife might be able to meet them when they reached Le Havre, and noting that for the first time he felt afraid of the sea: too big, he complained. On the night of November 16 they crossed over the border into Mexican waters, and Lowry spent hours leaning on the port taffrail, staring across at the land that had become the objective correlative of his own inner landscape. When they came abeam of Acapulco, Lowry brought Margerie up on deck to look with him at the white and apparently tranquil city. It seemed to them that they could just make out the Quinta Eugenia on the hillside above Caleta Beach.

On the morning of November 27 the *Brest* reached Balboa, and began its journey through the Canal. The passage was marred for Lowry by his fears that new passengers who were to come aboard in Cristóbal might cause him and Margerie to be separated, in order that enough room be made for everyone. This was not, after all, necessary, and the next day the ship set off across the southern Caribbean, bound for Curaçao.

Here Lowry was able to buy a case of Scotch, so that he no longer had to depend on an invitation to the captain's cabin for a drink; and he had by now eagerly accepted an invitation from the ship's engineers to mess with them instead of with the deck watch— since the engineers, working as they did in such heat, rated a double ration of wine with meals. From Curaçao the *Brest* headed due northeast through the Caribbean, and on December 2—the Lowrys' anniversary—passed by the island of Montserrat and entered the Atlantic, on the final leg of the voyage. Two days later they noticed storm clouds to leeward; and a day after that they were overtaken by a southwesterly winter storm that pursued and beat at them for almost two weeks:

> Low, wild sky with now and then a muted sun; gray, gray sea with a huge roll (grosse houle), but confused and breaking in every direction, some waves breaking like combers on a beach with a crash, with curving snowy crests from which

Curaçao, December 1947.

the wine lifts the spray like a fountain. Some waves collide,
rising to jagged peaks high above the ship, where the top
breaks, and even spouts. Most weirdly beautiful of all, once
in a long time a light comes throgh the top: beneath the
spray appears a pale luminous brilliant green like phospho-
rescence, as though the wave were lighted from within by a
green flame.

("Through the Panama," 80)

On the night of December 11 the ship's hydraulic steerage system
broke down, although they still managed to keep steerage way; and
at dawn all the starboard lifeboats were smashed. By December 12

395

Paris, May 1948.

the wind had reached 100 miles an hour, and Lowry began to suspect that it would be an "unusual bloody miracle" if they pulled through. The crew and passengers were exhausted. No one had slept for two nights, and it was impossible to lie down, or even sit down. They stood, bracing themselves and holding on to anything that was bolted in place. Then, slowly over the next three days, the wind abated, until shortly before noon on December 17, they spotted Bishop Light, off the English coast. Lowry's admiration for French seamanship was boundless.

The *Brest* docked first at Rotterdam, then moved down the coast to Antwerp; and on December 23, after 47 days aboard ship, the Lowrys went ashore at Le Havre. John Davenport was not there to meet them, so they went on to Paris. Lowry gave Margerie a brief introduction to pernod, after which they found a hotel room on the Left Bank. Early the next morning Lowry went out to get cash on the black market. Two days later Margerie, who had been left with no money with which to buy food, and who did not know where they were, and who could speak no French, crept down to the entrance of the hotel, to see her husband staggering up the street toward her, grinning happily. When Margerie told him that she had had nothing to eat for two days, he replied that he hadn't either, but felt quite well nevertheless. After Lowry had slept, and Margerie had eaten, they moved to a hotel on the Rue Saint-Benoît, off the Boulevard Saint-Germain, and called John Davenport, who had just arrived in the city. Margerie thought perhaps that he might be an ally in her struggle to keep Lowry from misbehaving too badly. If so, she was mistaken: an hour later Davenport appeared at their door, wearing a tuxedo jacket, a flannel shirt, and baggy, filthy trousers. He had no money, and was, he said, frightfully thirsty. He and Lowry were gone almost before Margerie could speak (but not before she could grab some money for food); and she saw them infrequently for the next two or three days. Once their binge was over, Margerie sent Davenport back to London, and put Lowry to bed.

A week later, Davenport wrote to suggest that they drive out to the town of Vernon, in Eure, 50 miles northwest of Paris on the road

Lowry and Joan Black, La Cerisaie, April 1948.

to Rouen. He had a friend there, an Irishwoman named Joan Black, who owned a lovely house called "La Cerisaie" (and who was soon to marry Viscount Churchill, later one of Lowry's closest friends). They went, and Joan Black welcomed them very graciously. She was a tall woman with a great deal of *hauteur*, but she and Lowry got on famously (indeed, it was her sudden death in 1957 that sent Lowry into his final, suicidal depression); and before their visit was over she had invited the Lowrys to come to stay at La Cerisaie. This they did, gladly, in the second week in January. Once there, Lowry met one of his staunchest allies: Julienne Lapierre, the cook. She and her husband had once owned and run a restaurant in Giverny, but they had come to work for Joan Black before World War II began. When Miss Black had been interned in the Vichy zone during the occupation, Julienne and her husband had taken care of La Cerisaie; and now they remained, looking on with amused tolerance at their chatelaine's often *outré* guests. Julienne took Lowry under her care, doled out to him his rations of red wine mixed with water, and said to him, "You are my bad egg, but I love you."

In the meantime the translators of *Under the Volcano* at the *Éditions de la Revue Fontaine* were struggling away at their offices in the Rue Gozlin with the novel's argot, its quotations (exact and inexact), its allusions to *Faust*, to Mexican folklore, to Elizabethan English, and so on.[9] They had not exactly given up, but they were very relieved indeed when, toward the end of January, Lowry called them from Vernon. He was anxious, he said, to do whatever he could to help their translation; so would they please send someone out to Vernon as soon as possible? Clarisse Francillon agreed (without much enthusiasm) to go the following Monday. Lowry met her at the train station, and, without saying anything to her, put her into an enormous cab and set off with her toward La Cerisaie. She, frightened, was as mute as he. At La Cerisaie they were met by Margerie and Joan Black, who took them inside for a drink. It was then, wrote Clarisse Francillon, that she really got a look at Lowry, as he stood by the fireplace with a glass of whiskey clutched in his small, plump hand, in his eyes a look that was at once attentive and distant. There was something, she saw, quite strange about him. A little later, when he had left the room, the two ladies explained to her that, yes, he was the Consul, and, yes, the story of *Under the Volcano* was partly his story. (One hopes that Lowry was somewhere nearby, eavesdropping: he would have loved this sort of thing.) By an extreme act of will, they went on, he had stopped drinking in order to write his novel; but now that the book was completed, he was again drinking—which meant of course that he was unable to write a single line. Only one thing could save him here in France: to work on the translation with Clarisse Francillon and her friends. She, naturally, accepted the invita-

9. The material in these paragraphs is drawn from two articles by Clarisse Francillon in *Les Lettres Nouvelles:* "Souvenirs sur Malcolm Lowry," 5:54 (November 1957), 588–603; and "Malcolm, Mon Ami," 8:5 (July–August 1960), 21–25. The French translators of *Under the Volcano* at this time were Mlle. Francillon, Stéphan Rorce, and Max-Pol Fouchet, the editor-in-chief at Fontaine. Rorce was subsequently replaced by Stéphen Spriel.

tion. She could not speak English very well, and he had almost no French; but she began to visit La Cerisaie almost every week-end through the rest of January and February, and would sit with Lowry in the library while he drank diluted wine and attempted to explain the subtleties of his novel to her.

Occasionally, when Margerie could not dissuade him, Lowry would go down to Paris, usually alone, sometimes with her. Clarisse Francillon would often meet him in the street outside the hotel in the Saint-Germain-des-Prés, pacing up and down in his disreputable, raglan-sleeved overcoat, with his collar turned up, and his hands deep in his pockets. Once, when she remarked to him that she had never seen him stagger, he had quite haughtily replied, "An Englishman never staggers."

They would usually go to the Fontaine offices, where she and her colleagues would sit around a table with Lowry, trying to elicit from him why, say, Señor Cervantes' menu should have appeared so hilarious to Geoffrey, Hugh, and Yvonne. Once, Mlle. Francillon brought in a journalist to conduct an interview with Lowry, who had drunk a great deal that day, and who had just found a guitar in an adjoining office. The reporter asked the ritual question: "Why do you write?" Lowry responded, "Out of despair. I am always despairing, then I always try to write, I write always except when I am too despairing." He reached for the cognac bottle which Clarisse Francillon was trying to hide, then continued, "If I should write again, I would write Under, Under, Under the Volcano . . . I write because I am a humorist. King Lear was also a humorist. . . ." Then he continued drinking and strumming on the guitar. It was his only interview in France.

Sometimes when Margerie went with him to Paris, he would play the same fox-and-hounds game he had played with Jan and the Calder-Marshalls in Cuernavaca eleven years earlier: from bistro to bistro, over many hours, until, just as his pursuers were giving up the chase, he would appear, grinning foxily. It never occurred to them that the quickest way of catching him was to stop looking for him.

Clarisse Francillon was saddened to observe that Paris interested

Lowry not at all. Never during this entire period did she see him bother to look at any object of architectural or historical interest. Even in the country, he never glanced at the sun, or the trees. Joan Black's garden was magnificent; but Lowry disdained it utterly, never bothering to look out the window. Strangest of all for a novelist, he seemed absolutely incurious about other human beings. The only thing he really cared about, she concluded, was his first glass of wine in the morning: he would, at La Cerisaie, sleep until close to noon, then dash out of his room, his gray pullover wound around his neck, and run toward the kitchen, where Julienne Lapierre had his glass ready for him.

Perhaps because even this routine was too much for him, or perhaps because Margerie discovered that John Davenport was about to reappear, Lowry went in early March into a hospital in Vernon run by Sisters of Charity, for an "extended rest." When Davenport arrived and went to visit Lowry, he found him quite complacent: the nuns, like Julienne Lapierre, had all fallen for him, and were catering to his every whim—which included the frequent administration of wine, with as well as between meals. The charm of which Conrad Aiken, Ralph Case, and Charlotte Haldane had spoken years before was still operative, evidently.

When Lowry returned to La Cerisaie after two weeks in the hospital, he and Margerie agreed that they needed a seaside vacation, and Joan Black suggested that they take a train down to Cassis, a little fishing village twenty-three miles east of Marseille. They did so, and were not happy: the beach was rocky and precipitous, and Lowry's *amour propre* was badly damaged when, walking out of the sea, he slipped and fell. He mumbled for the rest of the day about "the beastly Mediterranean," and refused to swim again. This sulking led promptly to a return to really heavy drinking. Margerie awakened one morning shortly after to discover that Lowry had fled once more. Before she could take off after him a porter from the luxury hotel on the hill above their *pension* came down to report that her husband was in the hotel bar fighting, and to ask that she come up and extricate him. She did so, and brought him back to their room. As soon as she closed their door, he turned on her, grabbed her by the throat, and begun trying very earnestly to strangle her. Margerie managed a shriek, at which the manager and a helper dashed upstairs and pulled Lowry away from her. Lowry collapsed on the bed, and the manager demanded that they leave the *pension* with all haste.

Later that evening, when Lowry had become relatively coherent (and, as usual, torn by remorse), Margerie suggested that they wire his oldest brother, Stuart, and ask him to come down to Cassis. Lowry, surprisingly, agreed. While they waited for Stuart, Margerie told Lowry of a plan she had formulated with Clarisse Francillon some weeks earlier. It was obvious, they had agreed, that Lowry needed immediate and intensive psychiatric care. When Margerie said that finding the right analyst would not be easy because her husband, being a genius, would require particularly sophisticated treatment, Clarisse Francillon suggested an acquaintance of hers in Zürich: Dr. C. A. Meier, a former *Mitarbeiter* of Jung's and a distinguished psychoanalyst in his own right. Margerie had actually written to Zürich while Lowry was dallying with the nuns, and had sent Dr. Meier a copy of *Under the Volcano*, along with a description of her husband's condition. After looking through the book, Dr. Meier wrote Margerie, and told her that analytic treatment did indeed seem highly indicated, and that he would be interested in taking her husband on. All Margerie had to do was convince Lowry to go to Zürich for the analysis, and find a way to pay for it. It was her hope that Stuart, as a member of the family, would help her with this.[10]

10. Margerie Lowry has for some time maintained that it was with Dr. Carl Jung himself that she spoke; that *he* read *Under the Volcano* and was so struck by its brilliance that he offered to treat Lowry for nothing if Lowry could afford to pay for a room in Zürich for the length of time an analysis would take. In an attempt to confirm this, I wrote in the winter of 1969-70 to Dr. Aniela Jaffé in Zürich, who acted as Jung's secretary, and who has maintained his correspondence files and his library. She could find no record anywhere, either of Malcolm Lowry or of *Under the Volcano*. Some months later I noticed the name of Dr. Meier in one of Lowry's pocket notebooks, found his address, and wrote him. On November 20, 1972, he answered, "I can only tell you that Malcolm Lowry has never been in touch with Jung and that I have only seen Mrs. Lowry once or maybe twice. She gave me the book which I read and then saw her again telling her that I would be interested in taking its author on for analytic treatment which indeed from her

Stuart, it turned out, had no intention of doing so. When he arrived with his wife later in the week, and took a room in the Lowrys' *pension* (the manager had given them a temporary reprieve), it seemed to him that the situation was urgent enough to call for something more immediate than long-term analysis in Zürich. Lowry, staring and dazed, had hardly acknowledged Stuart's arrival, and appeared on the verge of complete collapse. Margerie, however, refused to call a doctor: she was afraid that if she did so Lowry would become violent again, and possibly be deported. Stuart insisted, and a doctor came up from Cassis that afternoon. There was nothing he could do, he said; and recommended that they take him back to England. Stuart was not at all keen about this, and suggested to Margerie that she take him to the American Hospital in Paris. She and Stuart went to see the American Consul in Marseille, who arranged for Lowry's admission to the Paris hospital. While they were in Marseille, Lowry sat back at the *pension* in Cassis writing a note to Albert Erskine:

> Albert the good,
>   Sorry I haven't written.
>   Maybe I am a bit herausgeschmissen,
>   I don't eat my food,
>   and in my bed I have twice geshitten,
>   Anyhow I am living here
>   in a comparative state of mundial fear—
>   Also give my love to my dear Twinbad the bailer
>   I mean dear Frank Taylor.
>   This is written on the night of April 18th
>   Anyway or the other, there is no rhyme
>   Unless you can think of one above.
>   Save love,
>   Malcolm

---

own reports was very highly indicated. Apparently however Mr. Lowry did not have the guts and never turned up at my doorstep. . . ." Perhaps Margerie assumed that Dr. Meier was a sort of apprentice to Jung, and that, once the preliminaries were concluded, Jung himself would take over. This does not, however, seem to have been the case. The conclusion is unavoidable: there was never any correspondence with Jung himself; and Jung never read *Under the Volcano*.

Stuart declined to accompany them on the train to Paris, but escorted them to the station, his arm around his younger brother, who had been heavily sedated to insure his good conduct during the journey. It was the last time they saw each other.

The train left at midnight, and it was a tense trip for Margerie: Lowry kept coming out of the sedation in a rage and fighting it with all his strength, then lapsing for a few minutes back into a daze. A car from the hospital was supposed to have been waiting for them in Paris, but none was there, and Margerie did not dare leave Lowry alone long enough to look for a telephone. After perhaps an hour, a young American came up and offered his services. He drove them to the hospital, where a room was waiting for Lowry, and then he disappeared.

Lowry stayed in the American Hospital for two weeks, and appeared to make a rapid recovery, though it was at this time that a staff psychiatrist told Margerie that the wisest course for her would be to leave her husband, since he was certain eventually to kill either himself, or her. At any rate, by May 12 he had convinced Margerie that they should try another vacation. This time it was to be Italy. They left on May 15 for Florence, where they spent a relatively placid five days, with Lowry drinking only wine; and then moved over to the Adriatic, to Cattólica, a small fishing village south of Rimini. The weather was chilly, but Lowry swam every day, until the noise of the juke boxes in the cafés along the waterfront began to get on his nerves. They traveled on up to Venice, which Lowry found delightful. They did everything there that tourists are supposed to do: swam at the Lido, boated down the Grand Canal, were photographed with pigeons in the Piazza San Marco, toured the Doge's Palace, and looked at Byron's tiny cell in the dungeons by the Bridge of Sighs ("What a wonderful place to write!" Lowry exclaimed, and Margerie took him seriously). They stayed in Venice for perhaps a week, after which their schedule called for a trip to Rome. Lowry did not want to leave Venice, and became increasingly tense as their day of departure approached; but Margerie, who was looking forward very much to seeing Rome, insisted that they adhere to the schedule. On June 1, they left by train from Venice, and Lowry slept throughout most of the journey.

In Rome the following morning, they went to the Hotel Inghilterra, on the Via Bocca di Leone. Soon after they had checked in, Margerie walked up to the American Express office to look for mail. She was gone from the hotel for no more than half an hour. When she returned, she was stopped at the desk: her husband had gone into the hotel bar, become drunk, started screaming, and attacked someone. Margerie had some of the hotel staff wrestle Lowry to his room and lock him inside. They called a doctor. While they waited for him to arrive, they stood outside the door to the room, listening in horror as Lowry ran about inside, shrieking and banging his head against the walls. Finally the doctor arrived and gave Lowry a sedative. It was clear to him that Lowry was obviously in the midst of a severe breakdown, and ought to be hospitalized at once, before he became really dangerous to himself and others. With the doctor's help, Margerie found a sanitarium just outside the city that had space for Lowry. Their first week in Rome, then, was spent at this sanitarium where, for $50.00 a day, Margerie and Lowry had adjoining rooms. With the exception of the physician who cared for Lowry, no one in the sanitarium spoke English. Even though Lowry was heavily sedated throughout this time, a guard was assigned to his room 24 hours a day. Some time during their third night there, the guard fell asleep in his chair. Lowry leaped out of bed and raced for Margerie's room, where he tried once more to strangle her. The guard awoke and subdued him, not without a great deal of difficulty. Predictably, Lowry once again made what seemed to be a phenomenally rapid recovery during the next two days, so that his physician, who perhaps knew nothing of Lowry's past behavior, released him. I am at a loss to explain why Margerie allowed him to be released, unless perhaps she was convinced after each of Lowry's collapses that his robust constitution might this time pull him through. But her own journals from Acapulco and from Haiti show very clearly that she was in fact quite aware of the seriousness of Lowry's condition, and not, as his various doctors apparently were, deluded by the outward signs of vigorous good health that he could manifest so convincingly. Perhaps she was simply hoping against hope that each collapse would be the last, and that Lowry would finally be able to function with relative normality. In any case, she found them a room in a *pensione* just off the Via Veneto, and Lowry spent a pleasant few days sitting in trattorias and sunning himself as he continued his practice of filling up his little notebooks with random observations. He stopped by Keats's house on the Piazza di Spagna, and got the idea for his story "Strange Comfort Afforded by the Profession"; and went to the zoo in the Borghese Gardens, where he recognized one of the elephants as being Rosemary, whom the *Pyrrhus* had brought from the Far East during Lowry's first voyage, in 1927. This incident was to be the basis of "Elephant and Colosseum" (*Hear Us O Lord*, 115–73). Then, when Margerie judged that he had fully recuperated, she produced the touring itinerary, and they were off. Judging from her notebooks, Margerie was an indefatigable and enthusiastic tourist: wherever they went, she studied, pondered, and waxed appropriately ecstatic. This conscientious exuberance brought out a response in Lowry that one might call fond irony, or affectionate wryness. When they visited the Colosseum, and Margerie exclaimed, "Wow! Isn't it colossal!" Lowry remarked that it looked to him like the Albert Hall in a dentist's nightmare. At St. Peter's, as Margerie rhapsodized over the Pietà, Lowry, who had been walking about with his collar undone and his jacket carried over his shoulder, disappeared behind a column, to emerge moments later, jacket on and tie in place, to stand reverently beside her, hands clasped before him. And at the Vatican, they entered the Sistine Chapel, where they lay on benches in order to look up at Michelangelo's ceiling. After some minutes, Lowry looked over at Margerie and said, "My God, do you remember when we painted the ceiling in the shack?" Margerie got the point, but nonetheless remained the indomitable tourist.

On June 13 they left Rome for Naples on the *rapido;* and, after putting up at the Hotel Patria, hired a horse cab for a ride around the city. Naples was a disappointment after Rome: the people were neither so happy nor well-dressed as Romans, and the city itself had for Margerie a "shabby, bitter look." She was depressed by the ubiquitous slums, but Lowry seemed much more interested in them than in what Baedeker found noteworthy there. Two days after their arrival they joined a group of tourists in an ascent of Vesuvius. A chairlift took them from Pugliano to a point near the top of the volcano, and they climbed the rest of the way, until they reached the rim of the crater. If Lowry was thinking of the Consul's final vision, he said nothing about it.

After a one-day trip to Pompeii, from which eventually came "The Present Estate of Pompeii" (*Hear Us O Lord*, 175–200), they moved on to Capri, where Lowry found a hotel at the Grande Marina—not the smart place to go, but on the beach. Here they visited (of course) the Blue Grotto and climbed Monte Solaro. They succeeded also in meeting Norman Douglas, whose habit it was to come down from the Villa Tuoro every day at noon, and sit for a short time in a café that looked out over the bay toward Naples and Vesuvius. The Lowrys sat there with him on several occasions, very pleased that he should deign to notice them. The Capri vacation sounds pleasant enough, but apparently Margerie was beginning to see in Lowry signs of a new breakdown; for, when they heard from Albert Erskine that he would be in Paris, she jumped at this chance to return to the relative security of that city, where there were friends who could help her through any new outburst Lowry might make. The day after they heard from Erskine they returned to Paris, arriving in the evening of July 12. Lowry had bought a large bottle of chianti near the train station in Rome, and was able to keep himself comfortably drunk until they met Erskine—who had only twenty-four hours to spend in Paris, and was rather disappointed that Lowry was not really able to carry on any sort of useful conversation for the one day that was available to them.

When Erskine had gone, Clarisse Francillon took Lowry under her wing, so that Margerie could have a little time to herself. They went to her flat, and Lowry walked into the kitchen and immediately ferreted out a bottle of rum which she had hidden there. Almost in tears, she demanded that he give her the bottle. Lowry refused. She said that if he did not give it to her, she would never again speak to him. He answered, "Oh, you'll speak to me; you love me too much not to." And kept the bottle.

On July 21 Lowry and Margerie returned to La Cerisaie, and Lowry tried, with only partial success, to go back on the watered-wine regimen of a few months before. He was not violent, but it seemed to Margerie—and to Joan Black as well—that he was now sliding into a condition almost worse than violence: a sort of sad apathy, in which he simply sat for long hours without speaking, or hearing what was said to him. Albert Erskine called on August 1 to say goodbye before he returned to America, and both Lowry and Margerie managed to sound cheery enough. But Margerie wrote Erskine that afternoon, to say that she hadn't been able to speak freely when he had called, and to explain to him Lowry's condition as she saw it:

> The tragic fact is that Malcolm is losing his mind & now it is going quickly so that one can see the change from week to week. He has periods of apparent calm & brilliance followed by periods of blackness. And he is becoming actively dangerous: first to himself & me but now more savage to anyone who crosses him in any way. Of course when he drinks it becomes intensely aggravated.

The only chance, she said, was to get him to Switzerland to see Jung, "who may be able to help him unless his mind goes completely in the meantime." She felt that Lowry could be persuaded to go, but first they had to find money. She had written his family to ask for their help, but in case they should not be willing to send money, she was ready to try to find work in Europe to finance Lowry's therapy; or even to return to America, if nothing turned up in Europe.

Eight days later Margerie again wrote Erskine, to say that she was making arrangements for them both to go to Switzerland as quickly as possible. She still had not heard from Lowry's relatives, she said, but had learned that his European royalties would at least allow them to begin whatever treatment was possible. She enclosed a letter that "the poor old boy" tried to write Erskine, on a little scrap of flimsy paper, which he had covered with an almost indecipherable scrawl. It is of crucial importance to anyone who seeks to understand both the struggles and the weaknesses of its author:

> I have to confess . . . that I am going steadily and even beautifully downhill: my memory misses beats at every moment, & my mornings are on all fours. Turning the whole business round in a nutshell I am only sober or merry in a whisky bottle, & since whisky is impossible to procure you can imagine how merry I am, & lucid, & by Christ I am lucid. And merry. But Jesus. The trouble is, apart from Self, that part [which] used to be called: consciousness. I have now reached a position where every night I write five novels in imagination, have total recall (whatever that means too) but am unable to write a word. I cannot explain in human terms the incredible effort it has cost me even to write this silly little note, in a Breughel garden with dogs and barrels & vin kegs & chickens & sunsets & morning glory with an approaching storm and a bottle of half wine. And now the rain! Let it come, seated as I am on Breughel barrel by a dogs grave crowned by dead irises. The wind is rising too, both on the ocean & in the stomach. And I have been kind to in a way I do not deserve. I have to write pretty fast. . . .
> A night dove has started to hoot & says incessantly the word "dream, dream." A bright idea. I remember always your kindness and generosity.
>
> (*Selected Letters*, p. 165)

Here is the essential Malcolm Lowry: sick, more than half-drunk, afraid that he has lost the power to write—and yet still writing with beauty and even tragic intensity. And, what is more, capable of self-mockery ("The wind is rising too, both on the ocean & in the stomach"): partly, to be sure, the self-deprecation that alcoholics fall into in order to avoid seeming maudlin; but in Lowry's case indicative of his undeniable courage—a refusal to give in completely to the despair that threatened him daily. The "poor old boy" had written a scrap of a letter that was better poetry by far then his best poem.

Mont-Saint-Michel, October 1948.

They did not go to Switzerland. Instead, once again, Lowry came out of his depression and was eager to take Margerie on more tours. On October 2 they set off from Paris once again, to begin a journey through Brittany. Their first stop was Mont-Saint-Michel, where Lowry wrote Jimmie Craige that "Here the tide comes in at 60 miles an hour and 48 feet high—there are quick sands all around and the swimming is much better *home* in Dollarton. Please guard our beloved house and pier, and use it as you will" (*Selected Letters*, p. 166). From Mont-Saint-Michel they went to St. Malo, still devastated from Allied bombings and shellings during the war; then swung down along the south coast of Brittany to look at Carnac.

Lowry was somewhat better, now, but Margerie still wanted to pursue her plan to get him to Zürich. She was not particularly pleased when Julian Trevelyan came by one day to say hello, and to take Lowry out for a stroll. Trevelyan recalled (BBC "Portrait of Malcolm Lowry") that Lowry insisted they visit the Grand Guignol, which delighted him. Trevelyan had a hard time getting Lowry home, since, freed from Margerie's supervision, he obviously intended to stop in every bar in Montmartre. Finally back at St. Germain, they went into one last bistro, where Lowry said, "You know they say I ought to be psychoanalyzed." Trevelyan told Lowry that he didn't need a psychoanalyst; he simply needed to get to work. When Lowry repeated this to Margerie, she was furious with Trevelyan. Glaring, she said to him, "What you've undone, Julian, I can't say." She had spent months in convincing Lowry that he needed analysis, and was afraid that Trevelyan's matter-of-fact diagnosis had undermined all her work.

On November 20 she nevertheless flew from Paris to London, leaving Lowry once again in the care of Clarisse Francillon. In London she called Stuart Lowry at his home in Cheshire. Stuart was noncommital, and Margerie realized that her only real hope for financial aid lay in befriending Lowry's mother. She took a train to Liverpool, where Stuart met her and took her to the office of his solicitor. It seemed to her that Stuart was ashamed of the fact of his youngest brother's alcoholism and possible insanity, and so preferred simply not to think of it. She asked him to take her out to Cheshire so that she could meet the mother, who could have afforded to pay for Lowry's analysis ten times over. Mrs. Lowry was friendly enough, and quite pleased when Margerie showed her some of the reviews of *Under the Volcano* (which she had not read). She took Margerie upstairs to show her Lowry's room, and cried when Margerie tried to describe her son's condition to her. But when Margerie asked for money, Mrs. Lowry became vague, and referred Margerie back to Stuart. Realizing that she had failed, Margerie returned to Paris—to find Lowry busily and happily working away with the staff of Fontaine on last-minute revisions of their translation.

They spent Christmas of 1948 at La Cerisaie, and then began preparations for their return to Dollarton. Early in January they flew to London, where, because of a serious winter storm over the Atlantic, their flight to Montreal via Shannon and Gander was delayed for fourteen hours. Lowry telephoned John Davenport and Arthur Calder-Marshall, who showed up shortly afterwards at the airport. The three men sat in the airport pub and made a very long night of it, while Margerie, whose fondness for Lowry's friends was at the moment rather limited, sat alone in the transient lounge. This booze-up marked the beginning of a truly remarkable alcoholic odyssey for Lowry. When their plane finally left early the next morning (re-routed, because of the storm, to Iceland and Labrador), Lowry, who had drunk innumerable pints of beer, brandy, and rum with his friends in London, now continued with several brandies and rums. He was also taking large doses of sonoryl, a sedative that Clarisse Francillon's doctor had prescribed for him in Paris. They were snowed in for three days at the airport outside Keflavík, where they stayed in a large and drafty Quonset hut. Lowry somehow mustered up enough authority to demand the manager's office for himself, and sat in it in lordly solitude, requiring Margerie to fetch his meals. Not much in the way of liquor was available in the Quonset hut, but Lowry made up for this when the blizzard passed and they took off for Labrador. On this leg of the flight he consumed, as he afterwards wrote Clarisse Francillon (*Selected Letters*, p. 167), six double whiskies. At the bar in Goose Bay he drank three more, and swallowed more sonoryl. Then in Montreal, during the wait for their flight to Vancouver, he had several cocktails before dinner. On the long flight across Canada drinks were forbidden, but Lowry had brought along a bottle of whiskey, much of which he drank "right under the nose of the snooty stewardess." At Vancouver they went into a pub and drank beer, pouring the rest of Lowry's whiskey into it; then bought two more bottles of whiskey, caught the bus out to Dollarton, struggled through the snow down to their icy shack, and had a party—after which Lowry sent himself off to sleep with sonoryl.

If this record of consumption seems improbably Herculean, one must recall that Lowry had during the months prior to the trip been as it were getting himself in shape for it. In his letter of February 16, 1949, to Clarisse Francillon, he reminded her of this:

> For the last year I had averaged at least 2½ litres to 3 litres of red wine a day, to say nothing of other drinks at bars and during my last 2 months in Paris this had increased to about 2 litres of rum per day. Even if it ended up by addling me completely I would not move or think without vast quantities of alcohol, without which, even for a few hours, it was an unimaginable torture.

Now that they were back in Dollarton, he wrote, he had come around almost miraculously: eating well and drinking only occasionally, and smoking four instead of sixty cigarettes each day.

Soon after their return, Lowry made a firm resolution to pull himself together. He even drew up a statement, which he had Margerie duly witness, and which he put before him on his work table:

RESOLUTION OF THE HIGHER SELF

Tonight.

Try *not*, under any circumstances, to get tight; at the first sign of any obliviousness take a spirits of ammonia instead of a drink.

Do not provoke any arguments or *lose temper*. Be sympathetic to dear Margie but try to finish work.

Get off will and a note at a sober moment.

Do *not* argue about having more drinks when suppertime comes.

Try to enjoy, also so far as possible, *use* drinks, all this with leading the whole drink business to some real and wise *lasting* solution, such as that you may reach a position shortly where it is not *necessary* to drink, where you may abandon it altogether without feeling it to be a problem, or subsumed with guilt, or handle it without its using you or your feeling afraid of it. This has to be done sooner or later: why not NOW? Both for Margie's sake and your own.

NO GUILT!

He really meant it, of course; and for some time he did his best to adhere to his resolution. Inevitably the binge-drinking returned, and the day-to-day drinking once again intensified: Lowry was far too completely in the grip of alcoholism and the congeries of neuroses that caused and abetted it ever to break free. But for a while he was able to carry on rather well, and even to return to writing with some of the old industriousness that had got him through draft after draft of *Under the Volcano*. After he and Margerie had repaired the shack and the pier (which had partially collapsed), he set to work once more on *Dark as the Grave* and *La Mordida*, standing over his desk, leaning forward, sniffing and brooding over the journals which he hoped to transmute into fiction. He was hindered in his work, though; first by the fact that he could not perform the physical act of writing: his hand, though steady enough, refused to move; and secondly by his legs, which were more painful than ever: his varicose veins had never improved, and now both legs were discolored from the knee down.

Near the end of January 1949, Margerie took him up to Deep Cove, where a young general practitioner named Clarence McNeill had just opened a branch office.[11] Dr. McNeill found him to be "a short, sturdy pink-faced man with an absent manner," whose speech was chipped and slurred, and who paused frequently as he stopped for the right word. His legs hurt, he told Dr. McNeill. He was, he said, a writer, who had to dictate his work to his wife, since he had a mental block which prevented him from holding a pen or pencil. Margerie explained that her husband dictated standing up. "He leans," she said, "with the backs of his hands on the top of the desk. Sometimes he will stand that way for what seems an hour, thinking for the proper word. At the end of the day his legs are all swollen and aching. Show him your hands, Malcolm." Lowry showed his hands to Dr. McNeill. They were, he saw, short, stubby, muscular.

11. Dr. McNeill wrote an essay about this visit, called "Malcolm Lowry Visits the Doctor," which he has very kindly allowed me to use. I should note, however, that Doctor McNeill's memory errs in one point: his essay suggests that this visit took place before the completion of *Under the Volcano*. He had also forgotten about the eczema on Lowry's legs, which had to be cleared up before there could be an operation.

Bowen Island, British Columbia, May 1947.

On the backs of the knuckles and first joints of the fingers, he noticed, there were calluses. "But these are 'anthropoid pads,'" the doctor exlaimed. "The apes have these from leaning and dragging the backs of their hands on the ground. I have never seen calluses in this area before." Lowry seemed rather pleased at this evidence of his uniqueness.

When Dr. McNeill had Lowry strip, he saw immediately what his trouble was. The long periods of standing had given him a severe case of varicose veins that extended to mid-thigh, the condition now complicated by eczema on the calves and shins. He explained to Lowry that if he were to dictate while pacing, or with his feet up, either lying or sitting, then his discomfort would cease. Lowry replied that it was not possible for him to dictate while walking about, or lying or sitting: "The words will not come unless I am standing in just this position and leaning with the backs of my hands on the desk." Dr. McNeill then suggested that Lowry submit to a surgical procedure: ligation and stripping to remove the varicose veins from the groin to the ankle. When Lowry understood that this was a relatively minor operation, and that it would not impede his writing more than a few weeks, he agreed.

As he had been talking with Dr. McNeill, Lowry had dressed himself. Now seated on a low stool, he set about putting on his shoes and socks. He reached out for his right shoe and started to slip it over his toes. Margerie, who had spent years presiding over the arduous daily ritual of getting Lowry dressed, said, "No, dear, put your sock on first." Lowry stopped talking, looked down, grunted, and put on his sock, then his shoe. Then, Dr. McNeill recalls, "he reached out to the left side, groping, still talking to me. I was watching him fascinatedly and by golly, he did it. He picked up the other shoe and started to put it on his bare left foot." Once again Margerie corrected him, and once again he stopped talking, looked down, grunted, and put on his sock. Margerie and the doctor looked at one another and shook their heads. Here, Dr. McNeill thought to himself, was a man who needed a lot of looking after.

On February 28, 1949, Frank Taylor had written Lowry from Hollywood that he and another writer were hard at work on a script for F. Scott Fitzgerald's *Tender Is the Night*, which one film studio after another had been attempting to produce for thirteen years. The novel was, Taylor said, "magnificent material for a film," though far from easy to transpose. The Lowrys decided to read the book, and Margerie checked a copy out of the Vancouver library. She read it first, while Lowry spent most of early March looking back through *Under the Volcano* to see where it might after all be cut. Erskine had told him that it might be possible to bring it out as a Signet paperback if it were shortened, and presumably simplified. Lowry came up with a few ideas, but could not really take very seriously the idea of mutilating his novel, and the scheme was abandoned. Then, in mid-March, he entered the hospital for the operation on his legs. "It lasted two solid hours," he wrote to Earle Birney (*Selected Letters*, pp. 175–76) on March 26, "and I was able to watch most of it. It seems to have been successful—they put me in the maternity wing, to the alarm of an expectant father palely standing in the lobby. I explained that I was just one of those new, larger, as it were atomic babies just recently on the market."

He rested for most of that spring, and saw a good deal of the Birneys and the Kirks in the evenings, when he would often allow himself to drink as he had the year before. On the BBC "Portrait," Birney described Lowry's characteristic behavior at these get-togethers:

When he was moving from exhilaration into tipsiness and into drunkenness, which was a fairly rapid process, there would be moments in it when he would really be at the top of his form. Then he would start some extremely interesting and complex sentence, and stop in the middle of it, because there was a word he couldn't get. After a while we'd carry on the conversation. He'd be extremely annoyed and I had to stop until he got this word, and got this sentence finished. Then he'd go on to a further stage. We no longer existed really. He'd needed us as an audience, now he'd invented his own audience, and hallucination was beginning to take over, very often, so that these familiars that he felt were in his life, invisible to us, but animals, grotesque creatures, shades and spirits of various things, were in around the corners of the rooms and he would move over to a corner and sometimes he'd turn his back on us and go on with what he was saying, but it would become more and more directed to something in the corner that he was getting into an argument with. He would be so caught up in this that he would suffer and he would sweat and just be torn by that terrible inner drama going on and very shortly after that he would pass out, often as stiff as a board.

Or pretend to pass out, according to one school of thought about Lowry's drinking. The sort of thing that Birney describes could very well have been simply another instance of masterful acting on his part, with alcohol as a prop (in both senses of the word). If Lowry were not acting, however, if he were *really* hallucinating in this way, then his behavior could not be laid merely to alcoholism: it would have to be taken as evidence of a deep-seated and advanced form of delusional psychoneurosis, freed and exacerbated by alcohol. I am inclined to suspect a bit of both: the hallucinations were, finally, genuine enough; but they were probably summoned up more or less deliberately, auto-induced, as it were. It would be interesting to know how Lowry behaved when he drank alone, without benefit of audience.

When he had recuperated sufficiently from the leg operation, Lowry went back to work on *Dark as the Grave*. On July 1, 1949, he wrote to Frank Taylor: "I am absorbed in the new book to the extent of sometimes fifteen hours a day, and boy, it has some theme, being no less than the identification of a creator with his creation —Pirandello in reverse, or Six authors in search of his Characters; or otherwise stated, Every man his own Laocoön." On July 11, however, came the accident described earlier: while Margerie was away in Los Angeles visiting her mother, Lowry, drunk, fell from his pier onto the rocks below and injured his back. He managed to get to his feet and struggle up the path to Percy Cummins's store, and then was taken in to St. Paul's Hospital, where he was able to sign his own admission form.[1] He lay in bed for two days, when an intern came to question him but soon gave up because of Lowry's incoherence. X-ray spot films made on July 14 showed no injury. Later that day, Lowry "became violent and difficult to handle and had to be discharged from hospital." It was obvious that he was in the throes of delirium tremens, which is a common manifestation of alcoholics when deprived of liquor for two to three days— especially of chronic, as opposed to binge drinkers; but there was nothing the hospital could do for him. He was, however, admitted almost immediately afterwards to the North Vancouver Hospital, where his injury was diagnosed as a compression fracture of the fourth dorsal vertebra. He was given a Taylor brace to wear (which he wore more or less faithfully for the next six months, calling it his Beau Brummel), and taken home by Margerie, who had rushed back to Vancouver as soon as she heard about the accident. When he could write again, of course, Lowry began work on *The Ordeal of Sigbjørn Wilderness*, discussed earlier. This probably occupied him for the rest of the summer, after which he seems to have lost interest in it—as well he might have done, since the typescript of *The Ordeal* as it was when he dropped it shows very little promise of getting anywhere at all.

A more definite reason for his discarding plans for this work was that their reading of *Tender Is the Night* in February and March had convinced Lowry and Margerie that they, and no one else, should write the filmscript on which Frank Taylor was working. On

1. This information, and that which follows, was collected for me by Dr. McNeill from his own records, and from microfilmed records from Vancouver Hospital.

September 29 they wrote a joint letter to Taylor, which Margerie began by saying: "We have what we think is a real inspiration and a new angle on *Tender Is the Night*. Malc's genius is working on all sixty cylinders, and, I may say, he is thoroughly enjoying himself; —also, he says, he is learning a Lot About the Novel in tearing this one to pieces and recreating it." Lowry continued: "We have become possessed by *Tender Is the Night*. I believe we are distilling it, it offers a general and sometimes particular architectonic of a great film which if you do it will make your name for twoevers and a day. I myself have never felt so creatively exhilarated since writing the better parts of the *Volcano* so that by this I mean that what we are doing is essentially creative." Taylor responded to all this on October 7 by saying that MGM had shelved the whole project, but that they would be happy to have Lowry do a treatment of the film on speculation. This was not really very much in the way of encouragement, but the Lowrys were off and running anyway. Like almost all Lowry projects, it rapidly outgrew its original form: from a ten-page treatment it swelled to a simple scenario, and continued outward from there as 1949 ended. Lowry paused only momentarily to mourn the death of the Cabbalist Charles Stansfeld-Jones (off on his last astral journey, one is tempted to say) in January 1950; and he seems to have taken the time to behave very badly in the course of an evening at the Kirks'—enough so that he had to write a letter of apology to them (*Selected Letters*, p. 189). Except for these distractions, he and Margerie wrote on and on, in gloved hands through one of Vancouver's coldest winters, until, on February 14, they could write Taylor that they had "more or less finished the opus," except for final typing and correcting. On March 12 they wrote again, to say that they were on the home stretch, perhaps only a few weeks away from completion. Just as they were about to mail the script off, however, they were distracted once again: on April 6, 1950, Dylan Thomas, who had not seen Lowry since their days in the Fitzroy Tavern, arrived in Vancouver during his first tour of North America, escorted by John Malcolm Brinnin and pursued by every culture-vulture and eager-to-be-ravished vestal virgin British Columbia could muster. He was

Vancouver, Fall 1949.

particularly eager to see Lowry, who came in from Dollarton for Thomas's reading that night. The two tried their best to talk over drinks after the reading, but Thomas was finally hauled away by a young woman. Thomas subsequently told Robert Pocock (who recounted the anecdote on the BBC "Portrait of Malcolm Lowry") that he returned later to the hotel where the Lowrys had taken a room for the night, to find Lowry, drunk of course, throwing darts at a naked light bulb and calling out the name of James Travers, his old friend from Cambridge and London, dead in the war (but who had recently, if you will recall, returned in ghostly form to visit with Lowry as he lay delirious in St. Paul's Hospital). Margerie remembers no dart-throwing.

In spite of the disruption caused by Thomas's visit, Lowry and Margerie mailed the script of *Tender Is the Night* to Frank Taylor on April 12. They had never (they wrote him two days later) had "so much terrible fun doing anything." Taylor was stunned to see, when the script arrived, that it was perhaps 500 pages long, in five blue binders. He began reading it, and wrote the Lowrys on April 25 that "It requires my most careful attention, and I don't wish to speak or think lightly of it, but even the most superficial glance staggers me with your brilliant, cinematic conceptions." He was, in fact, really impressed by what they had done: he described it to Conrad Knickerbocker in 1964 as "a total filmic evocation—complete with critical remarks, attached film theory, directions to actors, fashions, automobiles: the only things like it are the James Agee scripts." It would have run six hours. In other words, it was brilliant, but impossible. MGM had already decided not to do it before the Lowrys began their work; if it were ever to be done, David Selznick intended to produce it as a vehicle for his wife, Jennifer Jones, and would doubtless have a script prepared as he wanted it prepared; and the Lowry script, while a remarkable achievement, was hopelessly impractical. It would nonetheless, Taylor reassured them, be invaluable to anyone who *did* write a workable script, as a reference point or source-book. (It was Taylor's private opinion, expressed years later to Knickerbocker, that Lowry had taken on the scriptwriting chore as an excuse not to do his own work.) That nothing was to come of all their labor did not really depress Lowry and Margerie as much as it might have done: they themselves knew its worth, and in the next couple of months they received enough encomiastic letters from Hollywood to keep them from any sense of having failed.[2]

Lowry was, in fact, now about to embark on his last real burst of creative energy. The trip that he and Margerie had made to Gabriola Island in 1946 had stuck in their minds, and they began in the summer of 1950 to collaborate on a short story called "October Ferry to Gabriola." They sent it off to Harold Matson in July, and while they were waiting to hear about it, Lowry began writing "Strange Comfort Afforded by the Profession," the story that had occurred to him during his visit to Keats's house in Rome. Before he had finished it, back came "October Ferry to Gabriola" from Matson: it had not seemed to him to be at all saleable. They decided that it could be done better if done singly rather than in collaboration, so Lowry undertook to rewrite it completely. By the middle of September it had become, predictably, a 100-page novella, a size at which it was to remain for several months more before growing even larger.

The pound had recently been devalued, and the Lowrys found that their monthly remittance from his father's estate was barely sufficient to live on. Early in September Lowry wrote to Stuart telling him of their plight, and asking for any kind of financial aid he might be able to give. Their worries were increased by renewed threats of eviction, which would have meant not only sorrow at losing the shack, but also increased financial burden, since wherever they had to move would undoubtedly be more expensive.

On September 21 Lowry sent "Strange Comfort Afforded by the Profession" to Matson, who returned it promptly, saying that it seemed more like a notebook than a fully realized story. Nothing daunted, Lowry wrote to Matson on November 14 that he was hard at work on several other stories: in addition to "October Ferry to Gabriola," he was well into "Present Estate of Pompeii," "Hom-

2. See Appendix Seven of *Selected Letters* for letters from Frank Taylor, Jay Leyda, Christopher Isherwood, and James Agee.

age to a Liberty Ship" (the embryonic form of "Through the Panama"), "Gin and Goldenrod"; and some that were never completed, or published — "Deep Henderson," about "a dying hot musician who takes a bus to Haiti" (obviously to be extracted from his and Margerie's notes on their own bus trip from Seattle to New Orleans), "The Course," a golfing story, and "A Heart-Warming Episode," which was to describe the visit of "an O'Neillish American dramatist to a puritanical English home." Most of these last were probably not much more than titles: in any case, Lowry never mentioned them again.

On December 6 Lowry's mother died, intestate. Whatever sorrow her death brought Lowry, it meant in practical terms that eventually, when all the legal problems were solved, he would come into a rather handsome income. In the letter telling Lowry of her death, Stuart informed Lowry that none of his English capital could possibly be released to him before the end of March 1951; but he did promise to get a little in advance sent in the next month or so. Finally, in June 1951, the advance (£190) arrived; and it was many months before Lowry saw any of the rest of his inheritance. He and Margerie survived during the winter and spring on his regular monthly check, and on $200 sent him by Albert Erskine.

While Margerie worked on her never-published novel, *The Castle of Malatesta*, Lowry was struggling along with his stories, only moderately impeded by his financial worries or by the continuing notices of imminent eviction. Though he wrote to Erskine on June 5 (*Selected Letters*, p. 241) that he had been "fairly gravely impeded by all these anxieties from accomplishing anything recently that is first rate or at the same time saleable," he had by this time largely written the novella, "Forest Path to the Spring," and begun toying with his master-plan for all his fiction, *The Voyage That Never Ends*. When not working on his stories, he was spending long hours writing lengthy and complex letters to foreign translators of *Under the Volcano*, to old friends like Philippe Thoby-Marcelin, and to young well-wishers like David Markson. It is possible to say, uncharitably, that these dozens of letters, many of which must have taken days to compose, were for Lowry, like *Tender Is the Night*, a way of avoiding his real work. In his defense it must be said, first, that he was certainly *not* avoiding his real work during this period; and second, that he was temperamentally a writer of enormous, rambling letters: he had neither the time [3] nor the discipline—nor, perhaps, the epistolary ability—to write short letters. To do so would have been as uncongenial to him as the writing of short fiction was.

In August 1951 a Vancouver bank was holding a contest in which they would award a cash prize to the author of a short-short story which would then be used in the bank's fall newspaper and magazine advertisements. Morley Callaghan had won the competition the preceding year, and Lowry decided he would have a try at it. The result of his attempt to produce a 1000-word story was "Elephant and Colosseum," which ran to more than eighty pages of typescript. He did not win the prize. Lowry sent the story along to Matson, with an accompanying letter: "I am sending you today . . . a comic classic, or at least a masterpiece of nature" (*Selected Letters*, p. 226). Obviously, these months were for Lowry a psychological high period, between the troughs of the European débâcle of 1948 and the bad period that was to come. It would have been next to impossible to discourage him now, no matter what agents, editors, and—presumably—bankers said about his work.

In the letter to Matson just cited, Lowry says also that he is thinking of a collection of short stories to be called *Hear Us O Lord from Heaven Thy Dwelling Place*, which would include "Through the Panama," "October Ferry to Gabriola," a never-to-be published piece called "In the Black Hills," which was essentially a story told him by Whitey, his fisherman friend, "Strange Comfort Afforded by the Profession," "Elephant and Colosseum," and "The Forest Path to the Spring." He had written James Stern years before that

> It is possible to compose a satisfactory work of art by the simple process of writing a series of good short stories, complete in themselves, with the same characters, interrelated,

3. On March 5, 1949, he began a letter to Erskine by saying: "Am very sorry I haven't written before. Have no excuse save that I wanted to write a long letter. Who was it said: I haven't time to write you a short letter?" (*Selected Letters*, p. 172).

correlated, good if held up to the light, watertight if held upside down, but full of effects and dissonances that are impossible in a short story, but nevertheless having its purity of form, a purity that can only be achieved by the born short-story writer.

(Selected Letters, p. 28)

Now, clearly, Lowry proposed to try what he had defined for Stern. His stories would have to be good not only in themselves, but considered as a unit, too. This reasonable ambition was to cause him (and his favorably inclined critics) some difficulty.

By November 1, 1951, he had completed another story, "The Bravest Boat," and was able to spend the next two weeks in preparing his impressive, confusing, and rather muddled fifty-page statement entitled *Work in Progress*. When he mailed it to Harold Matson on November 22, it contained, first, an outline of the way in which he conceived of his great literary continuum:

THE VOYAGE THAT NEVER ENDS
The Ordeal of Sigbjørn Wilderness, I
Untitled Sea Novel
Lunar Caustic
Under the Volcano: The Centre
Dark as the Grave Wherein My Friend Is Laid ⎫
Eridanus ⎬ Trilogy
La Mordida ⎭
The Ordeal of Sigbjørn Wilderness, II

Eridanus, he explains parenthetically, is to consist of the stories in *Hear Us O Lord*, the poems in *The Lighthouse Invites the Storm*, a play (presumably, his dramatization of Grieg's *The Ship Sails On*)—in short, everything not of novel length that was lying about the shack. The untitled sea novel would be "a complete rewriting of a twelfth-rate and derivative and altogether unmentionable early novel of mine that I would like in every way to forget" —*Ultramarine*, of course.

Lowry then goes on to include plot summaries of *Lunar Caustic*,

Dark as the Grave, Eridanus ("an idyllic intermezzo" to the trilogy noted above, in which Sigbjørn and Primrose Wilderness, seated after dinner in Laruelle's house in Cuernavaca, reminisce about their halcyon days and nights in "Eridanus," or Dollarton), and *La Mordida*. The remainder of his *Work in Progress* consists of a lengthy discussion of "The Forest Path to the Spring," followed by briefer descriptions of the rest of the *Hear Us O Lord* stories, as well as something called "Battement de Tambours" (probably a revision of "Deep Henderson," mentioned earlier), and two tales of the Canadian woods in winter, entitled "We're All Good Ducks Here" and "Nocturnal Genius." "October Ferry to Gabriola" is described now as "a short novel, about the length of 'The Forest Path.' "

Here, then, was the Lowry canon in 1951. Stripped of all of Lowry's optimistic rhetoric, what he had to offer was a projected total revision of an early novel (*Ultramarine*), a much-edited but still—to him—unsatisfactory novella (*Lunar Caustic*), *Under the Volcano*, seven or eight short stories, only one of which was in publishable form, several dozen poems of meager worth—and hundreds of pages of manuscript drafts at varying stages of development out of the journals that he and Margerie kept. If one excepts *Under the Volcano*, there was not really very much here to gladden the heart of a publisher: a bet on Lowry was obviously a long shot. Nevertheless, someone was impressed.

Matson sent *Work in Progress* and a typescript of *Hear Us O Lord* (with Lowry's notes indicating how he intended to complete the stories) to Robert Giroux at Harcourt, Brace, since Harcourt had an option on Lowry's work now that they had hired Eugene Reynal, who brought with him the Lowry account from the defunct firm of Reynal and Hitchcock; and Giroux wrote Matson that *Hear Us O Lord* was "an admirable collection." Furthermore, thought Giroux, "*The Voyage That Never Ends* promises what might be the most important literary project of the age" (*Selected Letters*, p. 445). Though Lowry had nothing against Giroux, he was most anxious to keep Albert Erskine as his editor, and now wrote Matson to give Erskine copies of *Work in Progress* and *Hear Us O Lord*, too, and to try to interest Random House, where Erskine was now an editor, to buy the Lowry account from Harcourt. Matson replied that they were ethically bound to give Giroux his option on the work, and suggested that Harcourt might very well offer Lowry a long-term contract for *The Voyage That Never Ends*. To show his faith in Lowry, Giroux sent him in early January 1952 an advance of $375 for *Hear Us O Lord;* for which Lowry was especially grateful, since the money allowed them to move out of the shack for the winter months, and into an apartment in Vancouver. He now sent Giroux a copy of *Lunar Caustic*, hoping that Harcourt would subsidize his revision of it. When they had heard nothing from Giroux by February 9, Margerie wrote Matson to tell him of their anxiety. They continued to hear nothing until March 13, when they received a letter from Giroux saying that Harcourt had decided not to take up the option contained in their contract: there was much that was good in *Lunar Caustic*, he said; but they simply did not feel it wise to advance Lowry money over the two years that it might take him to complete it (*Selected Letters*, pp. 449–50). Lowry responded with a long, gnarled, and ultimately gracious letter, which (if he read it all) must have made Giroux feel a little guilty for having raised such hopes in Lowry, and then dashed them so swiftly. In fact, Giroux was not really to blame for Lowry's sacking: Reynal, Giroux's superior, had made the decision, and left the sad task of informing Lowry up to Giroux.

In the meantime, Albert Erskine had received copies of *Work in Progress* and *Hear Us O Lord*, and given them to Robert Haas, his superior at Random House, along with a memo recommending enthusiastically that they offer Lowry a contract. On April 1 the Lowrys moved back to Dollarton. As they were at work repairing the damages done by winter, a wire from Erskine arrived: Random House was offering a generous long-term contract. Lowry accepted with joy, even though he was not at all certain that he could meet the terms of the contract, which called for two novels and a book of short stories to be delivered to Random House within the next two-and-a-half years. He was confident enough that he could produce an expanded *Lunar Caustic* and *Hear Us O Lord* in the allotted time; but he was in doubt as to which piece of unfinished work could be pulled into shape to serve as the second novel. *Dark as the Grave* seemed the likely choice. Anyway, he signed the contract; and his mood of optimism now reached its peak, where it seems to have stayed for most of that year. He had a real income, now; a publisher had expressed confidence in him; he had his favorite editor back; and the eviction warnings had, for the moment at least, stopped coming. All he had to do was write, and it seemed to him that he had more than enough material to keep him busy for the rest of his life. In fact, he actually saw published during what remained of his lifetime just two stories and a few poems; but he would have been the last person in the world to believe that so little would come of the mass of material he had in progress, and of the grandiose plans he had for *The Voyage That Never Ends*.

David Markson came west in July 1952, arriving in Dollarton on Lowry's birthday. He spent a week with them, swimming, rowing about Burrard Inlet in Lowry's leaky boat, and spending long boozy hours in conversations about Life and Writing. It seemed to Markson that Lowry was rather splendid, now: a drunk, certainly, and an almost hopelessly inefficient man—but happy enough, and absolutely self-aware, even when drunkest. He could be loonishly silly, and spend an entire evening sprawling about in the stern of his boat, while Markson—who, emphatically a New Yorker, knew nothing whatsoever about boats, or about large bodies of water—tried to row them in the dark from Port Moody at the end of Burrard Inlet back to the shack; but Lowry somehow contrived to indicate to Markson what he had to do, and where he had to go. Markson saw also something in Lowry that accounts for the large numbers of people who were willing throughout his life not just to tolerate him, but actually to love him: though Lowry was usually clumsy about human relationships, if one looked closely one could see that he was capable of extraordinary affection for those in whose company he could relax. His impulses were almost always gentle and friendly—unless he were in one of his "low" periods, when he fairly radiated misery, and could be really cruel. At his best, he was guileless, open, and trusting: not quite puppy-like, perhaps, because the evidence of complexity, of torment overcome for the time

Dollarton, 1953.

being by cheeriness, was always there; and because there was always the self-conscious, sly trickster just beneath the surface, watching to see how well the friendly-puppy act was going over.

After Markson's visit, the Lowrys got back to work: Lowry on the *Hear Us O Lord* stories, and Margerie on transcribing *Dark as the Grave*. On August 12 Lowry wrote Erskine to say that they had just deposited *Dark as the Grave*—700 pages of notes and drafts—in a Vancouver bank, and that Margerie had begun typing *La Mordida*. He himself was still battling *October Ferry to Gabriola*, trying to hold down its size even as he added page after page to it. In mid-November they moved into another flat in Vancouver to sit out the winter months, this time in the Baywater Apartment Hotel, at 1359 Davie Street.

The year 1953 started off well: Matson wrote Lowry on January 5 that *New World Writing* had accepted "Strange Comfort Afforded by the Profession." Lowry was pleased at this, but he was too concerned about the way which *October Ferry* was taking over his writing time and materials (even as he answered Matson, it was "greedily gulping" the material that belonged in *Eridanus*). The months allotted him in his contract with Random House were rapidly passing, and he knew he should have been completing the stories for *Hear Us O Lord* and *Lunar Caustic*; but *October Ferry* was all he could think of. In February he wrote Erskine to say that he hoped to send a hundred or so pages of *October Ferry* off to him soon, and to complete the other stories in the next few months. He was also beginning yet another story—like "The Bravest Boat," set in Stanley Park—called "Ghostkeeper." (Another of his writer-being-written-about pieces, it was abandoned after he had written only a few pages, and had made notes for possible resolutions for it.) He kept at *October Ferry* through spring and into summer, when he finally realized that it was, like it or not, going to become a full-length novel. Only now did it occur to him that it might very well serve as one of the novels called for by his contract, so that he could continue to work away at it without his conscience bothering him.

On June 28, however, his writing was stopped by another accident. It was a Saturday, and in mid-morning a young student of

Dollarton, Summer 1953.

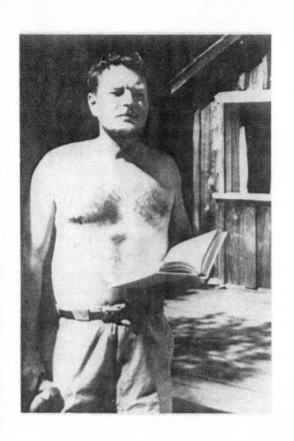

Earle Birney's called to pay his respects, bringing with him a bottle. He and Lowry sat down to work their way through it, and by mid-afternoon were quite drunk. The spring had dried up in the hot weather, and Lowry decided now that they needed water— which meant he would have to bring it down in buckets from Percy Cummins's store. He and the student set off up the steep path, singing and clanging about with their buckets. Suddenly Lowry tripped over a root and fell, twisting his leg as he did so. He was unable to stand, so the student dragged him back down the hill and into the shack, where he propped him up on the sofa. Margerie ran to the nearby cottage of their new neighbors, Harvey and Dorothy Burt, who came over to help. Lowry's ankle was swollen, and they bandaged it. He was too drunk to tell them (if he knew) where else he had been hurt, so they made him comfortable and left him there for the night. Early the next morning Margerie walked up to Percy Cummins's to telephone Dr. McNeill. Just as she reached the top of the hill, the Cummins's large black dog tore out of its pen and came after her. Before Cummins could rescue her, the dog had bitten her in the right thigh, ripping her green velvet slacks in the process. Bleeding badly, Margerie telephoned for an ambulance, requesting two extra men to help haul Lowry up the hill. She then walked down the hill to tell him help was on the way, then back up to meet the men and guide them down to the shack, then back up the hill with them as they carried her hungover husband to the ambulance—and then passed out. They were both in the North Vancouver Hospital for several days: Margerie under treatment for shock and possible infection, and Lowry for fractures of the tibia and fibula of the right leg.

When Lowry wrote soon afterwards to Erskine about the accident, he dramatized it slightly. He had tripped over a root that had been "deliberately upraised" by children who had been playing there (he may be forgiven for not having wanted to tell the publisher whom he owed considerable material that he had broken his leg while stumbling about in the woods, drunk); and Margerie, going for the telephone, "was suddenly sprung upon by a 'beast' (as she describes it) half husky and half wolf, who went for her throat, horribly tore her thigh and leg (which still after ten days is exuding pus) and was finally choked off by a bystander" (*Selected Letters*, p. 341). Percy Cummins did not see the Lowrys often after this incident: Margerie, especially, had cooled toward him.

The first batch of *October Ferry* went off to Erskine on October 14, 1953, with a letter of explanation which Erskine found undecipherable. Lowry failed to clarify matters with a rather cryptic "key" which he mailed to Erskine ten days later, on Halloween:

> You will be wondering at the length of this first chapter too—if it is a first chapter and which, if so, threatens to be the longest on record, so I will expound thus far the magic of Dr. Lowry's dialectical-Hegelian-spiritualism-Cabbalistic-Swedenborgian-conservative-Christian-anarchism for ailing paranoiacs: the first chapter (whether visibly such or not) is as the base to a triangle or a triad (and/or a radical having a valence of three): viz
>
>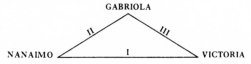
>
> As you observe, in this configuration it is difficult for chapter III not to seem to be going back to its starting point—or both ways at once—and in fact where does III start? And how is it solved? H'm; something that must have puzzled mightier minds than mine—but no more. On with the work; over those falls! through those weeds!
>
> (*Selected Letters*, p. 345)

On the perhaps reasonable assumption that this explanation did not clear things up as fully as was necessary, Lowry wrote Erskine again, later in the fall: not only because he had not succeeded in describing his novel well, but also because Erskine had, on December 18, 1953, sent him a warning letter:

> I have been reminded by the Keeper of the Contracts that we are now six weeks beyond the first delivery date. . . . It is therefore necessary to take stock, so to speak, and to learn from you just how much more remains to be done on *Octo-*

ber Ferry, of which I now have 159 manuscript pages, and how long you think it will take, etc. Also, please give me as clearly and briefly as possible some notion of where the story is going, what shape it is going to take, and how long you estimate the total manuscript will be. I know that you have it all planned and most of it on paper in one form or another, but the more specific the information you give me the better equipped I'll be to discuss it. All of this information is needed for a kind of "official review" of the situation, so please get it to me as soon as you can.

The Lowrys had just moved into Vancouver for the winter, for the third and last time (this year to the Caroline Court Apartments on Nelson Street); Lowry had been recuperating from the broken leg, which had had to be kept in a plaster cast until the end of September; and he had been elated in November to hear from Harold Matson that the *Partisan Review* had accepted "The Bravest Boat." He had been kept too busy, in other words, to notice the chill that was setting in at Random House. Even Albert Erskine, who had shown far more patience than Lowry had a right to ask, was growing irritated—and what is worse, *bored*—with what he was receiving from Dollarton. Anyone but Lowry, one suspects, would have sensed that the handwriting was already on this particular wall; but he noticed nothing, and when he wrote a third time to Erskine, it was to say that he was very busy catching a boat to stay with his friends the Neilsons on Bowen Island, and did not really have time for further explanations—after which he found time to write over three pages of single-spaced discussion of *October Ferry*, none of it appreciably more coherent than his preceding "explanations" had been. On January 4 he wrote Erskine a fourth letter, this time to say that £500 from his estate was on its way to him, and to ask that he be allowed to "buy time" from Random House—by which he meant that he wanted them to suspend his monthly payments for a period of time, so as to extend the deadlines called for in his contract. But before this letter could reach New York, Erskine wrote Lowry, on January 6, that Random House had decided to cut him off:

I wish that I could say that your statement of intentions about *Gabriola* had completely dispelled our feelings of uneasiness, based on readings of the first 159 pages of the manuscript, about the way the book is going. What you say *about* the book sounds, as far as I can understand it, interesting and exciting; but the question is whether all these themes are being communicated with sufficient clarity and with enough purely narrative and dramatic (surface) interest to make people want to read it and to feel rewarded for doing so. . . .

Because of these doubts it has been decided to suspend, for the time being, the monthly payments, and to review the question again when enough of the manuscript is available for us to get the real "feel" of it. I am sorry about this decision, but there is nothing that can be done about it at the moment.

This was, of course, nothing more than what Lowry had himself just proposed in his letter; but it hurt him almost past tolerating that Random House had decided on its own to suspend payment to him—and, what is worse, not because of Lowry's sudden windfall from England, which would allow him to live comfortably without his payments from Random House, but because of their lack of faith in the future of *October Ferry to Gabriola*. To Lowry, it seemed clear that his friend Erskine had betrayed him.

Suddenly all the tremendous amount of nervous energy and optimism that had been driving him since his return to Dollarton in 1949 was gone. For many months, now, Lowry had been arising at dawn, swimming (or doing calisthenics during the winter), then writing for as many as ten or twelve hours, and getting to bed long before midnight. He had continued to drink, but in what was for him moderation: his work came first, and he really believed that *October Ferry* and the stories in *Hear Us O Lord from Heaven Thy Dwelling Place* were—or were going to be—as good as *Under the Volcano.*

Were they? The answer is simple: no, not even close. Lowry did not stop writing after Erskine's letter, even though he never again wrote with the drive that had carried him through the preceding four years; and he was working on the novel and on four of the six stories in *Hear Us O Lord* up until the time of his death over three years later. But even if we look at *October Ferry* and the stories in their final, published form, we can see that, though they have their moments, they do not come anywhere near the brilliance of *Under the Volcano*.[4]

October Ferry's Ethan Llewelyn is Lowry's earnest attempt not, for once, to write about an artist: he is (or had been, until his premature retirement) a criminal lawyer of considerable skill and reputation. And his young wife Jacqueline represents Lowry's one real effort to create a woman character who is neither Jan nor Margerie, nor even an uneasy conflation of the two, like Yvonne in *Under the Volcano*. With neither Llewelyn nor Jacqueline does Lowry succeed. From his Vancouver friend William McConnell he gathered a few legal terms to salt here and there among his protagonist's thoughts; but, aware of his own almost total ignorance of the law, Lowry never really dares to show Llewelyn functioning professionally. The protagonist of *October Ferry* is finally yet another projection of the author's personality, well-intentioned, vulnerable, fumbling, tormented by the crassness and venality of the world, and wanting only to be left alone in sylvan solitude. Jacqueline has dark hair and eyes, and is a native Canadian with a rather bizarre and sad background (her mother, an unwed Scotch feminist, is a suicide; and her father, a potentially interesting sort whom Lowry never devel-

---

4. The problem, considered both textually and critically, is vexed by the fact that, with the exception of "The Bravest Boat" and "Strange Comfort Afforded by the Profession," neither the novel nor the stories were completed during Lowry's lifetime. Margerie edited them all for posthumous publication, and in many cases neatened them up and carried them forward in the directions Lowry had indicated in his working notes. Professionally speaking, then, in evaluating *October Ferry to Gabriola* and *Hear Us O Lord*, we are working with "corrupt" texts. On April 27, 1967, Margerie wrote me, in connection with our edition of *Dark as the Grave*, about fears that she might be introducing her own words into the novel: "I think it is ridiculous. I certainly wrote plenty of lines, and scenes, when I was editing "The Forest Path" and "Through the Panama"—both of which have received high praise and people write me about them all the time and no one has criticized me or suggested I wronged Malcolm's work in any way." When one considers how large a part she played in the composition of Lowry's works during his life (including *Under the Volcano*), one understands how she might fail to see any reason not to continue to do so after his death. Nothing Lowry wrote after 1939 was, strictly speaking, entirely his own.

ops, is a white magician named Angus McCandless), but she is still for the most part Margerie Lowry as seen by her husband: nervous, vivacious, moody, strong. Lowry has in his attempt at distancing even given the two a son, Tommy, who is so insubstantial as to be well-nigh invisible. Tommy cares little for his parents, which is under-standable: they appear to be able to traverse hundreds of pages of prose without so much as noticing his existence.

The Llewelyns meet in an art-film theater in Toronto, and it is love at first sight. They spend countless hours talking, usually in bars but occasionally during walks through the city's parks. She is reticent about her past, but Llewelyn is more than anxious to tell her about one particular skeleton in *his* closet that very nearly mad-dens him: he had been in some obscure way responsible for the sui-cide of a university friend of his, Peter Cordwainer. (Here we are, one more time, face-to-face with the unhappy "Wensleydale"; still shadowy and ambiguously presented, but obviously still very much on Lowry's mind.) Llewelyn has carried the burden of his guilt with him since his undergraduate days, until it bids fair to destroy not only his career, but his relationship with Jacqueline, too.

Though troubled by his recollections of Peter Cordwainer, Llew-elyn is able to get along reasonably well until his house in Niagara-on-the-Lake burns to the ground. No one is hurt, and insurance will pay for their loss. A misfortune, perhaps; but hardly a crippling tragedy—especially when one pauses to realize that in the very recent past (this all takes place just after World War II) many worse things have happened to worldwide multitudes. But the loss of their house damages both Llewelyn and Jacqueline grievously, and even imperils their marriage. They take to drink, and morosely watch their estrangement setting in: "was it not rather as if they'd become—or was this just the shock of the fire again and alcohol's mutual alienation?—all of a sudden like the hero and heroine of separate films, playing in separate but adjoining cinemas?" (*October Ferry to Gabriola*, p. 106).

Then, as if by magic, sudden and apparently causeless fires spring up all around them: other homes burn; a liquor store catches fire, as do a child's tree house and a parked car. Fireballs roll through

kitchens; lightning strikes a team of plowing horses. Hysteria begins
to grip the community, and increasingly curious phenomena are observed: a phantom sailing ship "with all its topmasts blazing with
corposants" is observed sailing through the sky in an easterly direction; a seamonster with horns like a goat is reported cavorting down
the Niagara River; people leave their doors open for Jesus to walk in;
and the innkeeper's setter gives birth to a blue dog. Ethan Llewelyn
takes all this—especially the fires—to mean that some alien "intelligence" is after him personally, toying with him before striking him
down. He reads a book which suggests to him that certain unex-
plained fires in the past had actually been *feared* into existence:
"that on occasion, feelings of sheer hatred or revenge toward other
human beings had been sufficient to cause, without admixture of
purposive 'magic,' disaster, otherwise inexplicable, to others. (So
why not to onself, Ethan thought, as psychiatry implied, by hatred
of oneself?)" (*October Ferry*, p. 139). Llewelyn has fears enough,
certainly:

> and out of the fears grew wild hatreds, great unreasoning
> esemplastic hatreds: hatred of people who looked at him so
> strangely in the street; long-forgotten hatreds of schoolmates
> who'd persecuted him about his eyes at school; hatred of the
> day that ever gave him birth to be the suffering creature that
> he was, hatred of a world where your house burned down
> with no reason, hatred of himself, and out of all this hatred
> did not grow sleep.

Such vehemence hardly suits the timid Ethan Llewelyn: it comes
obviously as a *cri de coeur* from the author himself, and tells us
more about him than almost any other autobiographical statement
he ever made. Fear does in truth breed hatred, and Lowry, fuller of
fears than most, must certainly have often felt consumed by the fires
of hatred (as, indeed, his London psychiatrist was eventually to
learn when he questioned the drugged Lowry in 1956). The operative term, once again, is paranoia, as Lowry, writing to Erskine
about Llewelyn in January 1954, himself recognized: "it is he and
no one else who produces the so-called coincidences and disasters

that happen to them: himself, as it were, the paranoiac black magician of their own lives." Llewelyn, now (again like his creator) totally obsessed with signs, portents, and coincidences, realizes that the fires will stop following him around only if he radically alters the way he lives. So he resigns from his law firm, sells his car, and heads with Jacqueline and their son for British Columbia—where, predictably, they buy a cottage on the beach at "Eridanus," and live very much as did Malcolm and Margerie Lowry.

But, of course, the threat of eviction comes, and the Llewelyns must search for a new home. The real villain becomes now not Ethan's own guilt, but Civilization, always encroaching, always sullying, always degrading. When Jacqueline wants to buy a piece of land, Llewelyn explodes:

> Your poor little bit of property won't be safe from desecration no matter where you are. And then, when they've finally ruined most of the beauty of the country with industry, and thoroughly loused up the watersheds and rainfall, and the last old sourdough has traded in his gold sifting pan for a Geiger counter and staked out the last uranium claim . . . some jeezly fool will drop an atom bomb on the whole business, and serve them damn well right too!

Finally they travel to Victoria, on the southern tip of Vancouver Island, then by bus (yet another Lowryan bus ride!) up the east coast of the island to Nanaimo, where they hope to find a ferry that will take them over to the smaller island of Gabriola. There, perhaps, they will find a house sufficiently isolated from the rest of the world. While he waits in a bar for Jacqueline to locate the ferry for them, Llewelyn torments himself with a new guilt: the newspapers are full of articles about the imminent hanging of a young boy who has committed a rape-murder, and Llewelyn knows that his forensic skills, should he offer them, could prevent the boy's execution. He must, he resolves, come out of retirement, get himself in shape, and go to the boy's defense.

It is a noble (if soap-operatic) stance for Llewelyn, but not really very convincing—especially when we see him a couple of hours later aboard the ferry to Gabriola, unable to open his bottle of gin, and full of the old fears:

> And now Ethan, finding a spot on the bridge where he was hidden from the wheelhouse, near a coil of rope, felt all the fear coming back with redoubled force; fear of the future, fear of himself—how could he fight it? It was as though his whole soul were shivering as great waves of cold fright rushed through it. He felt inwardly like a man who freezes halfway up the rigging, or on a mountain pinnacle, petrified by his own tremors.

The ferry must return briefly to Nanaimo before continuing its run, and the Llewelyns are startled to see in a newspaper they buy that they are not after all going to be forced out of their shack in Eridanus. They can go home again; they do not have to make the perilous journey (the channel water is rough, and the Grail imagery obtrusive) to Gabriola. But Ethan knows that Eridanus has been their Paradise, and that it is ordained that every Adam and Eve must leave the Garden of Eden. And, moreover, that to do so is a good, even beautiful thing: perhaps, says Ethan to Jacqueline, their life in Eridanus was something like a sunrise: "when it's at its very best you say, oh, if it would just stay like that forever, but if it did you'd never know what full noon was like, or midnight either. No, it was time to leave, no matter how much it hurts" (*October Ferry*, p. 325). This sentiment, a favorite with Wallace Stevens and Rainer Maria Rilke, seems also to please the Llewelyns, whose ferry is about to touch the dark, mysterious, and possibly promising island of Gabriola as the novel ends.

The characterization of *October Ferry to Gabriola* is clumsy, the dialogue often downright embarrassing, a sense of pace almost nonexistent, and the logic dubious, at best: the Llewelyns are, for instance, not leaving their Paradise to go into another world, but to try to find another Paradise (or, closer to the phrasing of Lowry's own psychology, another place in which to hide from the outside world)—and this, for all the busing and ferrying that goes on, hardly constitutes an *advance* in their condition. *October Ferry to*

Gabriola has its occasions of eloquence, humor, and—maybe—profundity; but it is by no means a good novel, not even after its further revision by Lowry after Erskine saw it in 1954, or after Margerie had cleaned it up as best she could for its publication in 1970. As *idea*, it might have been interesting; but Lowry had hardly even begun to develop that idea into a work of fiction with at least minimal "narrative and dramatic (surface) interest," as Erskine complained in his cutting-off letter of January 6, 1954.

Once again, one is tempted to think of the painting of Albert Pinkham Ryder, the late nineteenth-century American eccentric. The parallels are startling: the chronic eye infections in youth; the stuffy mercantile fathers; the habit of sitting abstracted for long periods; the writing of execrable poems (most of Ryder's were mercifully blown away by winds); the desire in both men to think of their works as musical compositions; and their lack of real technical ability. Neither Lowry nor Ryder was a "natural": it is said of Ryder that he never mastered his medium, only wrestled it into obedience; and the same might be said of Lowry. *October Ferry to Gabriola* is a beginner's novel written by a man who had already proved himself a master—but a master, like Ryder, not of the techniques of his art, but of his own singular vision and of an almost obsessive tenacity in revision. Ryder completed no painting: whatever he did, he worked and re-worked, for years if possible, until his canvas became so thickly textured that it was in danger of crumbling under the weight of the alcohol, candle wax, varnish, and oil that he had poured or scraped onto it. The same might be said of Lowry: with *Under the Volcano* he stopped in time, before (only *just* before) the canvas crumbled; and with *October Ferry to Gabriola* there was never time to do more than begin the layering. What the novel might have become, we shall never know. What exists is thin—a large canvas barely covered with lines indicating how the composition might ultimately have taken shape.

With *Hear Us O Lord from Heaven Thy Dwelling Place*, one need not be quite so glum. In these seven stories there are, to be sure, the inevitable Lowryan excesses and defects; but there are also minor triumphs. Short fiction was never his *forte:* with Lowry, a work almost invariably got better as it grew longer. There are four genuinely "short" stories in this collection, and they are at best only partial successes; but there are three novellas (or, let us say, short stories on their way to becoming novels) here, and two of them—"Through the Panama" and "The Forest Path to the Spring"—are of sufficient promise to merit our attention. One must also remember in evaluating *Hear Us O Lord* that Lowry was writing not just a group of stories to be flung together anyhow, but a *book:* something with a beginning, middle, and end, with continuity of characterization, symbolism, and theme (see his letter to James Stern mentioned earlier in this chapter).

Lowry included in his *Work in Progress* statement a paragraph in which he defined what he hoped would be the broad, unifying idea of the collection:

> Most of these stories deal, either humourously or seriously, but it is to be hoped not sentimentally, with those occasions of life when, either consciously or unconsciously, some act of charity or faith or understanding, or perhaps only a coincidence, or even a mistake, has unwittingly testified to the existence of something divine, or miraculous in human destiny.

More specifically, all of the seven stories deal with couples (though in two of them the wife is kept offstage) in love; and all seven have something to say about how such couples contrive to live and love in a world which is constantly throwing up obstacles against their happiness. Five of the stories, not very surprisingly, are about artists of one kind or another. Lowry's old standby Sigbjørn Wilderness is the protagonist of four,[5] but he is by no means always the *same* Sigbjørn Wilderness. In "Strange Comfort Afforded by the Profession" he is an American writer in Rome on a Guggenheim Fellowship. In "Through the Panama" he is the most literary of writers,

---

5. The narrator of "A Forest Path to the Spring" is a nameless composer; but Ethan Llewelyn in *October Ferry to Gabriola* (which was, remember, originally to have been the penultimate story in the collection) speaks of Sigbjørn Wilderness, his neighbor on the beach in Eridanus, as "an unsuccessful Canadian composer"; so it seems probable that the "I" of "Forest Path" is none other than Wilderness.

thinking almost incessantly about art of one kind or another in the most improbable and extreme of situations. In "The Forest Path to the Spring" he is an alcoholic jazz musician who is only now beginning to learn about literature. And in "Gin and Goldenrod" he is a drunk, period. For Lowry, the essential Sigbjørn Wilderness

> is not, in the ordinary sense in which one encounters novelists or the author in novels, a novelist. He simply doesn't know what he is. He is a sort of underground man. Also he is Ortega's fellow, making up his life as he goes along, and trying to find his vocation. . . . he is disinterested in literature, uncultured, incredibly unobservant, in many respects ignorant, without faith in himself, and lacking nearly all the qualities you normally associate with a novelist or a writer. . . . His very methods of writing are absurd and he sees practically nothing at all, save through his wife's eyes, though he gradually comes to *see*. I believe this can make him a very original character, both human and pathetically inhuman at once.
>
> (*Selected Letters*, pp. 331–32)

Though Lowry's description here applies primarily to the protagonist of *Dark as the Grave* and *La Mordida*, it encompasses most of the other Sigbjørn Wildernesses as well. If they differ from story to story, they do so only in so far as they represent different *personae* for Malcolm Lowry: the author, perhaps, as he thought he had been; or was; or might be.

The various wives are, whatever their names—whether Primrose Wilderness, Lovey L'Hirondelle Cosnahan, Tansy Fairhaven, or Astrid Storlesen—always the same gay, excited, passionate looking, slightly wild young heroine; understanding, patient, eager to travel, a perfect mate (for any man who wants to live with a cliché and not with a woman). Only in "Gin and Goldenrod," when she must coax and bully the hungover Sigbjørn through an unpleasant chore, is she really believable.

In addition to using similar or identical characters throughout, Lowry attempts also to link the stories by giving them common refrains and motifs, not always with success: the frequent reiteration of "Frère Jacques," for instance, ultimately seems mechanical, not organic, and thus comes only to irritate the reader. Eridanus, the fishing community in which the Wildernesses and Fairhavens (of "The Present Estate of Pompeii") live, figures in six of the seven stories. Liquor, actual, potential, or remembered, is of course a factor, as is the sea.

Considered according to the conventional criteria for evaluating fiction, *Hear Us O Lord* fails, in that Lowry in almost every instance neglects the fables, or plots, of his stories, and dwells almost exclusively on the other two elements deemed necessary to successful fiction: characterization and idea. Once again, we are liable to feel that nothing is *happening*, that no one *does* anything; that, properly speaking, these are not stories at all. And so they are not (except, perhaps, "Gin and Goldenrod," which is by far the most conventional of the seven)—which means that they must be something else; something for which we might wish to find our own label. Suppose we say that *Hear Us O Lord* is a collection not of short stories, but of *fictional meditations:* reflective pieces, more or less autobiographical in nature, on a common theme. (The religious connotation of the term "meditations" is intentional, because —as the title of the collection suggests—the work as a whole is, among other things, not only a series of religious reflections, but an appeal to God as well.) The common theme is the one which preoccupied Lowry during his entire career: it has to do with the struggle of man and woman who, having been expelled from the Garden, hope first to survive, and then, with luck, to return. The theme is at first existential: how are the exiled lovers to live at all in the noisy yet barren welter of civilization? It becomes a moral problem: how are they to live ethically, with regard to their fellow man? And, finally, the theme is religious: how are the lovers to find grace (which, for Lowry the lapsed Wesleyan, still meant the unmerited love and favor of God toward man)? If they are fortunate, the lovers will begin by loving each other—as, say, Geoffrey and Yvonne in *Under the Volcano* had been unable to do. At some point they will, wherever they are, go through a sort of epiphany: a small, apparently almost fortuitous experience, that carries them into a condition in which it is possible not only to survive, but to survive with happiness, perhaps even with grace. The solution, in every case, lies in *simplicity:* Lowry's lovers learn (or do not learn—the epiphany does not always come) that their best hope lies in returning to a life lived close to *things.* The enemy is not only a venal and loveless civilization (Sigbjørn Wilderness in "Through the Panama" says that the real cause of alcoholism is the "ugliness and complete baffling sterility of existence as *sold* to you"), but also a dangerous urge toward obsessive introspection: the barrenness of self-absorption, to which the alcoholic and the artist are so prone. There are, then, two enemies facing the lovers: one lies all around them, befouling and then devouring their garden; and the other, more insidious, lies within.

The stories, or meditations, in *Hear Us O Lord* are not quite so formulaic as this statement of theme would suggest: Lowry was, after all, an artist and not a writer of tracts. But the theme is there, and it is an ancient and potent one. Perhaps once or twice in the collection Lowry is able to provide the theme with a worthy vehicle, but mostly he is not. These are meditations on simplicity and goodness, and better writers than Lowry (one thinks, for instance, of Milton) have not known very well how to deal with such nearly ineffable qualities. It is easier, as Milton learned, to write well of evil; but Lowry, who was really the most innocent of men, wanted to do the harder thing: to write well of goodness.

The obvious danger in this is, of course, that of sentimentality. The first piece in the collection, "The Bravest Boat," is endearing (what a good man must have written this! we exclaim), but cloying. Sigurd and Astrid Storlesen are walking through what is obviously Stanley Park in Vancouver on a blustery March day. He is a seaman, presumably about to leave on a cruise; she, a "beautiful passionate girl," is close to tears. They walk hand-in-hand like young lovers (though he is thirty-nine and she twenty-four, and this is their seventh wedding anniversary) along paths that wind past a lagoon filled with swans and wild ducks. They watch a little boy and his father try to sail a toy boat in the lagoon. A forest lies nearby, and on its edge are gardens "with sheltered beds of snowdrops and here and there a few crocuses lifting their sweet chalices." (Could Lowry actually have written such things?) The park serves as the thematic garden in this meditation, though Eridanus itself lies in the distance, seen as "a few lowly little self-built shacks and floathouses, that might have been driven out of the city altogether, down to the water's edge into the sea itself, where they stood on piles, like fishermen's huts . . . all standing, even the most somber, with their fluted tin chimneys smoking here and there like toy tramp steamers, as though in defiance of the town, before eternity" (*Hear Us O Lord*, p. 17).

Opposed to the garden is Enochvilleport (Vancouver, of course), which is

> composed of delapidated half-skyscrapers, at different levels, some with all kinds of scrap iron, even broken airplanes, on their roofs, others being moldy stock exchange buildings, new beer parlors crawling with verminous light even in mid-afternoon and resembling gigantic emerald-lit public lavatories for both sexes, masonries containing English tea-shoppes . . . totem pole factories, drapers' shops with the best Scotch tweed and opium dens in the basement. . . .
>
> (*Hear Us O Lord*, p. 16)

Anyone "who had ever really been in hell," Lowry concludes "must have given Enochvilleport a nod of recognition."

The "something miraculous in human destiny" that was to play a part in each of these tales is here a little toy boat containing a message, set adrift five miles south of Cape Flattery by Sigurd Storlesen when he was ten. For twelve years the boat wandered, tossed about by tempests and tides, attacked by seabirds, until it was discovered on the beach at Stanley Park by the seven-year-old Astrid. Now, seventeen years later, the two still marvel at how they were brought together by the little boat. This "meditation" is, then, about the survival of apparently fragile things. The boat has actually had to be extremely well-constructed and tough in order to last long enough to accomplish the miracle of bringing Astrid and Sigurd together. A little squirrel that seems about to be caught by a caged lynx, and just manages to escape, is only apparently vulnerable, as they realize: it appears to be in mortal danger, but, like the boat, bounces along, happy and almost unaware of its peril. As they stand on the beach that is covered by debris, evidence of the ocean's destructive force, they are reassured: they know that their love is like the boat or the squirrel—small, insignificant against the ruthless and implacable power of nature as well as the ugly strength of the distant city; but strong enough to survive.

The tale itself is, unhappily, *not* strong enough to survive—not by itself, anyway. Perhaps Lowry chose to place it first in *Hear Us O Lord* (if it was Lowry who wanted to include it in the collection, and it might not have been) so that it could stand as a brief, almost tentative lyrical statement of the major theme, which would then be treated more vigorously as the book progressed toward its final, grand evocation of simple virtue in "The Forest Path to the Spring."

The tone of the second meditation, "Through the Panama," is certainly more vigorous than that of "The Bravest Boat." Now as Sigbjørn and Primrose Wilderness retrace the voyage made by Malcolm and Margerie Lowry from Vancouver to Europe (as described in the preceding chapter), we are on no simple journey from one geographical point to another. Sigbjørn's sorrow at leaving Eridanus is precisely the sorrow of Adam leaving the Garden of Eden, and he broods aboard the ship "as it takes him away inexorably from the only place he has loved, and perhaps forever." He thinks of himself as "the Protagonist, turning his face from damnation, as he thinks, and limping off into the unknown, and leaving his poor house, though he is making a great mistake as it happens, for his poor house was his salvation. . . ." To put it mildly, Sigbjørn's mind is cluttered: in addition to lamenting his exile, he must act protective toward Primrose (who is actually far braver and tougher than he), keep face before the crew, be available in case the captain thinks of asking him to his cabin for an apértif, fend off the scores of literary and musical allusions that leap out at him constantly— and, above all, work on his projected novel: an account of the journey of one Martin Trumbaugh, a novelist who has written a book set in Mexico, and who now is going back there for obscure but possibly morbid reasons, one of which is to become able to write a book about his return—to be called, naturally, *Dark as the Grave Wherein My Friend Is Laid*. If Sigbjørn Wilderness is Malcolm Lowry, then Martin Trumbaugh is Sigbjørn Wilderness—which means of course that Martin equals Malcolm, too.

No one could be more confused about all this than Sigbjørn, who sometimes speaks as "I," sometimes as "he," and sometimes as "Martin." Lowry was, after all, capable of self-parody; and "Through the Panama," in which he mocks his own confusions in trying to play off his journals against his fiction, is in this respect a real *tour de force*. The humor is qualified, however, by Sigbjørn's real fear that he, like Martin, has become enmeshed in the plot of the novel he has written—and what, he wonders, if he were to become so enmeshed as to be *killed* "by his own book and the malign forces it arouses"? As a typical Lowry protagonist, Sigbjørn already carries a crushing weight of guilt about with him; but "Through the Panama" suggests that the curse of being a writer is just as grievous a burden. Sigbjørn thinks of himself as the Ancient Mariner, and George Woodcock correctly calls Sigbjørn's albatross that of "literary creation and its attendant curse hung around his neck." [6] Specifically, the curse is one of confusion: Sigbjørn's mind has become so completely and quixotically baffled by the effort to create that he can no longer tell whether he is writing, or *being written*—presumably by some *daemon* perched above him invisibly, who controls his every move. This was the notion with which Lowry had begun to play in *Dark as the Grave*, and developed further in *La Mordida*.

The one-day journey through the Panama Canal is rather heavy-handedly a symbolic death-rebirth passage. In Los Angeles, a Mr. Charon had joined the cruise. As they head down the coast of Central America toward Panama, Sigbjørn has a nightmare in which he enters an indescribable dark something-or-other "with teeth that snap tight" behind him: the time-honored old *vagina dentata*, with

6. "Under Seymour Mountain," *Canadian Literature*, 8 (Spring 1961), 5.

all its terrors of birth and death and submersion of identity and castration. The Canal itself, when they reach it, is a series of locks that snap shut around their ship, and on either side is dense and fetid tropical forest: not very happy sexual symbolism, but sexual symbolism nonetheless. In the midst of their passage, Sigbjørn has an eerie sort of vision that teaches him the beginnings of humility: he observes in the marginal gloss which he, inspired by Coleridge, has been using intermittently through his journal, that a man is sitting in a control tower by the side of the Canal, and that this man

> has a model of the canal locks before him, carefully built, which registers electrically the exact depth of the water and every movement of every lever and thus is able—ghastly image of the modern world—to see what is happening at every moment—and has possibly even seen me taking notes. . . .
>
> (*Hear Us O Lord*, p. 61)

The passage through the Canal is not, then, just another symbolic death and rebirth: it is also a frightening encounter with Lowry's old foe, the Infernal Machine—and with the mysterious *daemon* who operates it. The gloss continues:

> it works, God how the whole thing beautifully and silently works, this celestial meccano—with its chains that rise sullenly from the water, and the great steel gates moving in perfect silence, and with perfect ease at the touch of that man sitting up in the control tower high above the topmost lock who, by the way, is myself, and who would feel perfectly comfortable if only he did not know that there was yet another man sitting yet higher above him in *his* invisible control tower, who also has a model of the canal locks before him, carefully built, which registers electrically the exact depth of everything I do, and who thus is able to see everything that is happening to me at every moment—and worse, everything that is *going* to happen. . . .

Somehow this disturbing vision comforts Sigbjørn, and, very gradually, a pattern of rebirth imagery begins. There is, once they reach the Western Ocean, the perilous storm to endure; but their ship, like the little boat in the first tale, is surprisingly sturdy. Still introspective as he is being pummelled about in the gale, Sigbjørn now comes to a kind of realization: he is no literary sophisticate. He may allude to Rilke, say, but he has never read a line of Rilke; if he refers to a painting by Bosch, Bosch is the only painter he can appreciate at all. He can understand nothing of what his fellow writers are saying; and though his room is full of old copies of *Kenyon Review*, *Partisan Review*, *Minotaur*, and so on, he is able to make precisely nothing out of their contents. Sigbjørn must face the fact that he will always be an intellectual primitive, a naïf who scarcely belongs on this earth, let alone in this age. He concludes by reflecting that "In short, at the bottom of his chaos of a nature, he worshiped the virtues that the world seems long since to have dismissed as dull or simply good business or as not pertaining to reality at all" (*Hear Us O Lord*, p. 87). Those virtues are compassion, courtesy, tact, humor, and a love for his wife so strong that it will make him loyal to her beyond death. The storm subsides, land is at last sighted, and the voyage from the Garden into the realm of death and beyond that into rebirth is complete. The rejuvenated Sigbjørn Wilderness resolves, like the Ancient Mariner once relieved of his albatross, "to teach by his own example, love and reverence to all things that God made and loveth." He has changed from a narrowly introspective artist into one whose first concern is now to serve his fellow man.

If one were a Jungian, it would be tempting here to speak of "symbols of transformation," and reflect about how consistently Lowry employs the sea as his agent of metamorphosis. Time after time in his works a protagonist is tested by the sea, and emerges from the contest radically altered in one way or another. But the sea as transformer is, after all, the hoariest of literary clichés, and there is no great profit in our saying here only, "Look, Lowry does it, too." What is different about Lowry is that for him the sea is not simply symbolic, but magical in a way that it has not been made to seem since, perhaps, *The Tempest*. Lowry's conversation was never far from things nautical, nor are any of his works: if his characters are not actually aboard a ship, tossed about like the Wildernesses aboard the *Diderot*, then they stand on shore and watch the surf, or sit in their beach cottages listening to the plangent reverberations of the waves as they strike the rocks below them. The sea in Lowry's writing is magical because it never kills, for all its vast and turbulent menace: it may exalt, bore, frighten, challenge, or transform one —but it never really harms Lowry's heroes, who are all (all but one: the hell-bound Geoffrey Firmin) striving consciously to be better men than they have been, and who are impelled toward their goal by the sea. For Lowry, finally, the sea was his one unfailingly positive symbol: the garden could be lovely, or corrupt; the forest could shelter, or devour; the mountain could be Himavat or destroying volcano—but the sea, for all its apparent fury, is always benevolent, always, as Lowry put it, "on the side of life."

There is little to be said for the four pieces that follow "Through the Panama." In "Strange Comfort Afforded by the Profession," Sigbjørn Wilderness, the American writer in Rome, takes notes as he explores Keats's house, being especially intrigued by the letters of Severn, Keats's friend, describing the poet's death agonies. Then, sitting in a nearby trattoria, he thumbs through the notebook and finds a few pages he has written at the time of his visit to Mamertine Prison. He comes next upon the notes which he had made long before, on his visit to Poe's home in Richmond, Virginia. Here he had seen on display a letter from Poe to his foster father, pleading in the most anguished way for financial aid: "For God's sake pity me and save me from destruction." Finally, in a second notebook Sigbjørn comes across a draft of a letter he, on his uppers in Seattle, had written years ago to his lawyer in Los Angeles, a Mr. Van Bosch (it is obviously something that Lowry himself had written in 1938–39 to Benjamin Parks). The letter describes his suffering in Seattle, and ends by saying, "Literally I am dying in this macabre hole and I appeal to you to send me, out of the money that is after all mine, enough that I may return." Sigbjørn is happy to think that he, after all, has something—misery—in common with the likes of Keats and Poe. And not only misery, but something else as well: the almost shameless self-consciousness that allows such poets to be aware of themselves *as artists* even as they are composing pathetic (and real) appeals for help. Sigbjørn suspects that Poe must have been thinking, as he looked at his letter to the foster father, "Damn it, I could use some of that, it may not be so hot, but it is at least too good to waste on my foster father." It is certainly true that Sigbjørn thought this way about *his* letter to Van Bosch—and sure enough, here it is, dropped entire into his story. "Strange Comfort Afforded by the Profession" is hardly a "meditation," in the sense that I have been using the word. A musing, perhaps, or simple flight of fancy.

"Elephant and Colosseum," though much longer than "Strange Comfort," is just as insubstantial. Now, still in Rome, we find an Americanized Manxman, Kennish Drumgold Cosnahan, sitting alone in a café, his newly published comic novel, *Ark from Singapore*, on the table before him. He is depressed: he misses his "pretty, gay, wild-looking" wife, Lovey; his mother, a benign witch, had died on the Isle of Man a month earlier; he speaks no Italian, and so is afraid to try to order a glass of wine; and he cannot bring himself to begin writing again. He wanders, terrified of the Roman traffic, until he comes to the zoo. He discovers that one of the elephants there is none other than Rosemary, whom he had taken care of years before on the voyage that had brought her from Malaysia to Rome, and who had been a central character in his novel. It is Cosnahan's joyous moment of epiphany: Rosemary's presence tells him not only that he can now write again, but also that all life is itself comic, complete with happy ending. Lowry manages to spin all this out to 58 pages.

"Present Estate of Pompeii" is simply Lowry's attempt to work the journal of his visit to the ruins into an extended *pensée*, and the result is certainly the most egregious failure in the collection. Now the protagonist is a gruff, dour Scots-Canadian schoolmaster named Roderick McGregor Fairhaven (obviously based on Lowry's friend Downie Kirk), and his wife, who is "pretty, a bit wild, delightful, enthusiastic," is called Tansy. She is eager to see Pompeii, but he misses his waterfront home in Eridanus, broods constantly about it (so that he misses most of what their guide is telling them), and thinks of travel in general as being a trip to a place where, pre-eminently, "you don't belong . . . something that slips through the hands of your mind, as it were, and that seen without seeing, you can make nothing of: and behind you, thousands of miles away, it is as though you could hear your own real life plunging to its doom" (*Hear Us O Lord*, p. 177). The burden of the meditation is muddled, but it might be simply that life is too short for man to waste his time staring at ruins; that life is altogether elsewhere—specifically, and perhaps uniquely, on the beach at Eridanus.

In "Gin and Goldenrod" Sigbjørn Wilderness, wracked by a ferocious hangover and consumed by remorse and shame, is walking through the woods near Eridanus with his angry Primrose, on his way to find a bootlegger from whom he has some nights earlier bought several bottles of liquor to supply an impromptu party. Now he must pay the man out of their slender savings. The land they walk through had been virgin forest, but it is now being destroyed to make room for a middle-class housing development called Dark Rosslyn. For Sigbjørn, to have to walk through this ugly development, with its tacky houses slammed down on scalped land, is tantamount to a journey through hell. They find the man, pay him his money, and return home. On the way back, Primrose relents, and admits to Sigbjørn that she has saved one bottle of gin from his orgy. The tale thus has a happy ending of sorts: "In the cool silver rainy twilight of the forest a kind of hope began to bloom again." The hope is perhaps spurious, based as it is on a return to a home threatened by the city's rage for expansion, and an alcoholic escape. But then, maybe a drink of gin on a dry, hot Sunday for a hungover man is no small affirmation.

"The Forest Path to the Spring" is Lowry's attempt "to write of human happiness in terms of enthusiasm and high seriousness usually reserved for catastrophe and tragedy" (*Hear Us O Lord*, p. 271). The mood throughout is one of muted exaltation, as the unnamed narrator tells of everyday life in the earthly paradise of Eridanus; and, though there are occasional lapses into lush and "poetic" writing ("Sometimes, too, on the seaboard of the night, a ship would stand drawn, like a jewelled dagger, from the dark scabbard of the town"), and the almost nonexistent dialogue is unfortunate, to say the least (the narrator's wife can look up at a winter night sky and say, "Like splinters of ice in a sky of jet"), Lowry manages for the most part to sustain his tone throughout the 68 pages of this genuine meditation.

The narrator is a former seaman, jazz musician, and alcoholic. One senses his fragility, his fatigue of spirit, as he writes. He has obviously been grievously damaged by life, and his equilibrium can be maintained only with the utmost care. (He is, in other words, rather like Malcolm Lowry during the final months in Ripe.) Once again, there is no real "plot": the meditation is one long paean to his wife and his constantly threatened little shack on the beach. Jimmie Craige, Whitey, and Sam (here called Quaggan, Kristbjørg, and Mauger) are shadowy figures in the background, not really substantial enough to be called "characters." There are finally only the couple, the woods, and the dangerous ugliness that lies outside. In the summer they swim, go for excursions in their rowboat, laze about in the sun. Then the first frosts come, and there is silver driftwood on the beach, and when it grows too cold to swim they take walks through the forest "where the ice crystals crackled like rock candy" under their feet. And then comes the season of fogs, and sometimes "the fog froze on the trees and the forest became a crystal forest." Winter, with its silence, is good:

> The wintry landscape could be beautiful on these rare short days of sunlight and frostflowers, with crystal casing on the slender branches of birches and vine-leaved maples, diamond drops on the tassels of the spruces, and the bright frosted foliage of the evergreens. The frost melted on our porch in stripes, leaving a pattern against the wet black wood like a richly beaded cape flung out, on which our little cat tripped about with cold dainty paws and then sat hunched outside on the windowsill with his tail curled round his feet.
>
> (*Hear Us O Lord*, p. 252)

But spring is best:

> The very quality of the light was different, the pale green, green and gold dappled light that comes when the leaves are

very small, for later, in summer with the leaves full out, the green is darker and the path darker and deeply shady. But now there was this delicate light and greenness everywhere, the beauty of light on the feminine leaves of vine-leaved maples and the young leaves of the alders shining in sunlight like stars of dogwood blossoms, green overhead and underfoot where plants were rushing up and there were the little beginnings of wild flowers that would be, my wife said, spring beauties, starflowers, wild bleeding hearts, saxifrage and bronze bells.

It is all quite lovely, and described with a simple eloquence that often approaches, but seldom falls into, sentimentality. It is just what Lowry always wanted: a life of grace and measure, order and quiet: utter simplicity, in fact.

The destroyer lurks, however, all around them. At the end of Indian Arm, in the forest at the end of the narrowing gorge where they once rowed for tranquil picnic lunches, is an inn "where you may even today, among the advertisements for dyspeptic soft poisons nailed to trees, have, for the equivalent of what used to be an English crown, a cup of chill weak tea with a little bag in it at a place called Ye Olde Totemlande Inne." Excursion boats float past their shack daily during the summer months, the guides aboard them pointing out the squatters' shacks at Eridanus with derision. Smog rises ever more heavily over the city, and spreads toward them. Civilization, "creator of deathscapes," may ultimately win in its battle to destroy nature, and on one occasion, as he heads homeward down the path that leads to their spring, the narrator is almost overcome by hatred of the despoilers of his green world. But after a few moments of intense rage, he realizes that there is no room in Eridanus for hatred. After all, he thinks, "it was not human beings I hated but the ugliness they made in the image of their own ignorant contempt for the earth"; and he picks up his buckets of fresh water, and goes back to his wife.

Some time later his real epiphany comes. Depressed once again about the multiple threats to their security, he is plodding along the same path when he becomes aware suddenly that a cougar is crouched in a tree in front of him, eyeing him fixedly. For long moments neither moves; then the man calmly tells the cougar to get going—and it does. Later that night, as he lies in bed with his wife, he remembers that he had felt no fear during his encounter with the cougar. This was, he realizes, because he had feared something else more than he feared the big cat—and he cannot remember what that greater fear was, save that it had to do with "something on the path that had seemed ready, on every side, to spring out of our paradise at us." The fear gone, he can now give himself wholly to enjoyment of life at Eridanus.

Old friends from his days as a musician bring him a second-hand piano, and he begins composing a jazz symphony. Their shack burns, and the symphony goes up with it. In their new shack, he writes a jazz opera, to be called *The Forest Path to the Spring*, which will be a celebration of their own life. The opera is a success, and they are drawn for a time into the outside world. But they return, because the man knows that out there he will be subject to the pride he feels in his accomplishment; and in Eridanus he can be his own simple fool. Wise fool, certainly, for what he has learned over the years is that he and his wife have progressed

> as if to a region where such words as spring, water, houses, trees, vines, laurels, mountains, wolves, bay, roses, beach, islands, forest, tides and deer and snow and fire, had realized their true being, or had their source: and as these words on a page once stood merely to what they symbolized, so did the reality we knew now stand to something else beyond that symbolized or reflected: it was as if we were clothed in the kind of reality which before we saw only at a distance. . . .
> (*Hear Us O Lord*, p. 281)

Here it all at last was, the experience of that which Lowry all his life had known was there, but had been unable quite to perceive: that what one needs to know about reality is only that it is real. Here are the Rilkean *things*, fully realized in their existential *thingness;* here are, at last, no empty abstractions, no frenzied need to symbolize, no whirling cerebral chaos. Here is only a quiet, green world on the edge of the life-bringing sea, where the Lowryan man may protect his fragile self, love his wife, and deal reverently and perhaps a little humorously with the *things* that surround him.

The idea of the *Hear Us O Lord* collection is a majestic one, marvelously elegant in its simplicity; and it is sad to know that Lowry only at the end of his final story (the last story he wrote, actually) was to discover the idea in its pure form. "The Forest Path to the Spring" should have marked the beginning, and not the end, of his career. Or perhaps one should say instead that the sanity and wisdom of "Forest Path" are the lessons of time alone: that they are granted only to the man who learns through complicated suffering to simplify (to become a fool, in Lowry's terms), and not to the man to whom simplicity comes easily. Lowry himself knew that this "meditation" should mark the end, and not the beginning of something, for his *Work in Progress* statement noted that the final section of "The Forest Path to the Spring" would eventually serve as the coda to the whole *Voyage That Never Ends* cycle.

It would be pleasant to leave Lowry here, assuming that he had learned what his narrator learns. But this is a biography, not a novel, and real lives (especially those of people like Malcolm Lowry) do not arrange themselves with such aesthetic neatness. One is bound to say, first of all, that *Hear Us O Lord from Heaven Thy Dwelling Place* is, even considered as a series of meditations instead of short stories, rather bad. "The Forest Path" has elements of greatness in it, and the neurotic boisterousness of "Through the Panama" is often fetching; but the other five pieces should either have been left unpublished, or else revised many more times before being let into print. There is, almost throughout, a fatal lack of energy in the book; and the number of digressions, the ultimately boring self-consciousness about writing, suggest that Lowry had the compulsion to write, without very much to write *about*—except, of course, for the single grand idea, which he did not really comprehend until the final piece.

One must resist the urge to end aesthetically, leaving a self-realized Lowry sitting securely in his waterfront cottage, writing simply and eloquently about his life of equilibrium in his Canadian paradise. What really happened is messier by far, and sadder.

He began his anticlimactic last months in Canada by writing an irate letter to Albert Erskine on January 26, 1954, which began "My God, you old rapscallion," and continued by accusing Random House in general and Erskine in particular of insensitivity and lack of judgment in cutting off the contract payments for the *Work in Progress*. Lowry ended, as he so often did in his correspondence, by almost forgetting his anger, and going into digressive discussions of other writers, other works.

Erskine, long out of patience with Lowry and his interminable projects, answered on January 29 as temperately as he could that he was very sorry if Lowry's pride had been hurt, but that there was nothing he could do about *October Ferry to Gabriola*, or any of the other material:

> I can only say that I read only with what equipment I've got, right or wrong. If that equipment seems inadequate to you there is nothing I can do about it. . . . Do you want me to say I understand and love it when I don't? Is flattery what you want? Don't bother to answer those questions. I don't get the whole business, but I know I'd prefer not to get any more letters like the last one. . . .

This letter did not reach Lowry, because Margerie intercepted it. She read it, then walked up to the Post Office and wrote Erskine from there.

> I don't dare leave Malc very long. I haven't shown him your letter, I didn't dare. This whole business has nearly killed him. He just managed to get the last installment and letter off to you and then collapsed. He's in bed, with a high fever, unable to keep anything on his stomach, & in such a desperate state of mind I'm frightened myself. I'm afraid the tone of his letter—half jocular, half angry—has misled you as to his real feelings. . . . He feels disgraced, cast out—"I know thee not, old man"—not only his ability but even his sense of responsibility questioned etc. etc. But finally and most importantly he is so despairingly *hurt* and heartbroken it would

move a brass mule to compassion. . . . No, Albert, he doesn't want flattery (well, he likes it) but he longs for faith in him and at this stage he needs encouragement more than food. You've never seen him in the throes of creation, feeling his way, unsure (even while sure in the long run) & super super sensitive about everything. . . . You may think (and so may I for that matter) that it is immature to attach so much importance to saving face, but he has a fantastic and touchy pride & what he cannot endure is humiliation. . . . I beg you to write him an affectionate letter. . . . I am doing all I can to bolster him up, but he waits every day for some help from you. Please give him a little help, so he can get up and go on. He *has* courage. He will. . . . Please, our brother.

Erskine answered this plea as honestly as he could, by writing to Lowry that he had not lost his admiration for, and faith in, him or his work, but that he still could not bring himself to admire the manuscript material that had been arriving from Dollarton.

Lowry now was spending most of his hours sitting in their apartment on Nelson Street, writing little and drinking steadily. From time to time he managed a sardonic letter to David Markson, most especially about a head injury he had sustained when trying to rescue a pigeon trapped in an air vent on the roof of their apartment (Margerie remembers no such rescue, but *does* recall that about this time Lowry fell in the bathtub and cut his head rather badly on a soap dish); but for the most part, he sat. At the end of February he and Margerie moved back to Dollarton.

In the second week in March Margerie flew to Los Angeles to see her mother. After she had been there for three days, a telephone call came from Norman Newton, a former student of Earle Birney's who was now living near the Lowrys in Dollarton. Newton told her that Lowry had disappeared two days before, and that he and his wife Gloria had found him walking in Vancouver's skid row, behaving insanely. Newton had called the Neilsons on Bowen Island, who had taken Lowry home with them. They had sat up with him all night, but by the morning of March 22 were frightened enough by his behavior to take him in to the emergency ward of St. Paul's Hospital, where X-rays were taken after Lowry told a physician that he had fallen and hit his side on a table some days earlier; and it was discovered that he had broken two ribs. An intern taped him up, then released him to the care of the Neilsons. Margerie arrived back in Vancouver the following day, and went out to Bowen Island, where she found her husband still raving and threatening anyone who came near him. He would not speak to Margerie. She stayed on at the Neilsons', and three days later, when he had calmed down sufficiently, she took Lowry back to Dollarton.

It was at about this time, Harvey Burt remembers, that Lowry, drunk and clad only in his swimming trunks, wandered down to the cabin of a neighbor of theirs, a carpenter. The man had several children, one of whom was severely retarded. Lowry accepted a drink from the carpenter, and his mood turned ugly. He began to stare (the man later told Burt) at the afflicted child, then suddenly turned to the carpenter and sneeringly asked, "What kind of man are you if this is the sort of kid you produce?" The man hit Lowry in the face as hard as he could, then pushed him out of the cabin onto the rocks that lined the shore. Lowry stumbled, bleeding and crying, back to his shack, calling out to Margerie for help.

His remorse for such miserable behavior could manifest itself strangely. Burt recalls another evening when Lowry had disgraced himself somehow, and he and Burt were walking down the path toward the shack. Lowry, crying with shame, threw himself onto the floor of the forest beside the path, rolled over onto his back, and stretched out his arms above his head. He was lying in a bed of tall ferns; and when he grasped some of their leaves, he stripped them of their bitter spores, which he thrust into his mouth with both hands, chewing and swallowing convulsively. A very paradigm of compulsive orality—and ominously prophetic of the manner in which, one evening three-and-a-half years later, he clapped handfuls of sodium amytal tablets into his mouth.

On May 20 Lowry pulled himself together sufficiently to write a long letter to David Markson, full of good-natured advice. But he could not keep from mentioning that the authorities were once again up in arms about the squatters' shacks in Dollarton, and had in fact already served eviction notices to many of his neighbors. He mentions his broken ribs, and comments that "It is the suspicious element of the possibly suicidal in all these constant small accidents that have plagued me which frightens me." He is almost afraid to swim any more, because of the unnecessary risks which he cannot help taking. And he and Margerie have, he says, "also taken to hitting the bottle, especially me, somewhat too hard—if not with consular vehemence or consistency—and though this can often be a joy too, there are few things worse than a bad hangover on a glorious day."

On May 22 Lowry, friendly again, wrote Albert Erskine to say that he and Margerie had decided to leave Dollarton. The evictions had stopped just short of them, but their own shack and the small piece of forest around it were now only an oasis of "greenwood and sea" surrounded by sub-section and oil refinery. "Eridanus" was gone. And, since they would have to pay $1000 income tax if they stayed in Canada, there could be no thought of a ferry to Gabriola or any other new hiding place in North America. Sicily seemed the likeliest place to try next, he said.

Then on July 10, already packing to leave, Lowry wrote David Markson one more note from Dollarton: "All is half gaily bloody and schizophrenic here but hopefully and even gaily forward." They had reservations on an Italian liner leaving New York in early September, and warned Markson to expect them in Manhattan on August 25.

In the meantime they made airline reservations to New York via Los Angeles, so that they could visit Margerie's relatives for a few days. By August 10 they were ready to leave. Just in case, Harvey Burt was to look after the shack, and store Lowry's library in his own cottage. There was no particular reason to dispose of the little amount of furniture they had accumulated, so they left the shack as it was. Early on the morning of the 11th, Harvey Burt and Jimmie Craige came by for them, and they walked up the path to the Dollarton Road one last time.

Lowry said almost nothing on the drive to the Vancouver airport. They all stood more or less silently at the boarding gate, and when the depature of their flight was announced, Lowry suddenly threw his arms around little Jimmie Craige, gathering the old man up as if he were a child, and began crying: "I'm afraid to leave. I'm afraid we'll never come back!" Then Margerie took her husband's arm and led him to the airplane, and they were gone.

EPILOGUE

The next journey was the last, the one recounted in the first chapter of this work: to New York, Italy, London, and finally to Ripe, the village in East Sussex. The Infernal Machine was about to make its final, predictable revolution, and the sad, funny life of Malcolm Lowry was to come to its inevitable conclusion.

I have said that Lowry was a man of "such awesome talent that the word *genius* must be used to describe him." Is this far too grand a claim to have made for this poor drunk, this frightened, clumsy, one-book author? I think not. If we ignore the modern bloat that has all but destroyed the word, and reach back via the *Oxford English Dictionary* for its more precise denotation in the eighteenth century, we can define genius as "native intellectual power of an exalted type; extraordinary capacity for imaginative creation, original thought, invention, or discovery." Now Lowry was, as I have said, in no sense a "natural" writer—compulsive, yes, but not natural: he was a writer not because words flowed effortlessly from him, but because he was damned if he were going to be anything else. To Lowry, not to write was unimaginable; not to write was death. Genius, in other words, was something which Lowry had to labor, often frantically, to attain. And attain it he did: for there is before us, after all, the monolithic and undeniable fact of *Under the Volcano;* and there are the occasional moments in a few of the other works —specifically, in *Lunar Caustic* and "The Forest Path to the Spring." Such achievement transcends the realm of mere talent. In the one majestic novel he created a work that was *sui generis*—

not really a novel at all, but something that I have called (for lack of anything better) a "monument to prodigality of vision"; and it is entirely possible that in "The Forest Path to the Spring" he was on his way to the discovery of another unique mode of fiction: fiction, perhaps, as act of devotion. About the last, of course, we shall never know: Ripe ended all that.

If, as good Freudians, we attempt to search for the source of Lowry's genius in his manifold and aggravated neuroses, we find all the usual stigmata one conventionally associates with the "creative" personality: the truly Gargantuan appetite for alcohol, the accident-proneness, the infantile behavior, the possible auto-erotism, the inability to complete projects, the simultaneous need for and fear of persons in authority (father-figures, to put it simplistically), the excessive dependence on his wife, the cyclic movement between exhilaration and depression, the urge to self-destruction—they are all there, presenting themselves with such obviousness that we very nearly feel ourselves faced with examining a clinically perfect specimen, a cliché of abnormal psychology.

I do not for a moment believe, however, that Lowry's genius (which after all lay not in his failures as a man but in his achievement as an artist) can be explained or circumscribed by his neuroses. Jung is closer to the answer than Freud, here:

> When the Freudian school advances the opinion that all artists are undeveloped personalities with marked infantile auto-erotic traits, this judgment may be true of the artist as a man, but it is not applicable to the man as an artist. In this capacity he is neither autoerotic, nor heteroerotic, nor erotic in any sense. He is in the highest degree objective, impersonal, and even inhuman—or suprahuman—for as an artist he is nothing but his work, and not a human being. [1]

1. C. G. Jung, *The Spirit in Man, Art, and Literature, Collected Works,* Vol. XV (New York, 1966), 101. Jung's essay from which I am quoting here, "Psychology and Literature," was originally written in 1930. I have also made use in this discussion of the following works: L. J. Hatterer, *The Artist in Society: Problems and Treatment of the Creative Personality* (New York, 1965); Ernst Kris, *Psychoanalytic Explorations in Art* (New York, 1952); L. S. Kubie, *Neurotic Distortion of the Creative Process* (Lawrence, Kansas, 1958); H. Sachs, *The Creative Unconscious* (Cambridge, 1942); and Leon Salzman, *The Obsessive Personality* (New York, 1968).

What made Lowry a writer of genius was not his neuroses but something which both Freud and Jung ultimately agree is inaccessible to psychological analysis; for such analysis is inherently a rational activity, and the origins of creative ability lie deep in the realm of the irrational. To cite Jung again:

> the creative urge which finds its clearest expression in art is irrational and will in the end make a mock of all our rationalistic undertakings. All conscious psychic processes may well be causally explicable; but the creative act, being rooted in the immensity of the unconscious, will forever elude our attempts at understanding.

In this same essay Jung supposes that there are two radically opposed modes of artistic creation. The first he labels *psychological*, and the second *visionary*. The psychological artist (Jung's editors suggest that "personalistic" would have been a more accurate term) is he who derives his material and his method from "the sphere of conscious human experience—from the psychic foreground of life." He is the artist of consciousness, whose values are order, discipline, and clarity, and whose materials are "crucial experiences, powerful emotions, suffering, passion, the stuff of human fate in general"—as understood by the conscious, reason-oriented mind. About the realm of the visionary artist, Jung waxes eloquent, almost lyrical:

> Here everything is reversed. The experience that furnishes the material for artistic expression is no longer familiar. It is something strange that derives its existence from the hinterland of man's mind, as if it had emerged from the abyss of prehuman ages, or from a superhuman world of contrasting light and darkness. It is a primordial experience which surpasses man's understanding and to which in his weakness he may easily succumb. The very enormity of the experience gives it its value and its shattering impact. Sublime, pregnant with meaning, yet chilling the blood with its strangeness, it arises from timeless depths; glamorous, daemonic, and grotesque, it bursts asunder our human standards of value and aesthetic form, a terrifying tangle of eternal chaos, a *crimen laesae majestatis humanae*. On the other hand, it can be a

revelation whose heights and depths are beyond our fathoming, or a vision of beauty which we can never put into words.

The visionary artist is the artist of the irrational, the obscure, the monstrous: his values lie not in order and discipline, but in inspiration, whether sublime or perverse. His subject matter is not the everyday world, but the ancient and dangerous archetypes which lie hidden in the deepest regions of the unconscious. If the danger to the psychological artist is barrenness, sterility, a vitality-destroying discipline, the danger to the visionary artist is incoherence, or even madness. To reside absolutely at one or the other pole means at the very least artistic death: either sanity bought at the price of sterility, or immediate experience of the unconscious at the price of psychosis.

For Jung, the source of the artistic process is not seen as lying in repression, or in any sort of aberration, but in psychic health. The successful artist for Jung is he who is powerful enough to move with confidence back and forth from the psychological and visionary poles, and to find a propitious place somewhere between those extremes. Ideally, the creative process functions something like this: the artist moves into the visionary realm for his inspiration, then travels back into consciousness toward the psychological pole, where he finds the organizing ability that is necessary to give his vision coherence. Finally he will occupy a point somewhere along the line between the two poles, and his art will consist of symbolic structures which possess both archetypal potency and aesthetic form. That artist is a genius who has dared to expose himself to the full impact of the vision, and still been able to return to the world of consciousness in order to lend the most satisfying shape to that vision. The genius is what he is, then, by virtue of both his courage and the strength of his intellect and will.

Perhaps we now have at least a basis from which we may begin tentatively to discuss the nature of Malcolm Lowry's artistic achievement. I submit that his early works are successful only in so far as they suggest Lowry's incipient awareness of the powerful forces available to the artist who is willing to risk the perilous journey into the dark interior of the visionary mode; and that these early works fail because he actually dared rather little, and because he lacked the necessary technical skill to manage even the little visionary material that he had perceived. *Ultramarine* strives to be more than the conventional seaborne *Künstlerroman*, and one respects the young Lowry for his attempts to turn the *Oedipus Tyrannus* into a sort of itinerant Inferno. But he was too much in thrall to Jack London, Eugene O'Neill, and Nordahl Grieg to escape the confines of a rather empty and facile tradition. *Lunar Caustic* comes closer to a realization of Lowry's potential: we are obviously now in the presence of a genuinely mythopoeic artist, one seeking to present a startlingly original vision in a highly unconventional manner. But he never completed the novella because he did not know how to organize and control his material.

Then came *Under the Volcano:* a stunning and final evocation of hell on earth, a magnificently controlled vision of a world which none of us knows, but which all of us recognize. There is no point now in trying to say any last evaluative words about *Under the Volcano;* but Jung, had he ever read the novel, would undoubtedly have recognized it as a work of genius as he understood the term: a supremely successful fusion of both modes of artistic creation. The vision is there, and so is the evidence of intelligent and sensitive shaping—ten years of it, to be exact.

After the one great work, there was nothing more of lasting value until "The Forest Path to the Spring." In his review of *Hear Us O Lord from Heaven Thy Dwelling Place* (in *The Nation*, May 27, 1961), George Steiner wrote, "Volcanoes that blaze high leave little life around them"; and this is as good a way as any of saying that the single triumph of *Under the Volcano* had exhausted Lowry. He had had his one great vision, labored mightily until he found precisely the means of expressing that vision—and then he was finished, with ten years of life still left. What remained to him was only the inevitable deterioration of his art, and the analogous deterioration of his self.

And yet: one senses (not, it is true, with absolute confidence) that

Lowry might just have been on his way toward the delineation of an entirely new sort of vision in "The Forest Path to the Spring." If in *Under the Volcano* he had given us his Inferno, and in *Lunar Caustic* had tried to depict his Purgatorio, here now was his vision of the Paradiso. It almost comes off, and might have done so had Lowry lived to complete it. It might, that is, have brought us closer than other fiction has done to Jung's "vision of beauty which we can never put into words." Was the serenity one senses in this last story simply the calm that accompanies one's final fatigue; or was it real, an outward and visible sign of some unique illumination, never to be fully expressed or realized? I myself believe that it was the former: "The Forest Path to the Spring" is uncommonly graceful for Lowry, but there is after all a certain grace to fatigue; and I believe that Lowry was a burnt-out case by the time he and Margerie left Dollarton in 1954, and that if there was a new vision, it faded away almost before Lowry caught a glimpse of it.

What destroyed Lowry's genius? If we refuse to agree with Freud that a writer's neuroses feed his art, then we may at least see that they can inhibit and disrupt it. Neurosis by definition is wasteful and destructive: it does not provide creative energy; it only expends it. I believe that Lowry's neuroses crippled him not only as a man, but also as an artist, in that they impeded him in his psychic journey between conscious discipline and unconscious experience. The root of neurosis is fear, and Lowry clearly feared his art: if its visionary aspect frightened him, so did its shaping aspect. He was, then, a man self-compelled to serve a vocation of which he was terrified; and this led him into the most elaborate and self-destructive ways of avoiding his art. Specifically, it led him ever deeper into introspection. Ultimately he was exhausted by this morbid self-absorption, and his art died. For most of his career he could write only about himself, in such a way that we cannot understand his writing without understanding him, and this, as Jung cautions us, must be counted as a failure in the art:

> The essence of a work of art is not to be found in the personal idiosyncrasies that creep into it—indeed, the more

there are of them, the less it is a work of art—but in its rising above the personal and speaking from the mind and heart of the artist to the mind and heart of mankind. The personal aspect of art is a limitation, and even a vice. Art that is only personal, or predominantly so, truly deserves to be treated as a neurosis.

A work of art is successful, then, in the degree to which it becomes autonomous, freed from the Self that is writing. Only once in his life was Lowry able to accomplish this: in *Under the Volcano*—and it took him ten years to give the book its freedom from him. With everything else he wrote, one must constantly be aware of the presence of Malcolm Lowry and his attendant swarm of demons moving across every page. Does this mean that we must consider Lowry to have been a failure as a writer? Let him who thinks so try to write an *Under the Volcano*. Lowry was a great author who happens to have written only one great book.

Those who do not care for visionary fiction may not agree that Lowry was a literary genius. I should like to suggest finally that, considerations of his work aside, Malcolm Lowry was quite another sort of genius as well: the true innocent, the Fool of God, the man who desires simply and wholeheartedly to be *good*. I do not mean to suggest that he was a saintly man. Far from it: when in one of his depressed periods, he could (as we have seen) be cruel, even dangerous. Or that he was a simpleton: for his intelligence was both lofty and subtle. Or always a buffoon: for he could be dignified, even austere. I mean that he was a man of simple and uncritical good will. He attributed the best of motives to everyone—at least until they had cheated him past ignoring. Most of what he touched became a muddle, but he would very much have preferred to do things well, so as to please others. He was a nuisance, a disgrace, a constant burden to those who cared for him. He could fairly roll in self-pity. He could strike tragic poses that at first amused, then annoyed. He could be, in short, impossible. But we must always hear him saying, sly grin on face, "Do not take me quite so seriously." He was, we must remember, a most loveable sort of man, in spite of (and perhaps because of) his many flaws. His friends speak of him today as though he were still with them, laughing and talking endlessly. He was able to inspire the most astonishing affection and loyalty on the part of almost everyone who came to know him. Crusty and irascible old men smile when they remember him. Mothers, maids, and wives of friends cared for him as though he were their own. Harvey Burt is as aware as any of Lowry's many exasperating defects, and will brook no romantic myth-making about the man; yet over Harvey Burt's mantelpiece in Dollarton hangs Lowry's old ukulele, and the eagle feather that Jimmie Craige once gave him. And we must remember the anonymous voice in a bar, saying of Lowry that "The very sight of that old bastard makes me happy for five days. No bloody fooling."

I imagine that most of us would be rather proud to be the sort of man of whom such a thing could be said.

BIBLIOGRAPHY

No attempt has been made here to be exhaustive. Reviews are not included, nor are foreign language editions of Malcolm Lowry's various works. Publications of individual poems or groups of poems are not mentioned. Lowry's numerous unpublished manuscripts are not listed. For more complete information, one should consult the following: *Canadian Literature* for Spring 1961, Summer 1961, Winter 1962, and Winter 1964 for bibliographies and supplements compiled by Earle Birney and Margerie Lowry; the list of holdings of the Malcolm Lowry collection at the library of the University of British Columbia; and *A Malcolm Lowry Catalogue*, edited by J. Howard Woolmer (New York, 1968).

I. THE PUBLISHED WORKS OF MALCOLM LOWRY

The following are arranged in chronological order. For complete bibliographical references to Lowry's writings for *The Leys Fortnightly*, see Suzanne Kim, "Les Œuvres de jeunesse de Malcolm Lowry," cited below in II.

"Port Swettenham," *Experiment*, 5 (February 1930), 22–26.

"Goya the Obscure," *The Venture*, 6 (June 1930), 270–78.

"Punctum Indifferens Skibet Gaar Videre," *Experiment*, 7 (Spring 1931). Published in *Best British Short Stories of 1931* as "Seductio ad Absurdum."

Ultramarine. London: Jonathan Cape, 1933. Revised edition, with introductory note by Margerie Bonner Lowry, Philadelphia: Lippincott, 1962. Paperback edition, McGraw-Hill: New York, 1962.

"On Board the West Hardaway," *Story*, III (October 1933), 12–22.

"In Le Havre," *Life and Letters*, X, 55 (July 1934), 642–66.

"Hotel Room in Chartres," *Story*, V, 26 (September 1934), 53–58.

Under the Volcano. New York: Reynal and Hitchcock, 1947; London: Jonathan Cape, 1947. Subsequent editions: New York: Vintage Books, 1958; London: Penguin Books, 1962; Philadelphia; Lippincott, 1965 (with a preface by Stephen Spender); London: Jonathan Cape, 1965; New York: Signet Books, 1966.

"Economic Conference, 1934," *Arena*, 2 (Autumn 1949), 49–57. Written 1934.

"Garden of Etla," *United Nations World*, IV (June 1950), 45–47.

"Preface to a Novel," *Canadian Literature*, 9 (Summer 1961), 23–29. Written 1948.

Hear Us O Lord from Heaven Thy Dwelling Place. Philadelphia: Lippincott, 1961. Contains seven stories, two published here for the first time: "Elephant and Colosseum" and "Gin and Goldenrod"; two that were published during Lowry's life: "The Bravest Boat" (*Partisan Review*, 1954) and "Strange Comfort Afforded by the Profession" (*New World Writing*, 1953); and three that were published posthumously: "The Present Estate of Pompeii" (*Partisan Review*, 1959), "Through the Panama" (*The Paris Review*, 1960), and "The Forest Path to the Spring" (*New World Writing*, 1961).

Selected Poems. San Francisco: City Lights Books, 1962. Edited by Earle Birney with the assistance of Margerie Bonner Lowry.

Lunar Caustic. *The Paris Review*, VIII, 29 (Winter–Spring 1963), 12–72. Edited by Earle Birney and Margerie Bonner Lowry, with a preface by Conrad Knickerbocker. Subsequent publication: London: Jonathan Cape, 1968. Begun 1934.

"Under the Volcano," *Prairie Schooner*, XXXVII, 4 (Winter 1963–64), 284–300. Written 1937.

Selected Letters. Philadelphia: Lippincott, 1965. Edited by Harvey Breit and Margerie Bonner Lowry, with a preface by Harvey Breit. Published also in London: Jonathan Cape, 1967.

"Bulls of the Resurrection," *Prism International*, V, 1 (Summer 1965), 5–11. Written 1933–34.

Dark as the Grave Wherein my Friend Is Laid. New York: New American Library, 1968. Edited by Douglas Day and Margerie Bonner Lowry, with a preface by Douglas Day. Published also in London: Jonathan Cape, 1969. Paperback ed., New York: Meridian Books, 1969.

October Ferry to Gabriola. New York: World, 1970. Edited by Margerie Lowry. A section from this work was published as "The

Element Follows You Around, Sir!" *Show Magazine* (March 1964), 45–103.

II. SELECTED WORKS CONCERNING MALCOLM LOWRY

The following are arranged in alphabetical order.

Aiken, Conrad. *A Heart for the Gods of Mexico.* London, 1939. A *roman à clef* in which Lowry appears as "Hambo."

———. "Malcolm Lowry—A Note," *Canadian Literature,* 8 (Spring 1961), 29–30.

———. *Ushant: An Essay.* New York, 1971 (originally published, 1952). An autobiography in which Lowry appears as "Hambo."

Benham, David. "Lowry's Purgatory: Versions of 'Lunar Caustic,' " *Canadian Literature,* 44 (September 1970), 28–37.

Birney, Earle. "Against the Spell of Death," *Prairie Schooner,* XXXVII, 4 (Winter 1963–64), 328–33.

———. "Glimpses into the Life of Malcolm Lowry," *Tamarack Review,* 19 (Spring 1961), 35–41.

Bonnefoi, Geneviève. "Souvenir de Quauhnahuac," *Les Lettres Nouvelles* (July–August 1960), 94–108.

Breit, Harvey. "In and Out of Books—Obituary," *New York Times Book Review* (July 14, 1947), 8.

———. "Malcolm Lowry," *The Paris Review,* VI, 23 (Spring 1960), 84–85.

Calder-Marshall, Arthur. "A Portrait of Malcolm Lowry," *The Listener,* 78, 2011 (October 12, 1967), 461–63.

———. "Malcolm Lowry," unsigned essay, *Times* [*London*] *Literary Supplement,* 3387 (January 26, 1967), 57–59.

Carroy, Jean-Roger. "Obscur présent, le feu . . ." *Les Lettres Nouvelles* (July–August 1960), 83–88.

Chittick, V. L. O. "*Ushant*'s Malcolm Lowry," *Queen's Quarterly,* LXXI, 1 (Spring 1964), 67–75.

Corrigan, Matthew. "Malcolm Lowry, New York Publishing, and the 'New Illiteracy,' " *Encounter,* 35, 1 (July 1970), 82–93.

Costa, Richard H. "Lowry's Overture as Elegy," *A Malcolm Lowry Catalogue,* edited by J. Howard Woolmer (New York, 1968), 26–44.

———. *Malcolm Lowry.* New York, 1972.

———. "Malcolm Lowry and the Addictions of an Era," *University of Windsor Review,* V, 2 (Spring 1970), 1–10.

———. "The Lowry/Aiken Symbiosis," *Nation,* CCIV, 26 (June 26, 1967), 823–26.

Costa, Richard H. "*Ulysses*, Lowry's *Volcano* and the Voyage Between: A Study of an Unacknowledged Literary Kinship," *University of Toronto Quarterly*, 36 (July 1967), 335–52.

Day, Douglas. "Malcolm Lowry: Letters to an Editor," *Shenandoah*, XV, 3 (Spring 1964), 3–15.

———. "Malcolm Lowry: Oscuro como la tumba donde mi amigo yace," *Revista Nacional de Cultura*, 29 (1968), 32–41.

———. "Of Tragic Joy," *Prairie Schooner*, XXXVII, 4 (Winter 1963–64), 354–62.

Dodson, Daniel B. *Malcolm Lowry* (Columbia Essays on Modern Writers, 51). New York and London, 1970.

Doyen, Victor. "Elements Towards a Spatial Reading of Malcolm Lowry's *Under the Volcano*," *English Studies*, L, 1 (February 1969), 65–74.

Durrant, Geoffrey. "Death in Life: Neo-Platonic Elements in 'Through the Panama,' " *Canadian Literature*, 44 (Spring 1970), 13–27.

Edelstein, J. M. "On Re-reading *Under the Volcano*," *Prairie Schooner*, XXXVII, 4 (Winter 1963–64), 336–39.

———. "The Legacy of Malcom Lowry," *New Republic*, CXLIV, 23 (June 5, 1961), 24–25.

Edmonds, Dale H. "The Short Fiction of Malcolm Lowry," *Tulane Studies in English*, XV (1967), 59–80.

———. "*Under the Volcano*: A Reading of the 'Immediate Level,' " *Tulane Studies in English*, XVI (1968), 63–105.

Epstein, Perle. "Malcolm Lowry: In Search of Equilibrium," *A Malcolm Lowry Catalogue*, edited J. Howard Woolmer (New York, 1968), 15–25.

———. "Swinging the Maelstrom: Malcolm Lowry and Jazz," *Canadian Literature*, 44 (Spring 1970), 57–66.

———. *The Private Labyrinth of Malcolm Lowry*: Under the Volcano and the Cabbala. New York, 1969.

Francillon, Clarisse. "Malcolm, mon ami," *Les Lettres Nouvelles* (July–August 1960), 8–20.

———. "Souvenirs sur Malcolm Lowry," *Les Lettres Nouvelles* (November 1957), 588–603.

Fouchet, Max-Pol. "No se puede . . ." *Les Lettres Nouvelles* (July–August 1960), 21–25. Translated in *Canadian Literature*, 8 (Spring 1960), 25–28.

Gabrial, Jan. "Not with a Bang," *Story*, XXIX, 121 (September–October 1946), 55–61. A short story in which Lowry appears as a character, "Michael."

Haldane, Charlotte. *I Bring Not Peace*. London, 1932. A novel in which Lowry appears as a character, "James Dowd."

Heilman, Robert B. "The Possessed Artist and the Ailing Soul," *Canadian Literature*, 8 (Spring 1960), 7–16.

Hirschman, Jack. "Kabbala/Lowry, etc." *Prairie Schooner*, XXXVII, 4 (Winter 1963–64), 347–53.

Kilgallin, Anthony R. "Faust and *Under the Volcano*," *Canadian Literature*, 26 (Autumn 1965), 43–54.

Kim, Suzanne. "Les Œuvres de jeunesse de Malcolm Lowry," *Etudes Anglaises*, XVIII (1965), 383–94.

Kirk, Downie. "More than Music: Glimpses of Malcolm Lowry," *Canadian Literature*, 8 (Spring 1961), 31–38.

Knickerbocker, Conrad. "Swinging the Paradise Street Blues: Malcolm Lowry in England," *The Paris Review*, IX, 36 (Winter 1966), 13–38.

———. "The Voyages of Malcolm Lowry," *Prairie Schooner*, XXXVII, 4 (Winter 1963–64), 301–14.

Lorenz, Clarissa. "Call it Misadventure," *The Atlantic*, 225, 6 (June 1970), 106–12.

Lowry, Margerie Bonner. "Biographical Note on Malcolm Lowry," Promotional Brochure for Lippincott (Philadelphia, 1961).

Markson, David. "Malcolm Lowry: A Reminiscence," *Nation*, CCII, 16 (February 7, 1966), 164–67.

———. "Myth in *Under the Volcano*," *Prairie Schooner*, XXXVII, 4 (Winter 1963–64), 339–46.

McConnell, William. "Recollections of Malcolm Lowry," *Canadian Literature*, 6 (Autumn 1960), 24–31.

Myrer, Anton. "Le Monde au-dessous du volcan," *Les Lettres Nouvelles* (July–August 1960), 59–66.

Nadeau, Maurice. "Lowry," *Les Lettres Nouvelles*, 5 (July–August 1960), 3–7.

New, William H. "Lowry's Reading: An Introductory Essay," *Canadian Literature*, 44 (Spring 1970), 5–12.

Noxon, Gerald. "Malcolm Lowry: 1930," *Prairie Schooner*, XXXVII, 4 (Winter 1963–64), 315–20.

Spencer, Victor Alexander, Viscount Churchill. *Be All My Sins Remembered*. New York, 1965.

Spriel, Stéphen. "Le Cryptogramme Lowry," *Les Lettres Nouvelles* (July–August 1960), 67–82.

Stern, James. "Malcolm Lowry: A First Impression," *Encounter*, XXIX, 3 (September 1967), 58–68.

Tiessen, Paul G. "Malcolm Lowry and the Cinema," *Canadian Literature*, 44 (Spring 1970), 38–49.

Woodcock, George, ed. *Malcolm Lowry: The Man and His Work*. Vancouver, 1971.

Woodcock, George. "Malcolm Lowry's *Under the Volcano*," *Modern Fiction Studies*, IV, 2 (Summer 1958), 151–56.

———. "Under Seymour Mountain," *Canadian Literature*, 8 (Spring 1960), 3–6.

Wright, Terence. "*Under the Volcano:* The Static Art of Malcolm Lowry," *Ariel*, I, 4 (October 1970), 67–76.

INDEX

Printed in the United States
126434LV00005B/79/P